ST/ESA/STAT/SER.M/67/Rev.2

Department of Economic and Social Affairs
Statistics Division

Statistical papers   Series M No. 67/Rev.2

Principles and Recommendations for Population and Housing Censuses

Revision 2

United Nations
New York, 2008

Department of Economic and Social Affairs

The Department of Economic and Social Affairs of the United Nations Secretariat is a vital interface between global policies in the economic, social and environmental spheres and national action. The Department works in three main interlinked areas: (i) it compiles, generates and analyses a wide range of economic, social and environmental data and information on which States Members of the United Nations draw to review common problems and to take stock of policy options; (ii) it facilitates the negotiations of Member States in many intergovernmental bodies on joint courses of action to address ongoing or emerging global challenges; and (iii) it advises interested Governments on the ways and means of translating policy frameworks developed in United Nations conferences and summits into programmes at the country level and, through technical assistance, helps build national capacities.

Note

The designations used and the presentation of material in this publication do not imply the expression of any opinion whatsoever on the part of the Secretariat of the United Nations concerning the legal status of any country, territory, city or area, or of its authorities, or concerning the delimitation of its frontiers or boundaries.

The term "country" as used in this publication also refers, as appropriate, to territories or areas.

The designations "developed regions" and "developing regions" are intended for statistical convenience and do not necessarily express a judgment about the stage reached by a particular country or area in the development process.

Symbols of United Nations documents are composed of capital letters combined with figures. Mention of such a symbol indicates a reference to a United Nations document.

ST/ESA/STAT/SER.M/67/Rev.2

UNITED NATIONS PUBLICATION
Sales No. E.07.XVII.8

ISBN: 978-92-1-161505-0

Preface

The first set of principles and recommendations for population and housing censuses was issued in 1958 at the request of the Statistical Commission of the United Nations in response to a need for developing international standards and as a cornerstone of the first World Programme on Population and Housing Censuses.

Over the years, the United Nations Statistics Division has played a pivotal role in the coordination of the World Programme by issuing and revising international recommendation, providing technical assistance to countries in census operations, and compiling and disseminating census results from countries or areas. The last global census recommendations were published in 1998 under the title *Principles and Recommendations for Population and Housing Censuses, Revision 1*[1].

For the 2010 World Programme on Population and Housing Censuses, the Statistical Commission, at its thirty-sixth session,[2] requested that the United Nations Statistics Division, through the United Nations Expert Group on the 2010 World Programme on Population and Housing Censuses, proceed with its work on the revision and update of *Principles and Recommendations for Population and Housing Censuses*.

For the revision of the principles and recommendations, the Expert Group established a Drafting Group, and the following three working groups and technical subgroups: (*a*) Working Group on Standards, Frameworks and a Core Set of Outputs comprising (i) Technical subgroup on internal and international migration statistics, (ii) Technical subgroup on human functioning and disability, (iii) Technical subgroup on a core set of outputs and tabulations for international dissemination, and (iv) Technical subgroup on housing census topics; (*b*) Working Group on Census Planning and Management comprising (i) Technical subgroup on integrated data collection and dissemination, and (ii) Technical subgroup on alternative designs; and (*c*) Working Group on Promotion of Censuses: Making Value Visible.

In addition, an electronic mail exchange system and an interactive web-based discussion forum were established by the United Nations Statistics Division to facilitate communication between members of working groups and technical subgroups.

As part of the revision process, the United Nations Statistics Division organized three meetings of the Expert Group and on the basis of discussions and deliberations in these meetings[3] the draft *Principles and Recommendations for Population and Housing Censuses, Revision 2* was finalized for submission to the Statistical Commission of the United Nations.

Revision 2 of the *Principles and Recommendations for Population and Housing Censuses* introduces several substantive changes. For example, it contains an introduction that emphasizes the importance of a census. The recommendations for the 2010 round of censuses are also more output oriented and introduce a set of recommended tabulations on population and housing characteristics that all national statistical/census authorities are requested to generate at least once during the 2010 census round. The recommendations also stress the importance and necessity of collecting and presenting metadata as an indispensable element in the accurate interpretation of census results.

[1] United Nations publication, Sales No. E.98.XVII.8.

[2] *Official Records of the Economic and Social Council, 2005, Supplement No. 4* (E/2005/24-E/CN.3/2005/27), chap. IV, para. 12.

[3] The reports of these expert group meetings are available at: http://unstats.un.org/unsd/demographic/meetings/egm/default.htm.

Furthermore, the revised recommendations include a section that describes various alternative approaches to generating data that are usually collected through the traditional approach to population and housing censuses. However, as there is still limited operational experience for some of the alternative approaches, the United Nations Statistics Division is maintaining a website describing national experiences with different approaches[4] during the 2010 census round.

The definition of "place of usual residence" has been revised to introduce a time dimension. The revised recommendations feature a new classification of housing units, as well as a more detailed one of institutions as collective living quarters. *Principles and Recommendations for Population and Housing Censuses, Revision 2* also introduces several changes to the designation of topics for population and housing censuses as either core or non-core. In this connection, some topics that were previously core are now non-core and vice versa, and some new core topics have been added to the recommendations.

Finally, the latest revision (1993) of the System of National Accounts and the updates published up to 2004[5], and the World Health Organization (WHO) International Classification of Functioning, Disability and Health[6] have been taken into account in preparing the revised *Principles and Recommendations for Population and Housing Censuses.*

At its thirty-eighth session, in 2007, the Statistical Commission considered the draft principles and recommendations for population and housing censuses, revision 2 and adopted them. The Commission also requested the United Nations Secretariat to publish the principles and recommendations[7].

The following publications and papers issued by the regional commissions provide useful guidelines on census operations relevant to countries in each region:

(*a*) Economic Commission for Europe and Statistical Office of the European Communities, *Conference of European Statisticians Recommendations for the 2010 Censuses of Population and Housing*;[8]

(*b*) Economic and Social Commission for Asia and the Pacific, "Report of the Expert Group Meeting on ESCAP Regional Census Programme, 27-28 November 2006, Bangkok, Thailand",[9] and "Strengthening national statistical capacity by promoting the 2010 round of population and housing censuses";[10]

(*c*) Economic Commission for Latin America and the Caribbean, "América Latina: aspectos conceptuales de los censos del 2000 (Seminario Censos 2000: diseño conceptual y temas a investigar en América Latina)"[11] and "América Latina: lecciones aprendidas de los censos de población de la ronda 2000: principales resultados derivados de la encuesta dirigida a Oficinas de Estadística en el año 2003";[12]

(*d*) Economic Commission for Africa, "Africa Principles and Recommendations for Population and Housing Censuses—Addendum to the United Nations Principles and Recommendations for Population and Housing Censuses, Revision 2";[13]

(*e*) Economic and Social Commission for Western Asia, "Report on activities of the ESCWA Taskforce on Population and Housing Censuses, Beirut, 7-9 November 2006"[14], and "Report of the Taskforce Meeting on 2010 Population and Housing Censuses, Cairo, 12-13 November 2005"[15].

[4] See: http://unstats.un.org/unsd/demographic/sources/census/alternativeCensusdesigns.htm.

[5] *Updates and Amendments to the System of National Accounts, 1993*, Studies in Methods Series F/2/ Rev.4/Add.1. (United Nations publication, Sales No. E. 04.XVII.8).

[6] World Health Organization. (2001).

[7] *Official Records of the Economic and Social Council, 2007 Supplement No. 4* (E/2007/24-E/CN.3/2007/30).

[8] United Nations (New York and Geneva, 2006).

[9] http://www.unescap.org/stat/meet/egm2006/egm2006_report.pdf.

[10] http://www.unescap.org/pdd/CPR/CPR2006/English/CPR3_4E.pdf.

[11] CELADE-CEPAL, LC/L. 1204-P/E (Junio de 1999), Santiago de Chile (Sales No. S.99.11.G.9).

[12] http://www.eclac.cl/celade/noticias/documentosdetrabajo/1/24371/encuesta-lecciones.pdf

[13] Forthcoming

[14] E/ESCWA/SCU/2006/1G.1/10.

[15] E/ESCWA/SCU/2006/1.

Acknowledgements

The Statistics Division wishes to acknowledge the contributions of the members of the working groups and technical subgroups of the Expert Group on the 2010 World Programme on Population and Housing Censuses who participated in the development and review of the draft *Principles and Recommendations for Population and Housing Censuses, Revision 2*. Special thanks go to the members as well as to the Chair of the Drafting Group for the final review of the draft recommendations.

Summary of contents

Table of contents

Explanatory notes

ASCII	American Standard Code for Information Interchange
EA	enumeration area
ECE	Economic Commission for Europe
EDI/EDIFACT	Electronic Data Interchange for administration, commerce and transport
ESCAP	Economic and Social Commission for Asia and the Pacific
FAO	Food and Agriculture Organization of the United Nations
FTP	File Transfer Protocol
GIS	geographic information system
GPS	global position system
ICF	International Classification of Functioning Disability and Health
ICIDH	International Classification of Impairments, Disabilities and Handicaps
ICLS	International Conference of Labour Statisticians
ICR	intelligent character recognition
ICSC	International Classification of Status in Employment
ICT	information and communication technology
ILO	International Labour Organization
ISCED	International Standard Classification of Education
ISCO	International Standard Classification of Occupations
ISDN	Integrated Services Digital Network
ISIC	International Standard Industrial Classification of All Economic Activities
IT	information technology
LAN	local area network
LPG	liquefied petroleum gas
OCR	optical character reading
ODA	official development assistance
OECD	Organization for Economic Cooperation and Development
OLAP	OnLine Analytical Processing
OMR	optical mark reading
PES	post-enumeration survey
PSTN	public switched telephone network
RDBMS	relational database management system
SNA	System of National Accounts
UNAIDS	Joint United Nations Programme on HIV/AIDS
UNESCO	United Nations Educational, Scientific and Cultural Organization
UNICEF	United Nations Children's Fund
WAN	wide area network
WHO	World Health Organization
XML	Extensible Markup Language

Introduction

The most important capital a society can have is human capital. Assessing the quantity and quality of this capital at small area, regional and national levels is an essential component of modern government.

Aside from the answer to the question "How many are we?" there is also a need to provide an answer to "Who are we?" in terms of age, sex, education, occupation, economic activity and other crucial characteristics, as well as to "Where do we live?" in terms of housing, access to water, availability of essential facilities, and access to the Internet. The answers to these questions provide a numerical profile of a nation which is the sine qua non of evidence-based decision-making at all levels, and is indispensable for monitoring universally recognized and internationally adopted Millennium Development Goals.

Some nations are capable of generating this numerical profile for small areas from administrative records or through a combination of data sources. The vast majority of countries, however, produce these data on population and housing by conducting a traditional census, which in principle entails canvassing the entire country, reaching every single household and collecting information on all individuals within a brief stipulated period.

The traditional census is among the most complex and massive peacetime exercises a nation undertakes. It requires mapping the entire country, mobilizing and training an army of enumerators, conducting a massive public campaign, canvassing all households, collecting individual information, compiling vast amounts of completed questionnaires, and analysing and disseminating the data.

In most cases, a traditional census is an opportunity for mobilizing the country and making statistical activity visible. For many people the census may be the only time that the State reaches them and asks them a question. In addition, successfully conducting a census becomes a matter of national pride for many countries.

Ensuring confidentiality is crucial for the census to succeed. Thus, it has to be made clear that the only reason for collecting individual data is for the production of statistics and that there will be no dissemination of individual information or any non-statistical linkage with existing records in other government databases and data collections. Indeed, principle 6 of the *Fundamental Principles of Official Statistics** states: Individual data collected by statistical agencies for statistical compilation, whether they refer to natural or legal persons, are to be strictly confidential and used exclusively for statistical purposes.

* *Official Records of the Economic and Social Council, 1994, Supplement No. 9 (E/1994/29), chap. V.*

The United Nations recommends that all countries or areas of the world produce detailed population and housing statistics for small area domains at least once in the period 2005-2014, around the year 2010. For most nations that means conducting a traditional census, and the present revision of the *Principles and Recommendations for Population and Housing Censuses* thus focuses on the traditional census while also describing other approaches for generating reliable statistics on population and housing.

The population and housing census represents one of the pillars for data collection on the number and characteristics of the population of a country. The population and housing census is part of an integrated national statistical system, which may include other censuses (for example, agriculture), surveys, registers and administrative files. It provides, at regular intervals, the benchmark for population count at national and local levels. For small geographical areas or sub-populations, it may represent the only source of information for certain social, demographic and economic characteristics. For many countries the census also provides a solid framework to develop sampling frames.

PART ONE

Operational aspects of population and housing censuses

Chapter I
Essential roles of the census

1.1.   Evidence-based decision-making is a universally recognized paradigm of efficient management of economic and social affairs and of overall effective governing of societies today. Generating relevant, accurate and timely statistics is a sine qua non of this model; producing detailed statistics for small areas and small population groups is its foundation. The role of the population and housing census is to collect, process and disseminate such small area detailed statistics on population, its composition, characteristics, spatial distribution and organization (families and households). Censuses are conducted periodically in the majority of the countries in the world; they have been promoted internationally since the end of the nineteenth century, when the International Statistical Congress recommended that all countries in the world conduct them. Since 1958, the United Nations has also been actively promoting the population and housing census by compiling the principles and recommendations for population and housing censuses.

1.2.   While the roles of the population and housing census are many and will be elaborated in detail throughout the present revision of *Principles and Recommendations for Population and Housing Censuses*, several of the essential roles are listed below:

(*a*)   The population and housing census plays an essential role in public administration. The results of a census are used as a critical reference to ensure equity in distribution of wealth, government services and representation nationwide: distributing and allocating government funds among various regions and districts for education, health services, delineating electoral districts at the national and local levels, and measuring the impact of industrial development, to name a few. Establishing a public consensus on priorities would be almost impossible to achieve if it were not built on census counts. A wide range of other users, including the corporate sector, academia, civil society and individuals, make use of census outputs, as described in paragraph 1.23;

(*b*)   The census also plays an essential role in all elements of the national statistical system, including the economic and social components. Census statistics are used as benchmarks for statistical compilation or as a sampling frame for sample surveys. Today, the national statistical system of almost every country relies on sample surveys for efficient and reliable data collection. Without the sampling frame derived from the population and housing census, the national statistical system would face difficulties in providing reliable official statistics for use by the Government and the general public;

(*c*)   The basic feature of the census is to generate statistics on small areas and small population groups with no/minimum sampling errors. While the statistics on the small areas are useful in their own right, they are important because they can be used to produce statistics on any geographical unit with arbitrary boundaries. For example, in planning the location of a school, it is necessary to have the data on the distribution of school-age children by school area, which may not necessarily be equal to the administrative area units. Similarly, small area data from the census can be combined to approximate natural regions (for example, watersheds or vegetation zones) which do not follow administrative boundaries. Since census data can be tabulated for any geographical unit, it is possible to provide the required statistics in remarkably flexible manner. This versatile feature of the census is also invaluable for use in the private sector for applications such as business planning and market analyses;

(*d*)   The census results are used as a benchmark for research and analysis. Population projections are one of the most important analytical outputs based on census data; future population projections are crucial for all segments of the public and private sectors.

1.3.   In addition to the roles outlined above, it is critically important to produce detailed statistics for small areas and small population groups as a building block for efficient governance at all levels. For a vast majority of nations in the 2010 World Programme on Population and Housing Censuses, the method of choice for assembling this building block will be by conducting a population and housing census through universal and simultaneous individual enumeration of each individual within the nation's boundaries. Some nations will adopt alternative approaches; yet, all of these methods must result in identical outputs: detailed statistics for small areas and small population groups at the same moment in time.

Chapter II
Definitions, essential features and uses of population and housing censuses

A. Definitions

1. Population census

1.4.   A population census is the total process of collecting, compiling, evaluating, analysing and publishing or otherwise disseminating demographic, economic and social data pertaining, at a specified time, to all persons in a country or in a well-delimited part of a country.

1.5.   Population is basic to the production and distribution of material wealth. In order to plan for, and implement, economic and social development, administrative activity or scientific research, it is necessary to have reliable and detailed data on the size, distribution and composition of population. The population census is a primary source of these basic benchmark statistics, covering not only the settled population but also homeless persons and nomadic groups. Data from population censuses should allow presentation and analysis in terms of statistics on persons and households and for a wide variety of geographical units, ranging from the country as a whole to individual small localities or city blocks.

2. Housing census

1.6.   A housing census is the total process of collecting, compiling, evaluating, analysing and publishing or otherwise disseminating statistical data pertaining, at a specified time, to all living quarters[1] and occupants thereof in a country or in a well-delimited part of a country.

1.7.   The census must provide information on the supply of housing units together with information on the structural characteristics and facilities that have a bearing upon the maintenance of privacy and health and the development of normal family living conditions. Sufficient demographic, social and economic data concerning the occupants must be collected to furnish a description of housing conditions and also to provide basic data for analysing the causes of housing deficiencies and for studying possibilities for remedial action. In this connection, data obtained as part of the population census, including data on homeless persons, are often used in the presentation and analysis of the results of the housing census.

[1] For the definition of "living quarters", see para. 2.412.

B. Essential features

1.8. The essential features of population and housing censuses are individual enumeration, universality within a defined territory, simultaneity and defined periodicity.

1. Individual enumeration

1.9. The term "census" implies that each individual and each set of living quarters is enumerated separately and that the characteristics thereof are separately recorded. Only by this procedure can the data on the various characteristics be cross-classified. The requirement of individual enumeration can be met by the collection of information in the field, by the use of information contained in an appropriate administrative register or set of registers, or by a combination of these methods.

2. Universality within a defined territory

1.10. The census should cover a precisely defined territory (for example, the entire country or a well-delimited part of it). The population census should include every person present and/or residing within its scope, depending upon the type of population count required. The housing census should include every set of living quarters irrespective of type. This does not preclude the use of sampling techniques for obtaining data on specified characteristics, provided that the sample design is consistent with the size of the areas for which the data are to be tabulated and the degree of detail in the cross-tabulations to be made.

3. Simultaneity

1.11. Each person and each set of living quarters should be enumerated as of the same well-defined point in time and the data collected should refer to a well-defined reference period. The time-reference period need not, however, be identical for all of the data collected. For most of the data, it will be the day of the census; in some instances, it may be a period prior to the census.

4. Defined periodicity

1.12. Censuses should be taken at regular intervals so that comparable information is made available in a fixed sequence. A series of censuses makes it possible to appraise the past, accurately describe the present and estimate the future. It is recommended that a national census be taken at least every 10 years. Some countries may find it necessary to carry out censuses more frequently because of the rapidity of major changes in their population and/or its housing circumstances.

1.13. The census data of any country are of greater value nationally, regionally and internationally if they can be compared with the results of censuses of other countries that were taken at approximately the same time. Therefore, countries may wish to undertake a census in years ending in "0" or at a time as near to those years as possible. It is obvious, however, that legal, administrative, financial and other considerations often make it inadvisable for a country to adhere to a standard international pattern in the timing of its censuses. In fixing a census date, therefore, such national factors should be given greater weight than the desirability of international simultaneity.

C.　Strategic objectives

1.14.　The development of plans for a census should include the early preparation of a set of strategic aims and objectives that may be used to guide the implementation of the plans, set standards and form a set of benchmarks against which outcomes can be assessed to help determine the success of the census. Ideally, the starting point for developing these objectives would lie in combining information derived from evaluating previous census experience, from understanding user requirements for information from the census and from assessing changes in both society and technology. In practice, some of this information is difficult to obtain and often provides conflicting guidance. Nevertheless, such objectives can be used to assist in planning major elements of the process. Although the strategic objectives of the census will be specific to individual countries and will differ according to local circumstances, they can be described under the headings census content, impact on the public and on the census staff, production of census results, and cost-effectiveness.

1.15.　*Census content.* The aim is to ensure that the topics are appropriate for meeting the demonstrated requirements of users, taking into account considerations of cost-effectiveness. Subsidiary objectives under this element relate to (*a*) suitable consultation with existing and potential users at all stages, (*b*) establishment of measurable standards of reliability incorporating user views on priorities, and (*c*) adequate testing of new topics to ensure successful collection and production of reliable results.

1.16.　*Impact on the public and on the census staff.* The aim *is* to ensure that all the aspects of collection operations and the dissemination of results are acceptable to the public and fully comply with legal and ethical standards for protecting the confidentiality of individual responses. The public should be fully informed about census objectives, content and methods, as well as about their rights and obligations with respect to the census. Similarly, all census staff must be fully aware of their responsibilities. Subsidiary objectives include such issues as (*a*) keeping completed forms and other records containing personal information secure and confidential, (*b*) ensuring that public support for all aspects of the census is as strong as possible, and (*c*) producing requested customized output in a manner consistent with preventing disclosure of personal information, adhering to established reliability standards for the release of data, and implementing policies designed to safeguard the access of all users to census results.

1.17.　*Production of census results.* The aim is to deliver census products and services and to meet legal obligations and users' needs with stated quality standards and a predetermined timetable. Subsidiary objectives include (*a*) producing outputs with a minimum of error suitable for the purposes for which the data are to be used, (*b*) providing standard outputs for the main results and services for customized output, (*c*) providing access to output, (*d*) using geographical bases appropriate for collecting and referencing data for output, (*e*) improving methods of enumeration, particularly in difficult areas so as to reduce levels of undercoverage and response error, (*f*) improving methods of evaluation and the means to convey findings to users, and (*g*) developing a measure of quality and targets.

1.18.　*Cost-effectiveness.* The aim is to plan and carry out a census as inexpensively as possible in a manner consistent with the content and quality requirements. Subsidiary objectives relate to (*a*) capturing data more cost-effectively, (*b*) using efficient, speedy and reliable processing systems that are no more complex than necessary, (*c*)contracting out appropriate parts of the operation where this would be both cost-effective and consistent with the other strategic objectives, particularly the need to retain public confidence in the confidentiality of individual responses, (*d*) exploring possible sources of alternative funding and, if appropriate, developing proposals for cost recovery and income-generation, and (*e*) using development resources efficiently to develop prototype systems that can accommodate change and give "value for the money" in the final systems.

1.19.   These objectives can be used as benchmarks to assess user requirements and may also be built into appraisal systems which, with suitable weighting, can be used to compare and review options.

D.   Uses in an integrated programme of data collection and compilation

1.20.   Population and housing censuses are a principal means of collecting basic population and housing statistics as part of an integrated programme of data collection and compilation aimed at providing a comprehensive source of statistical information for economic and social development planning, for administrative purposes, for assessing conditions in human settlements, for research and for commercial and other uses.

1.21.   The value of either a population or a housing census is increased if the results can be employed together with the results of other investigations, as in the use of the census data as a basis or benchmark for current statistics, and if it can furnish the information needed for conducting other statistical investigations. It can, for example, provide a statistical frame for other censuses or sample surveys. The population census is also important in developing the population estimates needed to calculate vital rates from civil registration data (see paras. 1.55–1.57). In addition, these censuses are a major source of data used in official compilations of social indicators, particularly on topics that usually change slowly over time.[2] The purposes of a continuing coordinated programme of data collection and compilation can best be served, therefore, if the relationship among the population census, the housing census and other statistical investigations is considered when census planning is under way and if provision is made for facilitating the joint use of the census and its results in connection with such investigations. The use of consistent concepts and definitions throughout an integrated programme of data collection and compilation is essential if the advantages of these relationships are to be fully realized. Of course, census-type information can also be derived from population registers and sample surveys without undertaking a complete enumeration. These alternative data sources are presented under "Methodological approaches" in paragraphs 1.58–1.75.

1.22.   A population and housing census also serves as the logical starting place for work on the organization and construction of a computerized statistical database to serve continuing national and local needs for data in the intercensal period.[3]

1.   Uses of population censuses

(*a*)   Uses for policymaking, planning and administrative purposes

1.23.   The fundamental purpose of the population census is to provide the facts essential to governmental policymaking, planning and administration. Information on the size, distribution and characteristics of a country's population is essential for describing and assessing its economic, social and demographic circumstances and for developing sound policies and programmes aimed at fostering the welfare of a country

[2] See, for example, *Handbook on Social Indicators*, Studies in Methods, No. 49 (United Nations publication, Sales No. E.89. XVII.6).

[3] For a fuller discussion of many of the technical and policy issues that arise in the construction and use of integrated statistical databases, see *The Development of Integrated Data Bases for Social, Economic and Demographic Statistics*, Studies in Methods, No. 27 (United Nations publication, Sales No. E.79.XVII.14).

and its population. The population census, by providing comparable basic statistics for a country as a whole and for each administrative unit locality and small areas therein, can make an important contribution to the overall planning process and the management of national affairs. Population censuses in many countries also represent the very foundation of their national statistical systems, with census data providing important baseline data for policy development and planning, for managing and evaluating programme activities across a broad range of sectoral applications, and for monitoring overall development progress. An emerging use for census data is the assessment of good governance by civil society groups. The performance of a democratically elected Government in improving the welfare of its citizenry can be monitored from one census to the other by ordinary citizens through the widespread and timely dissemination of census results. On the international front, the declaration of internationally agreed development agenda objectives like the Millennium Development Goals and the focus on poverty eradication with the formulation of poverty reduction strategy papers have created a huge demand for periodic, regular and timely data for the monitoring and evaluation of such programmes. The census is helping to provide such data. Further and more specific examples and applications are given, along with references to appropriate manuals and guidelines, in part three, chapter IX.

1.24.   Population censuses serve many needs by providing statistical information on demographic, human settlements, social and economic issues for local, national, regional and international purposes. For example, population censuses provide basic information for the preparation of population estimates and detailed demographic and socio-economic analysis of the population. The census also provides data for the calculation of social indicators,[4] particularly those that may be observed infrequently because they measure phenomena that change slowly over time, and those that are needed for small areas or small population groups.

[4] *Handbook on Social Indicators,* Studies in Methods, No. 49 (United Nations publication, Sales No. E.89.XVII.6).

1.25.   One of the most basic administrative uses of census data is in the demarcation of constituencies and the allocation of representation on governing bodies. Detailed information on the geographical distribution of the population is indispensable for this purpose. Certain aspects of the legal or administrative status of territorial divisions may also depend on the size of their populations.

(b)   Uses for research purposes

1.26.   In addition to serving specific governmental policy purposes, the population census provides indispensable data for the scientific analysis and appraisal of the composition, distribution and past and prospective growth of the population. The changing patterns of urban/rural concentration, the development of urbanized areas, the geographical distribution of the population according to such variables as occupation and education, the evolution of the sex and age structure of the population, and the mortality and fertility differentials for various population groups, as well as the economic and social characteristics of the population and the labour force, are questions of scientific interest that are of importance both to pure research and for solving practical problems of industrial and commercial growth and management.

(c)   Uses for business, industry and labour

1.27.   In addition to those uses given above, the census has many important uses for individuals and institutions in business, industry and labour. Reliable estimates of consumer demand for an ever-expanding variety of goods and services depend on accurate information on the size of the population in subnational areas and its distribution at least by sex and age, since these characteristics heavily influence the demand for housing, furnishings, food, clothing, recreational facilities, medical supplies and so forth. Furthermore, the census can be used to generate statistics on the size and characteristics of the supply of labour needed for the production and distribution of such commodities and services in conformity with International Labour Organization (ILO) Convention 160. Such statistics on the local availability of labour may be important in determining the location and organization of enterprises.

(d)   Uses for electoral boundary delimitation

1.28.   A compelling use of census data is in the redrawing of electoral constituency boundaries in most countries. This is often enshrined in the country's constitution and provides a legal basis for census taking. The current distribution of a country's population is thereby used to assign the number of elected officials who will represent people in the country's legislature.

(e)   Use as a sampling frame for surveys

1.29.   Population censuses constitute the principal source of records for use as a sampling frame for surveys, during the intercensal years, on such topics as the labour force, fertility, and migration histories.

2.   Uses of housing censuses

(a)   Uses for development of benchmark housing statistics

1.30.   The housing census produces benchmark statistics on the current housing situation and is vital for developing national housing and human settlements programmes. The housing census is also valuable for providing the sampling frame for special housing and related surveys during the intercensal years.

1.31.   Housing benchmark statistics are also critical for emergency planning for response to natural hazards (such as destructive storms, earthquakes, tsunami, and fires), or post-conflict situations. Following such situations, these statistics can be used to estimate the numbers of people and structures affected, the need for emergency response, and reconstruction requirements.

1.32.   The Statistical Commission at its ninth session directed the attention of national statistical services to the need to develop, from housing censuses, the sort of benchmark statistics in housing that could be supplemented by current building and construction statistics and would provide a continuous up-to-date picture of the housing position needed for the consideration of housing programmes.[5] Since not all the basic information required to assess housing needs or to formulate housing programmes can be obtained through a housing census, additional data must be obtained through the population census, special housing surveys and environmental surveys, and from vital statistics, economic statistics and so forth; but data obtained from the housing census will constitute the basic framework within which the estimates are made, indices computed and further statistical inquiries planned.

1.33.   When population and housing censuses are carried out as a single operation or independently but in a well-coordinated fashion, the combined information provided is of much higher value since the essential features of both censuses are interrelated. The information on housing censuses may be analysed in association with the demographic and socio-economic condition of the occupants and, similarly, the demographic characteristics of the population may be analysed in association with the data on housing conditions.

[5]   *Official Records of the Economic and Social Council, Twenty-second Session, Supplement No. 7 (E/2876), para. 117.*

(b)   Uses for the formulation of housing policy and programmes

1.34.   The formulation of housing policy and programmes represents one of the principal uses of housing census data. Housing policy is normally influenced by social and economic as well as political considerations and available factual data concerning the housing situation provide objective criteria, which it is important for policymakers to take into account.

1.35.   In most countries, housing programmes encompass both governmental and private activity. The data derived from a housing census are used by governmental authorities for making an analysis or diagnosis of the housing situation.[6] Housing conditions are analysed in quantitative and qualitative terms and data from previous censuses are used to indicate the changes in the housing situation that have occurred during the intercensal periods; the housing deficit and future housing requirements are estimated and compared with the rates of dwelling production being attained; the characteristics of the households in need of housing are considered in relation to the availability and cost of housing. As part of overall development plans, such an analysis is necessary for the formulation of national housing programmes and for their execution.[7]

1.36.   Commercial users also study housing census data. Those engaged by the construction industry as well as financing institutions and manufacturers of housing fixtures and equipment and household appliances assess the possible demand for housing and perceive the scope of their activities within the overall programme.

(c)   Assessment of the quality of housing

1.37.   The materials used for the construction of housing units (roof, walls, floor) are a significant pointer to the quality of life in different parts of a country. Trends indicated by census data with regard to the type of housing materials can show improvements in the welfare of the citizenry, as the percentage of poor quality or slum-like housing facilities is decreased.

3.   Relationship between the population census and the housing census

1.38.   An especially close association exists between population censuses and housing censuses. The two censuses may constitute one statistical operation or they may be two separate but well-coordinated activities, but in either case they should never be considered completely independently of each other because essential elements of each census are common to both. For example, an essential feature of a population census is the identification of each occupied set of living quarters and of the persons living therein, and an essential feature of a housing census is the collection of information on the characteristics of each set of living quarters in association with the number and characteristics of its occupants.

1.39.   In many countries, the population and housing censuses are taken concurrently, often with the use of a single schedule. In this way, the information on population and living quarters can be more readily matched, processing is facilitated and extensive analysis can be carried out. This also makes it possible to relate to the housing census data the information on demographic and economic characteristics of each household member that is routinely collected in the population census.

1.40.   The advantages of simultaneous investigation may be offset to some extent by the additional burden on the respondent and the enumerator resulting from the increased amount of information that must be collected at one time. In countries where this is likely to be a serious problem, consideration might be given to collect-

[6] For some statistical indicators for measuring housing conditions, reference may be made to Statistical *Indicators of Housing Conditions*, Studies in Methods, No. 37 (United Nations publication, Sales No. 62.XVII.7) and to *Handbook on Social Indicators*, Studies in Methods, No. 49 (United Nations publication, Sales No. E.89. XVII.6).

[7] *Improving Social Statistics in Developing Countries: Conceptual Framework and Methods*, Studies in Methods, No. 25 (United Nations publication, Sales No. E.79.XVII.12).

ing data for a limited number of topics on the basis of a complete enumeration in the population and housing census, with more complex data in both fields being collected on a sample basis only, either concurrently with or immediately following the full enumeration. Alternatively, consideration might be given to carrying out the housing census as part of the advance-listing operations of the population census.

1.41.   The relationship between the population and the housing census will affect the means by which data on homeless persons are obtained. In the case of simultaneous censuses of population and housing, data on homeless persons will be obtained as part of the population census. Where the housing census is carried out independently of the population census, it will be necessary to try to enumerate homeless persons in the housing census. Information collected from enumerating homeless persons will reflect, among other things, the magnitude of the housing problem in a given locality.

4. Relationship of population and housing censuses to intercensal sample surveys

1.42.   The rapidity of current changes in the size and other characteristics of populations, and the demand for additional detailed data on social and economic characteristics of population and housing characteristics that are not appropriate for collection in a full-scale census, have brought about the need for continuing programmes of intercensal household sampling surveys to collect current and detailed information on many topics.[8]

8 *Handbook of Household Surveys (Revised Edition)*, Studies in Methods, No. 31 (United Nations publication, Sales No. E.83.XVII.13).

1.43.   The population and housing census can provide the frame for scientific sample design in connection with such surveys (see paras. 1. 438–1.441); at the same time, it provides benchmark data for evaluating the reasonableness of the overall survey results as well as a base against which changes in the characteristics investigated in both inquiries can be measured. To permit comparison of census and survey results, the definitions and classifications employed should be as nearly alike as possible, while remaining consistent with the aims of each investigation. Because of the relative permanence of living quarters, the lists available from the housing census (with suitable updating) may also provide a convenient frame for carrying out inquiries dealing with topics other than population and housing.

5. Relationship of population and/or housing censuses to other types of censuses and other statistical investigations

(a) Census of agriculture

1.44.   While the population and housing censuses have a close relationship, their relationship with the agricultural census is less well defined. However, as the result of increasing integration within programmes of data collection, the relationship between the population and housing census and the agricultural census is now far closer than in the past and countries are increasingly looking at new ways to strengthen this relationship.

1.45.   One issue in relating the two censuses is that they use different units of enumeration. The unit of enumeration in the agricultural census is the agricultural holding, which is the techno-economic unit of agricultural production, while the unit of enumeration in the population census is the household and the individual within the household. In many developing countries, however, most agricultural production activities are in the household sector and households and agricultural holdings are very closely related, often in a one-to-one relationship. Establishing links between the two censuses is particularly relevant for such countries.

1.46.　The agricultural census collects various household/individual data for members of the agricultural holder's household. The *World Programme for the Census of Agriculture 2010*,[9] recommends the collection of data on household size and limited data on demographic characteristics and economic activity of members of the holder's household, as well as some limited information on persons working as employees on the holding. Users may find some agricultural activity data from the agricultural census more comprehensive than from the population census because the latter normally investigates only the principal economic activity of each person during a short time reference period and this may not identify persons connected with agricultural activity on a seasonal or part-time basis. On the other hand, the population census provides data on agricultural employment and agricultural population, which is not available from the agricultural census because it only covers households associated with agricultural holders. To get a complete picture, agricultural data users will need both agricultural census data and population census data.

1.47.　In planning the population and housing census, every opportunity for developing the relationship between this census and the agricultural census should be explored. This can take several forms. Definitions used in the population and housing censuses should be compatible with those used in the agricultural census so that meaningful comparisons can be made between the two data sets. The population and housing census can also be of use in the preparation of the agricultural census, such as in the demarcation of enumeration areas, the preparation of the frame for the agricultural census or, if applicable, the sample design.

1.48.　In planning the national census programme, consideration should be given to the possibility of collecting additional agricultural information as part of the population and housing census exercise that would facilitate the preparation of the frame of agricultural holdings in the household sector for a subsequent agricultural census. This could be done as part of the pre-census cartographic work and/or listing exercise or by adding an additional question to the census questionnaire. In the latter case, an additional item at the household level could be included on whether any member of the household is engaged in own-account agricultural production activities. Alternatively, additional data at the individual person level could be collected to identify persons involved in agricultural activities during a longer period, such as a year. These new items are included in the principles and recommendations (see para. 2.381–2.390). Where countries choose to adopt this approach of using the population and housing census to establish a frame for the agricultural census, the agricultural census should be synchronized with the population and housing census and conducted as soon as possible after the population and housing census, while the frame is still up to date.

1.49.　The opportunity for linking population and agricultural census data should also be explored. This could add considerable analytical value to data sets from both censuses and save on data collection costs. Much of the demographic and activity status data collected in the population census are also collected in the agricultural census. If data from the two censuses could be linked, it would no longer be necessary to collect these data again in the agricultural census.

1.50.　Some countries conduct the data collection for the population and agricultural censuses as a joint field operation. Normally, each census retains its separate identity and uses its own questionnaire, but field operations are synchronized so that the two data collections can be done at the same time by the same enumerators. Occasionally, the two censuses are merged into one. This may have a number of advantages, but its effect on field operations and data quality needs to be carefully considered.

[9]　Food and Agriculture Organization of the United Nations, Statistical Development Series No. 11 (Rome, 2005).

(b) Census of establishments

1.51.   Although the collection of information on industrial and commercial establishments does not constitute a part of the population census, some of the information that is collected regarding economic characteristics of individuals can be used for preparing listings of the proprietors of such establishments and/or of the establishments themselves. Experience shows that these listings can be used in a subsequent census of establishments or for supplementing the registers of establishments maintained by most countries and utilized in their establishment censuses. While most business registers cover at the least all establishments in which more than some minimum of persons (usually 5 or 10) are employed, the population census can be used to collect basic information (volume, activity and employment) of business establishments with employment below the minimum number of persons, particularly those operated by self-employed persons. However, special care should be taken in the choice of the unit of enumeration to ensure that there is no double counting of establishments owned by more than one person/household. It is essential that the information from the population census be available and used shortly after the enumeration is carried out because this information quickly can become outdated.

1.52.   The population census information needed for these purposes is the industry and the status (as employer, employee, own-account worker and so on) of economically active persons, the name and address of their establishment (if any) and (for employers) the number of employees. If all of this information appears in the census questionnaire, the data for small employers and own-account workers can be extracted from the schedule or from the processing documents after the enumeration. If only industry and status appear on the schedule, the remaining information may be obtained from the desired group at the time of the population census enumeration and entered in a separate schedule.

(c) Census of buildings

1.53.   It is necessary, as part of the housing census operation, to inquire whether or not all buildings (both residential and non-residential) are occupied. Thus, it may be convenient to record basic information for all buildings at the time of the housing census, even though detailed data may be collected only for those in which housing units or other sets of living quarters are located. The comprehensive list thus obtained sometimes provides the basis for a census of buildings, carried out concurrently with, or subsequent to, the housing census, or it may provide for the identification of special types of buildings significant for other inquiries, such as the census of establishments or the school census. If a listing of households is to be carried out before the actual enumeration, this would be most ideal for carrying out such an exercise.

(d) System of current housing statistics

1.54.   Current housing statistics refer to housing activity. They reflect the number of dwellings constructed and certain related information such as value, number of rooms, floor space, and so forth, as well as number of dwellings destroyed or demolished. These data are usually obtained from a system of data collection based on the administrative procedures required in connection with the activity in question. For example, construction statistics may be derived from permits issued for the construction of dwellings, from records of dwelling starts or completions, or from certificates of occupancy. Statistics on dwellings destroyed may be obtained from the records maintained for the levying of rates and the collection of taxes. Compiled monthly or quarterly, current housing statistics reflect changes in the housing inventory and, although they may serve other purposes, they are also used to update the benchmark data obtained from housing censuses.

(e) Civil registration and vital statistics

1.55.   Population census data serve as denominators for the computation of vital rates, especially rates specific for characteristics normally investigated only at the time of the census. Conversely, census results, time-adjusted by vital and migration statistics, can provide estimates of the future size, distribution and other characteristics of the population of the total country and subnational areas. Furthermore, census data on fertility can provide a benchmark check on the reliability of current birth statistics, and vice versa. It is consequently desirable that procedures for the collection of population census data, vital statistics and migration statistics be closely coordinated with regard to coverage, concepts, definitions, classifications and tabulations.

1.56.   It may be noted that some countries have linked individual census returns for infants under one year of age with birth registration reports for the year preceding the census date as a means of checking on the completeness of one or the other type of investigation. Linkage of death reports with census returns has been used to compare the information on characteristics of the deceased as reported in the two sources. While the many problems posed in the past by the one-to-one matching of two types of records have not been entirely solved, their severity has been mitigated by developments in computer technology. Before under-taking either of the procedures, however, countries should consider carefully the possible advantages of using household sample survey returns rather than census returns in the operation. Moreover, such operations have to be carried out in complete accord with national laws and policies governing the confidentiality of information obtained in the census if public confidence in the census is to be maintained.

1.57.   In the establishment of a vital registration system, census results on the geographical distribution of the population can be useful in the consideration of appropriate locations for registration offices.

E.   Methodological approaches

1.58.   As part of their preparation for the 2010 global round of population and housing censuses, some countries are developing, testing, and implementing alternative methods for collecting, processing and disseminating key statistics that used to be generated by the traditional approach to population and housing censuses. Even so, the crucial principle of providing detailed statistics at the lowest geographical level remains of paramount importance.

1.59.   While the present publication focuses on the traditional approach to taking a census, sections 1–4 below briefly describe the major approaches currently in use or development. Many of the principles and guidelines described, in particular the recommended definitions and tabulations, are applicable to all approaches.

1.   The traditional approach

1.60.   During the 2000 round of censuses, over 190 countries conducted a population census and an overwhelming majority utilized the traditional approach to a census. The traditional approach comprises a complex operation of actively collecting information from individuals and households on a range of topics at a specified time, accompanied by the compilation, evaluation, analysis and dissemination of demographic, economic, and social data pertaining to a country or a well-delimited part of the country. Members of the public respond to a census questionnaire, or interviewers are deployed to collect information from respondents. For interviewer-based censuses, enumerators assigned to different enumeration areas cover all households and persons in the enumeration area during a specified and usually short period of time in order to meet the requirements of universality and simultaneity. Both short and long forms may be used within the context of traditional censuses. The short form contains only questions intended for universal coverage, while the long form is used to collect information from only a sample of households and population. This form usually contains detailed questions on a particular topic in addition to covering complex topics such as fertility. Both forms are utilized during the same time frame of the census. While the long form estimates are not based on full coverage, they are regarded as census output. Overburdening the census form is likely to adversely affect response rates and the quality of data.

1.61.   Because various methods can be used for collecting the data, including a mailed or dropped-off questionnaire, the telephone, the Internet, personal visit follow-up, or a combination of such methods, countries employing the traditional design may utilize very different methodologies in doing so.

1.62.   The traditional census has unrivalled merit in providing a snapshot of the entire population at a specified period and the availability of data for small geographic domains. In that sense, the traditional census is perhaps unique in nature. This approach is particularly suitable for countries having a federal structure and having the requirement of producing population numbers by various social and economic characteristics simultaneously for all geographical levels to meet the needs of planning and the allocation of funds. The delimitation of electoral boundaries also demands simultaneity, and for that reason also the traditional approach may be better. But at the same time, traditional censuses have been singled out as the most elaborate, complex and costly data collection activity that national census offices undertake. In addition to costs, this complex task requires full awareness and agreement of the public to participate in it. Because of the complexity and expense of such censuses, they are usually mounted only once every 5 or 10 years, so that census data are often several years out of date. For measuring the current state of employment and similar indicators it is therefore necessary to conduct a sample survey during the intercensal period.

1.63.   The following is a list of the essential features of a census. Under each is a description of how the traditional census approach incorporates these features into its design and production:

Individual enumeration

Separate information is collected for each individual. Individual information may be reported by proxy.

Universality within a defined territory

Single form approach:

Where only one form is used, all persons within the defined territory who meet the coverage rules are enumerated.

Short form/long form approach:

Short form topics. All persons within the defined territory who meet the coverage rules are enumerated.

Long form topics. These are surveyed and some persons are not covered by the enumeration but are represented in the results. Since the collection is coincident with the short form, it is possible to relate them together and by convention this survey is included as part of the census.

Simultaneity

The census information is provided with respect to a census moment in time. In cases where the information refers to a longer period (for example the last week) that period is expressed relative to the instant.

Periodicity

In principle, the census is taken at least once in every 10-year period.

2. The register-based approach

1.64.   The concept of producing census-like results based on registers emerged in the 2000 round of censuses, although it has been debated and tested to various degrees since the 1970s, and several countries succeeded in using this approach to generate census data in the 1990 round of censuses. The philosophy underlying this concept is to take advantage of the existing administrative sources, namely, different kinds of registers, of which the following are of primary importance: households, dwellings and individuals. In the next iteration these are linked at the individual level with information on business, tax, education, employment and other relevant registers. While it is theoretically possible to link the records on the basis of the name of the individuals, the existence of a unique identification number for each individual, household and dwelling is of crucial importance, as it allows much more effective and reliable linking of records from different registers.

1.65.   One of the essential preconditions of this approach is that the country should have an established central population register of high quality and good coverage linked with a system of continuous updating. In the case of local registers, continuous updating along with communication between the register systems must be good. It is essential to harmonize the concepts and definitions when linking registers, and forming the linkages will be difficult when no universal personal identifier exists. Quality assessments should be conducted. If these conditions are not met, the country should rely on the population census as the primary source of benchmark population statistics.

1.66.   The primary advantages of a register approach are reduced cost for the census process and greater frequency of data. However, establishing and conducting administrative registers involve higher costs than the census alone may justify. It is a more useful and effective administration that must prove the need of a register, not the statistics alone. The use of administrative data sources also involves certain drawbacks that need to be taken into account. One such drawback is the fact that register-based descriptions have to rely exclusively on the information contents that can be formed on the basis of the registers available. In addition, in not a few countries, registers are legally restricted to use for another purpose, such as making statistics. This imposes some restrictions with respect to characteristics that are available for description, and may also undermine international comparability. When a registered data item is changed, new or updated information is not always registered immediately and at times it is not registered at all. In this case, accurate information is not adequately reflected in the register.

1.67.   Related approaches, such as the combination of traditional and register-based designs, and register-based censuses combined with sample surveys, are described at http://unstats.un.org/unsd/demographic/sources/census/alternativeCensusDesigns.htm.

1.68. The following is a list of the essential features of a census. Under each is a description of how the register-based census incorporates these features into its design and production.

Individual enumeration

Separate information is collected regarding the characteristics of each individual. Information may be provided to an administrative register for other purposes. Access to administrative data for statistical purposes is given by law and/or by agreement. Then (*a*) the data may be passed as individual records to the population register; or (*b*) the registers may be temporarily linked to form a proxy population register.

Universality within a defined territory

All persons within the defined territory who meet the coverage rules are enumerated. In concept the enumeration is taken from a population register in which the fields for attributes are populated from subsidiary registers relating to specific topics. Where a subsidiary does not have an entry for a person, the entry in the population register is imputed as zero.

Simultaneity

Information is extracted from the register as it reflects the situation of individuals at the census moment in time. The timing of the census extraction may require careful thought where register update cycles vary.

Periodicity

Extracts meeting the other three essential features can be taken at a desired frequency, including "at least once in 10 years" noting again the need to manage the updating cycles for the registers.

3. The rolling census approach

1.69. A "rolling census" represents an alternative to the traditional model of the census by means of a continuous cumulative survey covering the whole country over a long period of time (generally years), rather than a particular day or short period of enumeration. The two main parameters of a rolling census are the length of the period of enumeration (which is linked to the frequency of updates required) and the sampling rate (which depends on the available budget and the geographic levels required for dissemination purposes). For example, it is possible to build a sample framework in order to produce national results with one annual survey, regional results by cumulating three annual surveys, and small area results by cumulating data over five years. Annual surveys may be conducted over the full course of the year or in a particular month or other shorter time frame.

1.70. Implementation of such an approach requires highly complex sampling and modelling techniques; a high quality sampling frame in order to allow sampling at very low levels of geography (a master address file updated annually is indispensable); and successful consultation about the approach with major stakeholders, including national and local governments and the user community. The main advantage of this approach is the higher frequency for updating data: a traditional census provides an update every 5 or 10 years, whereas a rolling census provides annual updates. Another advantage is in smoothing the burden of the census, instead of the high cost and labour requirement of a traditional census. Further, it is possible to improve the process year after year and test new technologies. The central disadvantage is that this approach no longer provides a simultaneous snapshot of the whole population, complicating comparisons between areas owing to different enumeration times, even if data collected at different dates are adjusted to have the same reference period, which is usually lagged by two or three years to allow for the cumulation of the annual surveys. In addition, as the rolling census covers the whole country over a long period of time, some respondents move. Thus some people may be surveyed several times and some other people will not be surveyed. As a result, universality might not be ensured unless careful methodological adjustments are made.

1.71.   The following is a list of the essential features of a census. Under each is a description of how the rolling census approach incorporates these features into its design and production.

Individual enumeration

Separate information is collected regarding each individual. Information may be reported by proxy. Where the cycle does not cover all persons, it could be considered that each record is not for an individual but the group that the individual represents through the individual's selection in the sample.

Universality within a defined territory

A proportion of the population is sampled in each period. Two cases may pertain: (*a*) in some cases an area may be fully enumerated over one or more years; (*b*) in other cases every person in the population has a chance of selection but at no time is it possible to say the entire population has responded.

Simultaneity

A range of mathematical techniques (for example, averaging and/or projections and/or interpolation) may be employed so that the data are a statistical depiction of the average situation as of a period of time.

Periodicity

Information is collected at regular brief intervals. For very small geographic areas, periodicity of dissemination will be determined to some extent by the rate of sample accumulation.

4.   Traditional enumeration with yearly updates of characteristics

1.72.   This design is a variation on the traditional census design and focuses on counting the population and collecting only the basic demographic data in the census year. A very large household survey collects and tabulates detailed demographic, social, economic, and housing data every year throughout the decade, replacing a census-year long form to collect these detailed data from a sample of the population. It may not be necessary to collect data on all topics every year, since requirements of such data may vary from country to country. The survey samples a percentage of addresses each year to approximate a long form sampling rate over a certain period of the census cycle, such as five years. To improve the reliability of the estimates for small governmental units, a larger proportion of addresses is sampled. The sample is cumulated over time to produce the lowest levels of geographic detail similar to the long form sample in the traditional census. Survey data are weighted to reflect the sample design, to adjust for the effects of non-response, and to correct for survey undercoverage or overcoverage. This final weighting adjustment helps to ensure that estimates of the characteristics are comparable to the standard, which is the periodic census. Once the final weights are applied, the statistics are generated, including population estimates, proportions, means, medians and ratios.

1.73.   The primary impetus for this approach is twofold: to provide more frequent and relevant data on the population than are available when a census is conducted only once a decade and to reduce the operational risks associated with the census. Such a programme, however, is costly and technically difficult to mount, and requires a multi-year programme of comprehensive planning, development and testing. Particularly in countries with legal requirements for complete counts of the population at intervals, the complete count component of the census design is crucial. As with the previous case, publication of small area data has to be delayed by two to three years to allow for the cumulation of the annual surveys.

1.74.   The following is a list of the essential features of a census. Under each is a description of how the traditional enumeration with yearly updates approach incorporates these features into its design and production.

Individual enumeration

Separate information is collected regarding each individual. Information may be reported by proxy.

Universality within a defined territory

(*a*) All persons within the defined territory who meet the coverage rules are enumerated in the short census component; (*b*) a predefined proportion of the population is sampled in each update period but the update sample never covers the entire population although through sampling methods the entire population is represented.

Simultaneity

(*a*) The short form census component is taken with respect to a census moment; thus, all information in that component refers to the census moment; (*b*) the update component will utilize temporal reference periods appropriate to the enquiries undertaken. A range of mathematical techniques (for example, averaging, projections, interpolation and weighting) may be employed so that the data are a statistical depiction of the average situation as of a period of time relating to and/or updating the short form census information.

Periodicity

(*a*) The short census component is taken at least once in 10 years; (*b*) the update component is collected at regular brief intervals; (*c*) output is provided at such intervals as data of sufficient quality and lowest geographical coverage are able to be compiled.

5.   Further information about these and other alternative census designs

1.75.   The United Nations Statistics Division website on the 2010 World Programme on Population and Housing Censuses depicts the approaches of a number of countries to the traditional census design and alternative designs. Each participating country describes its approach, including a discussion of how the design meets the essential features of a census, and the necessary conditions (legal, policy and technical) for implementing such an approach. Additional Internet links are provided for further information about each design. To access this information go to: http://unstats.un.org/unsd/demographic/sources/census/alternativeCensusDesigns.htm.

Chapter III
Planning, organization and administration of population and housing censuses

1.76.   The present chapter deals primarily with the operational aspects of traditional population and housing censuses and the very lengthy and detailed preparations that must be made in order to take such censuses successfully. Because of the technical and administrative complexities involved, the principles of census management provided below should be considered a review of the points to be taken into account in planning and executing a traditional population and housing census rather than a comprehensive treatment of the subject.

1.77.   A population and housing census (or a population census by itself) is perhaps the single most extensive, complicated and expensive statistical operation, consisting of a complex series of interrelated steps that a country undertakes. Some of these steps, for example, the printing of the census questionnaires, may be massive in scale; other steps, for example, the training of the supervisory staff, must be carried out in a uniform manner in all parts of the country; and still others, for example, the actual enumeration, must incorporate both features.

1.78.   To ensure that the diverse operations occur in their proper sequence and in a timely manner, the entire census and its various component steps must be planned for carefully in advance. An apparently minor oversight in planning may lead to serious defects in the census results and to costly inefficiencies in the census operations. Careful planning is therefore critically important to a successful census, not only in countries with comparatively little statistical experience but also in those with a well-developed system of statistics. Coupled with the need for careful planning is the need for appropriate organizational and administrative arrangements and procedures. Such arrangements and procedures are necessary to ensure both that the extensive human and material resources mobilized for the census are effectively and efficiently used and that its very tight time schedules and massive logistic requirements are met.

1.79.   It must be stressed, however, that at each stage of census planning and implementation, the various administrative arrangements developed will need to be guided by sound technical considerations. The quality and timeliness of the census data will almost certainly suffer unless sufficient weight is given throughout the census to a wide range of subject-matter and statistical requirements. This is especially valid in the case of cross-cutting issues, such as information technology, present throughout many essential phases of the census. It is for this reason that the management of a large statistical operation, and especially a population and housing census, cannot be considered a routine administrative assignment.[10]

1.80.   All censuses do not follow a uniform pattern but there are certain major elements that must be taken into account in every one of them. In general, census operations can be divided into six phases: (*a*) preparatory work, (*b*) enumeration, (*c*) data processing, (*d*) building of needed databases and dissemination of the results,

[10] For a discussion of statistical management generally, see *The Organization of National Statistical Services: A Review of Major Issues*, Studies in Methods, No. 21 (United Nations publication, Sales No. E.77.XVII.5) and *Handbook of Statistical Organization, Third Edition: The Operation and Organization of a Statistical Agency*, Studies in Methods, No. 88 (United Nations publication, Sales No. E.03.XVII.7).

(*e*) evaluation of the results, and (*f*) analysis of the results. In addition, distinct sets of operations related to the systematic recording of census experience and the quality assurance and improvement programme must accompany and support the main census operations. It will be readily apparent that these phases are not entirely separate chronologically or mutually exclusive. For example, some census results are usually released before all data-processing activities are completed; the analysis and the dissemination of census results overlap quite extensively; and the systematic recording of census experience should start at the beginning of the preparatory work and continue through all the subsequent phases. Furthermore, certain elements that are discussed below under Preparatory work, such as the budget and staff, may have to be amended according to the circumstances arising at a later stage of operations. The elements of each of these phases are discussed below in terms of their implications for sound census management.

1.81.   When the housing census and the population census are carried out together, the planning, organization and administration of the two censuses should be considered separate aspects of a single, integrated field and processing operation, that is, the separate technical requirements of each census have to be taken into account in planning and carrying out the combined operation. A combined population and housing census will be more costly and complex than each census considered by itself but less expensive than the total operation of carrying out both censuses independently. Moreover, the combined census will be capable of providing a greater wealth of cross-tabulations than both censuses carried out independently. Each country will have to decide on the trade-offs involved in the light of its own needs and circumstances (see also paras. 1.38–1.41). However, from the perspective of overall census planning and management, the decision is not a critical one. Whether the census is a combined operation or a separate population or housing census, the basics of census planning, organization and administration as described below remain unchanged, except for the added cost and complexity of the combined operation.

A.   Preparatory work

1.82.   The preparatory work for the census is necessarily long in duration and involves many quite distinct activities. It should be noted, however, that many of these activities may be interrelated but they also overlap to a large extent. When planning these preparatory activities, techniques for project management should be employed.[11] For purposes of presentation, these preparatory activities are divided into 18 somewhat arbitrary elements:

1.   Legal basis for a census (paras. 1.83 and 1.84)
2.   Financial basis for a census (paras. 1.85–1.94)
3.   Budget and cost control (paras. 1.95–1.102)
4.   Census calendar (paras. 1.103–1.107)
5.   Administrative organization (paras. 1.108–1.111)
6.   Census communication activities: user consultations, census publicity and promotion of census products (paras. 1.112–1.116)
7.   Plans for the quality assurance and improvement programme (paras. 1.117 and 1.118)
8.   Mapping (paras. 1.119–1.163)
9.   Small-area identification (paras. 1.164–1.172)
10.   Living quarters and household listing (paras. 1.173–1.176)

[11] See, for example, *Handbook on Census Management for Population and Housing Censuses*, Studies in Methods, No. 83/Rev.1 (United Nations publication, Sales No. 00.XVII.15/Rev.1), p. 8 -16.

11. Tabulation programme and database design (paras. 1.177–1.180)
12. Questionnaire preparation (paras. 1.181–1.192)
13. Census tests (paras. 1.193–1.196)
14. Plan of enumeration (paras. 1.197–1.200)
15. Plans for data processing (paras. 1.201–1.205)
16. Plans for census outputs and dissemination (paras. 1.206–1.209)
17. Staff recruitment and training (paras. 1.210–1.215)
18. Avoiding gender biases and biases affecting data on minority populations (paras. 1.216–1219).

1. Legal basis for a census

1.83. Legal authority for the census is required for fixing primary administrative responsibility, for obtaining the necessary funds, for determining the general scope and timing of the census, and for placing a legal obligation upon the public to cooperate and give truthful answers and a legal obligation upon the enumerator to record the responses faithfully. In addition, the confidentiality of the individual information should be strongly and clearly established in the census legislation and guaranteed by adequate sanctions so as to provide a basis for the confident cooperation of the public. In countries that lack permanent legal authority for the taking of periodic censuses, it is important to act early to establish ad hoc legal authority or, preferably, legislation calling for a system of periodic censuses.

1.84. The principle of conceptual and organizational flexibility should be observed in drafting the census legislation. Thus, the inclusion of too rigid provisions regarding the type of data to be collected or the structure and relationships of the various parts of the census organization is undesirable. Rather, necessary details should be contained in the census regulations promulgated by the census authorities. Moreover, provision will have to be made, in either the legislation or the regulations, for sanctioning the use of simplified administrative procedures, including the appropriate delegations of authority for the procurement of equipment and supplies and the recruitment of personnel during the operational phase of the census.

2. Financial basis for censuses

1.85. A census is the primary source of data about the size and characteristics of the population; it provides a demographic profile of a country and is the basis for developing area sampling frames for use in surveys. Censuses, however, are one of the largest and most costly statistical activities that governments and/or their national statistical offices undertake, and costs are on the rise. As a result, countries have been forced to delay or even cancel a census owing to funding constraints. Countries that have been able to secure partial funds or secure funds but at a late stage of their census preparation have been forced to compromise their data collection, data processing and dissemination of census results. It is therefore recommended that all census operations including planning, enumeration, analysis and dissemination, be budgeted from the beginning and efforts made to mobilize the required funds. Inflation should be taken into account, keeping in mind that duration has an impact on cost.

1.86. Given the above, there is growing pressure to look into the solutions to census funding, taking into account the role of key stakeholders, namely, Governments and their statistical agencies, and the greater involvement of international donors and the private sector. Concurrently, cost-effective strategies need to be put in place that would reduce census costs without compromising the quality of census data.

1.87.   It should be emphasized, however, that censuses cannot be carried out merely by national statistical offices alone. Rather, conducting a census should be seen as a national task involving all stakeholders. Thus, governmental departments, non-governmental organizations and the private sector end-users should be consulted (in all stages) to ensure the legitimacy and need for conducting the census and, at the same time, to improve the advocacy for sufficient funding. Although the conducting of a census is principally financed by the Government, the census must be designed in partnership with all political actors so as to obtain their involvement in the census process. A high level committee which consists of the Government, the private sector and civil society, including non-governmental organizations, communities and donors could be formed to discuss issues related to the cost and funding of the census.

1.88.   National statistical offices need to advocate the importance of investing in censuses within their own Governments. The possibility of cost sharing with other government departments, such as education and health ministries, should be further explored. These institutions could be supportive in providing logistics arrangements for the census, such as the use of existing infrastructure, transportation, communications facilities and the sharing of employees of other government departments.

1.89.   Good planning is an essential prerequisite for not only achieving a cost-effective census but also securing comprehensive financial support for its funding. The census must bring out the links between the various components, which will include types of resources (such as manpower, cost of stationery or printing) as well as tasks using the resource, including data collection and capture, data processing, and data management and dissemination. Cost tags must be attached to each of these components together with a justification.

1.90.   For each stage of the census the costs must be optimized, which will be assisted by making careful choice of the appropriate technology. Recent advances in technologies such as scanning, data processing and data management may be of assistance in achieving significant reductions in cost (or doing more within the same cost). In addition, the use of such technologies will speed up the computation of results and enhance their preservation. However, the choice of technology should be made only after carefully evaluating the costs and benefits of possible options. Some potential risks to canvass include the following: some approaches only become cost effective for large operations; some are dependent on expensive and scarce inputs (for example very high quality paper); and others require significant upfront investments in high quality computers. The options examined in the benefit/cost analysis could incorporate consideration of leasing (rather than purchasing) equipment and/or sharing it between countries that are undertaking censuses at convenient times.

1.91.   Outsourcing with the private sector could be considered as another cost-saving option, particularly in the context of publicity or for systems development for data collection or data processing. While not necessarily less costly, it may contribute technical expertise or resources not available within the national statistical office. Paragraphs 1.220–1.227 present in more detail criteria for countries considering outsourcing some of their census activities.

1.92.   It is anticipated that international donors will continue to play a pivotal role in helping to fund census costs in many countries. Technical cooperation and assistance from international agencies have also contributed greatly to the success of censuses in many countries. However, pooling of these donor resources could be a cost-effective strategy for meeting the rising costs of censuses.

1.93.   It is worth noting that a population and housing census has some intangible positive values. It is an opportunity for mobilizing the whole country and reaching even the most remote corners of it. In the life of many citizens, a regular census is often the only time that the State reaches out to them and asks them some questions. Successfully conducting a census is a matter of pride in many countries and a welcome opportunity to recruit a massive labour force and generate jobs and train people in valuable tasks (such as data entry) or in other ways to add to the national infrastructure.

1.94.   In general, population and housing censuses are exclusively the responsibility of national Governments and structures; this is particularly true for funding the census. Thus, all activities related to funding need to be elaborated, documented, justified and presented to all stakeholders in a transparent and comprehensive manner.

3.   Budget and cost control

1.95.   While no universal system of census budgeting and cost control can be suggested since financial practices vary greatly among countries, a few generally accepted principles can be noted. First and foremost, effective planning and control of the various census operations are not possible without a very careful financial estimate of the cost of each census operation, including all of its components, no matter how small. It is recommended to draft a detailed list of activities related to censuses and, as much as possible, to draft the budget in such a way that it corresponds to this list of activities. Second, it is critical for this census plan and budget to be presented by national statistical agencies to their respective Governments with adequate lead time, to facilitate the appropriation of sufficient resources from national budgets, or where appropriate, from the international development community. Moreover, funding of the census must be accompanied and developed on a sound and adequate legal basis if effective national census operations are to be enabled.

1.96.   Information on expenditures from the previous census classified by census phases, starting with the expenditure for different elements of the preparatory work and ending with expenditure for the dissemination of the census results, provides an important basis for estimating the budget of the census. Figures from the previous census will of course have to be modified in order to take into account quantitative and qualitative change in hardware and software, changes in wage rates and the costs of equipment, supplies and so on, planned changes in census content, methods and procedures, and anticipated changes in the population itself (for example, total size, percentage urban, and average household size), all of which may affect the cost structure of the census. In most countries, several cost elements tend to increase (for example, wage rates and the size of population) so that there is considerable pressure to achieve economies in other items of the census budget.

1.97.   Census managers need to implement transparent accounting procedures to enable prompt release of periodic allocations of census funds by national Governments.

1.98.   In the case of external/donor funds, the required conditions should be established well in advance by discussion between the donor and the national statistical office. This will avoid delay in the release of such funds for census operations.

1.99.   National statistical offices should set up special financial management systems that will ensure speedy disbursement of funds, proper receipting of their expenditure and an efficient audit. A clean outcome from a financial audit adds credibility to the census process so that the Government and civil society are more likely to accept the final results.

1.100.   To obtain the information needed to monitor the costs of the current census and that needed to plan for the next, detailed and precise data will be required on the following: (*a*) number and cost of census staff classified by function and manner of payment; (*b*) type of equipment and material used for the census, manner of acquisition (in other words, purchase or rental) and cost; (*c*) office space (surface measurement), classified by use and type of cost (in other words, for construction or for rent); (*d*) type of services used for census operations. The usefulness of the above information would be enhanced if the information could be recorded by source of funding, in other words, in terms of whether the expenditure has come from (*a*) the official census budget; (*b*) other funds of the census office (for example, a regular annual budget not specifically intended for census purposes, or general funds of the governmental agency or department of which the census office is a part); (*c*) other parts of the Government; (*d*) non-governmental organizations. This information is needed not only for fiscal planning and control but also in order to examine the trade-offs in terms of costs and benefits among alternative ways of carrying out various census operations. Although cost experience from a previous census in a country may provide useful experience for planning the next census, considerably more caution should be exercised in using the cost parameters from other countries. Differences in census content, organization and operations, as well as in cost accounting, can introduce serious incompatibilities into such country-to-country cost comparisons.[12]

[12] See United Nations Statistical Commission and Economic Commission for Europe, Conference of European Statisticians, *Costing Aspects of Population and Housing Censuses in Selected Countries in the UN/ECE Region*, Statistical Standards and Studies, No. 46 (United Nations publication, Sales No. E.96.II.E.15).

1.101.   It is important that the persons at the administrative and supervisory levels who will be responsible for the execution of each operation participate in estimating the budget items. Such an organization of the work presupposes detailed advance planning and "cost-consciousness" on the part of those responsible for a census.

1.102.   The census plan as executed will certainly change in a number of respects after the making of the original calculations. Consequently, a perfect correspondence between the estimates and the final costs is not to be expected. Changes in the prices of major components of census costs should be monitored on a regular basis with either the census budget adjusted accordingly or the census plans modified. Indeed, the development of the census budget is usually an incremental process in which rough initial estimates are replaced by more detailed and precise statements of resource requirements. Throughout the period of census taking and compilation of census results, the budget will have to be re-examined and performance compared with plans. With detailed information on expenditure, the governmental and census authorities will be better able to exercise control over keeping the development of census operations within the census budget as well as to assess and control the effectiveness and efficiency of these operations. This information is also very useful for studying possible improvements in census techniques and census methodology.

4.   Census calendar

1.103.   An indispensable element in the planning of a census is a calendar or timetable indicating the sequence and estimated duration of each of the component operations of the census. At the early stages of census planning, a provisional calendar of selected key dates should be prepared as an overall framework for the census. The calendar should be revised and made more detailed as planning proceeds, with the aim of establishing final dates as soon as practicable.

1.104.   Such calendars are essential, since they indicate the dates on which each of the numerous operations that make up a census are to be started and completed, and they serve as a guide for measuring the progress of each stage of the census operation. Serious delays in work, or errors in time estimates, can be detected by comparing the calendar target dates with the actual dates of each operation. A census calendar is a very efficient instrument not only in the timing control of each census operation but also in the control of the complex of all census operations that are interdependent. Therefore, when modifications in the census timetable are necessary, all related operations should be taken into consideration in order to avoid disruptions in the whole census programme. Obviously, the time schedule will differ for each national census depending upon the general census plan and the resources that are available.

1.105.   The census calendar usually shows the various operations grouped into three broad sectors: (*a*) pre-enumeration, (*b*) enumeration and (*c*) post-enumeration. The last-named sector includes evaluation and analysis as well as processing and dissemination. The basic date on which the census calendar and the scheduling of all other operations hinge is the starting date for the general enumeration of the population. For purposes of control, many operations that in fact overlap are shown separately in the calendar. Census calendars sometimes take the form of a chart or graph, in addition to a detailed checklist of operations. Project management software may help in the preparation of the census calendar.

1.106.   In establishing the census calendar, it is necessary to consider the relationship of the population and housing censuses to one another as well as to other statistical projects or other large-scale national activities. Although a joint population and housing census operation is likely to constitute, for the period of its duration, the major statistical undertaking of the Government, care should be taken that it does not interfere unduly with the other regular statistical activities that may be going on at the same time. A balanced statistical programme should avoid having too many simultaneous competing inquiries which might place too heavy a burden on the statistical services and on the public, with a possible resultant loss of both administrative efficiency and public cooperation.

1.107.   It is often useful to draw up a comprehensive diagram showing the sequence, interrelationship and timing of all the various steps in the census programme. This type of analysis often reveals the consequences of a delay at one step in terms of delays at other steps in the programme. It can therefore be a useful instrument against which the actual progress of the census preparations may be compared. Indeed, some countries have attempted to use such critical path analyses not only as an aid to census planning but also as a tool for the ongoing management of their census operations. In these instances, it is essential to establish procedures for revising the critical-path analysis in response to actual progress. It should be stressed, moreover, that the usefulness of such devices depends on how soundly they are designed, applied and understood. A project management software can be useful in linking the diagrammatic structure of census operations with information about nodes and/ or centres of responsibility for individual broad or detailed operations so as to control the chain of responsibility. In such a case, other tools, commonly referred to as groupware and collaboration software as well as internet forums, can support census operations by providing an environment for exchange of information, files, and data among dispersed teams.

5.   Administrative organization

1.108.   In planning the organization and administration of a census, it is important to consider the role and relationship of the various executive and advisory organs. National, subnational and local commissions and committees are frequently useful in the planning and preparations of a census. Such bodies may be composed of representatives of governmental agencies and of non-governmental users of the census data, particularly those involved in policy-oriented analysis of census results and analytical studies of the social, economic and demographic situation of the country. It is important, however, that their advisory and promotional functions be clearly defined and that the final responsibility for planning rest with the executive agency.

1.109.   There are definite advantages in having an office continuously responsible for census work established as an integral part of the statistical system of a country. Such an office assures continuity in census work and is the principal centre for the formulation of the programme and the initiation of preparatory work for the next census. Its permanence permits the development of specialized and experienced personnel and the maintenance of statistical and cartographic information, including cross-cutting issues such as information technology, essential for planning the next census.

1.110.   At the pre-enumeration stage, the census office will need to be expanded to form the nucleus of the full census organization, which must be capable of directing the field organization during the preparatory work as well as during the enumeration. In order to provide immediate supervision in each area, field offices at various levels are needed for the later part of the preparatory work, including staff recruitment and training, as well as for the enumeration period. Supervisory personnel in such offices should be persons who, being familiar with the particular area and the local language, are able to deal with local problems. This does not mean, however, that all supervisory positions must be filled by persons from the area. Personnel may be transferred from the central office or from other areas as the need arises.

1.111.   Subsequent to the enumeration, the census organization is usually readjusted to meet the needs involved in compiling, evaluating, analysing and publishing the results and to provide the continuity desirable for promoting the continued use of census materials and the development of improved methods.

6.   Census communication activities: user consultations, census publicity and promotion of census products

1.112.   A comprehensive programme of communications for a population and housing census covers three distinct audiences: (*a*) major users of census data, (*b*) persons and institutions participating in the census operations and (*c*) the general public. Since the census is a national activity that is completely dependent for its success upon the wholehearted cooperation and assistance of the general public and many governmental and local organizations, the entire communications effort should be developed as a coordinated activity in close conjunction with the other substantive preparations for the census. These communications activities are valuable not only for informing others about the census but also for providing census authorities with early and continuing information about the reactions to census plans and activities of the general public in various parts of the country and of key persons, groups and institutions.

1.113.   Consultation with users of census data on topics, on definitions and, particularly, on planned tabulations and the development of the census database is an indispensable step in the preparations for the census that should be taken early. These consultations will assist the census authorities in planning for a census that, within the resources available, is as responsive as possible to user needs in terms of the collection, processing, tabulation, storage and availability of meaningful data. Such consultations can also serve to foster a wider and more informed understanding of and support for census plans and activities. The users to be consulted should be from governmental departments, ministries, universities and other research institutions, the private sector, and other organizations (or individuals) representing the economic, social, educational and cultural life of a country. It is often more useful to hold separate consultations with different types of users with common interests, such as administrators, policymakers, planners, demographers, researchers, users in the business community and so forth, rather than a simultaneous meeting of all data users. Such combined meetings frequently prove frustrating to participants because there are substantial differences among users in their technical background and in their concern with the details of census content and operations. Because of the importance of the census in providing data for local planning and administration, it is also often advisable to have consultations with users in provincial and local governments and institutions in various parts of the country. Particularly in large countries or countries where the provincial or local governments have a comparatively high degree of autonomy, consultations with users at the subnational level is essential if the full potential of the census is to be achieved.

1.114.   In order to complete the preparatory work for the census and to carry out the census enumeration itself, the census office will have to expand its staff substantially. In addition, numerous governmental and non-governmental organizations outside the census office may be called upon to provide personnel, equipment, supplies, space, transportation or communications facilities and so on to help in the census work. As a result, large numbers of temporary personnel will have to be trained (see paras. 1.210–1.215) and the contributions of a diverse group of national and local organizations will have to be effectively mobilized. A well-planned communications programme can contribute to both efforts.

1.115.   Arranging the publicity for the census is another of the important tasks in the census operation. This entails an educational campaign, the purpose of which is to enlist the interest of the general public and its cooperation. The aims, as a general rule, are not only to dissipate any anxiety regarding the purposes of the census but also to explain the reasons for the various questions in the questionnaire and to offer some guidance as to the manner in which these questions should be answered. The publicity campaign may also be an important tool for increasing the completeness of census coverage, particularly among hard-to-enumerate groups. It is desirable that planning for the general publicity campaign should start as soon as the census is authorized. The campaign itself should be closely synchronized with other census activities and full-scale publicity should not begin too far in advance of the date on which enumeration is scheduled to start. Plans for the publicity programme should be closely coordinated with those for the census tests (see paras. 1.193–1.196). The programme will have to provide the publicity needed to carry out the census tests. In addition, the programme can use these tests to study the impact of alternative publicity materials and methods. If either the cartographic or house-listing operations require extensive fieldwork and widespread contacts with the public, it should be recognized that personnel involved in these activities often provide the public with its first impression of the census. Training and publicity programmes should take this factor into account. The general campaign should be directed to all sections of the country and all segments of the population through the use of all available publicity media. The general campaign may be supplemented by a number of specialized campaigns aimed at specific segments of the population.

1.116.   An integral part of census communication and publicity is informing key census data users and the general public about the many uses of population and housing censuses (see paras. 1.23–1.37) and planned census outputs (see paras. 1.206–1.209). Making transparent why censuses are undertaken and what they are used and useful for helps alleviated possible misconceptions by the general public, thus increasing participation and census coverage, and the utilization of census results and products. It is critical that such communication strategies be developed as an integral part of census planning and not left as an optional add-on.

7.   Plans for the quality assurance and improvement programme

1.117.   Most countries conduct population and housing censuses, once in 10 years. Thus current experience is limited. But experience from previous population and housing censuses as well as other censuses such as agricultural census is very useful to plan for a quality assurance and improvement programme for the current one. Moreover, numerous activities that compose the census operation have to be carried out in a limited time period. This means that countries must employ a large number of persons for census work for a few weeks or months. Usually a different set of persons are employed on a temporary basis for each of these operations. As a result, the quality of work is likely to vary from person to person, from one area to another and from one time to another. It is therefore important to be able to measure how well each census operation is proceeding by building in quality assurance procedures throughout the census. It should be stressed that a major goal of any quality assurance programme is to detect errors so that remedial actions can be taken even as the census operations continue. Thus, a quality assurance programme should also be viewed as a quality improvement programme. Without such a programme, the census data when finally produced may contain many errors which can severely diminish the usefulness of the results. If data are of poor quality, decisions based on these data can lead to costly mistakes. Eventually the credibility of the entire census may be called into question.

1.118.   The quality assurance and improvement system should be developed as part of the overall census programme, and integrated with other census plans and procedures. The system should be established at all phases of census operations, including planning, pre-enumeration, enumeration, document flow, coding, data capture, editing, tabulation and data dissemination. Establishing a quality assurance and improvement system at the planning stage is crucial to the success of the overall census operation. For a more extensive discussion of the components of a quality assurance and improvement programme, see paragraphs 1.228–1.277 below.

8.   Mapping

1.119.   There is widespread recognition that it is important for national statistical agencies to develop a continuing cartographic capability to serve their specialized cartographic needs. Such a capability can make a major contribution to the population and housing census and other elements of the national statistical system. A continuing cartographic capability within the statistical agency can also contribute to the analysis and presentation of census results.

1.120.   Statistical agencies, however, are not mapping agencies and should not, for the most part, try to duplicate the functions of one. Likewise, mapping agencies are not statistical agencies and often may not fully appreciate the statistical value of the information they hold or how best to present statistical information in map-based products. Despite this, undertaking a census can provide a catalyst for the statistical and mapping agencies to work together to the benefit of both agencies and the community.

1.121.   It should be stressed that there is now a wide range of techniques and technologies available for use in a census mapping exercise (and it is likely that before the conclusion of the 2010 World Programme on Population and Housing Censuses further options will become available). The following sections do not make any recommendation as to which system would be most appropriate for any country or countries at any stage of development. Rather, these sections summarize the options available at the time of writing and note particular issues that should be addressed by countries in deciding the type of operation to be undertaken for their census.

(a)   Strategic basis for a census mapping programme

1.122.   The quality of maps used in the census has a major influence on the quality and reliability of census data.

1.123.   In the enumeration phase, maps play a vital role in guiding enumerators to dwellings and other places where people are likely to be during the enumeration period. They are important in ensuring full and unduplicated coverage of geographic areas.

1.124.   It is still the case that in many countries there are only a limited range of maps available and these often do not show sufficient detail to enable the boundaries of small areas to be clearly defined. This is particularly likely to apply in areas of unplanned settlement. It is thus common to supplement the maps with other material, such as (a) lists of households (preferably compiled by statistical agency staff as part of the process of delineating enumeration areas, but on occasion provided by local leaders) see paragraphs 1.173 to 1.176; and/or (b) a textual description of the boundary including roads, railway lines, power lines, rivers and other physical features. This description may also include obvious landmarks on the boundary (school buildings, water points and others).

1.125.   However, it is not appropriate for field staff to rely entirely on a list of households, written or verbal descriptions and directions, or on local knowledge of the area boundaries. Reliance on verbal descriptions or local knowledge very often leads to confusion and error because people tend to have mental images (or mental maps) of places and these images may not coincide with the area as it really is reflected in the design of the enumeration area. For the same kind of reason, the supervisor's mental map of an enumeration area may differ markedly from that of an enumerator. To overcome such problems, it is important that the best possible quality maps be the basis for census enumeration operations and that the collection staff receive comprehensive training in the correct use of the maps and associated textual material if that is provided.

1.126.   Similarly, maps, which are now commonly in the form of digital products, play an increasingly important role in the dissemination phase. Statistics compiled from census data can be geographically referenced and provide for methods of analysing the geographic characteristics of those statistics. Maps may then be used effectively to relate statistical data to the geographical area to which the census results refer. This makes the statistics easier to understand and more readily usable by both expert users and the general public.

1.127.   In addition to the maps required for the census, a systematic, complete and up- to-date listing of localities is required. Such a listing is needed for the coding of place names and for determining to what extent data for localities will be tabulated. In some regions, the establishment of a definitive list of localities is a major operation because of difficulties arising from the frequent fragmentation, disappearance or combination of small localities, and from changes in name, variations in spelling, the existence of more than one name for the same place or the use of identical names for different places. This listing should be held as a formal database or as an integral component of the databases forming part of a geographic information system (GIS).[13]

1.128.   Where a digital base map is prepared, this may be able to be used in conjunction with GIS technology as the basis for coding information supplied in the census. This could apply to address of usual residence now and/or in the past, place of work and similar topics.

[13] For further details on GIS mapping, see *Handbook on geographic information systems and digital mapping*, Studies in Methods, No. 79 (United Nations publication, Sales No. 00.XVII.12).

(b)   Conceptual planning for census mapping operations

1.129.   The types of maps required for census mapping include the following: (*a*) small-scale reference maps for use in the census agency to manage the overall operation; (*b*) large-scale topographic maps for use by enumerators; (*c*) maps of the subregions or administrative areas, for the use of managers, showing the location of small population settlements and dominant physical features, such as roads, rivers, bridges and the type of terrain.

1.130.   The lead times necessary to create, maintain, print and distribute enumeration area maps are significant, and careful consideration should be given to the mapping activity during the census planning and preparation phases. The duration of the lead time for a country will be determined by a wide range of factors, including the number of maps to be produced, the technology available to produce them, the availability of funds to acquire additional resources and the time required for distribution of the maps to field staff. However, as a working rule it could be suggested that the mapping programme be established working back from a deadline of reproducing the last map three months before the census day. This will provide sufficient time to distribute the maps prior to commencing the training of field staff. Particular care must be taken in this regard where consideration is given to using more advanced technologies (see paras. 1.135 to 1.142). Additional time may be required to gain the capacity needed to use the technology effectively.

1.131.   Prior to developing the mapping programme for the census, consideration needs to be given to the geographic classification to be used and the mapping infrastructure available to carry out the mapping tasks. As the geography on which the census is collected will determine the geography on which the census data can be disseminated, a geographic classification should be devised in conjunction with the development of census mapping. The details of designing a general geographic classification, including the definition of the various areas of the geographic classification and their relationship to one another, are more complex than those involved in census mapping and will not be covered further in this volume.[14] However, the design of enumeration areas and other census management areas are of crucial importance for the census and are outlined in the following paragraphs.

(i)   *Design criteria for enumeration areas*

1.132.   Enumeration areas (EAs) are fundamental to both the statistical areas structure and to the census management area structure. Issues that need to be considered include:

(*a*)   Achieving complete coverage by showing clearly that there are no gaps in the area to be enumerated;

(*b*)   Improving the ability of personnel to manage field operations effectively by recognizing the workload limits of enumerators and ensuring that EA boundaries are designed so that they follow easily recognizable features such as roads, waterways, established walking tracks and railway or power lines. The use of features such as village or local government boundaries should be carefully considered, taking into account the difficulty of identifying boundaries using features such as compass bearings or lines of sight;

(*c*)   To the extent possible the design of enumeration areas should avoid including significantly different types of housing within a single EA. This will facilitate dissemination of information on specific housing situations, such as slums (an issue specified as part of the Millennium Development Goals);

[14] For an example of a more detailed description of the units that are considered in one country's statistical geography, see Australian Bureau of Statistics, "Australian standard geographical classification" Bulletin 1216.0, chap.10. The range of units classified are shown in the structural chart in that chapter. Note that the lowest unit "census collection district" is equivalent to enumeration area.

(*d*) Dissemination objectives also require taking into account the demand for small area data, the confidentiality of personal information and the ability to be aggregated to present information on larger geographic units. For some defined boundary areas, an approximation formed by aggregating boundaries may be used for dissemination.

1.133.   Procedures should be developed that will allow a comparability listing of areas from one census to the next. In cases where this is not possible, the criteria can outline design principles that will allow users to easily compare EA-based data across censuses.

(ii)   *Design criteria for census management areas*

1.134.   Census management areas will consist of aggregations of enumeration areas brought together for ease of managing the enumeration staff. Where existing government staff and structure are used for enumeration purposes, the census management areas may be the same as the administrative regions. It should be noted that this may be a matter of administrative convenience and the particular hierarchy (or way of combining enumeration areas into larger areas) for this purpose need have no role in the design of areas for the dissemination phase, which must be driven by the needs of users.

(iii)   *Appropriate technology*

1.135.   Before census mapping commences, the census agency needs to determine the appropriate technology for mapping. An agency should assess existing maps, available in any format, that are known to be accurate, and use them with new maps prepared as required. The new maps can either be produced as hand-drawn maps of enumeration areas, or they can incorporate overlays or other technological assistance. Alternatively, a GIS could be implemented. These options are described in the following paragraphs.

1.136.   In circumstances where it has not been possible to acquire appropriate base maps for areas of geography, enumerators (or other enumeration staff) may produce hand-drawn maps, accompanied by a textual description of the boundary features, to enable a successful enumeration. Hand-drawn maps do not possess the level of accuracy offered by high-quality topographic maps, but are an option when maps for an area: (*a*) do not exist; or (*b*) are too small a scale to provide sufficient detail for an enumeration area map; or (*c*) are seriously out of date and cannot be updated in the time available.

1.137.   Where reasonable-quality topographic maps are available, they should be used as a base and hand-drawn enumeration area boundaries can be added as an overlay on transparent film and the combination photocopied for use by the enumerators. All base maps produced for census should be referred to a unique, consistent, geodetic reference system all over the country.

1.138.   Where accurate and current maps at relevant scales are not available for a country, or part of a country, the technological alternatives described in the following paragraphs could be employed subject to consideration of the constraining factors described in paragraphs 1.139–1.142:

(*a*) *Satellite images.* Although currently relatively expensive to acquire, the price of satellite imagery is declining in real terms. A satellite image typically covers a large area and can be cost-effective compared to other sources. Imagery should be pre-processed by the supplier so that it is rectified and georeferenced (a known scale and orientation, with some latitudes and longitudes, is printed on the face of the image);

(b)   *Aerial photography.* Acquisition of aerial photographs for large tracts of a country may be expensive. However, existing archives of photographs can be an excellent resource for preliminary counts of dwellings and as a base for basic maps. In some cases digital aerial photographs can be a cost-effective way of initiating some components of a geographic information system (GIS);

(c)   *Global positioning systems (GPS).* Making hand-drawn maps, or digital maps from a GIS for use by enumerators in the field can be greatly assisted by GPS. A simple, hand-held GPS receiver will give latitude and longitude coordinates with reasonable accuracy of key points. Depending upon the system selected, a GPS may also track linear features and thus be useful for mapping boundaries. Maps printed from a GIS or hand-drawn map can be enhanced by the addition of latitudes and longitudes recorded at key points to provide orientation, scale and absolute position. Such information will be particularly valuable for dissemination purposes or if the work is a component of developing a GIS for later use.

1.139.   The implementation of strategies using such technologies must be thoroughly planned with the guidance of staff or external experts with formal qualifications in the use of advanced mapping technology. It is particularly important that the cost of acquiring and maintaining the hardware required to use this technology is factored into the budget (and that a sound cost-benefit analysis has been undertaken to support such changes), and adequate plans are made to ensure the availability of sufficient quantities of hardware in time for the census.[15]

1.140.   It should be noted that there may be additional risks due to the need for equipment to be operated in suboptimal conditions, including poor weather, dusty conditions and/or poor lighting. Despite its versatility, GPS may not be able to differentiate the coordinates of overlapping or closely located dwellings in multi-storey buildings and in this circumstance should only be regarded as providing coordinates for the building rather than the dwelling units within it.

1.141.   It is important to ensure that where such systems are employed they are clearly understood by enumeration staff. This should be achieved by ensuring that the staff, whether at the cartographic update stage or enumeration stage, are given adequate training in the interpretation of the maps. Should the maps be incorporated in digital devices such as personal data assistants, the staff should be trained in the use of both the hardware and the software.

1.142.   As with all other significant changes to census procedures, it is crucial that census geographic and mapping processes are successfully included in tests prior to being used in the main operation. This is particularly the case where a change in level of technology is being considered.

(iv)   Geographic information systems

1.143.   In recent years, many countries have adopted the use of GIS to facilitate census mapping in the production of both enumeration maps and dissemination products. As the cost is declining and the basic technology is now well established, it is expected that this will continue. It is likely that the census could be a useful catalyst for increasing capacity within the statistical office (or the country as a whole). Adoption of GIS should thus be seen as a major strategic decision with impacts beyond the census operation, and many issues need to be considered.

[15] It is unlikely that suppliers in most countries will be able to supply several thousand GPS receivers or personal data assistants without considerable advance notice.

1.144.   The (potential) benefits and costs of GIS are summarized as follows:

(*a*)   Benefits

    (i)   A closer linkage between maps for enumerators and map-based products for users;

    (ii)   The cost of intercensal updating of the base map will be less with a digital base map;

    (iii)   Producing duplicate maps may be less expensive with a GIS solution;

    (iv)   GIS will have increased ability to undertake quality assurance of geographic boundaries;

    (v)   The census agency will have a greater ability to perform spatial queries under GIS;

    (vi)   Space needed to store input maps for digital purposes will be far less;

(*b*)   Costs

    (i)   GIS requires additional technical expertise;

    (ii)   GIS will require a higher level of computing infrastructure;

    (iii)   A clerical census system can proceed on the basis of basic maps. However, use of GIS in this task requires that a digital map base exists. If it is necessary to create the digital map base, significant lead times are required as well as significant funding. In both cases, more experienced technical staff are required;

    (iv)   In most cases, the preparation of maps and/or GIS will not be the core business of a statistical agency.

(v)   *Contracting out for census mapping*

1.145.   The development of a mapping project beyond rudimentary clerical systems requires considerable knowledge of mapping, cartography and geographic systems. In the event that a census agency cannot draw on such skills from within the agency, it may be required to contract out some or all of the elements of preparation of census maps.

1.146.   Mapping for field purposes under a contract or agreement basis requires the statistical agency to specify its requirements to the contractor. These may include the following: (*a*) acquiring the base map data; (*b*) creating (or obtaining) the statistical boundaries and aligning them to the base map; (*c*) providing a process for enumeration area designers to advise on changes to boundaries (and updates to associated spatial data); (*d*) producing hard copy maps as specified for field work.

1.147.   The statistical agency would undertake the enumeration area design work and validation of the associated aspatial data, as well as take delivery of the hard copy maps for quality assurance checks and subsequent delivery into the field logistics programme. The statistical agency must also accept full responsibility for the maps meeting the required quality standards and delivery of the maps to field staff as required. The statistical agency would also provide, after the census, any feedback received from enumerators about the base map that may be of use to the mapping agency.

1.148.   Mapping for dissemination purposes is more difficult because the outputs will involve representation of statistical information (with, or as part of, a map) and often be accompanied by analysis or commentary about the information.

Advances in mapping software have made it easier for census agencies to produce a wide variety of standard thematic maps. However, advanced mapping products may require the expertise of a contractor. In these cases, it may be better for the statistical agency to focus on the statistics and let the contractor provide the technical skills required to produce the actual products with tight quality assurance procedures in place to ensure that the output from the contractor satisfies the end users requirements described above.

(c) Operational implementation of a mapping programme

1.149.   The development of a mapping system within the census agency requires the coordination of a series of complex tasks with relatively long lead times. It is important that project plans are established to manage this process. The main activities to be reflected in such plans are discussed below:

   (a) *Establishing a mapping unit.* The census mapping project requires a specialized project team. Where mapping activities are outsourced, the mapping project teams will be responsible for specifying the requirements of the census for mapping products and coordinating arrangements with the provider of mapping services;

   (b) *Developing a timetable.* The critical date is the date that maps must be delivered to the field. The mapping programme must commence early in the census cycle to allow sufficient time to produce national coverage of maps well before the census date and before training of field staff;

   (c) *Sourcing of basic mapping and digital geographic data.* A major step in the mapping project is establishing a map base of the country, including digital map data if required. If a census mapping project already exists, the agency may still require updates to their existing holdings.

1.150.   It will be most helpful if the concerned governmental authorities freeze the boundaries of various administrative units at least six months in advance of the census date so that no further jurisdictional changes are effected until the enumeration is over. This is of considerable help in delimiting enumeration areas, minimizing chances of omission or duplication and disseminating preliminary census results quickly.

(i) Sources and types of hard copy maps

1.151.   Where a hard copy map base is to be used, official published maps may be available from national or provincial government mapping agencies, the local government or municipal bodies. Other sources of maps may be other government agencies or private companies. Where the maps are obtained from sources outside the census agency, permission to use the maps collected must first be sought from the original source and any copyright issues addressed.

(ii) Requirements for digital mapping data

1.152.   When establishing a digital geographic database, a major consideration is the determination by the census agency of data requirements. With increasing amounts of digital spatial data becoming available, it is also important that standards and a common data specification be produced to ensure data validity and consistency.

1.153.   The key rules to be followed in selecting data items for inclusion are to question whether (a) the data item will be useful to enumerators in navigating their way around their enumeration area, and/or (*b*) the data item is relevant to users. Assessing the utility of data items to users in a census mapping context must place significant emphasis on the users' needs for small and/or customized areas. Data items that meet neither of those criteria should not be included in the database.

(iii) Updating maps or digital mapping data

1.154. Preparing or updating base maps, or base map digital data, requires substantial resources. The final content of base maps will have a major bearing on the accuracy and completeness of enumeration area maps and, subsequently, the effectiveness of census enumeration. The updating of base maps should be scheduled according to priorities, based on areas in which changes to the number or characteristics of the people require the maps to be updated. Important features to be updated include (*a*) accurately named and presented roads and waterways, (*b*) administrative boundaries, and (*c*) landmark features, such as schools, churches, post offices, parks and large buildings.

(iv) Operational design for enumeration and supervisory areas

1.155. Whether a hard copy or digital base is employed, an enumeration area (EA) design manual should be produced that contains the design criteria and the procedures to be followed when designing EA. The manual can be used as a basis of training for those involved in the EA design process.

1.156. If possible, EA design should be conducted by regional statistical office staff who are primarily responsible for EAs in their province or region. This ensures that local knowledge can be utilized in the EA design process. A considerable part of the EA design process is the gathering of information on where population and boundary variations have occurred in order to determine the best way to design particular EAs. As a result of EA design, a list should be produced that provides the enumeration phase with all relevant field data for each EA, and the dissemination area with relevant geographical data.

1.157. The design of field supervisor and regional area boundaries can be determined at the completion of the process through the aggregation of EAs, and the allocation of geographic identification codes.

1.158. Quality assurance measures should be implemented to ensure that data are correct to a minimum standard, both for field navigation and technical correctness in cases where a digital base is to be used as an output medium.

(v) Printing and content of field maps

1.159. Careful consideration should be given to the (considerable) time required for printing maps when establishing the project plan for census mapping.

1.160. Maps should be provided to every level of field staff. At least one map must be printed for every EA in the country. It is recommended that two copies of the map be produced, one copy to be used by the enumerator and the other by the field supervisor for training and reference purposes (and subsequently retained by the statistical office as input to the following census cycle).

1.161. Other considerations for the preparation of enumeration maps (whether based upon hard copy or digital data) include the following:

(*a*) Enumerators may be required to navigate in poor lighting conditions and thus details should be easily read;

(*b*)   The maps must be easily interpreted with text and symbols readily identifiable and correctly placed, along with the information being presented in a standard format compared to other source maps;

(*c*)   Boundaries (such as EA boundaries) overprinted on the maps must be clear and unambiguous;

(*d*)   EAs must be distinguishable when compared to the surrounding area;

(*e*)   Folding or refolding of large maps (larger than A2 in size) is inefficient for staff;

(*f*)   Maps need to facilitate the addition of handwritten enumerator comments;

(*g*)   Production of the maps should be cost-effective;

(*h*)   The maps should be suitable for reprinting to meet dissemination purposes where this reflects user demands.

1.162.   Maps for supervisors or regional managers should be smaller scale, providing sufficient detail to identify major features but not be so large as to be impossible to manipulate easily while, for example, answering a phone call from an enumerator. In many cases, the use of inset or supplementary maps may be required if the map is to cover a relatively large area. For all levels of senior field staff, the maps should show the boundaries of all subsidiary units for which they are responsible.

(vi)   Maps for dissemination purposes

1.163.   While preparation of maps, typically as hard copy, for enumeration purposes rightly receives the highest priority and attention from census managers, the need for maps for dissemination purposes should also be accommodated in the process. Data users require maps as hard copy or in digital form to understand how the EAs fit together and build up to higher geographic levels. Therefore, dissemination maps need sufficient topographic details in order to allow the boundaries and social and cultural features, such as schools, hospitals and major retail and work areas to be identified. Other factors that should be considered include the following:

(*a*)   The formats chosen should be widely used within the country so that output products can be prepared readily to meet a wide market;

(*b*)   The data should be suitable for commonly available desktop mapping applications.

9.   Small-area identification

1.164.   Two somewhat different methods are available to provide the census with a flexible capability for generating tabulations in terms of a wide variety of geographical aggregations including those needed for public and private sector data uses at the local level. The first method simply extends the traditional hierarchical system for coding all major and minor civil divisions so as to cover at the lowest level the enumeration area (EA), sometimes referred to as the "enumeration district". The second method, which at greater cost permits finer geographical specificity, is usually based on some coordinate or grid system, such as that of latitude and longitude. This method is often referred to as a "geocoding system".

1.165.   Particularly in the absence of a comprehensive system of street names, numbers or similar addresses, the first method, which uses the EA as the key unit for the production of small-area data, is to be preferred. Proper administration and control of a census require that the EAs be well defined and their boundaries identifiable on the ground. It is useful to let EA boundaries coincide with natural dividing lines in the field—not just rivers and major roads, but also limits of neighbourhoods and city blocks in urban areas. Not only does this help enumerators clearly understand the boundaries of their territories, it also prevents difficulties later on when small-area statistics have to be produced. As a rule, the EA boundaries are also traced on maps and the maps can carry the EA code numbers. The EA code numbers can then be included, along with the other geographical codes and the statistical information, at data entry. This makes it possible to produce, from the census database, any kind of recorded information for any given EA or combination of EAs at minimum cost, subject to the constraints imposed by the need to protect the confidentiality of individual responses (see paras. 1.376 and 1.377, on privacy and confidentiality).

1.166.   The fact that census data, whether published or unpublished, are available by EA provides for considerable flexibility. Such flexibility can be of value given that the geographical divisions used by various branches of the administration or by other data users do not always coincide and may therefore require different regroupings. Moreover, when changes are planned in administrative boundaries, tabulation of census data by the planned new entities can also be facilitated through the EA approach. However, if these changes cross EA boundaries and it is decided to try to retabulate the census according to the new boundaries, very expensive recoding of individual records may be involved. As an alternative, statistical concordances, showing the quantitative relationship between the previous and current classifications could be used. Further, where buildings or housing units have been geocoded, these geocodes can be used to directly allocate each household to the correct area under either classification.

1.167.   The tabulation of population and housing characteristics by EA, which may be shown on statistical maps, is also a useful tool for analysis. On the other hand, the linkage of data from other sources is not usually possible on the EA level because of the difficulty of obtaining such information for individual census EAs. Moreover, comparison between successive censuses is possible only to the extent that EA boundaries remain unchanged.

1.168.   Countries may sometimes find it useful to have even greater flexibility in the regrouping of census data into different geographical aggregations than that provided by a coding system based on the EA. In these situations, the use of some system of geocoding may be considered.[16] Among the advantages of geocoding, particularly if based on the grid squares approach, are its permanence, clarity and uniformity, as well as the possibility that it offers of interlinking statistics from a wide variety of sources. It must be stressed, however, that geocoding is more expensive than traditional methods of area coding and its technical prerequisites may not be present in many countries.

[16] For further information on geocoding, see *Handbook on geographic information systems and digital mapping*, Studies in Methods, No. 79 (United Nations publication, Sales No. 00.XVII.12).

1.169.   On the next level above the EA (or the block faces or nodes identified in a geocoding system), the situation in urban areas is somewhat different from that in rural ones. Large urban municipalities are often divided into units (quarters, wards, barrios, and so on), which may have a well-known and relatively permanent administrative status. Data tabulated by such units are of great practical value for all planning and analysis. If such area units do not exist or if they are too large for fruitful analysis, other, intermediate units may be formed for statistical purposes. These should be made as homogeneous as possible. In either case, these intermediate areas must be identified in the codes entered for each record. Possibilities for data linkage and for comparisons over time are clearly greatest for area units that have administrative status. Purely statistical areas that lack such status are the more useful the more widely they are recognized and the more permanently they are kept from census to census.

1.170.   At a minimum, developing countries that are predominantly rural will certainly wish to be able to identify villages which are usually the most important local units in rural areas. In the past, however, the village has not been uniformly a higher-level geographical unit than the EA. Although no problem arises when larger villages are divided into several EAs (as long as a village identification code is included in the record), a serious problem does arise if a single EA is composed of two or more small villages. In this situation, the EA codes cannot be used to generate village statistics. It may therefore be advisable to limit each EA either to one village or to a portion of a village or to an area not included in any village, bearing in mind that an individual enumerator can always be given more than one EA to enumerate. There are other problems connected with identification and delimitation of villages, and these must also be dealt with in planning the cartographic work. Owing to the organic role it plays in rural life and development efforts in many developing countries, the village should not be neglected in census plans or in census statistics.

1.171.   The statistical value of the village is further enhanced when it is possible to link census village data with village data from other sources. In many developing countries a wide range of data is compiled for each village, such as location, altitude, road connections, communications, facilities of various kinds or distances from such facilities, cultural or ethnic characteristics of the population, major industries, major crops, and so forth. The village as a unit is relatively stable but in the course of time new villages are created and old ones may disappear or merge. A village directory and its cartographic base therefore require frequent updating. The use of GPS receivers to identify real-world coordinates for establishing and maintaining a village directory has great benefits (see para. 1.127).

1.172.   In rural areas there may also be a need to create an intermediate statistical level between the village and the minor civil division if the former is generally too small and the latter too large for local data uses. In such cases, the intermediate units should be made as homogeneous as possible and changes in their boundaries over time should be avoided. On the other hand, it may be necessary to identify areas smaller than EA or village, particularly in the case of isolated settlements.

10. Living quarters and household listing

1.173.   A list of sets of living quarters, structures containing living quarters or households that are available at the start of the census is an aid in the control of the enumeration, particularly in the absence of adequate and updated maps. Such a list is also useful for estimating the number of enumerators and the number of schedules and other census materials needed in an area, for estimating the time required for the enumeration and for compiling provisional results of the census. It is also very useful for determining the enumeration areas and for establishing necessary links between population and housing censuses when they are carried out separately.

1.174.   Consideration should be given to providing permanent identification to streets and buildings, which can be used for successive censuses and for other purposes. A listing of sets of living quarters, particularly in densely settled places, cannot be made unless streets have names and buildings have unique numbers. Individual apartments in multi-dwelling buildings need to be numbered or otherwise unambiguously identified. Where these prerequisites do not exist, numbering immediately prior to the census would prove useful.

1.175.   Where such information is available, it is useful to provide the enumerators with additional assistance in the form of lists of addresses to visit. Address lists will be essential if self-enumeration, whereby questionnaires are sent to the households by mail, is part of the plan. Some countries have population registers that allow more or less complete address lists to be generated relatively simply. The census can then not only use these lists, but also assist in further improving the population register by reporting any discrepancies found in the field. Where official population registers are not available, or insufficiently complete, it may be possible to obtain additional address lists from postal authorities, utility companies or the private sector (for example, mail-order companies). A definitive list for the enumerators could then be prepared by merging the lists obtained from these various sources.

1.176.   Where a good population register exists, it may be possible to pre-print the household questionnaires with information such as the names of the persons expected to be members of a household, already available from the register. This reduces the response burden, accelerates the information-gathering process, and helps to pinpoint deviations. On the other hand it might have a negative psychological effect if respondents believed that the authorities were monitoring them too closely. An approach using one or several registers as the point of departure for a census that still includes full-coverage field enumeration is sometimes called a register-based census. Differences between the register(s) and the field situation will necessarily come to light, and rules will be required to deal with such differences.

11.   Tabulation programme and database design

1.177.   In most countries, the tabulation programme represents a compromise between the full range of desired tabulations and the limits imposed by practical circumstances. To ensure that this compromise is made transparently and efficiently it is important that planning the census dissemination task is started at the earliest stage of the census development cycle by a round of user consultations. Once the census testing programme has identified a practicable range of data items to be included in the questionnaire, data users should again be consulted on the specific cross tabulations required and the relative priority for their production. It is essential that the programme be outlined sufficiently early so that the procedures and costs involved may be investigated thoroughly before a final decision is reached. The type of questionnaire and the method of enumeration may limit the kinds and amount of data that it is possible to collect. Publication time and costs, and the data-processing resources available, will determine the number and complexity of the tabulations that can be produced within a reasonable time. This will enable prospective census data users to make firm plans and the census data processing staff to complete all systems analysis, programming and testing work in a timely manner.

1.178.   The tabulation programme presented in revision 2 of the *Principles and Recommendations for Population and Housing Census* is that fulfilling the most essential and/or generally required tabulations. Other requests for statistical information by specialist users will be made subsequently. The databases of census information can be used throughout the intercensal period to address such needs.

1.179.   It is important to plan the tabulation programme in such a way that final results can be issued within a reasonable period of time after the enumeration and before the information has become out of date for current needs. It is desirable that the details of the tables be prepared and the order of their preparation be decided early in the planning so that the processing of the data will not be delayed.

1.180.   Special tabulations may be requested at any time after the census enumeration. Once the census database has been produced by recording, editing and correcting the raw data, tabulation software packages can be introduced. These packages allow fast and relatively inexpensive production of tables for selected subsets of the total database or for alternative aggregates, assuming the information has been preserved in the database in terms of the needed detailed classifications.

12. Questionnaire preparation

1.181.   The following paragraphs relate only to those approaches to provision of census information that involve direct, paper-questionnaire-based enumeration of the individuals covered by the census. While many of the principles of designing a statistical questionnaire will also apply to the design of the administrative instruments underpinning a register-based approach, those instruments may also be based upon specific requirements of the administrative programmes they address.

1.182.   Further, where countries utilize the Internet to collect a proportion of their census information, it is possible that the layout and organization of the data collection instrument may differ from that of the paper questionnaire. While many of the same principles (for example, clarity of wording, omission of unnecessary material) will apply to an Internet based collection of information, specialized advice should be sought regarding such issues as (*a*) the technology employed to present the questions to the respondent, (*b*) the method of capturing the response, and (*c*) quality assurance checks employed during the capture process.

1.183.   A crucial principle is that questionnaire design must be regarded as part of an integrated process of satisfying users' demands by collecting, processing and disseminating information provided by respondents.

1.184.   The type of questionnaire, its format and the exact wording and arrangement of the questions require the most careful consideration, since the handicaps of a poorly designed questionnaire cannot be overcome during or after enumeration. Among the many factors that should be taken into account in designing the questionnaire are the method of enumeration, the type of questionnaire, the data to be collected, the most suitable form and arrangement of the questions and the processing techniques to be employed.

1.185.   The method of enumeration (see paras. 1.197–1.200) governs to some extent the type of questionnaire that can be used (for example, single individual, single household or single set of living quarters, multiple household or multiple living quarters, combined population and housing). It may also impact upon where each type of questionnaire can be used and the framing of the questions and the amount of explanatory material that must accompany them.

1.186.   It is important that questions are free from ambiguity. Moreover, questions should not be offensive; in many cases this can be avoided by excluding extremely sensitive topics from the census questionnaire, but care must always be taken to consider the reaction of respondents when designing questions. In addition, it should be noted that the quality of information collected in a census will be reduced if the questionnaire is excessively long. These issues should be carefully assessed during the testing programme including the so-called *pilot census* (see paras. 1.195 and 1.196) since poorly worded questions will not only collect poor quality data, but, by confusing respondents and/or enumerators, may also impact upon subsequent questions in the questionnaire.

1.187.   Special provision will have to be made if two or more languages are used in the country. Several methods have been used to deal with this situation, such as (*a*) a single, multilingual questionnaire; or (*b*) one version of the questionnaire for each major language; or (*c*) translations printed in the enumerators' manual of the questionnaire in the various languages. The problem is more serious in the case of non-written languages. Information on the distribution of languages in the country is important for sound census planning and, if not available, will have to be collected at some stage of the census preparations. Staff recruitment and training procedures (see paras. 1.210–1.215) will also have to take language issues into account.

1.188.   If the housing census and the population census are to be carried out concurrently, it will be necessary to consider whether a single questionnaire should be utilized to collect information on both population and housing topics. If separate questionnaires are used, they should be uniquely identified in a way that links the component forms so as to permit subsequent matching, both physical and automated, of the data for each set of living quarters with the data that refer to the occupants thereof. This will be particularly important where a single housing form is used to cover separate personal forms for each individual.

1.189.   Use of many of the more technologically advanced processing techniques,[17] such as optical mark reading (OMR) and intelligent character recognition (ICR) will have a significant effect upon the questionnaire design. In the case of OMR, it is necessary both to allow for the spacing of response areas and to ensure printing is undertaken to precise tolerances so that the data capture software is able to capture all required data but not any of the material around the designated response areas. With regard to ICR, it is crucial to allow sufficient room for response areas and to ensure that these are designed according to the requirements of the processing system so that each response box contains only one character, and that the character is correctly formed (usually in upper case). In turn, many decisions regarding the detailed design of the processing system are dependent on the final content, form and arrangement of the questionnaires. As noted in paragraph 1.188, where the scanning process requires that a booklet questionnaire is separated into component pages, it is important that some form of linking (for example, by serial numbers or bar codes) is employed to ensure that the correct information is amalgamated in the computer records.

1.190.   Questionnaire design must be driven by a planning process based upon dialogue between the statistical agency and those demanding information. This is essential if the questionnaire is to be designed to provide the information needed by users. This will, in turn, determine the tabulation programme, as it is to some extent conditioned by the limitations imposed by the questionnaire.

1.191.   The final questionnaire(s) must be drafted in time to allow for printing (making allowance for the many contingencies, such as industrial action and breakdown of printing equipment, that can arise in these processes); undertaking quality assurance checks to ensure the printing is of sufficient quality to be used in the data capture regime; adequate training of census officials at all levels, and adequate publicity to be generated on the content.

1.192.   In view of the many issues to be addressed in designing a census questionnaire, it is not feasible to suggest specific model questions for the census topics covered in part two. However, images of all census questionnaires that have been made available to the United Nations Statistics Division have been placed on the Division's website (see http://unstats.un.org/unsd/demographic/sources/census/censusquest. htm) together with research papers relating to questionnaires used to collect information on the various topics recommended for collection.

13. Census tests

1.193.   The testing of various aspects of a census plan prior to the enumeration is a very useful practice for all countries, and an essential one for countries without a long history of census taking and for those in which fundamental changes in census

[17] See paras. 1.304 to 1.306 for a full description of these techniques.

methods are being considered. Census tests can be designed for different purposes and in different ways. To yield full benefits, tests should be employed for all stages of the census, including enumeration, processing and evaluation of results. Such tests can give important information on the adequacy of the field organization, the training programme, extent of respondent burden, the processing plan and other important aspects of the census. They are particularly valuable in probing for weaknesses in the questionnaire, in the instructions or in enumeration procedures that might affect the quality of the data. They can be designed to provide information on the relative efficacy of alternative methods of enumeration and on the average time required for enumerating a single household or a single set of living quarters, which information is useful in estimating staff and cost requirements. In addition, census tests serve as practical training for the nuclear staff of supervisors and other officials.

1.194.   The first kind of tests carried out during census preparations are questionnaire tests. Their purpose is to test the suitability of intended census questions, including their formulation and the instructions provided, as well as the suitability of the questionnaire design. Such tests can be particularly helpful in assessing the suitability of the proposed material for enumerating specific population groups, as well as the general public. These tests are also used for estimating the time requirements in enumeration. It is practical to carry out questionnaire tests on a small scale in several purposively selected places. Because they are relatively inexpensive, repeated rounds of questionnaire tests may be carried out until a satisfactory questionnaire has been evolved.

1.195.   A comprehensive test of all census procedures is often called a "pilot census". Such large scale tests should be designed and managed to thoroughly test the entire system. Essential features of a pilot census are coverage of one or more sizeable administrative divisions and encompassment of the preparatory, enumeration and processing stages of a census, by which it thus tests the adequacy of the entire census plan and of the census organization. In order to best serve this purpose, care should be taken for resemblance in conditions of conducting pilot census with the actual enumeration as closely as possible. For this reason, it is often taken exactly one year before the planned census so as to conform to the expected seasonal patterns of climate and activity. It is generally unwise to consider the pilot census a source from which to derive usable substantive data. Apart from the sampling problems involved, such a use inevitably detracts from the central purpose of the pilot, which is to prepare for the main census.

1.196.   It is critically important to undertake a set of tests of the information and communication technology (ICT) solutions that are planned to be applied in the census. Depending on the extent and characteristics of ICT, these tests should include all ICT components related to the field work, data entry and processing well ahead of the census itself. This is particularly important if a new technology is being introduced, such as scanning the questionnaires as a means of capturing data. Tests should include the testing of the equipment itself, as well as the underlying circumstances necessary to avoid equipment malfunctioning, such as climatization, or significant delays due to inadequate quality of paper causing paper jams. In the context of new approaches using hand-held devices, testing should include daily data transfers to the major depository of data. Testing the efficiency of editing and tabulation applications should be done based on results collected by the *pilot census.*

14. Plan of enumeration

1.197.   Several different approaches to enumeration are possible. Traditionally, each household is contacted and enumerated on a face-to-face basis. This approach is still used in most developing countries and for at least part of the population in many developed countries. In those circumstances where up-to-date and comprehensive address or population registers exist or can be established, the enumeration process often involves mailing out the census forms, or having the public mail back the completed forms, or both. Whatever approach is to be used, the complete enumeration plan should be prepared well before the enumeration begins. This involves (*a*) the determination of the enumeration method to be used and the basic procedures to be followed in the collection of the data and the control of the enumeration, (*b*) the procedures for the control of the quality of the data and (*c*) an estimation of the number of sets of living quarters and the probable size of the population to be enumerated so that the number of questionnaires and other materials required for the enumeration, and the number of enumerators and supervisors needed, can be properly ascertained.

1.198.   With the advent of the Internet, several countries have also employed enumeration methods that allow respondents to submit their questionnaires through the online equivalent of their paper census questionnaires. It should be noted that only contexts characterized by high penetration rates of information technology including the Internet have implemented this method, and always in conjunction with more traditional ones. It should also be mentioned, however, that these options may never entirely replace more traditional enumeration methods and that, even where the society enjoys a high degree of using information technology, the majority of the population cannot be reasonably expected to prefer this mode of self-enumeration.

1.199.   The universal enumeration of population and living quarters should be made exclusively on a geographical basis, that is to say, the country should be divided into census enumeration areas and each area should be small enough to be covered by one enumerator during the period of time allowed for the enumeration. Other sources of information, such as registers of population or registers of properties, could be used to produce census data in countries that have established continuously updated population registers of high quality and good coverage.

1.200.   Special attention should be given to the procedures to be followed for the enumeration of nomadic and semi-nomadic populations. These procedures should take account of the specific difficulties in locating such population groups, which are characterized by movement from place to place (see paras. 1.281–1.283). Special arrangements may also need to be made to enumerate homeless persons as well as the special categories listed in paragraph 2.41 below, to the extent that these categories are included within the scope of the census. Where their number warrants, additional information that would indicate the reason for homelessness may need to be sought.

15. Plans for data processing

1.201.   Plans for data processing should be formulated as an integral part of the overall plan of the census, and those responsible for the processing of the census should be involved from the inception of the planning process. Data processing will be required in connection with the results of census tests, compilation of preliminary results, preparation of tabulations, evaluation of census results, analysis of census data, arrangements for storage in and retrieval from a database, identification and correction of errors, and so on. In addition, data-processing technologies are playing an increasing role in the planning and control of field operations and other aspects of census administration. Data processing has an impact on almost all aspects of the census operation ranging from the selection of topics and the design of the questionnaire to the analysis of the final results. Therefore, data-processing requirements in terms of personnel, space, equipment and software (computer programs) need to be looked at from the point of view of the census as a whole and at an early stage in the planning.

1.202.   The existing data-processing staff will certainly need to be expanded somewhat and will probably need some upgrading in terms of skills, particularly if new computer hardware or software is to be used in the census. Any needed training should be completed early enough so that those benefiting from the training can play an active role in census planning and operations.

1.203.   Decisions will need to be made concerning the location of the various data-processing activities within the country, including the extent to which the processing work is to be decentralized. Acquisition of both equipment and supplies can require long lead times; estimates of both data capture and computer processing workloads must be made early to enable timely procurement. Closely related to the question of equipment is that of the provision of adequate space. Although the maintenance of most personal computer equipment no longer requires adherence to rigid standards in terms of temperature, humidity, dust and so on, attention to issues related to power supplies is still important. Inevitably, more important is the attention to be devoted to the maintenance of servers (especially heavy duty servers), where most of the information processing is likely to take place and saved, as well as the data-transmission infrastructure. The last issue is essential to ensure smooth and noise-less Internet and/or web communications between different units and centres engaged in census operations. Moreover, in the case of traditional archiving, well-protected space for the storage of the completed census forms before, during and after processing will have to be secured.

1.204.   In addition to considering the processing equipment to be used in the census, decisions will have to be made on the software to be used in editing and tabulating the census data. It is very costly and time-consuming to develop software for census editing and tabulation. Consequently, a majority of countries in recent years have turned either to one of the several portable software packages available for census editing or tabulation or to one of the commercially available personal computer spreadsheet, database or tabulation packages. These packages can substantially reduce the extent of the systems analysis and programming tasks involved, although sometimes at a price in terms of loss of flexibility. Each country may wish to assess its software requirements in the light of its own needs and resources and in the light of the general purpose and census software available. Regardless of the software used, sufficient time will have to be allowed for training staff in its use. Whatever software is chosen, it is certain that at least some degree of customization can be expected in order to meet the specific requirements of the census, especially with off-the-shelf, commercial software packages not specifically designed for census operations. Therefore, a sufficient information technology (IT) workforce has to be available for software implementation.

1.205.   Outsourcing some of the predominantly IT-related operations may be considered. Outsourcing should be implemented in such a way as to bring immediate economic and quality advantages to census operations. Furthermore, national statistical offices should take adequate measures to ensure that outsourcing of census operations does not compromise data confidentiality and that necessary steps are taken so that the contractor does not have free access to the basic census databases. It is worth mentioning that responsibility for hosting of census databases rests with the national statistical offices and that outsourcing of these activities is not recommended. In short, outsourcing should be implemented so as to facilitate a transfer of knowledge into the census organization and always in such a way that essential features, such as the privacy of individual respondents and the confidentiality of the data, are fully protected.

16. Plans for census outputs and dissemination

1.206.   A census is not complete until the information collected is made available to potential users in a form suited to their needs. A wide range of statistical products can be made available to the public, the private sector, government agencies, local authorities and the academic and research communities. The information may be included in published tables or reports for general distribution, produced as tables in unpublished form for limited distribution or stored in a database and supplied upon request either on magnetic and optical media or online. A detailed plan for producing different census outputs should be guided by early user consultations (1.112) to ensure data and information requirements will be met in a format commensurate with user needs and demands; such a plan will also be a useful guide to prioritizing data processing and tabulations.

1.207.   Not all of the processed materials need to be disseminated widely or in a single format. Tabulations required by only a few users can be supplied in unpublished form. Some data may not be tabulated until they are required at a later date. The information stored in the census database allows fast and relatively inexpensive production of additional tables. Countries may offer on-demand services to provide census information to users who require tables or other outputs not produced, or aggregates not available, through other means. If suitable electronic dissemination is available to the census organization, custom tabulations from a separate, purposely-built online dissemination database might also be designed and extracted directly by end-users. In this case, the census organization should prepare in advance and then implement an authorization and security policy, so that the risk of breaching confidentiality in data provided to outside users is avoided.

1.208.   Printed publications, despite their production cost, remain in most countries the preferred vehicle for dissemination of the main results. Target dates for publication should be determined well in advance and processing and printing programmes should be planned accordingly. In addition to traditional methods of printing, there are various methods of reproduction available that are fast, economical and good-quality, and these should be investigated. For an increasing number of users, computer-readable magnetic and optical media as well as online electronic data dissemination are a better means than printed paper, based on the factors of cost, storage capacity (and therefore weight of documents), ease of reproduction and direct availability of the data for further computer processing.

1.209.   Census maps, in printed or digital form, should be included in the overall dissemination programme of a population and housing census. The provision for needed resources should also be made in the budget from the initial planning stage. In addition to preparing maps for the census tables and reports, countries should also produce a population atlas and try to make most data available in a geographic information system on a CD ROM, at different and nested levels of administrative geography, thus exponentially increasing the usefulness and utilization of census data.

17. Staff recruitment and training

1.210.   Early arrangements are necessary to secure the proper number and type of personnel required for each of the various census operations. For reasons of efficiency and economy, it is important that the staff be selected on the basis of competence. Consideration may also be given to the use of the same staff for successive operations, thus reducing the turnover of personnel. While the preparatory and processing work generally calls for office employees possessing or able to learn certain specialized skills (cartographers, coders, data entry operators, programmers and so on), the enumeration stage usually demands a large number of persons capable of going to their assigned urban or rural enumeration areas and collecting the information according to specific definitions and instructions. It is essential that the enumerators and, to the extent possible, their immediate supervisors be conversant with the languages or dialects of the area in which they will be working. It is only prudent to recruit and train a somewhat larger field force than is required for the enumeration itself, as a certain amount of attrition is inevitable from the beginning of the training programme until the completion of the fieldwork.

1.211.   Once the cartographic preparations are substantially complete and the questionnaire has been sent for printing, perhaps the single most important means that the census authorities have for influencing the success of the census is the training programme. The contribution that a well-planned and executed training programme can make to the quality of the census results therefore cannot be stressed too strongly. Such a training programme must of course focus on the widely dispersed and difficult-to-supervise field staff (namely, the enumerators and their immediate supervisors) but it must also cover others (for example, the higher-level supervisors, editors, coders, computer operators).

1.212.   The entire census training programme should be designed to cover each phase of the work and provide an efficient and consistent means of effectively starting large numbers of employees in their work. The programme will need to correspond closely to the needs of the various operations and, where appropriate, may include both theoretical and practical instruction, with emphasis on the latter. In the case of the enumerators and their immediate supervisors, the training is most effective if it includes several opportunities for the trainees to participate in practice interviews and role-playing exercises , including in the use of adopted IT solutions. (In countries in which multiple languages are used, the method and content of the enumerator training programme will need to be suitably adjusted. For example, if the questionnaire is printed in another language, provision will have to be made for instructing enumerators on the correct formulation of the census questions in the vernacular). The training programme for editors, coders, operators of data recording equipment and so forth should also provide opportunities for the trainees to practice under the supervision of the trainers, the operations it is expected they will subsequently perform. The intermediate- and higher-level technical staff, such as programmers and system analysts, may also benefit from special training programmes. For them, the emphasis should usually be on recent technical developments of relevance to the forthcoming census and on the interrelationships among the various aspects of census plans and operations.

1.213.   The organization and conduct of training courses should be entrusted to those having the necessary qualifications to carry out this task successfully, taking into account not only their professional abilities but also their ability in teaching. This means that staff in charge of training should have certain qualifications that will enable them to stimulate the interest of trainees and to transfer the required knowledge, since otherwise well-qualified technical personnel who are unable to transfer their knowledge to the trainees in a satisfactory manner will be unsuitable as instructors for group training activities. This must be taken into consideration when selecting instructors and it is recommended that objective criteria should be used. In practice, however, it is difficult to find the necessary number of instructors who have both the professional and the teaching qualifications; for this reason, the instructors selected should themselves undergo training in how to organize and conduct training courses.

1.214.   It is important that each training programme be made available in manual (booklet) form and distributed to the census organizers and training instructors.

Such a manual would be a valuable guide and would help considerably in the efficient training of census staff. It would also contribute to the uniformity of training, which is an essential factor for a successful enumeration, taking into account the great number of census instructors who will be engaged in training. Simple audio-visual aids (for example, film strips, posters, tape recordings) can also be used to help make the training more effective and uniform throughout the country. If available, new multi-media technologies can facilitate the provision of training at distant locations (distant learning) and be effective and efficient supplementary tools for training.

1.215.　　It is very important to determine the time required to train staff for the various aspects of the census. This depends on several factors: the type of function for which they are being trained, the level at which they will be performing, the complexity of the census, the educational level of the trainees, the number of instructors available and the funds available. Usually, all courses last from one week to one month. It is strongly recommended that the training be carried out daily for a fixed period. The results are not as good if training is provided for a few days per week, since with this approach, which draws out the length of the course, previous work is often forgotten and has to be repeated. For this reason, it is also best to avoid completion of the training long before the start of the actual work. Any duration, however, may be fixed for the course, provided that the main principle—namely that training should be long enough to permit the assimilation of the syllabus—is not overlooked.

18. Avoiding gender biases and biases affecting data on minority populations

1.216.　　Gender-based stereotypes can introduce serious biases in census data and the conclusions drawn from these data. These biases are discussed in more detail in part two (see, for example, paras. 2.114–2.119 and 2.231–2.300 relating to household relationships and economic characteristics, respectively). There is much that can be done in the preparatory stages of the census to help minimize gender-based biases. These preparatory activities are of two broad types: those related to census content and those related to census operations.

1.217.　　Issues of census content, including what information is sought and how, the definitions and classifications used, and the manner in which databases and tabulations are specified, are important in generating data needed to examine questions of gender equity. In addressing these content issues, census planners and users will need to be alert to prevailing stereotypes so as to develop a census that both minimizes the influence of the stereotypes that respondents may hold and avoids further perpetuation of these stereotypes.

1.218.　　With regard to census operations, particular attention will need to be given to the selection, training and supervision of the field staff. This involves ensuring that both men and women are recruited to the field staff (both as interviewers and supervisors) and that manuals and training materials cover gender bias issues just as they do other important sources of error. Consultations with women's groups and others concerned with gender equity can help in addressing both content and operational issues.

1.219.　　Gender-related stereotypes and biases are concerns that have relevance for all countries. Census authorities in a number of countries must also be alert to the possibility of stereotypes and biases affecting data on minority population groups. Such groups may include ethnic, linguistic, national, racial and religious minorities and indigenous and nomadic populations. As with gender issues, the problem will need to be addressed in terms of both census content and census operations. Representatives of these minority groups can often provide census planners with important information and insights relevant to both census content and operations. Thus, special efforts should be made to consult with them when planning the census. In the case of minority populations living in isolated settlements or enclaves, such consultations are often critical for minimizing underenumeration among these populations.

B. Contracting out

1.220.   Today, many countries contract out some tasks or activities of the census as a way of increasing efficiency by utilizing the advanced methods and technologies not necessarily available in the national statistical office or public sector responsible for conducting the census. At the same time, cost reduction through a competitive selection process can be achieved. However, not all census tasks are appropriate for outsourcing or contracting out. The appropriateness of contracting out should be determined step-by-step and after subdividing the overall census tasks into stages. Throughout the overall process, activities should be conducted by a method (considering accuracy and timeliness of the results) that can best satisfy the general public. No part of the work tasks should be done by a method that may result in loss of trust of the general public. So, in judging the propriety of contracting out, it is recommended that national statistical offices should carefully consider the following criteria:

(*a*)   Strict protection of data confidentiality;

(*b*)   Method of confidentiality assurance that satisfies the general public;

(*c*)   Guaranteed measures of quality assurance;

(*d*)   Ability to manage and monitor the outsourced census tasks/activities;

(*e*)   Control over the core competence of the national statistical office, and appropriateness judgement, considering the specific situation of each country.

1.221.   Confidentiality assurance is the first and most important issue that should be considered by national statistical offices. National statistical offices are responsible for data confidentiality, in terms of both perception and reality. It is extremely harsh for national statistical offices to find leakage or misuse of confidential information by ex post facto monitoring and controls. Consequently, contracting out of tasks that have the risk of such an incidence should be avoided. For example, in the phase of data gathering, it is highly recommended that contracting out should be avoided because the task is closely related to the earning of trust from citizens and the strict protection of confidentiality. Where temporary enumeration staff are engaged under contract, this should be done in such a way that they are subject to strict measures of monitoring and control by the national statistical office. These enumeration staff should be engaged in such a way that their activities are governed by the relevant statistical legislation to preserve the confidentiality of the data they collect.

1.222.   The second important and related issue that should be considered carefully is conveying confidentiality assurance to the general public. As described in the "Essential roles of the census" (see paras. 1.1–1.3), a census should be undertaken by the method that can produce the most reliable results and in a manner that wins the trust of the general public in terms of both perception and reality. If either one of these attributes is not met, then the method used as well as the results obtained may not meet the approval of the general public and could result in the existence of the census itself being highly questioned. Thus, protecting data confidentiality refers not just to the actual protection of confidential data, but to protecting the perception of confidentiality among the general public and providing a sense of inward security.

1.223.   The third significant issue to be considered in outsourcing is the quality assurance that should be guaranteed. A key point is that the national statistical office is satisfied that the goods or services paid for are provided. Cost should not be the first priority in considering and judging the successful bidder in this respect. Although it is desirable to engage in fair competition among several companies to reduce costs, it is worth mentioning that merely considering low price bidding as a determinant factor may adversely affect the quality of the job to be done by the successful bidder. Low quality work could cause a significant loss of trust among the general public. To assess the quality of work, as part of the contract allocation process, potential contractors should be required to provide samples of their work (for example, for printing, manufacturing satchels, and other work), or if this is not possible, to list referees who could be contacted to verify their claims and/or sites at which previous work can be inspected. Once the contract has been awarded, continuous monitoring of the progress of work entrusted to the selected company is necessary and the national statistical office should ensure that a system for monitoring quality is built into the contract. Consequently, in considering the proper contracting-out procedures, national statistical offices should also take into account the costs for constructing a system of surveillance for monitoring progress of the work being contracted out.

1.224.   The fourth major issue in outsourcing census activities is the procedure of assessment and evaluation of the capabilities of the candidate companies. Through this procedure national statistical offices should fully assess both the capabilities and the disabilities of companies in order to select the winner to which the activity/ies in question are to be outsourced. It is highly recommended that practical and financial peculiarities of companies should be considered after the assessment of their capabilities. Each private company has a potential risk of bankruptcy or of changing the field of its activity. It should be kept in mind that if a selected company is unable to fulfil the assigned tasks, the probable problems might not be resolved by applying penalties. However, a very significant problem that could occur is that people might not be able to make use of accurate and timely census results. In such a case, national statistical offices might lose the trust of the general public in the census and even in future censuses or other routine statistical projects conducted by the statistical office. It is, therefore, very important for national statistical offices to adopt a method in which risks are as low as possible.

1.225.   In addition to managing the outsourced activities or tasks, the ability or the flexibility to cope with sudden or unpredicted change in the situation is also very important. It should be mentioned that contracting out does not necessarily mean lower costs; sometimes the burden of monitoring cost, emergency costs and other matters may jeopardize the census. It is recommended that some tasks and /or activities which are hard to manage should be done by the national statistical offices themselves. National statistical offices should judge and determine whether to contract out census activities from this viewpoint.

1.226.   It should also be recommended that for critical activities, such as the coding of education, occupation and industrial classification, special care should be taken to ensure adequate training of the personnel to undertake the task, particularly when it is contracted out. The same amount of care and training is required even when the task is performed by the national statistical office or the census organization. This is due to the fact that the coding depends on the minor differentiation and level of coding (general and detailed classifications according to different coding standards), as well as the coding manual and the education of the coders. In the light of such subtle criteria for judgement, it is difficult to prepare a complete coding manual in advance before checking the filled questionnaire.

1.227.   Censuses are large operations with massive quantities of data that require coding and editing. To reduce the staff resources required and to improve timeliness, uniformity and accuracy, automated coding procedures may be employed. Some countries have already implemented automated coding procedures for addresses, countries, education, occupation, and industry. The development of the application software could be contracted out although the rules to be followed must be carefully specified by the national statistical office, which should retain responsibility for implementing the system. The software application can often be used for other statistical collections undertaken by the national statistical office.

C.   Quality assurance and improvement programme

1.228.   There is general agreement that, ultimately, quality has to do with user needs and satisfaction. In statistics, quality used to be primarily associated with accuracy; in other words, taking mainly into account errors, both sampling and non-sampling, which influence the value of the estimates, and intervals based on such knowledge upon which precise confidence statements could be made. Such measures are still considered necessary, but it is now recognized that there are other important dimensions to quality. Even if data are accurate, they do not have sufficient quality if they are produced too late to be useful, or cannot be easily accessed, or conflict with other credible data, or are too costly to produce. Therefore, quality is increasingly approached as a multidimensional concept.

1.229.   It has been suggested that the output of any statistical exercise should possess some or all of the following attributes:

(*a*)   Relevance, understood as the degree to which statistics meet users' needs, and suggests the need to avoid production of irrelevant data, namely, data for which no use will be found;

(*b*)   Completeness, degree to which statistics fully cover the phenomenon they are supposed to describe;

(*c*)   Accuracy, distance between the estimated value and the (unknown) true value;

(*d*)   Comparability, degree to which statistics are comparable over space (between countries) and time (between different time periods);

(*e*)   Coherence, degree to which data from a single statistical programme, and data brought together across statistical programmes, are logically connected;

(*f*)   Timeliness, time elapsed between release of data and reference period;

(*g*)   Punctuality, degree to which pre-announced release dates are met;

(*h*)   Clarity, degree to which statistics are understandable for non-expert users;

(*i*)   Accessibility, ease with which statistical data can be obtained by users;

(*j*)   Metadata, availability of information describing sources, definitions and methods.

1.230.   Quality is the outcome of processes, and deficiencies in quality (for example, delays in processing or lack of accuracy in the results) are usually the result of deficiencies in process rather than the actions of individuals working in that process. Therefore, process should at least show:

(*a*) Methodological soundness, adherence to professional methods and (internationally) agreed standards;

(*b*) Efficiency, degree to which statistics are compiled in such a way that the cost and the respondent burden are minimized relative to output.

Quality will be better supported by sound institutional arrangements, such as:

(*a*) Legal environment, degree to which statistical legislation is enacted, in conformity with the Fundamental Principles of Official Statistics;

(*b*) Planning mechanisms, the degree to which countries have instituted procedures for systematic, long-term planning of statistical operations;

(*c*) Resources, the degree to which statistical systems are properly funded and staffed, taken in relation to (different types of) cost and to each other.

1.231.   In the census context, some attributes of quality assurance may be emphasized over the rest. The census should produce statistics that are relevant to data users. A census is a particularly expensive exercise to undertake and creates a burden on respondents. Therefore, it is crucial to ensure that any unmet demand for data is kept to a minimum and that topics for which there is little demand are not included on the census form. Consulting with users of census data as one of the first steps in designing the census process is a positive public relations undertaking and an efficient, transparent means of determining the demand for potential census topics.

1.232.   The *relevance* of data or of statistical information is a qualitative assessment of the value contributed by these data. Value is characterized by the degree to which the data or information serve to address the purposes for which they are produced and sought by users. Value is further characterized by the merit of those purposes, in terms of the mandate of the agency, legislated requirements and the opportunity cost to produce the data or information. In the context of a census it is important to note the importance of the concept of fitness for purpose as a measure of relevance. If it is only necessary that data are available at broad level (for example, national or major civil division level of geography; broad demographic level) it is possible that the user requirements could be met more cheaply and effectively through a sample survey.

1.233.   *Completeness* is an extension to relevance, for completeness means not only that statistics should serve user needs, but also that they should serve them as completely as possible, taking restricted resources into account.

1.234.   *Accuracy* of data or statistical information is the degree to which those data correctly estimate or describe the quantities or characteristics that the statistical activity was designed to measure. Accuracy has many attributes, and in practical terms there is no single aggregate or overall measure of it. Of necessity these attributes are typically measured or described in terms of the error, or the potential significance of error, introduced through individual major sources of error, for example, coverage, sampling, non-response, response, processing and dissemination.

1.235.   Data are most useful when they enable reliable *comparisons* across space, such as between countries or between regions within a country, and over time.

1.236.   *Timeliness* of information reflects the length of time between its availability and the event or phenomenon it describes, but considered in the context of the time period that permits the information to be of value and still acted upon. It is typically involved in a trade-off with accuracy.

1.237.   *Accessibility* reflects the availability of information from the holdings of the agency, also taking into account the suitability of the form in which the information is available, the media of dissemination, the availability of metadata, and whether the user has reasonable opportunity to know they are available and how to access that information. The affordability of that information to users in relation to its value to them is also an aspect of this characteristic.

1.238.   The cost of providing information is also a component of the trade-off with accuracy and timeliness. If this were not so, data could achieve (near) perfect accuracy with little or no time delay.

1.   Need for a quality management system for the census process[18]

1.239.   The essential quality attribute of relevance of census output, and how to assure it, has been discussed above together with the need for consideration of accuracy, timeliness and cost. Quality is relative, and in the end is based on what is acceptable or fit for the purpose, rather than a concept of absolute perfection.

1.240.   Deficiencies in quality (for example, delays in disseminating output) are usually the result of deficiencies in process rather than the actions of individuals working in that process. The key to quality assurance and improvement is to be able to regularly measure the cost, timeliness and accuracy of a given process so that the process can be improved when a fall in quality is indicated. The focus of quality assurance is to prevent errors from reoccurring, to detect errors easily and inform the workers so that they do not continue. This simple feedback loop is represented in figure 1.

Figure 1
Quality assurance circle

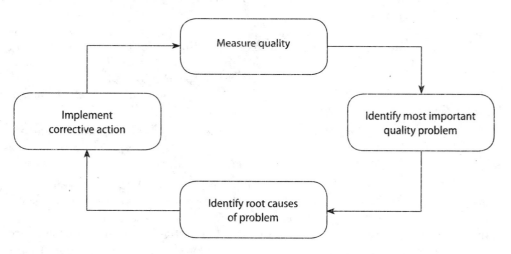

1.241.   Being iterative, the quality circle is particularly applicable to tasks that are highly repetitive, such as the processing phase of the census. However, the general principle applies to all processes. For example, there is less opportunity to evaluate performance, identify problems and implement corrective actions in phases such as enumeration owing to time constraints, the once-only nature of some of the processes and communication issues. However, it still can be established with careful planning and documentation in advance of the census.

1.242.   It is important that a complete evaluation takes place at the end of each phase of the census. This should be done particularly for phases such as enumeration, so that the organizational learning inherent in the quality circle is carried forward to the next census.

[18] This section draws heavily upon material in *Handbook on Census Management for Population and Housing Censuses*, Studies in Methods No. 83 (United Nations publication, Sales No. 00.XVII /Rev.1), chap. 1C.

1.243.　Since people play a key role in most census processes, they are in a good position to identify problems with quality and provide solutions. Quality is therefore not just the outcome of mechanistic applications of predetermined measures but relies on a combination of:

(*a*)　Established, documented processes;

(*b*)　Systems to monitor the outcomes of these processes;

(*c*)　Active encouragement by management to involve staff undertaking the processes in identifying and resolving deficiencies with quality.

1.244.　While elements of the quality circle, such as mechanisms to monitor quality, may have some superficial resemblance to some of the elements of traditional quality control approaches, they are quite different[19]. Traditional quality control is based on correction of error after the event, whereas the emphasis of the quality circle is on improving the process that caused the "error", which may be any of the cost, timeliness or accuracy attributes falling below specified levels. A simple error correction process may suffer from any of the following:

(*a*)　It adds significantly to the cost of the operation;

(*b*)　Errors in the inspection process can fail to detect true errors or falsely identify errors;

(*c*)　The correction process can introduce errors into the data;

(*d*)　Operators take less responsibility for the quality of their work, believing it to be the responsibility of the inspectors;

(*e*)　Where a sample of units is inspected, the quality of data is only ensured for those units that are inspected.

1.245.　The emphasis should be on process improvement rather than correction. Therefore, an important aspect of quality management may be to not correct errors detected through the quality monitoring process unless they are of a severe nature or are generally applicable. For example, a generally applicable error could be a systems error that miscodes every occurrence of a common event. Resources are thus better focused on improving processes and thus overall quality.

2.　The role of managers

1.246.　Managers have a vital role in establishing quality. The biggest challenge to managers is first to establish a culture within the census agency that has a focus on quality issues and to obtain the commitment of staff to strive to achieve high-quality goals. At the same time, managers need to be aware that to achieve high-quality outcomes they need to give their staff responsibility to achieve these outcomes. Managers who do not delegate responsibility will find it difficult, if not impossible, to establish teams that strive for high-quality outcomes.

1.247.　Managers must ensure that staff understand the philosophy behind the approach to quality. As mentioned above, staff involvement is a vital ingredient to quality improvement. Therefore, an environment needs to be established in which staff contributions are expected.

1.248.　The second part of their role is to ensure that clients' expectations are known and that these expectations are built into planning objectives and into the systems that are to deliver them.

1.249.　Thirdly, processes need to be documented and understood by the staff implementing them. Systems and processes for implementing the quality circle also

[19] *Handbook on Census Management for Population and Housing Censuses*, ibid., contains in annex IV a case study of a system combining the quantitative components of the traditional system within a conceptual framework of a quality management approach. Annex IV also illustrates the important differences between the two approaches.

need to be documented and put in place. Questions such as how quality is going to be measured, who is involved in identifying root causes of problems with quality, and how the process improvements are going to be implemented need to be answered. These will vary greatly depending on the nature of the process. Appropriate quality assurance techniques for each phase of the census are summarized below.

1.250.   The greatest test of management commitment to genuine quality improvement will occur in how management approaches problem solving. Staff will monitor management responses closely and adjust their own behaviour accordingly. Staff will act in accordance with how they see managers behave rather than what they hear managers say.

1.251.   Managers who always react to problems by seeking out people to blame, or who establish systems that focus disproportionately on the merits or demerits of individuals at the expense of the team, are sending messages that are contrary to the thrust of quality improvement. An environment where the emphasis is on fault finding, rather than on finding solutions to problems, or on excessive competition, will assure that staff cease to be part of the solution and become part of the problem. Managers need to take upon themselves the responsibility for problems, as they are ultimately responsible for the systems that caused the problems. They should not seek to transfer the problems to lower-level staff.

1.252.   However, even in the best managed processes, there are circumstances where individuals can be justifiably blamed for impacting on quality. These may be individuals who are incapable of performing their duties, deliberately flaunt procedures or even deliberately sabotage the process. These individuals need to be dealt with by management and in some circumstances their employment should be terminated. Managers must deal quickly with these cases and act in a consistent manner. By doing so, managers will demonstrate to all other staff their commitment to quality.

1.253.   To be successful, it is necessary to create a culture in which everyone has the opportunity to contribute to quality improvement. Most of the staff engaged in census operational work undertake routine tasks, and it is up to management to help them see the bigger picture, to motivate them and to encourage them to assume ownership of their work. This can be done by promoting a commitment to quality improvement and by adopting a consistent approach to management.

3.   Quality improvement and the census

1.254.   The quality circle can be applied to the entire census cycle with:

(*a*)   Performance in the previous phase being evaluated at any given level of detail;

(*b*)   Problems with quality ranked in order of importance;

(*c*)   Root causes identified and corrective action implemented.

1.255.   The dependencies in the census cycle are represented in figure 2.

1.256.   It is worth noting that it is possible to start at any point in the diagram and achieve the same result.

1.257.   The following sections outline the way in which the concept of a quality circle is superimposed over the census cycle. Much of the discussion on form design, enumeration, processing and dissemination is in terms of relevance and accuracy. However, these are subject to constraints of time and cost that may be established prior to commencing the census cycle. These are discussed briefly below.

Figure 2
Quality circle dependency chart

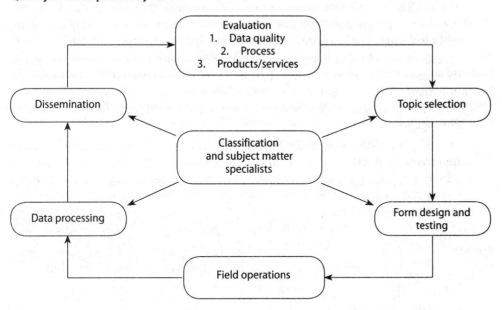

(*a*)   Topic selection

1.258.   The first step in managing the quality of the product (namely, the statistics to be produced) is to ensure that the product will be relevant. The key process is extensive consultation with actual and potential users of census information. The key success factor in this process is full, frank and open communication with users and all areas concerned with the census (in particular, subject matter and classification experts). As should be expected, users are reluctant to propose their needs for a future census until they have been able to assess the extent to which their current needs have been satisfied by the output from the previous census. This should be seen as an evaluation process feeding into the current cycle, the first step of quality management.

(*b*)   Form design and testing

1.259.   The next quality management task concerns the testing of each census question and the testing of the design of the form. Again, the quality circle approach is used, with the results of each test being analysed and evaluated before being fed into further design and testing. The following areas are the key internal stakeholders of the form design process and their requirements need to be taken into account:

(*a*)   The dissemination team, to ensure that the questions asked will deliver the data to meet the needs of users;

(*b*)   The subject matter specialist team;

(*c*)   The team responsible for development of the processing system. For example, positioning of text and delineation of response areas will be dependent on data capture and the processing methodology to be adopted. It is critical that there is ongoing coordination between the form design and processing areas;

(*d*)   The field operations team, which is responsible for training the enumeration workforce and printing the form.

(c) Field operations

1.260. The quality management process continues throughout the design of the census field operations. These are tested, as far as possible, in conjunction with form designs testing. The key internal client of field operations is processing. However, field operations can also impinge on other areas, such as dissemination and classification and subject matter areas where certain concepts, such as what constitutes a dwelling, are implemented during the field operations phase. Several components of field operations can be subject to specific quality circle mechanisms as these are likely to take some time and involve iterative processes. These components include:

(a) Demarcation of enumeration areas;

(b) Map production;

(c) Form printing, where a sample of forms is rigorously tested for adherence to standards.

1.261. Quality monitoring should be established for each of these components and mechanisms put in place to ensure that the outcomes of the monitoring are used to improve processes. It is more difficult to implement the quality circle during actual enumeration owing to the very tight time constraints. However, this can be achieved by:

(a) Clearly establishing the aims of the field operations phase;

(b) Applying thoroughly documented procedures;

(c) Ensuring that the enumerators understand their role through appropriate training and providing inspection of corrupted forms;

(d) Providing opportunities for field staff to be observed operating on the job so that feedback can be given and retraining undertaken.

1.262. However, it has to be acknowledged that during the actual carrying out of the enumeration this approach tends to identify "problem enumerators" rather than systemic or process errors. This means that evaluation following collection is vital. The evaluation should attempt to capture the experiences and suggestions of a range of enumerators and other field staff so that improvements can be made to the subsequent census.

1.263. A general overview of the quality of enumeration can be obtained through:

(a) The use of techniques such as post-enumeration surveys to gauge the level of underenumeration of people and dwellings;

(b) Feedback from field staff;

(c) Measures of the quality of any coding undertaken by field staff;

(d) Mechanisms that may be in place to handle queries from the public.

1.264. The effectiveness of the public communication strategy may be assessed by the amount of press coverage (positive and negative) of the census and follow-up surveys to test the reaction to particular advertising.

(d) Processing

1.265. The key clients of processing are the dissemination area and the areas of the country's statistical agency responsible for maintaining standard classifications and those with specialist subject matter knowledge. The dissemination area depends on the processing team to obtain data in an agreed format and compiled to agreed quality standards. This is necessary so that the data can be used in dissemination systems.

1.266.　Since the census is part of an overall national statistical system, data from the census are likely to be used in conjunction with data from other collections. Thus the classification and subject matter specialist areas, which are responsible for those other collections, need to be satisfied that the coding, editing and other data transformation processes are conceptually sound and deliver data of acceptable quality.

1.267.　Extensive testing of processing systems must be undertaken in advance of the census. Coding processes and training packages need to be prepared and tested using the type of staff likely to be involved in the operations. The processing phase gives the fullest scope for the use of quality improvement techniques, as many of the processes in this phase are repetitive and take a reasonable amount of time. This enables the quality circle to go through much iteration. It is vital that structures are put in place not only to monitor quality but also to involve processing staff in the identification of problems with quality and in proposing solutions.

1.268.　It is generally not possible for processing to improve the accuracy of census data. At best, processes such as editing may reduce some inconsistencies within the data. However, in the end, the data coming from the processing system will not be of any better quality than the information supplied on census forms. Much effort can be expended in correcting apparently inconsistent or inaccurate census data with no real improvement in the fitness for the purpose of the data. It may be a better strategy to educate users to accept slight inconsistencies in census data, rather than developing highly complex procedures that may introduce other errors and impose heavy costs in terms of delay in release of the data and cost to the community.

(e)　Dissemination

1.269.　Census dissemination can easily be overlooked in the chain of providing a quality outcome for the census as management attention is diverted to the costly and risky enumeration and processing operations. The dissemination area is responsible for the timely delivery of products and services to the census data users. Therefore, insufficient planning and resources for this phase can have the effect of delaying the release of the data and thus compromising the overall achievement of the census objectives. The dissemination phase should also be regarded as an ongoing process that will service the needs of users over a long period of time.

1.270.　Management of the quality in census dissemination is driven by concerns to (a) deliver relevant products and services while (b) maintaining accuracy of the data, and (c) timeliness and predictability of data release within agreed cost constraints.

1.271.　The first of these objectives is to provide relevant products and services. This can only be done by reviewing the experiences of the previous census products and services and by user consultation processes with both current and potential users of census data.

1.272.　The second objective is to ensure that the data supplied from the processing system are accurately transformed into output products. A quality assurance strategy to ensure that data tabulations and transformations are carried out accurately needs to be documented and followed. The quality circle approach to these processes needs to be applied and any gaps identified and corrected through extensive testing prior to the census and ongoing process improvement during the dissemination phase.

1.273.　The third quality objective for dissemination is the timely and predictable release of data from the census. While this is the responsibility of all phases of the census programme, special responsibility resides with the dissemination area. The dissemination area needs to be realistic about release dates and ensure that these are communicated to clients early so as to manage client expectations. The involvement of staff actually responsible for the dissemination phase in devising these dates is recommended where this is possible. Dissemination systems and processes need to be available, documented and tested prior to the release of data from the processing phase.

(f)   Evaluation

1.274.   Evaluation is usually considered the last stage in the census cycle. However, it is also possible to consider the evaluation of one census cycle as being the first step in the following census cycle. Similarly, evaluation of one process within a census cycle could be the first stage in the next process of the same census cycle. All aspects of the census programme should be evaluated. The strengths and weaknesses of each task should be identified and action points proposed for future census managers.

1.275.   Evaluation of the accuracy of the census data should also be undertaken, to the extent possible, by comparing the census results with similar data from other sources. These sources can include surveys in a similar time frame or previous census results. The purposes of evaluating the accuracy of the data are to inform users of the quality of the current census data and to assist in future improvements. Future improvement may be achieved by (*a*) improving processes; and (*b*) establishing performance benchmarks against which the quality of the data from subsequent censuses can be measured.

1.276.   Evaluation of data accuracy may have two parts. Preliminary evaluation will enable the identification of any problem areas that have not been previously detected through the quality management processes in earlier phases of the census. More extensive evaluation should be undertaken on data items where problems have been identified or where new questions or processes have been attempted.

1.277.   The results of the evaluations should be made available to census data users.

D.   Enumeration

1.   Method of enumeration

1.278.   There are two major methods of enumeration. In the canvasser (or enumerator) method, information for each individual (in a population census) and for each set of living quarters and the occupants thereof (in a housing census) is collected and entered in the questionnaire by a census official designated to perform this operation in a specified area. In the householder method, the major responsibility for entering the information is given to a person in the unit being enumerated (usually the head of the household), although the questionnaire is usually distributed, collected and checked by a census official. In some countries, postal distribution of the questionnaire, with or without postal return, is used in conjunction with the householder method. This mail-out and mail-back procedure can be used exclusively or combined with on-site checking by a census official.

1.279.   Each method has its own advantages and limitations. The canvasser method is the only method that can be used in largely illiterate populations or in other population groups that may be unwilling to complete the census forms themselves or find it difficult to do so. On the other hand, in countries where literacy is virtually universal and educational attainment relatively high, the householder method may often yield more reliable results at substantially lower costs, particularly if a mail-out/mail-back procedure can be used. However, the postal services may be used to distribute the census forms only when a comprehensive and up-to-date list of addresses is available or can be prepared. Another consideration is the emphasis to be placed in the census on obtaining responses, whenever possible, directly from the person concerned. The householder method allows for, and its instructions may encourage, at no extra cost to the census organization, consultations among family members when they complete the census form. In contrast, with the canvasser method it may be prohibitively expensive to encourage enumerators to go beyond even the "first responsible adult" they encounter in each household. In the light of these considerations, it may sometimes be desirable to rely on one method for enumerating most of the population and to use another method in certain areas or for special groups of the population. New hardware and software technologies have made possible other enumeration methods, such as self-enumeration on the Internet, or computer-assisted personal interviews. While these new methods can supplement and not replace more traditional approaches, caution about their adoption should be exercised. However, overly complex designs should be avoided and adequate quality checks, especially to avoid double counting and fraud cases, in case of coexisting enumeration methods have to be considered.

1.280.   The decision regarding the method of enumeration to be employed should be taken at an early stage on the basis of thorough testing of the various alternatives in terms of their costs, the quality of the data produced and their operational feasibility. Even where a method has been followed traditionally, it is well to periodically reassess its relative advantages in the light of current census needs and changing techniques. An early decision is required because the method of enumeration used affects the budget, the organizational structure, the publicity plan, the training programme, the design of the questionnaire and, to some extent, the kind of data that can be collected.

1.281.   To successfully carry out the enumeration of nomads, it is particularly necessary to pay full attention to the preparatory work in order to determine the suitable enumeration techniques. It should be pointed out that there is no absolute methodology for the enumeration of nomads and conditions vary from country to country. The particular method suitable for a country undertaking to enumerate nomads as part of the census should be determined only after a detailed preliminary study and after field testing. Some of the methods used to enumerate nomads and semi-nomads may be classified as follows: (*a*) group-assembly approach, (*b*) tribal or hierarchical approach, (*c*) enumeration-area approach, (*d*) water-point approach and (*e*) camp approach. Sometimes a combination of two or more methods may be used.

1.282.   In the group-assembly approach, the nomads are asked to assemble at particular interview sites on certain fixed dates. This method can be adopted only through the administrative and/or tribal authorities. The tribal or hierarchical approach is a favourite method, since the nomads usually follow what is dictated by the tribal or hierarchical chief. The enumeration work can be carried out as a kind of administrative census by contacting the tribal chief and collecting, sometimes from memory and sometimes from a register, all the needed information on the chief's followers. The other approach is to contact those followers with the assistance of the chief or a representative and to collect the necessary data directly from the household. In this case, the unit of enumeration is not areal but tribal. The enumeration-area approach presupposes creating conventional census enumeration areas and then contacting each nomadic household that happens to be staying in the enumeration area during the census. In the water-point approach, a list of all water-points available to the nomads during the period of enumeration is prepared. Since numerous temporary water-points are created during the rainy season, a meaningful list of water-points may be prepared with reference only to the dry season. The enumerator is given the task of locating and visiting every nomadic household that may be using a certain water-point. In the camp approach to enumerating nomads, a list of camps is prepared together with the approximate location of each within the country, and enumerators are sent to visit all the households in each camp.

1.283.   For more detailed information on the methods described above and for other methods of enumerating nomads, reference may be made to the study presented to the Conference of African Statisticians at its tenth session.[20]

2.   Timing and length of the enumeration period

1.284.   The choice of the time of year in which the census will be taken is of great importance. The main consideration should be to select a period in which the census is likely to be most successful and to yield the most useful data. This may depend on a number of factors. First, it is necessary to avoid those seasons in which it will be difficult to reach all inhabited areas because of rains, flooding, snow and so forth or in which the work will be particularly arduous, as is the case during extremely hot weather. Second, a time should be chosen when most people are staying at their place of usual residence; such a choice will simplify the census operations both in a de jure and in a de facto enumeration, and it can make the results of a de facto enumeration more meaningful. Seasons of peak agricultural activity should be avoided because it is difficult to interview persons who work late every day and who may even stay nights on their land if the land is far from home. Great traditional festivals, pilgrimages and fasting periods are also unsuitable times for census work. Since in many developing countries the bulk of the field staff is recruited among schoolteachers and older students, the conduct of the census may be feasible only during school holidays, though, as already indicated, the days of major festivals should be avoided.

1.285.   In a country that includes areas of sharply contrasting seasonal patterns of weather or activity or in which potential census personnel are in very short supply, it may be necessary to enumerate different parts of the country at different times or to enumerate the nomads or other special population groups at a different time from that established for the settled population. This, however, is generally not a very desirable solution both because the nomads cannot always be clearly differentiated and because there may be mobility among the settled inhabitants. Furthermore, such a solution creates complications in respect of the use of the census data.

1.286.   When a census has been taken and the census date is found to have been on the whole satisfactory, the next census should be taken at the same time of the year, unless there are strong reasons for changing this date. A regular census date enhances the comparability of the data and facilitates analysis. The tradition of a fixed census date in a country also provides administrative discipline, motivating all those involved in the census to make necessary preparations in a timely manner.

1.287.   It is desirable to keep the enumeration period short in order to avoid double counting and omissions, which can occur in spite of a single reference date. On the other hand, the shorter the enumeration period, the greater the number of field staff that have to be recruited, trained and supervised. This increases the cost and may lower the quality of the data. How these different considerations should be reconciled depends on the size and nature of the country and on the resources at its disposal. The length of school holidays is sometimes a restricting factor, although Governments of

[20] Economic Commission for Africa, "Study on special techniques for enumerating nomads in African censuses and surveys" (E/CN.14/CAS.10/16).

several developing countries, recognizing the great national importance of a census, have prolonged the school holidays in the census year in order to allow teachers and students to work on the census as long as required.

1.288.   In recent censuses, most developing countries have allowed about one week to 10 days for the training of enumerators, while the enumeration period has generally varied from a few days to two weeks. Short periods are often feasible in small countries while longer periods may be necessary in large countries with poor communications.

1.289.   One method sometimes used to allow sufficient time for enumeration and yet make the census simultaneous is first to enumerate the population over a longer period, say a week or more, and then, in one single day, to recanvass all households, deleting and adding persons as needed to update the files. This procedure is, however, not practicable in very sparsely settled areas.

3.   Supervision

1.290.   Adequate supervision of the enumeration is essential. When the enumeration lasts only a few days, control of the quantity and quality of the work accomplished after the first day of enumeration is recommended, in order to facilitate the correction of inefficiencies and to maintain satisfactory progress during the enumeration period. Where the enumeration extends over more than a few days, periodic and systematic assessment should be organized.

4.   Use of sampling in the enumeration

1.291.   Sampling may be employed in the enumeration for collecting information on any topics that need not be tabulated for small areas or small population groups. Questions designed to apply only to a sample of the population or of the living quarters may be included on the regular questionnaire or a special sample questionnaire may be used in addition to a complete enumeration questionnaire. For a discussion of the use of sampling in the enumeration, see paragraphs 1.408–1.437 below.

E.   Data processing

1.292.   No matter how thorough and accurate the census enumeration is, the usefulness, quality and timeliness of the census tabulations will suffer unless the collected data are properly processed. An important element of a successful processing operation is the close and continuing collaboration, at all levels, between the data-processing staff, and the subject-matter and the general statistical staff. At a minimum, the subject-matter and the general statistical staff will need to become familiar with and take a continuing interest in the processing plans and operations, while the processing staff will need to become familiar with and take a continuing interest in the substantive aspects of the census.

1.293.   The most common procedure is to have the census documents arrive in the processing centre in batches by enumeration area (EA). Maintenance of these batches throughout the data processing is recommended, since documents for a given EA reflect the work of one enumerator and may contain a series of errors typical of that person. To ensure the integrity of the batches, the census documents should be stored in a specially designed census document storage facility. The batch for each EA should first be checked for completeness, geographical identification codes and other characteristics of acceptability before being sent to the next stage of data processing, like coding. Transcribing all coded data onto another sheet (for example, the coding form) should be avoided since it may add transcription errors. The same considerations apply to the case of electronic transmission of questionnaires or when the first phase of data processing consists of the scanning and text/image recognition of census questionnaires. In the case of questionnaires transmitted electronically, it is appropriate to set up a *metadata model* where the EA can be recorded. As far as storage is concerned, if paper questionnaires are scanned, their digital version, not only the originals in paper, should be recorded onto secure media for backup.

1. Method of processing

1.294. The choice of an appropriate method of processing is determined by the circumstances of each country. Rapid advances in data-processing technology have greatly increased the speed and reliability of producing detailed tabulation, thereby making computer processing the standard method of processing around the world. Furthermore, an alternative to mainframes, whose computational power was necessary before the advent of lighter and more scalable IT hardware solutions, is the use of a client-server environment. Several lighter tasks, including editing and tabulation of data files, can very well be done on small-sized desktop systems which can be placed in substantive departments and in field offices. On the server side, most of the heavier computing operations, such as scanning, aggregation and analysis of large sets of microdata, coordination of data transmission, Intranet web hosting and so forth, can be executed more reliably than on microcomputers. However, a client-server environment to handle census data must operate over a robust and secure local area network (LAN) or wide area network (WAN). Therefore, computer work is not necessarily dependent on a centralized data-processing facility, provided that a robust LAN or WAN interconnects workstations dispersed over various offices, buildings and different parts of the country.

1.295. In a census office that utilizes a networked computer environment, the file servers allow both data and program files to be stored in a central location. This system economizes on storage space for client computers and removes the need for much physical movement of programs and data on computer media, such as diskettes. Data storage requires frequent backups of the system information to avoid major data loss due to hardware or software faults. Thus, having servers does have such a strategic importance that their location and administration must be well defined and secure enough to ensure data protection.

1.296. In determining the type of equipment to be employed and the advisability of a new machine installation (either complete or partial), or of additions or upgrades to existing equipment, consideration should be given to all the processing requirements of the data-collection programme for which the population and housing census is but one part. Only on this basis can a reasonable decision be made. Decisions on the type of data recording equipment and computer equipment should be made at least one year in advance of the scheduled date of enumeration in order to allow appropriate questionnaire design and proper preparation of instructions to enumerators, development of coding schemes, specification of data handling controls and procedures, and recruitment and training of data-processing personnel. Rapid processing of pre-test or pilot census data is particularly important for identifying improvements needed in the census questionnaire, instructions to enumerators or whatever other preparations may be needed. It is recommended, therefore, that arrangements for using appropriate equipment and software be made well in advance of such tests.

## 2.	Coding

1.297.	Whenever possible, pre-coded responses should be used in census questionnaires with numerical or alphanumeric codes being printed next to each category. Since computer editing and tabulation of textual material are not practical, verbal responses will have to be replaced by a code. This can be done by a coder (possibly computer-assisted) or by a dedicated computer program for automatic coding. There are obvious advantages to directly coding the respondent's answer into the questionnaire during the interview, since the respondent is still present to provide clarifications if necessary. Unfortunately, in most cases this is not practical because enumerators are normally insufficiently trained and they cannot be expected to carry the required code books and manuals during census enumeration.

1.298.	A coder normally works with one or several code books for various items in the questionnaires. Coders may specialize in certain variables, with one group of coders handling only geographical references, another responsible for detailed occupation and industry coding, and so forth. In any event, this is tedious work and can be an important source of errors. To avoid new sources of errors, coders should not rely only on their memory; they must base their function on the use of the *code books*. Automatic or computer-assisted coding may support efficiently the coding activity, by enhancing the quality of operations, reducing coding errors, and speeding up the coding process.

1.299.	*Computer-assisted coding* uses personal computers to assist the coders. The process requires that all the codes be stored in a database file and be accessed by coders during the coding operation. Computer-assisted coding is based on at least two general approaches. In the first one, coded answers are matched to a set of keywords. Textual information from the census questionnaire is parsed and compared to an indexed list of keywords, and then the likelihood of matching between found keywords and coded answers is measured and scored. If the score results are over a certain (high) threshold and there is no ambiguity, a sorted list of coded answers is presented to the coder, who retains the ultimate decision of accepting or refusing the system's proposed answers. In using this method, it may be advantageous to change the order of activities so that the capture of pre-coded information in the questionnaire occurs first, followed by the capture and computer-assisted coding of the remaining information.

1.300.	In the second approach, which is mainly used in image processing of data (intelligent character recognition method) for non-Latin or multilingual countries, owing to the difficulty and existing problems in character (alphanumeric string) recognition, the procedure is as follows: After the scanning and during the coding operation phase, the image of the text will be shown on the monitor, and at the same time, a pull-down menu from a coding database will present the coder with the ability to enter as few key entries as possible to get to the full textual and coding content of a specific case. When the coder selects a code, it will be allocated and saved in the database for that specific case. Although this approach is more time consuming and costly in comparison to the first approach, the quality of coding is much higher than in the traditional way of coding.

1.301.	On the other hand, both techniques have several similar advantages: (*a*) capturing the pre-coded information at an early stage leads to some data files becoming rapidly available, which opens up the possibility of generating and releasing preliminary census results; (*b*) the computer-assisted coding process provides an opportunity for a computer system to alert the operator to problems with data supposedly already captured, for example, missing information for a fully pre-coded variable;

(*c*) the coder works directly on the computer screen; (*d*) information from other variables may be helpful in determining applicable codes for write-ins.

1.302.   *Automatic coding* is a process in which the decision about the code to be assigned is delegated to a computer program. The main difference from computer-assisted coding consists in the automatic acceptance of the answer if its score is over a predetermined threshold and relatively higher than possible identified alternatives. Both computer-assisted and automatic coding systems may exploit self-learning capabilities of neural networks to fine tune their capacity of detection. A human operator becomes involved only in those cases where the software cannot resolve the issue. Computer coding may use, in addition to the written response for the item in question, other relevant information available in the record or the questionnaire. Therefore automatic coding is more applicable in cases where the data capturing process has already been completed, either manually or by some form of automatic reading. Developing computer software for automatic coding is a complex task. The error rates and rates of unsolvable cases for difficult variables tend to be high. Automatic coding methods need to be complemented by computer-assisted or conventional coding methods for unresolved responses.

3.   Data capture

1.303.   Converting the information obtained in the census to a format that can be interpreted by a computer is called data capture. It is possible that several simultaneous and different methods for data capture are being used in a census. They include *keyboard data entry*, optical mark reading, optical character reading and imaging processing techniques. Computer-assisted keyboard data entry is usually carried out using personal computer data entry programs with built-in logical controls. Some of the tasks accomplished by the programs are (*a*) verifying that EA codes are valid, and copying them automatically from one record to the next; (*b*) assigning a number to each person in a household automatically (and perhaps to each household within an EA); (*c*) switching record types automatically if the program's logic requires it; (*d*) checking that variable values are always within pre-determined ranges; (*e*) skipping fields if the logic indicates doing so; (*f*) supporting keyboard verification of the information entered earlier; and (*g*) generating summary statistics for the operator and the batch. In order not to delay the data capture task, data entry applications should limit checking to problems that are either very serious (for example, wrong EA code), or likely to be caused by a simple misread or key entry mistake. More sophisticated checking is deferred until the editing stage.

1.304.   *Optical mark reading* (OMR, often called optical mark recognition) equipment has been available for many years and has nowadays reached very good levels of reliability. OMR is the simplest of commonly available form processing technologies. Owing to relatively stringent requirements for the successful processing of the paper, countries with very dusty or humid climates and poor transport infrastructures are discouraged from using OMR. It is necessary to heed special questionnaire design restrictions as well as consider the quality of the paper and adhere to precise specifications regarding the printing and cutting of the sheets. In some developing countries, this may mean that local production of the questionnaires will be problematic. The need to reserve a relatively large space for marking areas and to adhere to other limitations imposed by OMR equipment sometimes makes it difficult to design the best questionnaire from the point of view of the enumeration process.

1.305.   OMR questionnaires can be marked by the respondent or by the enumerator. Marking by respondents is attractive from a cost perspective, but it depends on the presence of a cooperative spirit and relatively universal literacy. A practical problem is that most OMR devices put restrictions on the writing instrument and the colours that can be used in the marking. Assuming the rules are followed, the rejection rate for marked forms is often low, especially if the forms have been inspected visually before being fed into the readers. Converting a manually completed census questionnaire to OMR format after it has been received in the census office is inefficient and becomes a source of errors, and should therefore be avoided.

1.306.   *Optical character reading* (OCR; also called optical character recognition) and Intelligent Character Recognition (ICR) consist of the use of special equipment to read characters at specific locations in the questionnaire. These two terms identify very similar technological approaches. Specialized sources tend to identify with OCR the capability of recognizing printed characters only, whereas ICR would extend this capability to handwritten text. There is no agreed definition of ICR. In the context of censuses, therefore, this would require that handwriting of text in questionnaire forms by the enumerators be as uniform as possible to common "model" handwriting so as to enable the work of the recognition software engine. In general, only numerals will give acceptable results in an uncontrolled environment, that is to say, one where the machine has not been adapted to the writing style of a particular person. Nevertheless, letters or other writing symbols may also give good recognition rates, as experimented within a multitude of past censuses, if all enumerators comply to use a common handwriting style. OCR/ICR technology has progressed very much and it is still improving thanks to the implementation of more sophisticated recognition algorithms and the use of neural networks for self-learning of the system. Even OCR restricted to numbers represents a considerable step forward when compared with optical mark reading (OMR). Clear number writing instructions have to be provided for the enumerators.

1.307.   *Imaging techniques* and *scanner devices*, together with OCR software, have recently been used by several countries for data capture. Several countries, at different levels of development in their statistical infrastructure, find the modern imaging technology increasingly cost-effective. Experience shows that significantly low error rates are achieved in recovering marks or ticks from questionnaires. *Numerical and alphanumeric characters* written by trained enumerators can also be captured with an acceptable error rate. However, *alphanumeric characters* are more prone to higher error rates. The equipment developed recently has shown an expanded tolerance to variations in paper quality. Nevertheless, extensive testing must be conducted well in advance to determine the best type of equipment and paper. The use of imaging techniques is also dependent on the availability of local maintenance and support capabilities. Whatever methods of coding and data capture are chosen, it is essential that they be carefully tested before final adoption. Recognition engines can be customized to recognize various sets of characters and scripts, but unless good experience is available at the census office, careful planning and preliminary work are needed in conjunction with the OCR/ICR system providers.

1.308.   In addition to the benefits of the scanning technology for capturing the information, an important by-product of scanning census questionnaires is that this allows for the possibility of digitally filing and naming the scanned questionnaires. This increases the efficiency of storage and retrieval of the questionnaires for future use, particularly during subsequent data editing operations.

1.309.   The quantity and type of data entry equipment required will depend on the method of data capture selected, the time available for this phase of the census, the size of the country, the degree of decentralization of the data capture operations, and a number of other factors. For keyboard data entry, the average input rates usually vary between 5,000 and 10,000 keystrokes per hour. Some operators have stayed well below that range, while others have surpassed it significantly. Among the factors that affect operator speed are (*a*) the supporting software and program; (*b*) the complexity of the operators' tasks; (*c*) the ergonomic characteristics, reliability and speed of the equipment; (*d*) the question whether work is always available; (*e*) the training and aptitude of the recruited staff; and (*f*) the motivation of the workers.

1.310. Several options are available to help ensure that data entry operations are completed in a timely manner. They include (*a*) procuring more equipment, (*b*) increasing the number of working hours by working double or even triple shifts and during weekends and (*c*) applying independent verification to varying extents. With the increasing safeguard of data quality by data entry programs, complete verification has become less necessary. Full independent verification may be applied only in the initial stage of data entry and may be reduced when each worker has achieved an acceptable level of quality. After that, a sample verification plan can be applied. Operators may be assigned to sample verification depending on their observed error rate. The work of reliable operators may be verified only for a small sample of the EAs, while more extensive verification is continued for the more error-prone operators. Data entry operators should be retrained or removed if they are obviously lacking in talent for the work (see paras. 1.252 and 1.253 on quality assurance techniques).

4. Data editing[21]

(*a*) Micro-editing

[21] For further details on census data editing, see *Handbook on population and housing census editing*, Studies in Methods, No. 82 (United Nations publication, Sales No. 00.XVII.9).

1.311. Raw data files contain errors of many kinds, some generated by the respondents and others caused by enumerators who misunderstood the respondent's answer. Further mistakes are introduced in the data processing operations and during coding and data entry, or in the course of the transcriptions that take place. From an operational point of view, such errors are of two types: (*a*) those that have the potential of blocking further processing (critical errors), and (*b*) those that introduce distortions into census results without interrupting the logical flow of subsequent processing operations—non-critical errors. All of the first type of errors and as many as possible of the second type must be corrected. Prior to error correction operations and in case there is a need to go back over work, precautionary action should always be taken by making a back-up copy of the original data file at every stage, in case there is a need to go back over the work.

1.312. Since for large censuses, manual correction is rarely economically feasible, the conditions for such corrections are usually specified in specially designed computer programs for automatic error scrutiny and imputation based on other information for the person or household or for other persons or households. Whenever imputation is used, a flag should be set so that analysts are able to distinguish between reported information and that imputed by the editing system. For cases where sufficient information is unavailable for the specific persons or household to correct apparent errors, the *hot-deck imputation* method can be used. This technique uses information obtained from previously processed persons, families or households with similar characteristics as the "best suited" value in replacing missing values or values that have failed processing edits. However, this technique requires careful programming work, considering the fact that search for appropriate information in the census database would slow down computer program execution.

1.313. In some cases, the best solution will be to move out-of-range or clearly inconsistent values into a special category, prior to deciding how such cases should be edited and classified. In this way, the pitfalls of introducing statistical biases are considerably reduced. But precautionary measures should also be defined and set for the fact that overambitious automatic editing programs may cause the so-called corrected data to be significantly flawed. In this respect, it would make sense to have an acceptable cut-off value for error rates at the enumeration area level. If a data scrutiny program finds that more than a certain percentage of the records in a particular batch have one or more serious problems, the whole batch should be rejected and subject to human and/or field work verification.

1.314.   Editing and imputation rules should be formulated by subject-matter specialists, not by computer programmers; also, an error scrutiny and editing plan should be elaborated at an early stage of the census. A set of consistency rules and corrective measures should be put in writing and made available to the programming staff, leaving no room for confusion, misinterpretation or unwarranted independent initiative. The computer programmers should implement these editing rules by working as a part of a team with the subject-matter specialists.

(b)   Output or macro-editing

1.315.   The outcome of micro-editing is a set of records that are internally consistent and in which person records relate logically to other person records within the same household. This process does not, however, provide the full range of assurance necessary to accept the data set as the best possible. A range of conditions could cause errors that cause the data to be consistently wrong: for example, perhaps a condition in the editing suite itself is set incorrectly; proportions in an imputation program may be set wrongly; or enumerators may complete a collection control panel incorrectly. To identify such consistent errors it is necessary to critically review some key aggregate tables to isolate outlier aggregates and identify the cause of the unusual values. These key tables may be a subset of those intended for output or may be tables specifically designed for this purpose.

1.316.   It is recommended that a bottom-up approach be used in this process. That is, the tables should first be examined for a selection of enumeration areas (EAs), then the next level up and so on up to the first set of national tables. There are two reasons for this:

(a)   The first EA will complete the processing cycle well before any other geographic level. Thus, commencing at this level gives the earliest possible warning of a problem, enabling corrections to be made before a large amount of reprocessing is required;

(b)   It is far simpler to examine a few hundred hard copy records within an EA than to attempt to resolve the problem in the millions of records in a national file.

1.317.   A crucial stage in the process is designing the analytical tables. One way of approaching this could be to identify a set of variables which are conceptually consistent with those in the previous census (or a major survey). Thus a set of benchmark values could be constructed before the census operation commences and compared with those from the current enumeration. The content of the benchmark set will depend upon the content of the enumeration and much of this must therefore be determined by each country. However any census will include the variables age and sex so a comparison of the age pyramid and sex ratio for each 10 year age cohort would be basic elements of such analysis.

1.318.   A second component of the analysis is the compilation of a set of information regarding expected changes since the benchmark survey. For example:

(a)   It is possible that in the due time (since the previous collection) improvements in maternal health care programmes have led to an increased survival rate for women. Thus a decreased sex ratio around the childbearing ages may be noticed;

(b)   If literacy is included in the analysis and government policy has been to strongly support increased school attendance, an increase in the proportion of literate people could be expected.

1.319.   There will be a need for careful judgement when the analytical tables show a significant and unexpected difference from the benchmarks. While it may be found that the difference is due to a problem with the current collection, it could also be due to:

(a)   A problem in the collection that has generated the benchmarks;

(b)   A genuine and previously undetected social change that is being correctly revealed by the current collection.

1.320.   In the latter two cases it would be wrong to make any change to the current data set. However, it is crucial that details of the investigation are made known to users (by preparing suitable metadata) so that they would be able to treat and analyse the data correctly. If the analysis indicates that there is a problem with the current collection it will also be a matter for judgement as well as how to react to it. One proposition is to revise the input processing system in order to prevent the problem from being continued. After applying such changes, and in order to avoid introducing further problems, it is essential that they be fully tested and accepted. The second proposition is to make decision in regard to whether to reprocess the records which have already been processed or not. This decision should be guided by the following:

(a)   Significance of the error;

(b)   Number of questionnaires that have already been processed;

(c)   Time duration for the reprocessing;

(d)   Impact of such a decision on other consecutive phases of the census (such as tabulation and dissemination);

(e)   Cost and expenditure of that decision.

5.   Processing control

1.321.   Careful planning and control are required to ensure an uninterrupted flow of work through the various stages from receipt of the census questionnaires through preparation of the database and final tabulations. The plan should provide for the computer edit to follow closely the coding/checking/recording of the data so that errors can be detected while knowledge related to them is fresh and appropriate remedial actions may be taken.

1.322.   Countries may wish to establish a computer-based processing management and control system to check individual forms or groups of forms for each EA or for other processing units. Such a system should link the databases for EAs and other geographical entities with the control information. The system would check and manage progress from process to process so as to ensure the completeness of records at each stage of the processing operations. As specified earlier, project management software may support the formal description of different processes, and provide an environment to control the execution of all operations connected to an individual phase or status of the census. This system should be fed into the overall quality assurance and improvement system whose management is elaborated in paragraphs 1.246–1.253.

6.   Master file for tabulation

1.323.   When data editing is in progress, new files consisting of *clean* data records for each person are produced; these can be assembled so as to build a master file for later tabulations (often called the micro-data file). This master file, like the raw data files, can have a simple rectangular sequential format. There is usually no need for (but neither should it be discouraged) having the master file organized with a database structure with index files. However, the master file should usually be maintained in geographical order, starting with the lowest geographical entity, sorted by housing unit, household or family. Another way commonly used to generate tabulations involving both the individual and the family, household or housing unit is to include in the head of household's record selected characteristics of these latter units. Alternatively, a single hierarchical file can be created involving, for example, person, family and housing unit records. Whatever the chosen structure, the master file must allow for easy checks, controls, and computations to be performed.

1.324.   One of the most common and problematic errors in census files is that different EAs carry, for one reason or another, the same identification codes. Upon sorting the file, these EAs may have been merged, generating households with two heads of household, twice the usual number of members, two housing records, and so on. To avoid this problem, the EA geocodes should be checked carefully prior to the editing phase. This is best done by keeping a check file of all expected code combinations, and marking a code as "used" once an EA using the code has been processed. A module of this functionality can be part of the editing program. The check file will serve to flag impossible or double identification codes, and towards the end will show which EAs were expected but have not been processed.

1.325.   Census master data files may become large. Nowadays servers are much more powerful and able to process files of such size. Well-equipped desktop systems have also higher computational power and are equipped with much bigger and cheaper mass-storage devices. Nonetheless, the hardware infrastructure available to several countries is older, thus two strategies are applied to reduce file size and to make data management simpler. The first involves working with the next lowest geographical entity as a basis, processing the data on this level and aggregating later to obtain national results. The second remedy is to apply on-the-fly compression/decompression to the storage medium. Census files can be compressed quite significantly to less than 20 per cent of their original size. Since tabulation programs access the data in sequential order, using the compressed data will result in a faster reading process.

7.   Methods of tabulation

1.326.   Preparing the tabulation plan is the substantive responsibility of the demographers and other subject-matter specialists who have the necessary expertise in interpreting the census results. This will require consultation with principal users of the census information (see paras. 1.112–1.116). The duties of the data-processing department should be limited to checking the logic of the various accumulations, designing the required programs and producing correct results within the shortest possible time. It is possible that the need for initially unforeseen tables will become apparent, so the census organization should always be prepared to produce additional aggregations. This may involve newly defined classes for certain variables, new types of cross-classifications, differently defined geographical subdivisions, and so on. If the master file is organized according to the principles of relational databases in a relational database management system (RDBMS), original and additional aggregations can be designed according to the relatively easy Structured Query Language statements. In case of a list of records with a rectangular structure, online analytical processing (OLAP) tools might be used to generate multidimensional tabulations. However, if the information needed to produce these aggregations is not available in the master file, it will usually be prohibitively expensive to attempt to add this information at a later date.

1.327. The use of software packages specifically designed to produce census tabulations is highly recommended. These packages will make the job of preparing a useful program much simpler (and thereby help prevent errors). Usually designed for maximum execution speed (given that large files are to be processed), these systems are often available free of cost, or for just a nominal fee.

1.328. Tabulation work can also be easily done by software belonging to either of two other classes: statistical analysis and database software. However, these packages have not been designed with large-scale sequential or geographical processing in mind. They may require substantially more computer time than a specialized census tabulation system. In countries with a limited capacity of powerful computers, this can be an important consideration.

1.329. Other factors that should be taken into consideration when selecting software packages for tabulation work include:

(*a*) The availability of expertise in the census office. It makes no sense to switch to a software system that is only marginally better when this would require a major retraining effort;

(*b*) The need for customisation of the software to perform advanced functions, such as random perturbation to preserve confidentiality.

Moving to a different software environment should be the result of a careful analysis of all the factors concerned.

8. Provisional census results

1.330. Based on the summaries prepared by enumerators, provisional census results may be processed manually or by computer and issued soon after the enumeration is completed. For reasons of efficiency and quality, the use of computers is always preferable. Provisional results will normally cover information only on total population by sex and by major division. The number of households and housing units may also be derived easily from this exercise. Since provisional and final results may differ (for example, the summaries on which provisional results were based might contain errors), it is important that users be warned about the possibility of such differences. The final census results will be the output of the main tabulation program (see chap. IX below). Tabulations may be based on all of the returns or on a sample. If some of the topics are collected on a sample basis only, proper weights will have to be applied in the tabulation stage to produce valid national estimates. In addition, the census office should be prepared to facilitate the production of tables requested by researchers and users (see paras. 3.49–3.54).

F. Databases

1.331. In order to expand the life and usability of the data, and as a complement to the standard production of tables, national statistical offices are encouraged to store the census data in various computerized database forms so as to better satisfy the full range of needs of internal and external data users. Census databases assist data users by providing easy access to a wide range of census data.

1.332.   The establishment of such databases can enhance the dissemination of the census results as well as increase their usefulness by combining census data together with related information from other demographic inquiries in a common format. (An important special case is bringing together the data from prior censuses into a single database.) In addition, such databases can improve the coherence of the input and output processing systems.

1.333.   Needs vary widely from user to user according to specific interests and circumstances. There is therefore no preferred approach to setting up a census or population database. For example, a basic decision must be made whether to provide micro-data, aggregated data or both. Other basic design issues to be considered include whether an effort is to be made to incorporate the new census results in an existing database structure or whether one or more new census databases are to be established, and if the latter is the case, whether the new database(s) will be exclusively in the form of a census database or constitute instead the nucleus of one or more population databases incorporating data from other sources. Consideration will also have to be given to such issues as identification of the different types of users, their information requirements, types of information to be stored in the database, sources and maintenance/update of information, processing of user queries, identification of the appropriate commercial software or, alternatively, whether it is feasible to develop such software, and selection of the appropriate hardware capable of supporting the current database and its anticipated growth.

1.334.   Since building a census or population database requires careful planning and can be time-consuming, such implementation should fit within the global statistical framework of the organization, and be seen as an ongoing process both complementing the data dissemination strategy and strengthening the statistical capacity of the organization.

1.   Database for micro-data

1.335.   Micro-data (records of individual persons and households) collected in the census can be stored either in their raw form, or in their final edited form, or in a file that combines both raw and edited records. To limit problems of conservation, the data should be stored preferably on a medium of excellent reliability such as, currently, compact disk read-only memory (CD-ROM) or a digital versatile disk read-only memory (DVD-ROM), which has much more capacity than a CD-ROM. As time goes by, new technologies for mass storage will undoubtedly evolve. Such new technologies present two issues for census managers and technicians: (*a*) the issue of when it will be appropriate to adopt a new technology as the standard and (*b*) that of the need to convert materials stored in older media to the new standard or otherwise provide accessibility to the older materials.

1.336.   With technological advances in mass storage devices and media, it is now feasible to store the full census data file (one character per byte) as a single large rectangular file. After adding a data dictionary that describes the data format and a tabulation module, one obtains a set that could be described as a census database. The micro database requires a cross-tabulation program which can be either part of the package or external. The software normally used for census tabulation still requires some prior training and may be confusing to inexperienced users. More intuitive tabulation software is available, but may be either too slow in processing or too limited in its options to be fully satisfactory.

1.337.   The organization of the micro-database may take several formats, for example the software may allow for reorganizing the data in a transposed format (for example, one separate file per variable). This can substantially reduce the need for storage space and increase the speed of tabulations. However, establishing this kind of database is more complex, technically demanding and time-consuming. There would be advantages in storing census micro-data with standard commercial databases. This approach has the advantage that many users are already familiar with such software and so it is easier to find programmers and system analysts in the labour market. Even though the storage space required would be comparatively larger, today's market for mass storage has made available very large and fast hard disks at much cheaper prices than a few years ago and the hardware market seems to continue to follow this trend.

1.338.   One of the main advantages of a micro data base is that it permits the retrieval of data, at least in principle, at any level of detail. Since micro-data could be used to obtain information on individual persons, families, households or family enterprises, privacy concerns must always be taken into consideration. In most countries, the use of the census data to identify individuals is prohibited by law. Moreover, the long-term reputation of national statistical authority may well be jeopardized if such disclosures occur.

1.339.   There are a range of methods (such as sampling, introduction of random disturbances, recoding and aggregation) that can be used to make such micro-data available while still protecting individuals' rights to privacy. All have in common the fact that they sacrifice some information in order to eliminate or greatly reduce the risk of disclosure. However, it is important that census organizations interested in disseminating micro-data to outside users should take the appropriate precautions to protect privacy and confidentiality.

2.   Database for macro-data

1.340.   Aggregated census data can be stored in many formats, either as the results for one census, as a database covering more than one demographic inquiry, or in a broad database of statistical information. Whereas micro-data are saved to allow aggregations to be made that were not programmed initially, macro-data are stored to preserve earlier aggregations, to provide the broad public with readily usable information, and to prevent double work by those who may find that the summary data they require have already been produced.

(a)   Publication equivalents

1.341.   The simplest form of what could be called a database for macro-data is a straight copy of a publication on a computer medium, usually on an optical disk (CD-ROM or DVD-ROM) or on the website of the census office. A machine-readable publication-equivalent database may have the advantage of being less expensive to prepare than its hard copy counterpart. In addition, electronic or paper copies can be made quickly, with copying of only part of the publication if only part is required. A disadvantage is that a user needs a computer, and one possibly provided with compatible software, in order to have access to the census information.

1.342.   The original printed publication can be captured on the computer medium by (*a*) exporting the camera-ready output to some portable file formats or scanning the printed pages, which generates raster-type images, or (*b*) copying the original computer files American Standard Code for Information Interchange (ASCII) text form and/or worksheet/database formats. The former approach makes it extremely simple to retain all the formatting and to include graphs and other illustrations. The latter solution has the big advantage of allowing the user to process the information further by computer without having to re-enter the data. This, as noted before, economizes effort and prevents transcription errors. The information content in this case is usually limited to tables, perhaps with some explanatory texts. Because of the important advantages of each of these storage methods, census organizations can use both. The user receives a computer medium holding the camera-ready output file or the scanned images as well as ASCII files of the tables. If tabulated data are provided in readable format, they may also be organized with some kind of data-browsing software. In this case, the software should always allow for downloading in a variety of non-proprietary and the most popular spreadsheet formats. This is possible especially when the medium has a large capacity, as in the case of CD-ROM or DVD-ROM.

(*b*) Table-oriented databases

1.343. More advanced users may prefer that a census database of macro-data offer more than an equivalent of the printed publication. They might like to be able to manipulate the tables in various ways in order to obtain views or results that represent their specific requirements more precisely. Associated graphing and thematic mapping capabilities may also be welcome. Several statistical offices have successfully filled this need. However, a major problem often encountered is that there is no generally accepted definition of what constitutes a statistical table and of the rules that should be followed when designing one.

1.344. In a controlled environment, such as that of a given census or national statistical organization, it is possible to standardize table definitions. The most common way is to design a basic layout having a number of attributes that together fully describe a table. Appropriate software will then give users access to a number of operations that process the table or several tables at the same time. Examples of such operations are reclassifying a variable (for example, from one- to five-year age groups), eliminating a dimension from a multidimensional table or joining tables that have a dimension in common.

1.345. The availability of a standard table description language offers important advantages in exchanging tables as data-processing objects among national and international organizations. However, as mentioned before, some statistical tables are not easily pressed into the mold provided by formal descriptions. In this respect, it should be noted that statistical tables have little in common with the structures known as relational tables in popular database management systems.

1.346. Nevertheless, census offices should be aware of the potential offered by Extensible Markup Language (XML). XML is not, as a matter of fact, a language itself but rather a metalanguage system designed to be used on the Internet. With XML, users can define their own "tags" to structure the information within a document. XML thus offers the potential of precisely describing all elements composing a statistical table: title, subtitle, units of measure, indicators, values, the time dimension and footnotes and in short the metadata. Other solutions, such as EDI/EDIFACT (electronic data interchange for administration, commerce and transport), are a set of internationally agreed standards, directories and guidelines for the electronic interchange of structured data between independent, computerized information systems.

(c) Time-series and indicators databases

1.347. Databases can also cover more than one demographic inquiry, and census results can be integrated with various other data sets, including the results of earlier censuses. In developing databases that are aimed at serving a heterogeneous user community, the issue of a number of basic trade-offs will have to be addressed. For example, on the one hand, the number of variables should be kept as small as possible to make the database easy to use; on the other hand, it should be as comprehensive as possible to address the broadest possible requirements. A minimum data set of versatile indicators should consist of those variables that are useful for a wide range of applications and consistently available across space and time, and whose characteristics are clearly defined. In developing such a database, not only storage of the key indicators and variables themselves, but also the inclusion of some basic figures (absolute numbers or basic data) as a way of standardizing the basic statistical framework, is recommended.

1.348.   It would be ideal to have a broadly accepted storage format that could improve interchangeability between producers and users. The principal problem is that series usually contain a number of descriptive attributes that have not been standardized. Metadata such as key code, definition of the variable, periodicity, unit of measure, universe covered, number of terms recorded, base year (for an index), adjustment applied, and so on, are required to interpret the series properly.

1.349.   In addition, various processing modules (custom-made or commercial) can be attached, allowing seasonal adjustment, interpolation and extrapolation, model building, and adding or subtracting of series if relevant, and so on. Spreadsheet manipulation, as well as graphing and mapping capabilities, can greatly enhance data presentation and analysis.

(d)   Graphing and mapping databases

1.350.   By having associated graphing and mapping capabilities, databases will greatly increase their usefulness. Ideally users should be able to generate the graphs and/or maps required by themselves and then print or plot them, paste them into a report or make the images available for other uses.

1.351.   Several census organizations have produced this kind of product, sometimes in cooperation with a commercial company. Many users want data for relatively small areas concerning such matters as home ownership, educational profiles, and the labour market. While the database may be for one census, some historical information can be included to allow users to observe prevailing trends over time.

1.352.   Both micro- and macro-data can be at the basis of these dissemination products. However, owing to disclosure problems as well as in order to increase processing speed, some form of prior aggregation is usually applied, for example by using summary data. Such summary data could also be combined with the general-purpose graphing and mapping software. However, this would result in a reduction of the user community to those able to handle rather more complicated processing jobs. Making available a census database with tightly integrated graphing and mapping capabilities (which usually implies a tabulation function) is an excellent way to improve the effectiveness of census information dissemination. If it is to be commercially successful, the product must be easy to use.

3.   Geographic information systems

1.353.   A geographic information system (GIS) can be seen as a system of hardware, software and procedures designed to support the capture, management, manipulation, analysis, modeling and display of spatially referenced data.[22] In practical terms, such a system may range from a simple desktop mapping facility to a complete GIS system that is capable of solving complex planning and management problems or producing detailed georeferenced inventories. Its ability to use space to integrate and

[22] For further details on GIS mapping, see *Handbook on geographic information systems and digital mapping*, Studies in Methods, No. 79 (United Nations publication, Sales No. 00.XVII.12).

manipulate data sets from heterogeneous sources can make its application relevant to planning and managing the census process itself. For example, a GIS provides functions for the aerial interpolation of statistical data in cases where the boundaries of aerial units have changed between censuses. However, the development and implementation of such a repository of georeferenced data are not easy tasks to accomplish, and simple desktop mapping systems generating thematic maps from a database of base maps and indicators will satisfy the needs of most census organizations.

1.354.   GIS technology should be considered only at a level appropriate to the skills and resources available, and constitute an integral part of the overall work of the organization. Cooperative arrangements with other agencies should be pursued particularly with regard to the acquisition and maintenance of base map data, which should not be the responsibility of the statistical organization. Statistical organizations should proceed with GIS development or implementation only where it is feasible to maintain such a system during the intercensal years and where there is no dependence on external support.

1.355.   Statistical offices may nevertheless develop GIS applications with population data and other georeferenced data from other sources for more advanced forms of spatial analysis. The task could be shared with other institutions, or be delegated completely to specialists elsewhere. The role of the census office would then consist in supplying census data at the right level and in the right format for such a system. Census offices provide vital information on current demographic conditions and future trends for policymakers in a range of sectors such as health care, education, infrastructure planning, agriculture and natural resources management; and the provision of spatially referenced census databases is an essential prerequisite of the facilitation of the use of demographic data in these fields.

1.356.   In this regard, it should be noted that the GIS should be capable of generating additional geographical delimitations beyond those used in the census, such as school districts, water catchment areas or power service units. These entities will have to be constructed from the smallest geographically identified units available in the census (for example, block faces, grid squares, or EAs). If (as is the case in most developing countries) EAs are the smallest unit, this will have important implications for the establishment of EA boundaries. Cooperation with the authorities responsible for these geographical entities before the boundaries of EAs are drawn can reduce later problems.

1.357.   Being a rather complex technology and a resource-consuming one, GIS needs to be introduced in developing countries carefully and gradually. As an alternative to immediately launching full-scale GIS applications, countries may start with a simple and robust design that is likely to be understood and maintained by a wide array of users, transferable to a wide range of software packages and independent of any hardware platform. GIS implementation in a developing country may follow a hierarchical strategy, with the national statistical office employing a high-end commercial GIS with extensive capabilities for handling and analyzing large amounts of spatial data. Widespread dissemination of databases can then be achieved by creating a version of the finished databases using a low-end mapping software format for distribution at low cost and through web dissemination of macro-information in an online GIS.

G.   Dissemination of the results

1.358.   A census is not complete until the information collected is made available to potential users in a form suited to their needs. The information may be included in published tables and reports for general distribution, produced as tables in unpublished form for limited distribution or stored in a database and supplied upon request, or disseminated online (in this case it will be available only to connected populations).

1.359.   All dissemination is subject to issues of (*a*) quality assurance, (*b*) possible disclosure of information about identifiable respondents and (*c*) copyright and ownership. In addition, the issue of cost recovery has become important to many statistical organizations. Each medium of dissemination offers respective advantages and limitations, and the choice of using one or several of them depends on the context, and on the intended categories of users. In most instances, these methods complement each other and can provide effective ways to reach out to the public and private sectors.

1.360.   When data are provided in electronic form, special attention should be given to providing users with easy means for data retrieval. The options for obtaining the relevant meta-information and the data should be accessible in standard format (ASCII text), comma separated value format as well as in common database and spreadsheet format for easy retrieval and manipulation.

1.   Publication of printed tables and reports

1.361.   Printed publications remain in most countries the preferred choice for the dissemination of the main census results. At least for the present, they reach out to the largest number of potential census users. Paper media do not require that the user have any particular equipment, software or technical skills.

1.362.   It is important that plans be made and sufficient funds be allocated to ensure publication of the tabulations of widespread interest. The final tabulations should be presented and explained in a way that will facilitate their widespread use. The data should be shown for appropriate geographical and administrative divisions and classified by important demographic variables. The census publications should also contain information on how the data were collected and processed, results of available evaluation studies, and appraisals of the substantive significance of the results presented. In addition, a sufficient number of maps should be provided in the census publication to allow the identification of the geographical units for which the statistics are presented.

1.363.   Using tabulation programs to produce output directly for publication allows the traditional method of dissemination of statistics through printed reports to be integrated more closely and more inexpensively with the statistical production process. If the software used for tabulation cannot produce camera-ready output, the files containing output tables can be moved into a document that could be assembled using desktop publishing or word-processing software. Manual retyping of tables once generated should be avoided as much as possible to prevent transcription errors and delays.

1.364.   The choice of how the actual printing is to be done entails in fact a trade-off involving quality, cost and speed. The best results can usually be obtained by sending the documents in computer-readable format to a professional printing plant. This will allow high-quality typesetting and the use of supporting colours. Alternatively, master printouts can be made in the census office and sent to the printer for cheaper duplication or offset printing. There are also affordable high-speed printing systems that can be directly controlled by the microcomputers in the census office.

1.365.   Target dates for publication should be determined well in advance and processing and reproduction programmes should be planned accordingly. In addition to traditional methods of printing, there are various methods of reproduction available that are rapid, economical and legible, and these should be investigated.

1.366.   As a cheaper alternative to printing, census reports can be reproduced on microform (microfilm or microfiche). This technique allows broadening the publication programme without incurring proportionally higher costs. A drawback is that microform requires special reading equipment, and even then most users do not find it easy on the eyes. Dissemination of census publications on microform has largely given way to the electronic alternatives described below.

2.   Dissemination on computer media

1.367.   For an increasing number of users, computer-readable magnetic and optical media are the preferred medium of dissemination. This is because data in this form are often cheaper to obtain, copy and store. In addition, they are directly available for further computer processing and analysis. Magnetic media are usually diskettes, but they are becoming rapidly obsolete owing to the advent of CD-ROMs and DVD-ROMs. Important drawbacks of diskettes are their limited capacity and vulnerability. Adequate storage and frequent recycling are necessary to avoid demagnetization and loss of data. CD-ROMs have a capacity of up to 700 MB, while DVD-ROMs have a capacity from 4.7 to 17 GB.

1.368.   Technologies such as CD-ROM, and the emerging DVD-ROM, provide a much better medium of distribution for large data sets that are not subject to frequent change or updating. Standard CD-ROMs and DVD-ROMs are read-only optical media. They have a very large storage capacity, they are durable and they can be produced inexpensively. Because the results of a particular statistical inquiry such as a census are supposed to be final, dissemination on a read-only support should be satisfactory.

3.   Online dissemination

1.369.   With the surge in importance of the Internet and the World Wide Web, online dissemination of all kinds of information, including statistical information, has gained a new impetus. The advantages of online dissemination are found primarily in terms of speed, flexibility and cost. The information is available to the user as soon as the provider has loaded it on the server and cleared it for access by users. Information can be static or dynamic. The cost to the user is limited to the expenses of communication with the Internet service provider plus whatever charge the information provider is placing on top of these. There is no expense involved in the production and distribution of printed materials or other data supports.

1.370.   Online dissemination of data had been common well before the Internet gained prominence. The simplest option open to statistical organizations had been bulletin board systems (BBS), now largely replaced by Internet and Intranet websites. One could use the same website for both internal and broad community communication, with the granting of access rights in certain areas to privileged users only. Security measures, including passwords, callback procedures and so on can be used to exclude unauthorized users from reaching these areas. However, this is risky, since resourceful hackers may find their way around the barriers and gain entrance to confidential information. Firewalls are hardware and/or software security systems that limit the exposure of a computer or network to malicious infiltration from an external location. The census office website is probably the first dissemination medium where Internet connected users would look for census information. It is recommended that microdata should not be stored on a website in direct contact with the public. It is also recommended that a powerful firewall constitute a security layer between the website that is visible to the public and the working network of the census office. Websites of public administrations are under constant attack from hackers and very sophisticated security measures must be adopted when "opening up" on the Internet. Internet security, despite being an issue of a technical nature, has to be mandated, demanded and provided resources for by the highest levels of management of the census office.

1.371. An Internet website can be used not only to make information available as soon as it has been cleared, but also for other forms of communication with users. Possibilities include online ordering of publications and one or more receiving areas for questions that would be answered later through the same medium by appropriate specialists. One such area could be the census forum or "chat room".

1.372. Internet websites may support "door" or "gateway" applications that allow users to run outside programs on the computer on which the Internet web server operates. Interactive access to census outputs can be offered to most types of databases and census products, including reports, publications, tables, maps and graphs. For example, there may be a database of aggregated census data for small areas or a micro-data database that users can access in this way. When the required data are not readily available, users could run an on-the-spot query to obtain and retrieve results that satisfy their needs. This can be done by offering to Internet users census microdata samples and an interactive tabulation system. Users can then select records from these data sets that satisfy certain parameters and compute statistical information, such as two-dimensional cross-tabulations of either original or recoded variables. Program execution by users on the outside, however, raises important questions of cost, efficiency and confidentiality, which have to be resolved. For reasons of efficiency, it is recommended that information which is provided or likely to be heavily requested by users accessing the census website be made available in a static format, which is faster to download. Letting the user run data extraction on online databases, which would be a dynamic way of accessing the census information, is more resource-consuming and should be the second choice for those users needing more detailed data than those available through static pages.

1.373. Another electronic dissemination method, limited in depth but broad in accessibility, is television videotext. Quite a few statistical offices already maintain on certain television channels a number of pages of actual information that are accessible by anyone having a television set with videotext capability. From a public relations point of view, this is an excellent way to bring the work of the statistical office to the attention of a very broad audience. Since the taxpayer generally still funds an overwhelming part of the costs of official statistics, such a consideration is not to be neglected. Similarly other media are useful in disseminating census information targeted at different sectors of the population. More generalist media, such as the radio, television programmes, newspapers, press conferences and so forth offer the possibility of reaching out to sectors of the population not otherwise reachable.

1.374. A hybrid solution for data dissemination that appears to combine the advantages of several approaches is one whereby the statistical or census organization makes basic data available to users on a computer-readable medium, usually through a website or optical media, while additional information may be provided by telephone or some other online protocols, such as File Transfer Protocol (FTP) sites. This will usually take the form of a package that contains basic data, metadata and data browser software. The basic data may contain existing time-series, report files and the like, as well as country and region maps that can be used to generate thematic maps with various indicators. Maps made available to general users need not ensure the same geographical detail as maps used for EAs. Lighter versions of maps at any subnational level may be provided to the general public, and more sophisticated and detailed ones to those fewer users who would actually need an increased level of detail. It is thus important that the website specify the instructions on how to contact officers responsible for special dissemination needs.

1.375. For some users, if the particular statistical information is not yet available on the physical distribution medium, special access may be granted, provided that adequate screening of their credentials and security checks are performed, to protected areas of the Internet site where up-to-date census information becomes available. Since "opening up" online resources to users has to be planned carefully and a clear policy established in advance (so that criteria for deciding whether or not to grant access are unambiguous), it is not recommended. Instead, provision of an online data tabulation system for expert end users is advised.

4. Privacy and confidentiality

1.376. All the information stored in the census database allows the production of tables not only for very small areas (such as enumeration areas or villages) but for all individual units in these areas. Therefore, when a census database is constructed, not only technical considerations but also the maintenance of confidentiality and the protection of individual privacy—which must be a primary consideration in designing the data-collection and data-processing programme—must be taken into account. Accordingly, micro-data, such as name and local address, or the unique characteristics that permit the identification of individual respondents, must be removed from the database or otherwise altered.

1.377. The same care must be taken if a transcription of information from original questionnaires (that is to say, from a representative sample) is needed for use by qualified agencies and research institutes engaged in special studies beyond the purview of the regular census programme. Such needs have sharply decreased with the almost universal use of computer technology. However, when such a procedure is possible under the census law, individual privacy should be ensured and no exception should be authorized.

5. Acceptance of results

1.378. In countries with limited prior census experience and without a well-functioning civil registration system, where population data are based largely on estimates, it is important to inform the users, particularly the governmental authorities, that the census results could differ from such estimates and to explain the reason for these differences. In some cases, there may be doubts expressed about the census results; usually those doubts focus narrowly on the total population of the country, major subdivisions or population sub-groups, rather than on the bulk of the census data relating to characteristics of the population or on the data for local areas. In this situation, it may be possible to take such doubts into account by modifying the census evaluation programme or by adding appropriate qualifications to the text of the census reports or in tabular footnotes. Nevertheless, the Government may proceed with the processing and dissemination for official purposes. In any case, every effort should be made to process and evaluate the full census and to make appropriate use of as many of the census tabulations as possible.

H. Evaluation of the results

1. Purpose of census evaluation

1.379.   The quality of population and housing census data is very important for many reasons, building public trust and understanding in the national statistical system. The purpose of census evaluation is to provide users with a level of confidence when utilizing the data, and to explain errors in the census result. It is therefore important to choose an appropriate way of sending out these messages to the right group of people.

1.380.   It is universally accepted that a population census is not perfect and that errors can and do occur at all stages of the census operation. Errors in the census results are classified into two general categories—coverage errors and content errors. Coverage errors are the errors that arise due to omissions or duplications of persons or housing units in the census enumeration. The sources of coverage error include, *inter alia*, incomplete or inaccurate maps or lists of enumeration areas, failure on the part of enumerators to canvass all the units in their assignment areas, duplicate counting, persons who for one reason or another will not allow themselves to be enumerated, erroneous treatment of certain categories of persons such as visitors or non-resident aliens, loss or destruction of census records after enumeration, and so forth. Content errors are errors that arise in the incorrect reporting or recording of the characteristics of persons, households and housing units enumerated in the census. Content errors may be caused by poorly phrased questions or instructions, or enumerator errors in phrasing the census questions; inability or misunderstanding on the part of respondents in respect of answering specific items; deliberate misreporting; errors due to proxy response; coding or data entry mistakes, and so forth.

1.381.   Many countries have recognized the need to evaluate the overall quality of their census results and have employed various methods for evaluating census coverage as well as certain types of content error. Comprehensive evaluation should however also include assessment of the success of census operations, in each of its phases, including such activities as the census publicity campaign. Countries should ensure, therefore, that their overall census evaluation effort addresses the census process, as well as the results. The present section is devoted to evaluation of the results. However, the section on the quality assurance and improvement programme (paras. 1.228–1.277) provides further recommendations relating to controlling and assessing the quality of census operations.

1.382.   Evaluation efforts focused on census results should generally be designed to serve one or more of the following main objectives: first, to provide users with some measures of the quality of census data to help them interpret the results; second, to identify as far as is practicable the types and sources of error in order assist the planning of future censuses; and third, to serve as a basis for constructing a *best estimate* of census aggregates, such as the total population, or to provide census results adjusted to take into account identified errors. As discussed below in the following subsection, a number of methods exist for carrying out census evaluation. In practice, many countries use a combination of such methods in order to fully serve these objectives.

1.383.   The final publication of census results should include an estimate of coverage error, together with a full indication of the methods used for evaluating the completeness of the data. The publication should also provide users with some guidance on how they might use the evaluation results. It is also desirable to provide, as far as possible, an evaluation of the quality of the information on each topic and of the effects of the editing and/or imputation procedures used.

1.384.   The range and quality of editing in regard to the correction of the inconsistent data and imputation possible in a population census are greatly enhanced by the use of computer edit programmes that permit inter-record checks (for example, the replacement of missing values based on one or more items on the basis of reported information for other persons or items). If any imputation is made, the topics affected, the methods used and the number of cases affected should be clearly described in the census report.

1.385.   The process of census evaluation should not be permitted to delay the prompt publication of the principal results of the census. Evaluations of the completeness and accuracy of the data can be issued after the initial census results are published.

2.   Methods of census evaluation

1.386.   The choice of evaluation methods to be used depends upon the evaluation objectives. These, in turn, depend on national census experience in terms of past and anticipated errors, user and public concerns, and the financial and technical resources available for evaluation. The decision whether to measure coverage error, content error or a combination of the two must be made. In addition, both gross and net error must be taken into account in developing the overall evaluation plan. Gross coverage error in a census is defined as the total of all persons omitted, duplicated or erroneously enumerated. Net coverage error takes into account the underestimates due to omissions and the overestimates due to duplications and erroneous inclusions. When omissions exceed the sum of duplications and erroneous inclusions, as is usually the case in most countries, a net undercount is said to exist; otherwise, a net overcount results. Similarly, both gross and net content errors have to be considered in the evaluation design.

1.387.   Numerous methods are available to estimate the coverage and content error of censuses. These include simple techniques of quality assurance such as internal consistency checks. Comparisons of results with other data sources including previous censuses, current household surveys and/or administrative records are also useful techniques. Such comparisons may be made in aggregate, that is to say, by comparing the overall estimates from two sources (net error only). Alternatively, record-checking, in which individual census records are matched against alternative sources and specific items of information are checked for accuracy, may be used. Both gross and net errors can be estimated in record checks, which may involve field reconciliation of differences, a costly exercise that cannot be overlooked. An important but complicating factor in the use of record checks is the requirement of accurate matching. It is essential to plan carefully for this aspect, since the operation can be tedious and costly. It should be noted that record checks are best employed to study the coverage of certain segments of a population, such as children whose birth records are complete, since these checks are, by definition, limited to subpopulations with complete, accurate records.

1.388.   Demographic analysis and post enumeration surveys[23] are two very important methods for evaluating census data, and these are discussed in further detail in the following two subsections.

[23] Note that for the purposes of this publication, a post-enumeration survey, or PES, is defined as being a post-census evaluation survey.

3.   Demographic analysis for census evaluation

1.389.   Demographic analysis offers a powerful methodology for evaluating the quality of a census and countries are encouraged to use demographic analysis as part of their overall census evaluation methodology. A wide variety of demographic techniques have been developed and used, ranging from visual inspection of census data to comparative analysis of two census age distributions. A basic procedure for assessing census quality on age-sex is graphical analysis of the population pyramid. Age-heaping or the tendency of respondents to report a particular ending digit is a useful internal consistency check, as are sex ratios by age and certain summary indices of age-sex data, including the United Nations Age-Sex Accuracy Index which extends age-sex ratio analysis by observing deviations of the observed age-gender ratios from the ones expected for each five-year age group and combining the results into a single score.[24] Other summary indices are Whipple's Index and Myer's Blended Index, used for judging age-heaping.

1.390.   Stable population theory is also used to assess the quality of census distributions by age and sex. It is based upon measuring the reported age-sex distribution against that of an appropriately chosen stable population. Its usefulness is demonstrated by the fact that the conditions assumed under the model, constant fertility and constant or recently declining mortality, are satisfied in a number of countries. Recent declines in fertility in a given country render the technique somewhat less useful as an evaluation tool, however, since the technique is sensitive to changes in fertility levels.

1.391.   The methods mentioned above, while useful in providing overall assessment of census quality, cannot differentiate the sources of census error in terms of the relative contributions from undercoverage (or over-coverage) or content error. Better information about coverage error, through demographic analysis, derives chiefly from comparative analysis of data from successive censuses, in which four methods are used.

1.392.   The four methods include (*a*) derivation of an expected population estimate taking account of vital registers of births, deaths and net migrants between censuses, as compared with the latest census, (*b*) population projections based on the results of the prior census plus data on fertility, mortality and migration from various sources and comparing the projected estimates with the new census results (cohort component method), (*c*) comparison of two census age distributions based on intercensal cohort survival rates and (*d*) estimates of coverage correction factors using regression methods to make the age results from the two censuses mutually consistent (cohort survival regression method).[25] It should be noted that the first two methods would likely have to be restricted to evaluation studies of coverage at the national level, especially in countries that do not have good subnational data on migration.

4.   Post-enumeration survey

1.393.   The post enumeration survey (PES) can be defined as the complete re-enumeration of a representative sample of the census population and matching each individual who is enumerated in the post-enumeration survey with information from the main enumeration. The objectives of the post enumeration survey can be summed up as follows:

(*a*)   To assess the degree of coverage during census enumeration;

(*b*)   To examine the implications of coverage deficiencies, if any, on the usefulness of the census data;

(*c*)   To obtain information for the design of future censuses and surveys;

(*d*)   To examine the characteristics of persons who may have been missed during census enumeration.

PES, a special kind of survey designed to measure census coverage and/or content error, has been used effectively in a wide range of countries in recent decades.

[24] See *Methods of Appraisal of Quality of Basic Data for Population Estimates: Manual II* (United Nations publication, Sales No. E.56.XIII.2).

[25] Detailed methodologies including step-by-step procedures for applying all the demographic techniques mentioned above, plus others, are contained in *Evaluating Censuses of Population and Housing* (Washington, D.C., United States Department of Commerce, Bureau of the Census, 1985), chap. 5. Numerical examples are also given in the chapter regarding the application of these techniques in many developing countries. The complete publication is also useful as an overall census evaluation reference.

1.394.   While a PES can be designed to provide a comprehensive evaluation of coverage and content error especially when supplemented by and integrated with detailed demographic analysis of census quality, the methodology of a sound PES is complex, so that countries must accordingly weigh with care the demanding technical requirements and the costs of conducting a successful PES, and elaborate a clear statement of its objectives, before deciding to undertake such a survey. Careful advance planning is crucial. To be valid, a PES has to function within a number of operational and statistical constraints. These include the requirement that the PES be carried out within a few months of the end of the census to ensure that the impact of natural population changes (births, deaths and migration) and lapses in respondent recall do not hopelessly complicate the exercise.

1.395.   The methodology for a PES may entail either a single or a dual system estimation procedure for estimating the "true" total population and hence, the coverage error which is typically an undercount. When dual system estimation is used, an essential property in terms of design is PES independence of the census. Independence implies the presence of many features that are often difficult to introduce in actual practice, including the use of a frame for PES sampling that is unrelated to the census operation, a PES staff of enumerators and other field personnel who are different from the census staff, and organizational management of the PES operation that is under the general supervision of someone other than the census director. When sufficient independence cannot be achieved, a PES design that relies upon single system procedures may be usefully employed. Even though the sampling frame is then based on the census and the PES managed by the census director, this methodology still assumes that the PES, with its better trained enumerators and more intensive field procedures, will give results superior to those of the census. However, unlike the dual system approach, this method cannot account for those persons missed in both the census and the PES, and so the degree of undercoverage is usually understated when a single system PES is used.

1.396.   Another basic property of PES design and execution, irrespective of whether single or dual system estimation is used, involves matching and reconciliation. Matching the PES person-record or household-record against the corresponding census record is an operation whose performance must be of very high quality to ensure that inaccuracies in the PES itself do not effectively ruin the estimate of coverage error. Matching is especially difficult in countries where many surnames are identical and well-defined street addresses do not exist. Part of the matching operation usually involves a field visit to reconcile differences between the census and the PES as regards either coverage or content. Reconciliation of course adds another dimension of cost and complexity, since it entails a second visit to the field for PES-related purposes.

1.397.   Clearly defining the objectives of a PES is the first and most crucial step in planning the survey. The objectives might include estimation of coverage error at the national level; estimation of coverage error for major subnational domains or population sub-groups, each with its own specified level of precision; and/or measurement of content error for specific census items.

1.398.   As mentioned, the design of a post-enumeration survey is complex and there are various alternatives, primarily depending upon whether single or dual system estimation is to be utilized. A number of excellent references are available that set out highly detailed procedures for designing a PES and the conditions under which they may or should be considered.[26]

[26] The most comprehensive material is found in *Evaluating Censuses of Population and Housing* (Washington, D.C., United States Department of Commerce, Bureau of the Census, 1985) chap. 2; *Developments in Dual System Estimation of Population Size and Growth*, K. Krotki, ed. (Alberta, Canada, University of Alberta Press, 1978), is also highly recommended for its exposition of the use of PES in census evaluation; especially relevant therein are: E. Marks, "The role of dual system estimation in census evaluation," chap. 10; E. Marks and J. Rumford, "The 1974 post-enumeration survey of Liberia: a new approach" chap. 11; and C. Scott, "The problem of independence and other issues," chap. 12.

5. Re-interview surveys

1.399. Sometimes a post-census survey is designed to measure content error only, in which case it is usually known as a re-interview survey. The advantage of a well-designed re-interview survey is that the results are more accurate than those of the census insofar as the operation is much smaller and can be more effectively controlled. Estimates of relative response bias can be obtained from a re-interview survey, which (rather than the census) is generally taken as the standard in this area on the grounds that the survey, with its better-trained interviewers and more intensive survey procedures, yields superior results.

1.400. As part of the design of some post-enumeration surveys, a sample of the original census enumeration districts, blocks or areas is chosen and recanvassed for the PES. As regards methodology, this constitutes a useful *re-interview* technique for measuring content error, and such an element in the design is often put into practice because the matching operation between survey and census records is then dramatically simplified. When this technique is also used to estimate census coverage error, the single system estimation methodology has to be employed since the PES and census are not independent.

I. Analysis of the results

1.401. In order to ensure the fullest possible utilization of census results by national and local governmental authorities, by academic researchers and by others, it is advisable to draw up a comprehensive and coordinated programme of analytical studies, phased over a period of several years. This will help allocate effort and resources in such a way as to ensure that important policy needs are adequately met, undue duplication of research effort is avoided and priorities are observed as far as possible. In these studies, the data of the current census should be examined not only by themselves but also as complemented by relevant data from other sources and from earlier censuses, in order to obtain a broader context, improve the estimates and establish trends.

1.402. The analytical studies to be included in such a programme will vary according to the needs and circumstances of the country. The programme may include descriptive summaries of results, policy-oriented analyses of census results and detailed analytical studies of one or more aspects of the demographic and social situation of the country. Some of these studies may be undertaken by the census organization itself, but others, particularly the more time-consuming studies, can most effectively be carried out in cooperation with other research organizations. In any case, it is desirable to invite specialists from other governmental offices and experts outside of the Government to take part in drawing up this programme of studies and it is natural that they would play an important part in the execution of various parts of the analytical programme.

1.403. One important aspect to be considered in establishing a programme of analysis is the possible use of census results in achieving the goals and objectives of population, human settlements or similar policies and strategies at the national and local level and in applying available resources effectively towards the improvement of conditions in these fields. For this purpose, it will be necessary to analyze population and housing census results within the framework provided by other available information so as to achieve an integrated approach to the solutions of population, human settlements and similar problems.

1.404.   A permanent census office should be the central repository of all census results; it would thus be equipped with the information needed for comparative studies, which will indicate long-term trends in the phenomena investigated. However, to facilitate the fullest possible use of census results by others, subsidiary depositories should be established that serve different substantive or geographical groups of users.

1.405.   Aside from the studies that are part of the overall census programme, additional analyses carried out on their own initiative by research organizations, universities or other experts should be encouraged.

J.   Systematic recording and dissemination of census experience

1.406.   It is recommended that every country should prepare and, if possible, publish a methodological and administrative report providing specimens of the census questionnaires and forms, instructions for the enumeration, and detailed information on the cost of the census and on the implementation of the census budget, as well as information on the manner in which the census was planned, organized and conducted, the important methodological and other problems encountered at the various stages of the programme, and points to be considered in future censuses. It is important that the report be as comprehensive as possible, covering all stages and aspects of census planning and operations, including fieldwork, processing, analysis, dissemination, evaluation, and so forth. This report would both assist the users of the census results in appraising and interpreting the data and facilitate the proper planning of future data-collection programmes, including population and housing censuses.

1.407.   The cumulative experience of past censuses in a country is definitely of great help in the preparation of a new census. Because of the lapse of time between censuses and the likelihood of changes in upper-echelon personnel even in a permanent census office, it is most useful to assemble complete records on the methodology of each census, an evaluation of the techniques employed and detailed records on costs and implementation of the census budget. These records should be arranged in such a way as to ensure that information on each aspect of the census operation may be found easily (see para. 1.90 for an indication of the information required on costs and resources). Setting up or implementing a programme of knowledge management in the census office may thus support a rationale and efficient manner of modelling flows of information, centres of responsibility, and map essential working processes connected with the execution of the census. Knowledge management tools and techniques help in preserving institutional memory in a codified way so that lessons learnt from the past may be used for better management of future census planning and execution.

Chapter IV
Use of sampling in population and housing censuses

1.408.   The potential role of sampling in population and/or housing censuses is extensive. On the one hand, sampling can be an integral part of the planning, data collection and operations, analysis and evaluation of the census. On the other hand, the census may serve as a sampling frame for subsequent sample surveys or survey programmes.

1.409.   Important aspects of the use of sampling in connection with the census are set forth below in three sections: the first on features of acceptable sampling operations, the second on sampling as an integral part of the census and the third on the census as a frame for subsequent sample surveys.

A.   Features of acceptable sampling operations

1.   Accuracy and precision

1.410.   The use of sampling in a census entails an awareness of the precision desired in sample estimates. The higher the levels of precision, the larger and/or more complex, and hence the more expensive, the sample. A distinction is to be made between the precision of a sample estimate and its accuracy. Precision can be measured by the standard error (which gives a measure of the error due to sampling compared with a complete enumeration under the same general conditions of inquiry), while accuracy is measured by the difference between the true value (which is generally unknown) and that obtained from an inquiry, whether on a sample or complete enumeration basis.

1.411.   Sampling methods employed in census taking, with the exception of pilot tests, should make use of probability samples as opposed to judgemental, purposive or other non-scientific methods. For the successful execution of a probability-based sampling plan, it is essential that scientifically designed selection procedures be strictly followed. The sampling procedures must be such that a known positive probability of selection can be assigned to every unit in the population. The inverse of these probabilities must be calculable so that they can be used to estimate population values and to calculate the measure of precision of the estimates (in other words, their sampling error). Selection procedures must be faithful to the design so that deviations from prescribed standards or instructions are minimal.

1.412.   Of course, estimated results based on samples are subject to sampling errors in addition to various types of non-sampling errors that are also present in a complete enumeration. The smaller scale of a sample operation may make it possible, nevertheless, to employ interviewers of higher calibre, to devise and pose questions of greater detail and to minimize response errors. As a result, non-sampling errors, which affect the accuracy of the estimates, are likely to be fewer in a well-executed sample than in a complete enumeration.

1.413.   Whenever sampling is used in the census data collection, provision should be made for computing estimates of sampling error (variances), at least for the major items of interest. While a variety of techniques can be employed to estimate variances, the particular technique adopted should be one that reflects the actual sample design used.

2.   Census resources

1.414.   Effective planning of sample operations consists to a large extent in making judicious use of whatever expert knowledge and equipment are available in a particular country. Specific sample plans aimed at the same objective may vary from country to country, depending on the quality and quantity of census resources. In planning a sample operation as part of the census effort, it is important to bear in mind considerations of cost and competent direction.

1.415.   The question of cost in sampling is of crucial significance and cost may be the reason why it was decided not to collect the same information through a complete enumeration in the first place. Numerous factors govern the cost of sampling and it is essential that these be fully weighed before a decision is made to associate a sample plan with a complete count. One important factor, for instance, is the size and complexity of the sample, which in turn is governed by the objectives of the survey and the procedures that are regarded as most efficient.

1.416.   Sample operations should be conducted under the direction of a competent statistician who is conversant with the theory of sampling and of statistical analysis from sample data, and the practical operations of carrying out sample surveys in the field. The advice of such a sampling statistician is indispensable at all stages of the sample operations from planning and sample design to estimation and calculation of variance.

1.417.   In order to ensure that the sample is selected strictly according to the design and to avoid any possibility of bias in sample selection, it is strongly recommended that the actual selection of the sample units should be carried out either in the central office or in regional offices under the direct supervision of a sampling statistician.

B.   Sampling as an integral part of the census

1.418.   Depending on the types of problems to be tackled, a country may consider applying sampling methods in one or more of the following phases of a population census: tests of census procedures, data collection for (usually) a subset of topics in addition to those for which universal coverage is required, post-enumeration field checks, quality assurance of data-processing, advance tabulation of selected topics, and final processing and tabulation. Each phase is discussed below.

1.   Tests of census procedures

1.417.   Planning the various phases of a census often involves choosing among several alternative procedures. Tests conducted on a sample basis provide the best means of determining which alternative to use. The results of such tests facilitate a more desirable allocation of available census resources than is possible otherwise.

1.420.   The nature and extent of census testing depend on the information that is available from previous censuses or other sources. If, for example, prior housing statistics are lacking in a country, a pilot survey may be called for to assess in advance the practical problems that will be involved in including specific housing topics in the census.

1.421.   When carrying out census tests, probability samples are not usually necessary. Since the purpose of most census pilot and pre-tests is to judge the operational feasibility of a proposed course of action for the main census rather than make population estimates, purposive samples can usually be used for such tests. Purposive selection of one or a few geographical areas is generally preferable for such feasibility testing. Purposive samples are also particularly useful when it is necessary to test census questionnaires and methods in areas with particularly difficult conditions. On the other hand, when overall quantitative measures are needed for comparing efficiencies of different procedures (for instance, in examining the anticipated response errors arising from different systems of enumeration), random sampling procedures must be used.

2.   Enumeration of topics in addition to those for which universal coverage is required

1.422.   The expanded needs in most countries for extensive and reliable demographic data have made the use of sampling a cost-effective part of census taking. Sampling is increasingly being used to broaden the scope of the census through the asking of a number of questions of only a sample of the population and households. This use of sampling makes it feasible to obtain urgently needed data of acceptable precision when factors of timing and cost would make it impractical to obtain such data on a complete-count basis.

1.423.   It is important to bear in mind, however, that national legal requirements may make it mandatory to collect certain information on a complete-count basis. Legislation in many countries prescribes complete population enumerations at particular times or makes certain political or administrative dispositions dependent on particular results from a complete enumeration. For example, the apportionment of seats in the legislature among the civil divisions of a country often depends on the number of persons actually enumerated in each division. The data needed for this and similar purposes may not be collected by sampling.

1.424.   Census information that is collected for only a sample of the population and/or housing units is usually obtained by one of two different methods. The first pre-designates a systematic subset of census households to receive a so-called long form, or the census form that contains the detailed questions on all topics. Depending on the sample requirements which, in turn, take account of considerations of cost and precision, the systematic subset that is designated for the long form may represent, for example, 1 in 4, or 1 in 5, or 1 in 10 of the census households. Under such a sampling scheme, all other households in the census will receive a short form containing only those questions intended for universal coverage. If countries choose this option, it is recommended that the pre-designation of the sample households that are to receive the long form be carried out at a central location by supervisory statistical staff, since it has been shown that when the enumerators themselves actually identify the sample households the results are often biased.

1.425.   The second method of sampling often used involves designating a sample of enumeration areas to receive the long form. In this approach, all households in the designated enumeration areas receive the long form and all households in the remaining enumeration areas receive the short form. The advantage of the first method over the second is that the sampling precision of results is greater in the former because clustering effects increase the sampling variance when whole enumeration areas are used as sampling units. On the other hand, the advantage of the second method is that different enumerator staffs may be trained more easily, since one set of enumerators can be trained only for the long form and the other set only for the short form.

1.426.   It is important to make certain that asking questions that are not asked of all persons does not give rise to legal, administrative or even political issues, since census information is required under statute and often with penalty for refusal.

1.427.   The suitability of particular questions for a sample enumeration depends on the precision with which results are needed for small areas, and small population groups, and on the enumeration costs involved.

3.   Post-enumeration surveys and field checks

1.428.   As discussed in the section on the evaluation of census results, it is universally recognized that census taking is not perfect and that errors can and do occur. A highly useful method of evaluating the census results discussed in that section is the use of post-enumeration evaluation surveys (PES). An independent quality check such as a PES can be critical in validating the census count. Whenever a PES is utilized for census evaluation, it is important of course that the design of the PES be based upon sound probability sampling methods.

1.429.   The sample design for a PES must duly take account of the measurement objectives of the evaluation study. These usually include the need to estimate census undercoverage with a certain degree of reliability. In addition, the estimates of undercoverage may be wanted for geographical areas such as provinces or States, and large cities, for urban rural comparisons and so forth. Such requirements also greatly affect the sample design of a PES, as the necessary sample size is increased substantially when estimates of subnational coverage (or undercoverage) are wanted. When designing a PES it is important that:

(*a*)   Time between the census and the PES be minimized to avoid as much recall error as possible;

(*b*)   The PES must be independent of the census. PES interviewers must not have census information about the areas they are working. When interviewers have knowledge of census responses, they tend only to confirm what the census recorded;

(*c*)   To preserve the independence of the PES, its data collection and processing operations must be completely separate from the census data collection and processing;

(*d*)   Dual system estimation should be used because it requires assuming that the PES is only a second independent enumeration, and not that it is a higher quality (or perfect) enumeration than the census;

(*e*)   The members of households interviewed in the PES should be matched to the census on a case-by-case basis to determine whether they were enumerated in the census;

(*f*)   The PES must have a rule for people who move between Census Day and the survey interview. For example, the independent sample may be the people who are residents of the sample areas on Census Day, which includes the out-movers.

4. Quality assurance and improvement programmes

1.430. As mentioned earlier, sampling can be used effectively for measuring and controlling the quality of many phases of census operations (see paras. 1.228–1.277). The quality assurance measures start with pre-enumeration (designing questionnaires and pilot tests), and continue through enumeration and post-enumeration. Under post-enumeration this includes, in particular, the editing and coding of questionnaires, data entry and tabulation. Even in a country of medium population size, these operations involve millions of questionnaires.

1.431. Every effort should be made to keep operational features as simple as possible. In general, a systematic pattern of selection with random starts is preferable to a random pattern. Measures of quality must be adaptable to simple record-keeping systems.

5. Advance tabulation of selected topics

1.432. A complete national census is a huge undertaking and several months, or even years, may elapse before some of the tabulations are published. It is therefore natural that some countries, particularly those with very large populations, should consider advance, provisional tabulations as a way to ensure that key data are available and are disseminated in a timely manner. Sampling can be availed to serve this need in countries that decide to prepare advance tabulations.

1.433. Preparing advance tabulations through sampling has certain disadvantages, however. For the final results to be given, the results tabulated for the sample units have to be integrated with those tabulated for the non-sample units. These operations may increase the total tabulation time of the census and its cost. Precautions are necessary in order to minimize the delay that may be caused in the preparation of the final results. Moreover, issues concerning the differences between the advance tabulations (which are *estimates* based on a sample) and the final tabulations (which for some topics may be complete counts, while for others estimates based on the long-form sample) must be resolved to the satisfaction, and with regard to the comprehension, of users. Finally, the need for an extensive set of advanced tabulations has been reduced in recent years because the widespread use of microcomputers has reduced the time that was being taken to process the census in many countries. In these circumstances, advanced tabulations programmes are likely to be needed only by very large countries that anticipate extended data-processing operations.

1.434. If sampling has been used as an integral part of a complete enumeration to secure information for a subset of topics, as described above, the same sample of units (persons, households or enumeration areas) can also provide a sample for advance tabulations of the census proper. Such a sampling scheme, if it is devised efficiently, with a view to securing additional census information by small administrative units, may offer excellent opportunities for conveniently obtaining advance tabulations for the same administrative units.

1.435. Even when no sampling has been used in the actual enumeration, a sample design for advance tabulations may be comparatively simple to achieve because the complete census returns provide a sampling frame which can then be used to select the sample for the advance results.

6. Final processing and tabulation

1.436. The principal limitations of complete processing and tabulation of all the information collected in a population census and/or housing census are the length of time it takes and the costs. Consequently, a country may decide that CSPro and IMPS should be used as processing and tabulation programmes that provide complete tabulation of a set of core items, such as those on the short form (for countries that use sampling for long-form items), while certain other characteristics are processed and tabulated only on a sample basis. In addition, countries should keep in touch with the latest technology to be used for data processing and tabulation.

1.437. In considering the advisability of using sampling in connection with the final processing operations, the following considerations may also be taken into account. There are certain population and housing characteristics about which information is needed only by large areas and for the country as a whole. Sampling makes it possible to obtain detailed tabulations for large areas, with reasonably small sampling errors, at a much reduced cost and in a shorter time than that needed for tabulations on a complete basis. However, since one of the purposes of a census is to serve local interests, the feasibility of sampling is determined to some extent by the size of the smallest localities for which separate tabulations can be reliably produced.

C. The census as a basis for subsequent sample surveys or survey programmes

1.438. An essential ingredient of probability sample design is the existence of a complete, accurate and up-to-date sampling frame. A sampling frame is a list of all (or most) of the N units in the universe. A sampling frame may be a list of small areas. It may also be a list of structures, households or persons. The census can be used to construct either type of frame, or both; indeed, most countries do use their census for such purposes. The census frame is almost always the departure point for the design of a household sample survey. It is important to note that an old census—even one that, in rapidly changing or growing countries, is one or two years old—may be unsuitable as a frame. In such cases, it is essential to update the census frame with current fieldwork before using it as a frame for a household sample survey.

1.439. It is important to give careful consideration to the construction of a census for subsequent use as a survey sample frame when the census is in the planning stage. The above-mentioned requirements—accuracy, completeness and up-to-dateness—must be addressed. This means, for example, that care must be taken to ensure that the entire country is divided into enumeration areas (EAs), and that all land area belongs to one and only one EA. In terms of their size, the EAs are important not only for the census itself but also for later uses as a potential stage of sampling for surveys; this feature should therefore also be given due consideration by census planners.

1.440. Maps and prior census information concerning small areas are very important for the devising of a good sample plan. The maps are particularly valuable if they unambiguously indicate boundaries of small areas that can be used as primary or secondary sampling units. Population and household counts for the enumeration areas, taken from the census, are also a highly useful ingredient for post-census sample survey design planning. This information is often used to establish measures of size for the selection of first- or second-stage sampling units, or to help in various stratification schemes. Early developments in sampling theory and methods concentrated on efficient designs and associated estimation techniques for population totals or means. In consequence, it is generally believed that while censuses covering total population and housing provide statistical information on a uniform basis for small areas and subgroups of the population, large sample sizes may have to be considered to produce similar results for the long-form topics.

1.441.   More recently, however, the methods for analysis of survey data that take into account the complexity of the sampling design (both sampling and non-sampling errors) have developed rapidly. Therefore, even though sample surveys used alone cannot provide data for small areas or small population groups, they can be used in combination with a census on specific topics. For instance, aggregates of variables recorded on every individual in the population, which are often used for stratification of enumeration areas, may in turn be used as calibrator or independent variables when models are fitted and used in estimation of aggregates of variables recorded for samples only, and for small areas not in the sample. Information users, however, must be made aware whenever results obtained in this fashion are published. Related techniques have been used in some census operations when checking information for internal coherence and in some approaches for imputation of missing or incoherent information.

Chapter V
Units, place and time of enumeration for population and housing censuses

A. Units of enumeration

1.442.   Since individual enumeration is an essential feature of a population and housing census, clarity about the unit of enumeration is an essential element of census planning. In the case of the population census, the primary unit of enumeration is the person. There are two general frameworks within which individuals are identified: (*a*) households and (*b*) institutions, as a subset of collective living quarters. The household is a general framework within which most individuals are identified, since the majority of the population live in households, and the household is also a unit of enumeration in its own right. Because the household is also a unit of enumeration for the housing census, careful identification as a preliminary step in the enumeration can facilitate the efficient collection of the data and the control of its completeness in both types of census.

1.443.   As mentioned above, the second framework within which individuals are identified comprises "institutions", as a subset of collective living quarters. In addition to persons identified within households, there are persons living in institutions who are not members of a household. This group constitutes the "institutional population", which is also investigated in population censuses.

1.444.   For the housing census, the household is one of the three units of enumeration; the other two units are living quarters (in other words, housing units and collective living quarters) and buildings. It is important to bear in mind that, in conceptual terms, these three units are clearly distinguishable. There is not necessarily an identity or exact correspondence among these concepts nor are the terms themselves interchangeable. Several households may live together in one set of living quarters and one household may occupy more than one set of living quarters. Similarly, several sets of living quarters may together occupy one building and one set of living quarters may occupy more than one building.

1.445.   It is recognized that there may be difficulty in some countries in maintaining independent concepts of "household" and of "housing unit".[27] However, the advantages in terms of the usefulness of the data that result from preserving separate concepts usually outweigh the additional effort required in maintaining them.

1.446.   In carrying out a census, it is essential that the units of enumeration be clearly defined and that the definitions be included in manuals of instruction for the enumeration and, to provide appropriate guidance for users of the resulting statistical information, in census reports. In order to reduce the possibility of difficulties in applying the definitions recommended below, countries may find it necessary to expand the definitions and to illustrate them in terms of national conditions and circumstances. Post-enumeration field checks can provide a useful means of determining

[27] For further discussion on the concepts of households and housing units, see paras 1.448 and 1.451; also, for the definition of "housing unit", see para. 2.418.

to what extent the national definitions of the units of enumeration have been applied in the field and the consequent effects on census results.

1.   Person

1.447.   For census purposes, the term "person" denotes each individual falling within the scope of census. As emphasized above (para. 1.442), a person can be identified as belonging to the household population (that is to say, the population living in households) or to the institutional population (that is to say, the population living in institutions, as a subset of collective living quarters) as defined in paragraph 1.454 below. Although each person must be included in the count of the population, there will be some variation in regard to the persons for whom information is collected on different topics. The variations usually depend on the person's age (for example questions relating to economic activity in which case the age boundary may be driven by national legislation), sex (for example, questions relating to children born) and/or relationship to the head or other reference member of the household. It may be recommended that information on a particular topic should be investigated for less than the total population, and the group of persons for which a given topic should be investigated is indicated below under the definitions and specifications of such topics presented in part two, chapter V, section C. In addition, each tabulation presented in annex I is accompanied by a description of the population to be included in the tabulation.

2.   Household

1.448.   The concept of household is based on the arrangements made by persons, individually or in groups, for providing themselves with food and other essentials for living. A household may be either (*a*) a one-person household, that is to say, a person who makes provision for his or her own food and other essentials for living without combining with any other person to form a multi-person household or (*b*) a multi-person household, that is to say, a group of two or more persons living together who make common provision for food and other essentials for living. The persons in the group may pool their resources and may have a common budget; they may be related or unrelated persons or constitute a combination of persons both related and unrelated.

1.449.   The concept of household provided in paragraph 1.448 is known as the "housekeeping concept". It does not assume that the number of households and housing units are or should be equal. A housing unit, as defined in paragraph 2.418., is a separate and independent place of abode that is intended for habitation by one household, but that may be occupied by more than one household or by a part of a household (for example, two nuclear households that share one housing unit for economic reasons or one household in a polygamous society routinely occupying two or more housing units).

1.450.   Some countries use a concept different from the housekeeping concept described in the previous paragraph, namely, the "household-dwelling" concept, which regards all persons living in a housing unit as belonging to the same household. According to this concept, there is one household per occupied housing unit. Therefore, the number of occupied housing units and the number of households occupying them are equal and the locations of the housing units and households are identical. However, this concept can obscure information on living arrangements, such as doubling up, that is relevant for evaluating housing needs.

1.451.   Households usually occupy the whole or a part of, or more than, one housing unit but they may also be found in camps, boarding houses or hotels or as administrative personnel in institutions, or they may be homeless. Households consisting of extended families that make common provision for food, or of potentially separate households with a common head, resulting from polygamous unions, or households with vacation or other second homes may occupy more than one housing unit. For more discussion of household occupancy, see paragraphs 2.463–2.466.

1.452.   A household may also consist of one or more homeless people. The definition of the homeless can vary from country to country because homelessness is essentially a cultural definition based on concepts such as "adequate housing", "minimum community housing standard", or "security of tenure" (see para. 2.536–2.539) which can be perceived in different ways by different communities. The following two categories or degrees of homelessness are recommended:

(*a*)   Primary homelessness (or rooflessness). This category includes persons living in streets or without a shelter that would fall within the scope of living quarters;

(*b*)   Secondary homelessness. This category may include the following groups:

(i)   Persons with no place of usual residence who move frequently between various types of accommodation (including dwellings, shelters or other living quarters);

(ii)   Persons usually resident in long-term (also called "transitional") shelters or similar arrangements for the homeless.

These definitions should be supported by a data collection strategy that ensures, for example, that dwellings are properly identified as shelters and not households.

1.453.   For some topics investigated in housing censuses, the household may serve more efficiently than living quarters as the unit of enumeration. For example, tenure, if investigated in the census, should be collected with reference to households rather than living quarters. Information about household possessions that are normally included as part of the equipment of living quarters (radio and television receivers, for example) should be collected with reference to households. Information on rent, an item of significance in relation to both living quarters and households, would of necessity be collected in relation to the household.

3.   Institutional population

1.454.   As emphasized in paragraph 1.442, institutions represent the second general framework within which persons, as major units of enumeration, are identified. The institutional population comprises persons who are not members of households. These include persons living in military installations, correctional and penal institutions, dormitories of schools and universities, religious institutions, hospitals and so forth.[28] Personnel responsible for the running of an institution and not living in dormitories or similar accommodations should be excluded from the institutional population.

1.455.   Persons living in hotels or boarding houses are not part of the institutional population and should be distinguished as members of one- or multi-person households, on the basis of the arrangements that they make for providing themselves with the essentials for living.

4.   Living quarters

1.456.   The principal units of enumeration in a census of housing are living quarters. Only by precise recognition of these identities, data that will data provide a

[28] For more detailed definition and specifications of institutions as a subset of collective living quarters, see paras. 2.444–2.454.

meaningful description of the housing situation and a suitable basis for the formulation of housing programmes and policies can be obtained.

1.457.   Living quarters are structurally separate and independent places of abode. They may (*a*) have been constructed, built, converted or arranged for human habitation, provided that they are not at the time of the census used wholly for other purposes and that, in the case of improvised housing units and collective living quarters, they are occupied or (*b*) although not intended for habitation, actually be in use for such a purpose at the time of the census.[29]

5.   Building

1.458.   The building is regarded as an indirect but important unit of enumeration for housing censuses since the information concerning the building (building type, material of construction and certain other characteristics) is required for proper description of the living quarters located within the building and for the formulation of housing programmes. In a housing census, the questions on building characteristics are normally framed in terms of the building in which the living quarters enumerated are located, and the information is recorded for each of the housing units or other living quarters located within it.

1.459.   A building is any independent free-standing structure comprising one or more rooms[30] or other spaces, covered by a roof and usually enclosed within external walls or dividing walls[31] that extend from the foundations to the roof. However, in tropical areas, a building may consist of a roof with supports only, that is to say, one without constructed walls; in some cases, a roofless structure consisting of a space enclosed by walls may be considered a building.[32]

1.460.   In some countries, it may be appropriate to use the "compound" as a unit of enumeration, either in addition to the building or as a substitute for it. In some areas of the world, living quarters are traditionally located within compounds and the grouping of living quarters in this way may have certain economic and social implications that it would be useful to study. In such cases it may be appropriate, during the census, to identify compounds and to record information suitable for linking them to the living quarters located within them.

B.   Place of enumeration

1.   Concepts relating to place of residence

1.461.   In general, "usual residence" is defined for census purposes as the place at which the person lives at the time of the census, and has been there for some time or intends to stay there for some time.

1.462.   Generally, most individuals enumerated have not moved for some time and thus defining their place of usual residence is clear. For others, the application of the definition can lead to many interpretations, particularly if the person has moved often.

1.463.   It is recommended that countries apply a threshold of 12 months when considering place of usual residence according to one of the following two criteria:

(*a*)   The place at which the person has lived continuously for most of the last 12 months (that is, for at least six months and one day), not including temporary absences for holidays or work assignments, or intends to live for at least six months;

[29] For a more detailed discussion of the definition of "living quarters" and of the concepts of separateness and independence as used in the definition, see paras. 2.419–2.420.

[30] For the definition of "rooms", see para. 2.472.

[31] The term "dividing walls" refers to the walls of adjoining buildings (for example, of row houses) that have been constructed so as to be contiguous.

[32] For a more detailed discussion of the definition of "building" and related concepts, see paras. 2.511–2.513.

> (*b*) The place at which the person has lived continuously for at least the last 12 months, not including temporary absences for holidays or work assignments, or intends to live for at least 12 months.[33]

1.464. Persons who move frequently and do not have a place of usual residence should be enumerated at the place where they are found at the time of the census.

1.465. Regardless of the criteria used to define the 12-month period, countries should ensure that each person should have one and only one place of usual residence. Furthermore, countries should document the definition of place of usual residence that they have adopted for their census and also provide explicit instructions on how this definition should be applied at the time of enumeration to enumerators for use during an interview or to respondents when filling in self-administered questionnaires.

1.466. A number of special cases may be encountered in which the application may require some additional explanation as to the place of usual residence. Two of the more common examples where special consideration is required are as follows:

(*a*) Students at boarding schools and living away from family homes at universities;

(*b*) Persons working away from their family home: this situation covers a wide range of cases including:

(i) People who spend the working week (five days) in the area close to their work and weekends and holidays at the family residence;

(ii) Workers who constantly travel to different places, such as travelling salesmen, truck drivers and short-term consultants;

(iii) Workers on long term, or semi-permanent assignment to a location away from the family home. In many cases these workers will support the family by remitting portions of their wages to their families.

1.467. In some situations, the concept of usual residence may be referred to as though it is synonymous with the concept of de jure residence. The term "de jure" carries with it a requirement that the person's residence at that place has a basis in the legal system applicable to that place. In turn this implies that people without such a legal basis should not be enumerated in that area. It is not recommended that censuses of population and housing enumerate only those people with a legal right to be in a place but rather, as described in section 2 below, should include either all those present at the place on census night or all those whose usual residence on census night was at the place.

1.468. A further term which has recently come into use in literature is the "floating population". For census purposes this term should be defined as referring to those people usually resident in an area without a legal basis for their residence. Thus the term might include, depending on the circumstances of the country concerned, people from rural areas who have moved to a city for employment purposes without complying with rules for permits to do so, and people who reside in a city while having an official address elsewhere in the country.

2. Operational issues relating to place of residence and place of enumeration

1.469. In a population census, information about each person can be collected and entered in the census questionnaire either where he or she is (or was) present on the day of the census or at his or her usual residence.

[33] This approach is also recommended in the Economic Commission for Europe and Statistical Office of the European Communities, *Conference of European Statisticians Recommendations for the 2010 Censuses of Population and Housing*. United Nations (New York and Geneva, 2006). It is also consistent with what is recommended in the *Recommendations on Statistics of International Migration, Revision 1*, Statistical Papers, No. 58, Rev. 1 (United Nations publication, Sales No. E.98. XVII.14).

1.470. In compiling the census results by geographical areas, however, each person who is part of a household can be included in either (*a*) the household (and hence the geographical area) where the person was present on the day of the census or (*b*) the household (and the geographical area) where he or she usually resides. The same should apply for the institutional population. This allocation is not necessarily dependent upon the place at which information was collected for the individual but it can be simplified by the proper choice of a place of enumeration.

1.471. If a "present-in-area" population distribution is wanted, it is logical to enumerate each person at the place where he or she is (or was) present at the time of the census. If a distribution by usual residence only is required, it is more satisfactory to collect the information about each person at the person's place of usual residence. It should be noted, however, that it is not always possible to collect information about each individual at his or her usual residence, as, for example, when an entire household is away from its usual residence at the time of the census. Some provision must therefore be made for collecting information about such persons at the place where they are found at the time of the census.

1.472. With the growing need for information on households and families and on internal migration, it is becoming increasingly desirable to prepare tabulations on the basis of usual residence rather than on place where present, since the latter is often temporary and so is not useful for the investigation of the above-mentioned topics. It is comparatively simple to enumerate each person where present on the day of the census and thus to obtain a present-in-area population distribution of the population. However, a usual-residence distribution of the population is likely to be more useful for presentation and analysis of the resulting information than that of the population present-in-area during the enumeration.

1.473. If it is also desired to obtain information on both the usually resident population and the present-in-area population, then either each person present in each household or institution on the census day or each person present and each usual resident temporarily absent can be enumerated at the appropriate household or institution. A clear distinction must then be made in the questionnaire, as applicable, among (*a*) persons usually resident and present on the day of the census, (*b*) persons usually resident but temporarily absent on the day of the census and (*c*) persons not usually resident but temporarily present on the day of the census.

1.474. Depending on the categories of persons enumerated at any given place, information may then be collected on the usual residence (address) of those only temporarily present and on the place (address) at which each temporarily absent person can be found. This information can be used for the purpose of allocating persons to the household (or institution) and geographical area within which they are to be counted and of checking to be certain that no person is counted twice (namely, at both the usual residence and the place where present). The procedures to be followed at the enumeration and through the subsequent allocation of persons must, however, be very carefully planned and strictly adhered to if the allocation is to be accurate.

1.475. With the exception of mobile housing units (see discussion in para. 1.477), living quarters and buildings have a fixed location and therefore the place where they are to be enumerated does not have, therefore, to be considered in taking a housing census. Information on households, however, and the persons in households can be collected and entered in the housing census questionnaire either where they are (or were) present on the day of the census or at the usual residence. The procedure followed in the housing census should be governed by that adopted in carrying out the population census if the two censuses are carried out simultaneously. If the housing census is an independent operation, however, the procedure to be followed should be carefully considered since it may have a significant effect on the validity of the results of the housing census.

1.476. Where persons and households are allocated to the place of usual residence, they should also be allocated to the living quarters that they usually occupy. The living quarters that they are actually occupying at the time of the census should be counted as vacant if they are conventional dwellings or they should be excluded from the census if they are non-conventional dwellings.[34]

1.477. Mobile housing units represent a special case as far as the place of enumeration is concerned. They should be enumerated where they are found on the day of the census; however, in accordance with the procedure adopted for the allocation of the population, mobile housing units may also be allocated to the area where the occupants usually reside provided that they are the usual living quarters of the occupants in the area of usual residence. Where they are not the usual living quarters of the occupants in the area of usual residence, the occupants will be allocated to their usual living quarters and the mobile housing unit will be excluded from the census.

[34] To be considered as living quarters, non-conventional housing units and collective living quarters are required to be occupied in order to be included in the census.

C. Enumeration point of time

1.478. One of the essential features of population and housing censuses is that each person and/or each set of living quarters must be enumerated as nearly as possible in respect of the same well-defined point of time. This is usually accomplished by fixing a census "moment" at midnight at the beginning of the census day if there is only one census day.

1.479. For the population census, each person alive up to the census moment is included in a census schedule and counted in the total population, even though the process of completing the schedule does not take place until after the census moment or even after the census day, and the person may have died in the interim. Infants born after the census moment are not to be entered in a schedule or included in the total population, even though they may be living when the other persons in their household are enumerated.

1.480. For the housing census, each set of living quarters that has reached an established stage of completion and is not scheduled for, or in the process of, demolition should be included in a census schedule and counted as a part of the housing inventory even though the process of completing the schedule does not take place until after the census moment or even after the census day, and the living quarters may have been scheduled for demolition in the interim. Living quarters that have attained the prescribed state of completion after the census moment are not to be entered in a schedule (unless special instructions are issued for recording living quarters under construction) nor should they be included in the total number of sets of living quarters.

1.481. Where the amount of time allotted for enumeration in the census is considered to be so long that the population is not likely to be able to supply information as of a single moment in the past, it may be necessary to employ different points of time in the enumeration, even to the extent of using the night before the visit by the enumerator. If such a procedure is followed, it should be clearly explained in the census report and the total duration of the enumeration should be stated. For ease of reference and for the computation of intercensal indices, it is useful to designate a single date in the enumeration period as the official "census date". This date could be, for example, the day by which half of the population was enumerated.

D. Time reference period for data on the characteristics of the population and of living quarters

1.482.   The data collected about the characteristics of the population and of living quarters should be pertinent to a well-defined reference period. The time-reference period need not, however, be the same for all of the data collected. For most of the data, it will be the census moment or the census day; in some instances (as is the case for current economic characteristics and rental arrangements), however, it may be a brief period just prior to the census or (as is the case for fertility questions, usual economic activity and information on the period of construction of the building in which living quarters are located) a longer period of time.

PART TWO

Topics for population and housing censuses

Chapter VI
Topics to be investigated in population censuses

A. Factors determining the selection of topics

2.1.   In line with the overall approach of revision 2 of *Principles and Recommendations for Population and Housing Censuses*, the selection of census topics is based on outputs expected to be produced by the census. Thus, the first step involves clear identification of expected outputs, and then the core and additional topics are decided on that basis. For each of the core topics there is a recommended tabulation. It is recommended that countries collect data on the core topics and also produce the recommended tabulation, as this would improve the international harmonization and comparability of statistics through the use of common concepts, definitions and classifications. Use of an agreed international approach would also enhance the capacity of countries to generate statistics for monitoring the socio-economic situation of their populations, including for the provision of data for the Millennium Development Goals. The topics to be covered in the census (that is, the subjects regarding which information is to be sought for each individual) should, however, be determined upon balanced consideration of (*a*) the needs of the broad range of data users in the country (*b*) achievement of the maximum degree of international comparability, both within regions and on a worldwide basis (*c*) the probable willingness and ability of the public to give adequate information on the topics and (*d*) the total national resources available for conducting the census. Such a balanced consideration will need to take into account the advantages and limitations of alternative methods of obtaining data on a given topic within the context of an integrated national programme for gathering demographic and related socio-economic statistics (see paras. 1.20–1.57 in part one above).

2.2.   In making the selection of topics, due regard should be paid to the usefulness of historical continuity in providing the opportunity for comparison of changes over a period of time. Census takers should avoid, however, collecting information that is no longer required simply because it was traditionally collected in the past, bearing in mind changes in the socio-economic circumstances of the country. It becomes necessary, therefore, in consultation with a broad range of users of census data, to review periodically the topics traditionally investigated and to re-evaluate the need for the series to which they contribute, particularly in the light of new data needs and alternative data sources that may have become available for investigating topics hitherto covered in the population census. Each of the four factors that need to be taken into account in reaching a final decision on census content are briefly reviewed in the following paragraphs.

1.   Priority of national needs

2.3.   Prime importance should be given to the fact that population censuses should be designed to meet national needs. In defining national data needs for population census data, the full range of national uses (for example, policy, administration and research) and national users (for example, national and local government agencies, those in the private sector, and academic and other researchers) should be considered. Each country's decision with regard to the topics to be covered should depend upon a balanced appraisal of how urgently the data are needed and whether the information could be equally well or better obtained from other sources. Global and regional census recommendations can help in this appraisal by providing information about standard census topics and related definitions and concepts based on a wide range of national census experience.

2.   Importance of international comparability

2.4.   The desirability of achieving regional and worldwide comparability should be another major consideration in the selection and formulation of topics for the census schedule. National and international objectives are usually compatible, however, since international recommendations, based on a broad study of country experience and practice, are recommendations for definitions and methods that have successfully met general national needs in a wide range of circumstances. Furthermore, the analysis of census data for national purposes will often be facilitated if, by the use of international recommendations, it is possible to compare the data with those of other countries on the basis of consistent concepts, definitions and classifications.

2.5.   If the particular circumstances within a country require departures from international standards, every effort should be made to explain these departures in the census publications and to indicate how the national presentation can be adapted to the international standards.

3.   Suitability of topics

2.6.   The topics investigated should be such that the respondents will be willing and able to provide adequate information on them. Thus, it may be necessary to avoid topics likely to arouse fear, local prejudice or superstition, and questions too complicated and difficult for the average respondent to answer easily in the context of a population census. The exact phrasing of each question that is needed in order to obtain the most reliable response will of necessity depend on national circumstances and, as described in paragraphs 1.193 and 1.194 above, should be well tested prior to the census.

4.   Resources available

2.7.   The selection of topics should be carefully considered in relation to the total resources available for the census. An accurate and efficient collection of data for a limited number of topics, followed by prompt tabulation and publication, is more useful than the collection of data for an overambitious list of topics, which cannot be investigated, processed and disseminated in a timely, reliable and cost-effective manner. In balancing the need for data against resources available, several additional factors will enter into the decision, including the extent to which questions can be pre-coded.

B. List of topics

2.8.   The list of topics included in these global recommendations for population censuses are based on the global and regional census experience of the last several decades. The topics included here are, with minor revisions, the same as those included in the previous United Nations population census recommendations,[35] with the addition of a topic on agriculture, indigenous peoples, informal employment, cause of deaths in broad categories and deaths of children born alive in the last 12 months.

2.9.   It should be stressed that no country should attempt to cover all the topics included in the list of population topics (see para. 2.16). Rather, countries will need to make their selection of topics in the light of the considerations discussed in paragraphs 2.1–2.7 above, bearing in mind current regional recommendations pertaining to census topics. In using the classifications of different topics presented in part two of the *Principles and Recommendations for Population and Housing Censuses*, it is necessary to outline that all the one- and two-digit classification levels are recommended, while those at the three-digit level are incorporated for illustrative and guidance purposes.

2.10.   Evolving census experience over the past several decades globally and in the regions has demonstrated that a set of topics exist on which there is considerable agreement in regard both to their importance and to the feasibility of collecting the data for them in a census. Data on those within this set likely to present difficulties in terms of data collection or processing are probably best collected for only a sample of the population. The exceptions to this consensus occur, at one extreme, among the countries with the most developed statistical systems, where adequate data on a number of the topics listed, including some of the core ones, are available from non-census sources; and, at the other, among the countries in which data-collection opportunities are limited and it is felt that advantage must be taken of the possibilities offered by the census to investigate topics that, under better circumstances, might be investigated more suitably by other means.

2.11.   Although the set of topics covered in these recommendations is quite comprehensive in terms of topics generally considered suitable for inclusion in a population census, it is also recognized that a few countries may find it necessary to include one or more additional topics of particular national or local interest. However, before the final decision is made to include any such additional topics, their suitability should be carefully tested.

2.12.   To assist countries in using the present publication and in determining their own priorities, lists of recommended population topics are summarized in paragraph 2.16, with the core topics shown in boldface. These core topics correspond to those that were included as "priority topics" in the majority of the regional recommendations in previous census decades.

2.13.   The topics listed in paragraph 2.16 are grouped under nine headings: "Geographical and internal migration characteristics", "International migration characteristics", "Household and family characteristics", "Demographic and social characteristics", "Fertility and mortality", "Educational characteristics", "Economic characteristics", "Disability characteristics" and "Agriculture".

2.14.   Within each heading, a distinction is made between topics collected directly (those that appear in the census schedule or questionnaire), and derived topics. The former are those for which data are collected by a specific item on the census. Although data for the derived topics also come from information in the questionnaire, they do not necessarily come from replies to a specific question. "Total population", for example, is derived from a count of the persons entered in the questionnaires as

[35] *Principles and Recommendations for Population and Housing Censuses, Revision 1,* Statistical Papers No. 67 (United Nations publication, Sales No. E.98. XVII.8).

persons present or resident in each geographical unit. Such derived topics may perhaps be more correctly considered as tabulation components, but they are listed as topics in order to emphasize the fact that the questionnaire must in some way yield this information.

2.15.   The paragraph numbers in parentheses after each entry in paragraph 2.16 refer either to the paragraphs in which the group of topics as a whole is discussed in section D below or to the paragraphs in which the definition and specifications of individual topics are discussed.

2.16.   In the following list of population census topics, core topics are shown in bold and are represented by ◆ for topics that are collected directly, and by ❑ for those that are derived. Additional topics are represented by ○.

Legend:
◆ Core topic
❑ Core topic, derived
○ Additional topic

Table 1
List of population census topics

	1. Geographical and internal migration characteristics (paras. 2.44–2.88)	
(a)	**Place of usual residence** (paras. 2.46–2.51)	◆
(b)	**Place where present at time of census** (paras. 2.52–2.56)	◆
(c)	**Place of birth** (paras. 2.57–2.63)	◆
(d)	**Duration of residence** (paras. 2.64–2.66)	◆
(e)	**Place of previous residence** (paras. 2.67–2.68)	◆
(f)	**Place of residence at a specified date in the past** (paras. 2.69–2.70)	◆
(g)	**Total population** (paras. 2.71–2.77)	❑
(h)	**Locality** (paras. 2.78–2.80)	❑
(i)	**Urban and rural** (paras. 2.81–2.88)	❑
	2. International migration characteristics (paras. 2.89–2.106)	
(a)	**Country of birth** (paras. 2.93–2.96)	◆
(b)	**Citizenship** (paras. 2.97–2.102)	◆
(c)	**Year or period of arrival** (paras. 2.103–2.106)	◆
	3. Household and family characteristics (paras. 2.107–2.132)	
(a)	**Relationship to head or other reference member of household** (paras. 2.114–2.123)	◆
(b)	**Household and family composition** (paras. 2.124–2.131)	❑
(c)	Household and family status (para.2.132)	○
	4. Demographic and social characteristics (paras. 2.133–2.167)	
(a)	**Sex** (para. 2.134)	◆
(b)	**Age** (paras. 2.135–2.143)	◆
(c)	**Marital status** (paras. 2.144–2.151)	◆
(d)	Religion (paras. 2.152–2.155)	○
(e)	Language (paras. 2.156–2.159)	○
(f)	Ethnicity (paras. 2.160–2.162)	○
(g)	Indigenous peoples 2.163–2.167)	○
	5. Fertility and mortality (paras. 2.168–2.201)	
(a)	**Children ever born alive** (paras. 2.180–2.185)	◆
(b)	**Children living** (paras. 2.186–2.187)	◆
(c)	**Date of birth of last child born alive** (paras. 2.188–2.191)	◆

(d)	**Births in the past 12 months** (para. 2.189)	❑
(e)	**Deaths among children born in the past 12 months** (para. 2.191)	❑
(f)	Age, date or duration of first marriage (para. 2.192)	○
(g)	Age of mother at birth of first child born alive (para. 2.193)	○
(h)	**Household deaths in the past 12 months** (paras. 2.194–2.198)	◆
(i)	Maternal or paternal orphanhood (paras. 2.199–2.201)	○

6.   Educational characteristics (paras. 2.202–2.230)

(a)	**Literacy** (paras. 2.202–2.208)	◆
(b)	**School attendance** (paras. 2.209–2.214)	◆
(c)	**Educational attainment** (paras. 2.215–2.222)	◆
(d)	Field of education and educational qualifications (paras. 2.223–2.230)	○

7.   Economic characteristics (paras. 2.231–2.349)

(c)	**Activity status** (paras. 2.240–2.300)	◆
(e)	**Occupation** (paras. 2.301–2.305)	◆
(f)	**Industry** (paras. 2.306–2.309)	◆
(g)	**Status in employment** (paras. 2.310–2.321)	◆
(h)	Time worked (paras. 2.322–2.329)	○
(j)	Income (paras. 2.330–2.334)	○
(k)	Institutional sector of employment (paras. 2.335–2.336)	○
(l)	Employment in the informal sector (paras. 2.337–2.341)	○
(m)	Informal employment (paras. 2.342–2.345)	○
(n)	Place of work (paras. 2.346–2.349)	○

8.   Disability characteristics (paras. 2.350–2.380)

	Disability status (paras. 2.351–2.352)	◆

9.   Agriculture (paras. 2.381–2.390)

C.   Population count

2.17.   The main objective of a population census is to provide a reliable basis for an accurate count of the population of a country at a point in time. An accurate population count is essential for the efficient planning and delivery of services, distribution of resources, defining of boundaries for electoral representation and policy development.

2.18.   Countries are most interested in the count and distribution of usual residents because usual residence is generally the best indication of where people will demand and consume services, and a count of usual residents is therefore most relevant for planning and policy purposes.

2.19.   Some countries will supplement the population count from their census with information from other sources, for example on usual residents temporarily outside the country at the time of the census, to produce population estimates. Other countries will rely solely on the population count from the population census.

2.20.   Information about each person can be collected and entered in the census questionnaire either where he or she is (or was) present on the day of the census or at his or her usual residence. Paragraphs 1.461–1.477 describe the place of enumeration basis for the census.

2.21.   Population counts may be required on a population present, usual resident population, or service population basis. The choice of population count required will depend on national circumstances and some countries will require more than one. The information collected about each person by the census will need to enable the required population count(s).

2.22.   The aim of the census is to achieve unduplicated, full coverage of the population. In practice, countries face a range of challenges in enumerating the population on the basis they decide (where present on census day or where usually resident), and in producing the population count(s) they require. Many of these challenges relate to hard to enumerate groups of the population and persons for whom usual residence is not easily defined.

2.23.   In developing strategies for enumerating the population and collecting information to support the required population counts, it is important to consider consistency with the standards for international migration statistics described in paragraphs 2.89–2.92.

1.   Population present count

2.24.   A population present count is the simplest form of population count from a population census. People are counted at their place of enumeration, usually the dwelling where they will spend census night. Foreign residents who are in the country at the time of the census will be included and usual residents of the country who are absent at that time will be excluded. A population present count can be used with information on migration flows to produce an estimate for the national resident population of a country.

2.25.   A population present count removes complications associated with the application of the concept of place of usual residence, and can reduce the incidence of double counting or missing people by the census. Apart from these benefits of simplicity, a population present count offers a cost advantage because the census does not need to collect additional information about usual residents not at their usual residence at the time of the census.

2.26.   The major disadvantage of a population present count is that it does not provide a full count of usual residents and may not provide a true geographic distribution of usual residents for effective planning and policy purposes.

2.27.   A population present count may be a good proxy for a count and distribution of usual residents, particularly if nearly all the population will be at their usual residence at the time of the census, or if the characteristics of those persons present are very similar to the characteristics of usual residents. However, in many countries significant numbers of people will not be at their usual residence at the time of the census, and the characteristics of absent usual residents will be different from non-residents present, so that a population present count is not a good proxy for a count of usual residents. Large seasonal movements of people due to weather changes, holidays and other factors can add to this problem. The ability to produce accurate information on families and households is also reduced to the extent that persons are not enumerated with their families or households.

2.28.   To produce a population present count, information is required on all persons present and the address where they are enumerated. It is also very useful to collect information to identify those persons present who are not at their usual residence and those persons who are not usual residents of the country.

2.29.　Ideally a population present count should include all the difficult to enumerate groups set out in paragraph 2.41 below, except for categories (*b*), (*e*) and where applicable (*g*). For some of these groups the concept of "at the time of the census" may need to be extended to allow enumeration to take place. Collecting on a place of enumeration basis in these situations may increase the risk of either overcount or undercount. Persons who are at multiple locations during this extended period may be counted at more than one location, or alternatively they may not be counted at any location.

2.　Usual resident population count

2.30.　Countries increasingly prefer a usual resident population count because this count offers better information for planning and policy purposes on the demand for services, households, families and internal migration.

2.31.　**A usual resident population count** is a count of all usual residents of a country at the time of the census. Although countries determine the definition of a usual resident according to their circumstances, it is recommended that in defining a usual resident and the place of usual residence, countries apply the definition contained in para. 1.463. Usual residents may have citizenship or not, and they may also include undocumented persons, applicants for asylum or refugees. Usual residents then may include foreigners who reside, or intend to reside, in the country continuously for either most of the last 12 months or for 12 months or more, depending on the definition of place of usual residence that is adopted by the country. Persons who may consider themselves usual residents of a country because of citizenship or family ties, but are absent from the country for either most of the last 12 months, or for 12 months or more, depending on the definition adopted, should be excluded. Conversely, persons who are normally resident in the country but who are temporarily absent should be included in the usually resident population. Countries applying a different definition of a usual resident for national purposes should produce a usual resident population count using the recommended 12-month definition for the purposes of international comparability.

2.32.　A usual resident count provides a better count of the permanent population of a country for long-term planning and policy purposes, and a better distribution of the resident population within the country for planning and service delivery purposes at subnational geographic levels.

2.33.　To achieve a usual resident count, the population can be enumerated either on a "place where present" basis or on a "where usually resident" basis, as described in paragraphs 1.469–1.477.

2.34.　Ideally a usual resident population count should include all the difficult to enumerate groups set out in paragraph 2.41 below, except for categories (*e*) and (*e*).

2.35.　To produce a usual resident population count, information is required on all usual residents and the address of their usual residence. If the census is enumerated on a place present at census basis, then the information collected needs to differentiate clearly between persons enumerated at their usual residence, persons usually resident who were elsewhere at the time of the census, and persons present who are usually resident elsewhere. Information should also be collected to identify those persons who are not usual residents of the country. If the census is enumerated on a usual residence basis, then information about all usual residents needs to be collected at their usual residence, regardless of whether they are present at the time of the census or not, to ensure full coverage.

2.36. There are difficulties in obtaining information from those usual residents who are absent from the country at the time of the census, particularly where no other person is present at the time of the census to provide information about those people. Estimates of the number and characteristics of these usual residents not enumerated by the census will be used by some countries to supplement the census population count.

2.37. There can be challenges in applying the concept of usual resident if a person could be considered to have more than one usual residence, sometimes in different countries. There may also be those who do not consider themselves to have a usual residence, such as nomadic peoples or undocumented persons. Countries will need to develop appropriate operational rules for resolving cases where it is not clear whether a person is a usual resident of the country, or where the usual residence of the person within the country is not clear.

3. Service population count

2.38. **A service population count** may be required if a population present count or usual resident population count does not accurately represent the demand for, or provision of services in a country or part of a country. Service populations are relevant where a significant proportion of the population providing or using services in an area are not usual residents of that area. Types of service population counts include daytime populations, working populations and visitor populations. In some countries there may also be an interest in foreign service populations, consisting of foreign residents who cross the border regularly to provide or consume services. This is particularly important in the planning and provision of transport services.

2.39. A service population count may include some or all of the difficult to enumerate groups depending on the type of service population required. For example, daytime service populations may include civilian foreigners who cross the border daily to work or consume services in the country.

2.40. To produce a service population count, in addition to an estimate of usual residents, information is required about where people provide or demand services. For seasonal populations (holiday, resort), information is needed on the destination and timing of seasonal trips. Some countries will produce service population counts by supplementing the population present count or usual resident population count with information from other sources, such as visitor information from hotels and resorts, to produce visitor populations. Alternatively, additional information may be collected by the census.

4. Difficult to enumerate groups

2.41. The following difficult to enumerate groups are relevant to the production of any population count:

(a) *Nomads and persons living in areas to which access is difficult.* Making contact with these groups to enumerate them can be difficult, particularly as part of a point in time count. Enumeration may need to be done at a different time, over an extended period, or by using alternative methods to enable contact with these groups. For example, countries might consider asking those who provide services to these groups to assist with their enumeration. Seasonal movements may be identified in advance and this information can be used by collectors to enable contact. There needs to be planning and consultation, particularly with influential members of these groups, prior to the census to organize for their enumeration. Communication publicizing the benefits of the census, and engaging appropriate leaders in support of the census may assist coverage. Awareness of cultural issues relevant to specific groups should also be considered in developing enumeration strategies;

(b) *Civilian residents temporarily absent from the country.* As these persons will be absent from the country at the time of the census, they will be excluded from a population present count. Countries may collect information on these people from another family or household member present at the time of the census, but where a complete family or household is outside the country at the time of the census, it may not be possible for the census to collect information about these people. Estimates for usual residents temporality absent from the country based on other sources may be required to produce reliable estimates of usual residents for planning and policy purposes;

(c) *Civilian foreigners, who do not cross a frontier daily and are in the country temporarily, including, undocumented persons, or transients on ships in harbour at the time of the census.* These groups may be in the country at the time of the census and therefore form part of the population present count. It is important to include these groups in the population count if their demand for services is to be considered for planning and policy development purposes. However, these groups may prefer not be counted, either because they fear ramifications from being counted or they do not identify themselves as part of the population for the country. Language and communication may present challenges. Countries need to develop strategies, appropriate for their context, to include these groups in their enumeration;

(d) *Refugees.* Refugee populations in camps should be enumerated and their numbers presented separately, allowing calculation of country population excluding refugees, when such population count is required for non-demographic purposes;

(e) *Military, naval and diplomatic personnel and their families located outside the country and foreign military, naval and diplomatic personnel and their families located in the country.* Apart from the difficulties mentioned in (b) and (c) that are common to groups who are absent from their own country, enumeration of these groups is subject to diplomatic protocols. Detailed counts and characteristics of these groups may be considered sensitive on security grounds in some countries. Counts of these groups may be available from administrative records;

(f) *Civilian foreigners who cross a frontier daily to work in the country.* This group should be excluded from a usual resident population count. The practice of counting people where they spend census night removes much ambiguity and reduces possible duplication. The difficulty then is trying to include them in a service population if countries want to consider this group in policy development and in planning service delivery;

(g) *Civilian residents who cross a frontier daily to work in another country.* These persons are usual residents of the country and should be included in the population count;

(h) *Merchant seamen and fishermen resident in the country but at sea at the time of the census (including those who have no place of residence other than their quarters aboard ship).* Identifying that the ship will be at sea at the time of the census may be problematic, so countries will need to develop strategies to ensure inclusion of this group in the population count. This may include providing this group with census forms before their ship goes to sea or enumerating the ship before the time of the census.

5. Population subgroups for which counts are required

2.42.   Accurate population counts, required for the efficient planning and delivery of services, distribution of resources, defining of boundaries for electoral representation, policy development and the design and analysis of household surveys, are required for various population subgroups within a country. These subgroups are typically based on geography, age and sex. There may also be a need to identify other populations such as the school population, working population, indigenous population or disadvantaged populations to enable more informed policy formation and better targeted service provision. A range of characteristics will be required to identify these populations and population subgroups, depending on the services being planned, the resources to be distributed and so on. The need for population counts for particular subgroups will determine the questions asked in the census.

D.   Definitions and specifications of topics

2.43.   The present section contains the recommended definitions and specifications of all topics presented in the order in which they appear in paragraph 2.16 above. It is important that census data be accompanied by the definitions used in carrying out the census. It is also important that any changes in definitions that have been made since the previous census be indicated and, if possible, accompanied by estimates of the effect of such changes on the relevant data, in order to ensure that users will not confuse valid changes over a period of time with increases or decreases resulting from changed definitions.

1.   Geographical and internal migration characteristics

2.44.   It should be noted that "place of usual residence" and "place where present at time of census" may be considered alternative topics when countries do not have the resources to investigate both topics for general census purposes. Some countries, however, will want to investigate both topics for general purposes. The relationship between the two topics and their further relationship to the topic of "place of enumeration" are set forth in chapter IV (see paras. 1.469–1.477).

2.45.   It is recommended that countries investigating only "place where present at time of census" for general purposes should also obtain information on "place of usual residence" for all persons who do not usually reside in the household where they were enumerated, to be used in connection with the information on "place of birth", "duration of residence", "place of previous residence" and/or "place of residence at a specified date in the past" in determining internal migration status. If, in the compilation of the population of geographical units, persons are allocated to the place where they were present at the time of the census, information on the four above-mentioned migration characteristics will be irrelevant for persons who were only visiting, or transient in, the place at which they were present. Since such persons must, in any case, be identified in the questionnaire as non-residents so that they will not be erroneously classified as recent in-migrants, a question on their place of usual residence can be easily put and will make it possible to include the entire population in the tabulation of internal migration characteristics.

(a)   Place of usual residence (core topic)

Recommended tabulations: all population tabulations

2.46.   Information on the number of people usually residing in an area is basic to most informed decision-making about the area, whether it be a country, an urban agglomeration or a civil division. The number of residents determines the levels of most services required in an area.

2.47.   The **place of usual residence** may be the same as, or different from, the place where the enumerated person was present at the time of the census and/or his or her legal residence. For a definition of place of usual residence, see paragraphs 1.461–1.463.

2.48.   Although most persons will have no difficulty in stating their place of usual residence, some confusion is bound to arise in a number of special cases, where persons have more than one residence. These cases might include persons who maintain two or more residences, students living at school, members of the armed forces living at a military installation but still maintaining private living quarters away from the installation, and persons who sleep away from their homes during the working week but return home for several days at the end of each week (see also para. 1.466). In some other circumstances referring to the person's intentions for the future may assist the determination of the place of usual residence.

2.49.   Problems may also arise with persons who have been residing at the place where they are enumerated for some time, perhaps for more than half of the preceding 12 months, but do not consider themselves to be residents of that place because they intend to return to their previous residence at some future time, and also with persons who have left the country temporarily but are expected to return after some time longer than 12 months from the departure. In such instances, clearly stated time limits of presence in or absence from a particular place must be based upon the 12-month limit and used to determine whether or not the person is usually resident there.

2.50.   If each person is to be entered in the questionnaire only at his or her place of usual residence, the topic need not be investigated separately for each person, because the information will be available from the location information entered for the questionnaire as a whole.

2.51.   Information on the place of usual residence should be collected in enough detail to enable tabulations to be made for the smallest geographical subdivisions required by the tabulation plan and to meet the requirements of the database within the cost limits and operational procedures required to code to a fine degree of detail.

(b)   Place where present at time of census (core topic)

Recommended tabulations: all population tabulations

2.52.   In cases where the census is taken on the basis of "place where counted" this topic may fulfill some of the functions of place of usual residence.

2.53.   The **place where present at the time** of the census is, in theory, the geographical place at which each person was present on the day of the census, whether or not this was his or her place of usual residence. In practice, the concept is generally applied to the place where the person slept on the night preceding the census day, because many persons appearing in the questionnaire were not physically present at the place of enumeration during most of the day.

2.54.   As mentioned in chapter V (see paras. 1.471 and 1.472), the concept is sometimes further extended to apply to the night preceding the day of actual enumeration in cases where the enumeration extends over a long period of time and persons are not likely to be able to supply information as of a single moment in the past. Other departures from the definition may be necessary to deal with individual cases, such as persons traveling during the entire night or day of the census and persons who spent the night at work.

2.55.   If each person is to be entered in the questionnaire only at the place where he or she was present at the time of the census, the topic need not be investigated separately for each person, because the information will be available from the location information entered for the questionnaire as a whole.

2.56.   Information on the place where each person was present should be collected in enough detail to enable tabulation to be made for the smallest geographical subdivisions required by the tabulation plan and to meet the requirement of the database.

(c)   Place of birth (core topic)

Recommended tabulation: 1.4-R

2.57.   Information on the place of birth is a major input to development of policies relating to migration and the related issues of service delivery to migrants.

2.58.   The place of birth is the civil division in which the person was born or, for those born in other countries, the country of birth. For persons born in the country where the census is taken (the native-born population), the concept of place of birth usually refers to the geographical unit of the country in which the mother of the individual resided at the time of the person's birth. In some countries, however, the place of birth of natives is defined as the geographical unit in which the birth actually took place. Each country should explain which definition it has used in the census.

2.59.   The collection of information distinguishing between the native-born population and those born elsewhere (foreign-born) is necessary where any inquiry on place of birth is made. Even countries where the proportion of foreign-born population is insignificant, which therefore desire to compile information only on the place of birth of the native-born population, must first separate the native-born from the foreign-born population. It is therefore recommended that place of birth be asked of all persons. For further information on country of birth for the foreign-born population, see paragraphs 2.93–2.96 below.

2.60.   Information on the place of birth of the native population is usually used primarily for the investigation of internal migration. For countries that have been recently formed from parts of previously separate entities, however, such information may be of use in assessing the relative size of the population segments from each of those entities and their distribution throughout the country.

2.61.   For the latter purpose, it is usually sufficient to collect information only on the major civil division (state, province or department, for example) in which the place of birth is located. If desired, more detailed information on the subdivision of a specific locality can be collected and used for accurate coding of the major division or for presenting data for smaller areas.

2.62.   For studies of internal migration, data on the place of birth of the native population even in terms of major civil divisions are not adequate in themselves. For an understanding of the movements of people since birth it is necessary to collect information at the smallest possible geographic level, bearing in mind that (*a*) the boundaries of administrative units such as cities and other civil divisions will change over time, which may give rise to ambiguity in data reported; and (*b*) the costs of coding reported data to these smaller units may be prohibitive especially where there are many units and the population is highly mobile. To overcome the first problem, to the extent possible both national and subnational boundaries should refer to the boundaries applying at the time of the census. Countries must address the second problem in the light of their own circumstances.

2.63.   It is recommended that, for the study of internal migration, the data on place of birth be supplemented by information collected on duration of residence (see paras. 2.64 to 2.66) and place of previous residence (see paras. 2.67 and 2.68) or of residence at a specified date in the past (see paras. 2.69 and 2.70).

(*d*)   Duration of residence (core topic)

Recommended tabulation: 1.5-R, 1.6a-R

2.64.   The **duration of residence** is the interval of time up to the date of the census, expressed in complete years, during which each person has lived in (*a*) the locality that is his or her usual residence at the time of the census and (*b*) the major or smaller civil division in which that locality is situated.

2.65.   In collecting information on duration of residence, it should be made clear that the concern is with length of residence in the major or smaller civil division and the locality, but not in the particular housing unit.

2.66.   Data on the duration of residence have only limited value in themselves because they do not provide information on the place of origin of in-migrants. Therefore, when the topic is investigated, the place of previous residence should also be investigated, if at all possible, so that the data can be cross-classified.

(*e*)   Place of previous residence (core topic)[36]

Recommended tabulation: 1.6a-R

2.67.   The **place of previous residence** is the major or smaller civil division, or the foreign country, in which the individual resided immediately prior to migrating into his or her present civil division of usual residence.

2.68.   Data on the place of previous residence have only limited value in themselves because they do not provide information on the time of in-migration. Therefore, when the topic is investigated, the duration of residence should also be investigated, if at all possible, so that the data can be cross-classified.

(*f*)   Place of residence at a specified date in the past (core topic)[36]

Recommended tabulation: 1.6b-R

2.69.   The **place of residence at a specified date in the past** is the major or smaller division, or the foreign country, in which the individual resided at a specified date preceding the census. The reference date chosen should be that most useful for national purposes. In most cases, this has been deemed to be one year or five years preceding the census (or both of these time frames in cases where internal migration is of particular importance to users and resources are sufficient to code the data). The former reference date provides current statistics of both internal and international migration during a single year, while the latter may be more appropriate for collecting data for the analysis of international migration. Also to be taken into account in

[36] Place of previous residence and place of residence at a specified date in the past are alternate core topics, that is to say, countries should collect data on at least one of them and not necessarily on both unless there is a strong national interest to do so.

selecting the reference date should be the probable ability of individuals to recall with accuracy their usual residence one year or five years earlier than the census date. For countries conducting quinquennial censuses, the date of five years earlier can be readily tied in, for most persons, with the time of the previous census. In other cases, one-year recall may be more likely than five-year recall. Some countries, however, may have to use a different time reference than either one year or five years preceding the census because both of these intervals may present recall difficulties. National circumstances may make it necessary for the time reference to be one that can be associated with the occurrence of an important event that most people will remember. For foreign-born persons, the collection of information on year of arrival in the country is recommended (see "International migration characteristics", paras. 2.89–2.106).

2.70.   No matter what previous date is used, provision must be made for the treatment of infants and young children not yet born at that date. Tabulations of the data should indicate the nature of the treatment of this group.

(g)   Total population (core topic)

Recommended tabulations: all population tabulations

2.71.   For census purposes, the **total population** of the country consists of all the persons falling within the scope of the census. In the broadest sense, the total may comprise either all usual residents of the country or all persons present in the country at the time of the census. The total of all usual residents is generally referred to as the de jure population and the total of all persons present as the de facto population.

2.72.   In practice, however, countries do not usually achieve either type of count, because one or another group of the population is included or excluded, depending on national circumstances, despite the fact that the general term used to describe the total might imply a treatment opposite to the one given any of these groups. It is recommended, therefore, that each country describe in detail the figure accepted officially as the total, rather than simply label it as de jure or de facto.

2.73.   The description should show clearly whether each group listed below was or was not included in the total. If the group was enumerated, its magnitude should be given; if it was not enumerated, an estimate of its size should be given, if possible. If any group is not represented at all in the population, this fact should be stated and the magnitude of the group should be shown as "zero". This may occur particularly with groups (*a*), (*b*), (*d*) and (*n*) described below (see also paras. 2.41 and 2.42 for more information).

2.74.   The groups to be considered are:

(*a*)   Nomads;

(*b*)   Persons living in areas to which access is difficult;

(*c*)   Military, naval and diplomatic personnel and their families located outside the country;

(*d*)   Merchant seamen and fishermen resident in the country but at sea at the time of the census (including those who have no place of residence other than their quarters aboard ship);

(*e*)   Civilian residents temporarily in another country as seasonal workers;

(*f*)   Civilian residents who cross a frontier daily to work in another country;

(*g*)   Civilian residents other than those in groups (*c*), (*e*) or (*f*) who are working in another country;

(*h*) Civilian residents other than those in groups (*c*), (*d*), (*e*) (*f*) or (*g*) who are temporarily absent from the country;

(*i*) Foreign military, naval and diplomatic personnel and their families located in the country;

(*j*) Civilian foreigners temporarily in the country as seasonal workers;

(*k*) Civilian foreigners who cross a frontier daily to work in the country;

(*l*) Civilian foreigners other than those in groups (*i*), (*j*) or (*k*) who are working in the country;

(*m*) Civilian foreigners other than those in groups (*i*), (*j*), (*k*) or (*l*) who are in the country temporarily;

(*n*) Refugees in camps;

(*o*) Transients on ships in harbour at the time of the census.

2.75. In the case of groups (*h*) and (*m*), it is recommended that an indication be given of the criteria used in determining that presence in, or absence from, the country is temporary.

2.76. In those countries where the total population figure has been corrected for underenumeration or overenumeration, both the enumerated figure and the estimated corrected population figure should be shown and described. The detailed tabulations will of necessity be based only on the actual enumerated population.

2.77. The population of each geographical unit of the country, like the total population of the country (see para. 2.71), may comprise either all usual residents of the unit (see para. 2.47) or all persons present in the unit at the time of the census (see paras. 2.52 and 2.53).

(*h*) Locality (core topic)

Recommended tabulations: all population tabulations

2.78. For census purposes, a **locality** should be defined as a distinct population cluster (also designated as inhabited place, populated centre, settlement and so forth) in which the inhabitants live in neighbouring sets of living quarters and that has a name or a locally recognized status. It thus includes fishing hamlets, mining camps, ranches, farms, market towns, villages, towns, cities and many other population clusters that meet the criteria specified above. Any departure from this definition should be explained in the census report as an aid to the interpretation of the data.

2.79. Localities as defined above should not be confused with the smallest civil divisions of a country. In some cases, the two may coincide. In others, however, even the smallest civil division may contain two or more localities. On the other hand, some large cities or towns may contain two or more civil divisions, which should be considered as segments of a single locality rather than separate localities.

2.80. A large locality of a country (that is to say, a city or a town) is often part of an urban agglomeration, which comprises the city or town proper and also the suburban fringe or thickly settled territory lying outside, but adjacent to, its boundaries. The urban agglomeration is therefore not identical with the locality but is an additional geographical unit, which may include more than one locality. In some cases, a single large urban agglomeration may comprise several cities or towns and their suburban fringes. The components of such large agglomerations should be specified in the census results.

(*i*)　Urban and rural (core topic)

Recommended tabulations:　all population tabulations

2.81.　Because of national differences in the characteristics that distinguish urban from rural areas, the distinction between the urban and the rural population is not yet amenable to a single definition that would be applicable to all countries or, for the most part, even to the countries within a region. Where there are no regional recommendations on the matter, countries must establish their own definitions in accordance with their own needs.

2.82.　The traditional distinction between urban and rural areas within a country has been based on the assumption that urban areas, no matter how they are defined, provide a different way of life and usually a higher standard of living than are found in rural areas. In many industrialized countries, this distinction has become blurred and the principal difference between urban and rural areas in terms of the circumstances of living tends to be a matter of the degree of concentration of population. Although the differences between urban and rural ways of life and standards of living remain significant in developing countries, rapid urbanization in these countries has created a great need for information related to different sizes of urban areas.

2.83.　Hence, although the traditional urban-rural dichotomy is still needed, classification by size of locality can usefully supplement the dichotomy or even replace it where the major concern is with characteristics related only to density along the continuum from the most sparsely settled areas to the most densely built-up localities.

2.84.　Density of settlement may not, however, be a sufficient criterion in many countries, particularly where there are large localities that are still characterized by a truly rural way of life. Such countries will find it necessary to use additional criteria in developing classifications that are more distinctive than a simple urban rural differentiation. Some of the additional criteria that may be useful are the percentage of the economically active population employed in agriculture, the general availability of electricity and/or piped water in living quarters and the ease of access to medical care, schools and recreation facilities. For certain countries where the facilities noted above are available in some areas that are still rural since agriculture is the predominant source of employment, it might be advisable to adopt different criteria in different parts of the country. Care must be taken, however, to ensure that the definition used does not become too complicated for application to the census and for comprehension by the users of the census results.

2.85.　Even in the industrialized countries, it may be considered appropriate to distinguish between agricultural localities, market towns, industrial centres, service centres and so forth, within size-categories of localities.

2.86.　Even where size is not used as a criterion, the locality is the most appropriate unit or classification for national purposes as well as for international comparability. If it is not possible to use the locality, the smallest administrative unit of the country should be used.

2.87.　Some of the information required for classification may be provided by the census results themselves, while other information may be obtained from external sources. The use of information provided by the census (as, for example, the size-class of the locality or the percentage of the population employed in agriculture), whether alone or in conjunction with information from other sources, means that the classification will not be available until the relevant census results have been tabulated. If, however, the census plans call for the investigation of a smaller number of topics in rural areas than in urban areas or for a greater use of sampling in rural areas, the classification must be available before the enumeration takes place. In these cases, reliance must be placed on external sources of information, even if only to bring up to date any urban-rural classification that was prepared at an earlier date.

2.88.   The usefulness of housing census data (for example, the availability of electricity and/or piped water) collected simultaneously with, or not too long before, the population census should be kept in mind. Images obtained by remote sensing may be of use in the demarcation or boundaries of urban areas when density of habitation is a criterion. For assembling information from more than one source, the importance of a well-developed system of geocoding should not be overlooked.

2.   International migration characteristics

2.89.   Interest in the movement of people across national boundaries, namely, international migration, has steadily grown among countries concomitant with the increase in international migration. The present section on international migration supplements and expands the topic "geographical and internal migration characteristics", which is covered above. Definitions of international migration and specific ways of applying them in population censuses, consistent with the United Nations *Recommendations on Statistics of International Migration, Revision 1,*[37] are presented in this section.

[37] Statistical Papers, No. 58 (United Nations publication, Sales No. E.98.XVII.14).

2.90.   The revised United Nations *Recommendations on Statistics of International Migration* deals with both migrant flows and immigrant stock, and underscores population censuses as being the best source for collecting data on the immigrant stock and its characteristics. This section is therefore concerned chiefly with the topic of immigrant stock.

2.91.   Given the general definition of "international migrant" presented in the revised *Recommendations on Statistics of International Migration* (para.32), the logical definition of the stock of international migrants present in a country would be "the set of persons who have ever changed their country of usual residence; that is, persons who have spent at least a year of their lives in a country other than the one in which they live at the time the data are gathered". However, it is common to find that the need for information relates not to the generality of international migrants as characterized above, but rather to population groups such as those who were not born in that country and those who do not have the citizenship of the country where they live.

2.92.   Consequently, for the study of the impact of international migration using the population census, two sub-groups of the population represent the primary focus of interest. The first group consists of the foreign-born and the second comprises foreigners living in the country. In order to identify members of those groups, two items must be recorded in the census: (*a*) country of birth, and (*b*) country of citizenship. In addition, it is also important to record year of arrival in the country so as to establish length of stay in the country of international migrants.

(*a*)   Country of birth (core topic)

Recommended tabulations: 2.1-R, 2.2-R, 2.3-R

2.93.   The **country of birth** is the country in which the person was born. It should be noted that the country of birth of a person is not necessarily the same as his or her country of citizenship, which is a separate census topic dealt with below. It is recommended that place of birth be asked of all persons first to distinguish the native-born from the foreign-born population. The collection of this information is necessary even in countries where the proportion of the foreign-born population is small. For the foreign-born population, the collection of additional information on the specific country of birth is recommended so as to permit the classification of the foreign-born population by country of birth. For respondents who are born outside of the country of enumeration and cannot name their country of birth, at least the continent or region where that country is located should be ascertained.

2.94. For purposes of both internal consistency and international comparability, it is recommended that information on the country of birth be recorded according to national boundaries existing at the time of the census. If there have been boundary changes affecting the country of birth of a person, it is important that persons who have remained in the territory where they were born, but whose "country of birth" may have changed because of boundary changes, not be counted as foreign-born because of the failure to take account of the new configuration of the country where they live. It is essential that the coding of information on the country of birth be done in sufficient detail to allow for the individual identification of all countries of birth that are represented in the population of the country. For purposes of coding, it is recommended that countries use the numerical coding system presented in *Standard Country or Area Codes for Statistical Use*[38]. The use of standard codes for classification of the foreign-born population according to the country of birth will enhance the usefulness of such data, including an international exchange of foreign-born population statistics among countries. If countries decide to combine countries into broad groups, it is recommended that the standard regional and subregional classifications identified in the above-mentioned publication be adopted.

2.95. Countries with a significant number of immigrants may want to collect information on the country of birth of parents. Information on the country of birth of parents (father and mother) should be asked of all respondents following the same guidelines given for country of birth. The decision to collect and disseminate information on country of birth of parents in a census is dependent upon a number of considerations and national circumstances, including for example the suitability and sensitivity of asking such a question in a country's census.

2.96. This topic permits the identification of the group of descendants of the foreign-born population, and could be used, in combination with the country of birth information, to identify the migration background of respondents. Information from this topic permits the identification of native-born children of the foreign-born population, and can be used to study the integration processes and outcomes of immigrants and their descendants. Moreover, in countries that have experienced return migration, information from this topic allows for the group of foreign-born children of native-born parents to be identified. When studying integration processes, it can be particularly important to make separate analyses for this group and the group of foreign-born from foreign-born parents.

(b)   Citizenship (core topic)

Recommended tabulation: 2.3-R

2.97. **Citizenship** is defined as the particular legal bond between an individual and his/her State. A citizen is a legal national of the country of enumeration; a foreigner is a non-national of the country (that is, a citizen of another country). Because the country of citizenship is not necessarily identical to the country of birth, both items should be collected in a census.

2.98. Additional information on citizenship could be collected so as to permit the classification of the population into (*a*) citizens by birth, (*b*) citizens by naturali-

[38] United Nations publication, Sales No. 98. XVII. 9.

zation whether by declaration, option, marriage or other means, and (*c*) foreigners (citizens of another country). In addition, information on the country of citizenship of foreigners should be collected. It is important to record country of citizenship as such and not to use an adjective to indicate citizenship, since some of those adjectives are the same as those used to designate ethnic groups. It is essential that the coding of information on country of citizenship be done in sufficient detail to allow for the individual identification of all countries of citizenship that are represented among the foreign population in the country. For purposes of coding, it is recommended that countries use the numerical coding system presented in *Standard Country or Area Codes for Statistical Use*. The use of standard codes for classification of the foreign population by country of citizenship will enhance the usefulness of such data and permit an international exchange of information among countries on their foreign populations. If countries decide to combine countries of citizenship into broad groups, it is recommended that the standard regional and subregional classifications identified in the above-mentioned publication be adopted.

2.99.   In some cases people may have more than one citizenship and where there are needs for this information to assist informed decision-making within a country, details should be collected of all citizenships held, including the case of nationals of that country holding multiple citizenship. If this information is to be published, care will have to be taken to explain to readers of the table how the possibility of people being included in the table more than once affects the marginal totals on the table.

2.100.   For countries where the population includes a significant proportion of naturalized citizens, it may be useful to ask additional questions on previous citizenship, method of acquisition of citizenship and year of naturalization.

2.101.   The reliability of reported citizenship may be doubtful in the case of persons whose citizenship has recently changed as a result of territorial changes, or among the population of some newly independent countries where the concept of citizenship has only recently become important. Clear guidelines issued by the national statistical authority can help improve the quality of the data collected. As an aid to the analysis and interpretation of the results, notations indicative of the likelihood of these and other possible causes of misstatement should accompany tabulations based on citizenship. For the purpose of preparing tabulations on citizenship, all countries should be shown separately to the extent possible and a category of stateless persons should be presented.

2.102.   Enumeration and processing instructions should indicate the treatment of stateless persons, persons with dual nationality, persons in the process of naturalization and any other groups with ambiguous citizenship. The treatment of these groups should be described in the census reports and included in the metadata for accompanying tabulations.

(c)   Year or period of arrival in the country (core topic)

Recommended tabulation: 2.2-R, 2.4-R

2.103.   Recording the calendar year and month of arrival of a foreign-born person to the country of enumeration permits the calculation of the number of completed years between the time of arrival in the country and the time of inquiry, usually the census date. Information on the month and year of arrival also provides the flexibility of classifying foreign-born persons by period of arrival in terms of any prespecified period, such as 1975–1979, 1980–1984 and so forth. It is thus recommended that the period of arrival be shown, in any tabulations in which the variable appears, in terms of the actual year of arrival.

2.104.   It is possible to collect information on the date of first arrival in the country or the date of the most recent arrival in the country. Each has its own advantages and disadvantages. In making the choice of which information to collect, countries should be guided first and foremost by their policy needs.

2.105.   Note that information on the year and month of arrival is focused mainly on persons born outside of the country of enumeration, that is to say, persons who must have arrived in that country at some time after their birth. However, countries having experienced important migration outflows or that have population groups that maintain links to other countries, migrating to or from another country at different life stages (for example, as students or pensioners), may have an interest in collecting information on returning migrants: in this case, the question on year and month of arrival could also be asked to native-born respondents.

2.106.   Information on time since arrival can also be collected by asking how many years have elapsed since the time of arrival, instead of in what calendar year and month the person arrived. However, use of such a question is not recommended because it is likely to yield less accurate information.

3.   Household and family characteristics

2.107.   In considering the topics related to household characteristics, it is important to be aware of the differences between the concepts of household and family as used herein.

2.108.   A **household** may be either:

(a)   A one-person household, that is to say, a person who makes provision for his or her own food or other essentials for living without combining with any other person to form part of a multi-person household;

or

(b)   A multi-person household, that is to say, a group of two or more persons living together who make common provision for food or other essentials for living. The persons in the group may pool their resources and have a common budget; they may be related or unrelated persons or a combination of persons both related and unrelated. This arrangement exemplifies the "housekeeping" concept.

Some countries use a concept different from the housekeeping concept, namely, the "household-dwelling" concept, which regards all persons living in a housing unit as belonging to the same household. According to this concept, there is one household per occupied housing unit. Therefore, the number of occupied housing units and the number of households occupying them are equal and the locations of the housing units and households are identical. Countries should specify in their census reports whether they used the "housekeeping" or the "household-dwelling" concept of a private household.

2.109.   A household may be located in a housing unit (see para. 2.418) or in a set of collective living quarters such as a boarding house, a hotel or a camp, or may comprise the administrative personnel in an institution. The household may also be homeless. For more discussion on homeless households, see paragraph 1.452.

2.110.   The family within the household, a concept of particular interest, is defined as those members of the household who are related, to a specified degree, through blood, adoption or marriage. The degree of relationship used in determining the limits of the family in this sense is dependent upon the uses to which the data are to be put and so cannot be established for worldwide use. See paragraph 2.125 for a definition of the nucleus family.

2.111.   Although in practice most households are composed of a single family consisting of a married couple without children or of one or both parents and their children, it should not be assumed that this identity exists; census tabulations should therefore clearly indicate whether they relate to households or to families within households.

2.112.   From the definitions of "household" and "family", it is clear that household and family are different concepts that cannot be used interchangeably in the same census. The difference between the household and the family is (*a*) that a household may consist of only one person but a family must contain at least two members, and (*b*) that the members of a multi-person household need not be related to each other, while the members of a family must be related. A household can contain more than one family, or one or more families together with one or more non-related persons, or it can consist entirely of non-related persons. A family typically will not comprise more than one household. However, the existence of polygamous families in some countries, as well as shared child custody and support arrangements in others, means that individual countries should decide how best to derive and report data on families.

2.113.   It is recommended that the household be used as the unit of enumeration (as defined in paras. 1.448–1.452) and that the family be a derived topic only. The place of usual residence is recommended as the basis for assigning persons to households where they normally reside. Where the de facto approach is used as the method of enumeration (see paras. 1.469–1.477), household lists should, where feasible, also include usual residents temporarily absent. The place of usual residence is where a person usually resides and it may or may not be the person's current or legal residence. The latter terms are usually defined in the laws of most countries and need not correspond to the concept of place of usual residence which, as employed in the census, is based on conventional usage. In published reports, countries should indicate whether or not household information refers to usual residents and also what the time limits are in respect of being included or excluded as a usual resident. For a more detailed discussion and the difficulty of collecting information on place of usual residence, see paragraphs 2.46–2.51.

(*a*)   Relationship to head or other reference member of household
          (core topic)

Recommended tabulations: 3.1-A, 3.2-A, 3.3-A

2.114.   In identifying the members of a household (as defined in paras. 2.108 and 2.109), it is useful to identify first the household reference person or household head and then the remaining members of the household according to their relationship to the reference person or head. Countries may use the term they deem most appropriate to identify this person (household reference person, head of household, householder, among others) as long as the person so identified is used solely to determine relationships between household members. It is recommended that each country present, in published reports, the concepts and definitions that are used.

2.115.   With respect to selecting the household reference person, it is important to specify criteria for choosing that person in relation to whom household members would be best distinguished, especially in polygamous, multi-family and other households, such as those composed only of siblings without a parent and those composed entirely of unrelated persons. This information should be included in training materials and instructions to enumerators.

2.116.   The traditional notion of head of household assumes that most households are family households (in other words, that they consist entirely, except possibly for domestic servants, of persons related by blood, marriage or adoption) and that one person in such family households has primary authority and responsibility for household affairs and is, in the majority of cases, its chief economic support. This person is then designated as the head of household.

2.117.   Where spouses are considered equal in household authority and responsibility and may share economic support of the household, the concept of head of household is no longer considered valid even for family households. In order for the relationship among members of the household to be determined under these circumstances, it is essential that either (*a*) the members of the household designate one among them as a reference member with no implication of headship, or (*b*) provision be made for designation of joint headship where desired. In any case, it is important that clear instructions be provided in the census as to how this situation is to be handled.

2.118.   Even in the many countries where the traditional concept of head of household is still relevant, it is important to recognize that the procedures followed in applying the concept may distort the true picture, particularly with regard to female heads of households. The most common assumption that can distort the facts is that no woman can be the head of any household that also contains an adult male. Enumerators and even respondents may simply take such an assumption for granted.

2.119.   This common sex-based stereotype often reflects circumstances that may have been true in the past but are true no longer, insofar as the household and economic roles of women are changing. It is therefore important that clear instructions be provided as to who is to be treated as the head of the household so as to avoid the complications of enumerator or respondent preconceptions on the subject. The procedure to follow in identifying a head when the members of the household are unable to do so should be clear and unambiguous and should avoid sex-based bias.

2.120.   After identification of the reference member of the household, each of the remaining members of the household should be distinguished in relation to that person, as appropriate, as one of the following: (*a*) spouse, (*b*) partner in consensual union (cohabiting partner), (*c*) child, (*d*) spouse of child, (*e*) grandchild or greatgrandchild, (*f*) parent (or parent of spouse), (*g*) other relative, (*h*) domestic employee or (*i*) other person not related to the head or other reference member. Where this classification is considered too detailed for successful collection of the information, categories (*f*) and (*g*) may be consolidated as "Other relative" and (*h*) and (*i*) can be consolidated as "Other unrelated person".

2.121.   As an aid to the identification of conjugal family nuclei (as defined in para. 2.127) within the household, it might be helpful if persons were recorded in the census form to the extent possible in the order of nuclear relationship. Thus, the first person entered after the head or other reference person would be the spouse of that person, followed by unmarried children and then by married children, their spouses and children. For polygamous households, the order of entry could be such that each wife and her unmarried children appeared in succession.

2.122.   For estimating fertility by the *own children* method (see para. 2.171), the natural mother of each child under 15 years of age should be identified if she appears in the same questionnaire as her child. One way of doing this is to provide the line number of the mother alongside that of the child, if both are living in the same household. The information is not relevant for stepchildren, adopted children or foster children under permanent or temporary care.

2.123.   In order to meet increased data needs on households and families, countries may wish, while conducting their population censuses, to collect more detailed information on relationships. In households where the relationship structure is complex, including those with foster children, obtaining accurate information on the relationships between household members may be difficult. Some countries may supplement information on relationship to the head of household with information on direct relationships between household members by, for instance, relating a child to its parents even when neither parent is the head of household. Enumerators should be encouraged to probe for a clear relationship (such as child, niece, aunt and so forth). The recording of non-specific responses such as "relative" should be avoided. It is recommended that specific guidance be provided on allowable answers, that relationships be specified completely in the census questionnaire, and that any pre-coded categories used should be sufficiently detailed to produce desired outputs.

(b)   Household and family composition (core topic)

Recommended tabulations: 3.3-A

2.124.   Household and family composition can be examined from different points of view, but for census purposes it is recommended that the primary aspect considered should be that of the family nucleus.

2.125.   A **family nucleus** is of one of the following types (each of which must consist of persons living in the same household):

(*a*)   A married couple without children;

(*b*)   A married couple with one or more unmarried children;

(*c*)   A father with one or more unmarried children;

(*d*)   A mother with one or more unmarried children.[39]

Couples living in consensual unions may, where appropriate, be regarded as constituting a family nucleus.

[39] In countries where a different definition of family nucleus is used, it should be clearly stated in the census report.

2.126.   The concept of family nucleus as defined above limits relationships between children and adults to direct (first-degree) relationships, that is to say, between parents and children. In some countries, numbers of skip generation households, that is to say, households consisting of grandparent(s) and one or more grandchild(ren) with no parent of those grandchild(ren) present, are considerable. Therefore, countries may include such skip generation households in their family nucleus definition. The census report should clearly state whether or not skip generation households are included in the family nucleus definition.

2.127.   The family nucleus is identified from the answers to the question on relationship to the reference member of the household, supplemented where necessary by information on name and marital status. The identification of offspring and their mother and the order in which persons are entered in the questionnaire may be of additional assistance in this respect. The identification of family nuclei is likely to be more complete in de jure than in de facto enumerations, because the latter do not take account of temporarily absent household members who may constitute part of a nucleus.

2.128.   For census purposes, a child is any unmarried individual, regardless of age, who lives with his or her parent(s) and has no children in the same household. Consequently, the definition of a child is primarily a function of an individual's relationship to other household members, regardless of age. In accordance with the above definition, a household consisting of a married couple, their two never-married children, one of their children who is divorced, and a married daughter and her husband would be considered to be composed of two family nuclei, with the divorced child being regarded as a member of the parents' family. As used here, the term "child" does not imply dependency, but rather is used to capture household living arrangements of persons who are in a parent-child relationship. Countries need to be clear in their metadata how they treat foster and adopted children.

2.129.   The family nucleus does not include all family types, such as brothers or sisters living together without their offspring or parents, or an aunt living with a niece who has no child. It also excludes the case of a related person living with a family nucleus as defined above, for example, a widowed parent living with her married son and his family. The family nucleus approach does not, therefore, provide information on all types of families. Countries may extend the investigation of families beyond that of the family nucleus, in accordance with their own interests.

2.130.   Households should be classified by type according to the number of family nuclei they contain and the relationship, if any, between the family nuclei and the other members of the household. The relationship should be through blood, adoption or marriage, to whatever degree is considered pertinent by the country (see para. 2.123). Given the complexity of this item, it is important that information on relationship to the household reference person be properly processed. The types of household to be distinguished could be:

(*a*)   *One-person household*;

(*b*)   *Nuclear household*, defined as a household consisting entirely of a single family nucleus. It may be classified into:

    (i)   Married-couple family:

        a.   With child(ren);

        b.   Without child(ren);

    (ii)   Partner in consensual union (cohabiting partner):

        a.   With child(ren);

        b.   Without child(ren);

    (iii)   Father with child(ren);

    (vi)   Mother with child(ren);

(*c*)   *Extended household*, defined as a household consisting of any one of the following:[40]

    (i)   A single family nucleus and other persons related to the nucleus, for example, a father with child(ren) and other relative(s) or a married couple with other relative(s) only;

    (ii)   Two or more family nuclei related to each other without any other persons, for example, two or more married couples with child(ren) only;

    (iii)   Two or more family nuclei related to each other plus other persons related to at least one of the nuclei, for example, two or more married couples with other relative(s) only;

    (iv)   Two or more persons related to each other, none of whom constitute a family nucleus;

(*d*)   *Composite household*, defined as a household consisting of any of the following:[41]

    (i)   A single family nucleus plus other persons, some of whom are related to the nucleus and some of whom are not, for example, mother with child(ren) and other relatives and non-relatives;

[40] The subdivisions in this category should be modified to suit national circumstances.

[41] The subdivisions in this category should be modified to suit national circumstances.

(ii)   A single family nucleus plus other persons, none of whom is related to the nucleus, for example, father with child(ren) and non-relatives);

(iii)   Two or more family nuclei related to each other plus other persons, some of whom are related to at least one of the nuclei and some of whom are not related to any of the nuclei, for example, two or more couples with other relatives and non-relatives only;

(iv)   Two or more family nuclei related to each other plus other persons, none of whom is related to any of the nuclei, for example, two or more married couples one or more of which with child(ren) and non-relatives;

(v)   Two or more family nuclei not related to each other, with or without any other persons;

(vi)   Two or more persons related to each other but none of whom constitute a family nucleus, plus other unrelated persons;

(vii)   Non-related persons only; .

(e)   *Other/unknown.*

2.131.   In the census tabulations, all countries should at least distinguish between one-person, nuclear, extended and composite households. Where feasible, some or all of the subcategories shown above should also be distinguished, although countries may find it appropriate to modify the classification according to national circumstances. For example, in countries where almost all households contain only one family nucleus at most, the distinction between nuclear, extended and composite households may be applied only to households containing one nucleus or no nucleus; multinuclear households may then be shown as an additional category without any further classification by type. In countries where multinuclear households are comparatively common, further breakdowns of extended and composite households, distinguishing between those with three, four or more family nuclei, may be helpful.

(c)   Household and family status

2.132.   For purposes of determining household and family status and identifying how a person relates to other household or family members, persons may be classified according to their position in the household or family nucleus. Classifying persons according to household and family status has uses in social and demographic research and policy formulation. Census data could be presented according to both household and family status for a variety of purposes. Although status itself is based on information derived from responses to the item on relationship to the head or other reference member of the household and other items, the classification of persons by their household and family status is a relatively new approach: it is a different approach from the traditional one of classifying household members solely according to their relationship to the head or reference person. The following household and family status classifications illustrate how such an approach may be used.[42] Care should be taken at the planning stages to relate this item to the classification of households by type as recommended in paragraph 2.130.

Persons are classified by household status as:

1   Person in a household with at least one family nucleus

   1.1   Husband

   1.2   Wife   .

[42] To date, only the population and housing census recommendations for the Economic Commission for Europe region contain household and family status classifications.

[43] Person living with children, without spouse.

[44] Ibid.

[45] The subdivisions in this category should be modified to suit national circumstances.

[46] Persons classified as spouse, lone parent or child are by definition members of a family nucleus.

    1.3   Partner in consensual union (cohabiting partner)
    1.4   Lone mother[43]
    1.5   Lone father[44]
    1.6   Child living with both parents
    1.7   Child living with lone mother
    1.8   Child living with lone father
    1.9   Not a member of a family nucleus
        1.9.1   Living with relatives
        1.9.2   Living with non-relatives
2   Person in a household with no family nucleus
    2.1   Living alone
    2.2   Living with others[45]
        2.2.1   Living with sibling(s)
        2.2.2   Living with other relatives
        2.2.3   Living with non-relatives

Persons are classified by family status as:[46]

1   Spouse
    1.1   Husband
        1.1.1   With child(ren)
        1.1.2   Without child
    1.2   Wife
        1.2.1   With child(ren)
        1.2.2   Without child
2   Lone parent
    2.1   Male
    2.2   Female
3   Child
    3.1   With both parents
    3.2   With lone parent
        3.2.1   With lone father
        3.2.2   With lone mother
4   Not member of a family nucleus
    4.1   Relative of husband or wife
        4.1.1   Parent of husband or wife
        4.1.2   Sibling of husband or wife
        4.1.3   Other relative of husband or wife
    4.2   Non-relative

4.   Demographic and social characteristics

2.133.   Of all the topics investigated in population censuses, *sex* and *age* are more frequently cross-classified with other characteristics of the population than are any other topics. Aside from the importance of the sex-age structure of the population in itself, accurate information on the two topics is fundamental to the great majority of the census tabulations. Possible difficulties in securing accurate age data are often not recognized because the topic appears to be a simple one. The difficulties are therefore stressed in paragraphs 2.135–2.143 below.

(a) Sex (core topic)

Recommended tabulations: all population tabulations except 3.3-A

2.134.   The sex (male or female) of every individual should be recorded in the census questionnaire. Sex disaggregation of data is a fundamental requirement for gender statistics. For many socio-economic and demographic characteristics that could be collected through a census, such as education, economic activity, marital status, migration, disability and living arrangements, there are generally variations by sex. In this context, the presentation of data disaggregated by sex is important because of its utility for gender studies. The Platform for Action of the Fourth World Conference on Women recommends the presentation of data disaggregated by age and sex to reflect problems, issues and questions related to women and men in society for utilization in policy and programme planning and implementation.[47] Sex, together with age, represents the most basic type of demographic information collected about individuals in censuses and surveys, as well as through administrative recording systems, and the cross-classification of these data with other characteristics forms the basis of most analyses of the social and demographic characteristics of the population as it provides the context within which all other information is placed.

[47] Report of the *Fourth World Conference on Women, Beijing, 4-15 September 1995* (United Nations publication, Sales No. E.96.IV.13), Chap. I, resolution I, annex II.

(b) Age (core topic)

Recommended tabulations: 1.4-A, 1.5-A, 2.1-A, 2.2-A, 2.3-A, 3.2-A, 4.1-A, 4.2-A, 5.1-A, 5.2-A, 5.3-A, 5.4-A, 6.1-A, 6.2-A, 6.3-A, 7.1-A, 7.2-A, 7.3-A, 7.4-A, 7.8-A, 8.1-A, 8.2-A, 8.3-A

2.135.   **Age** is the interval of time between the date of birth and the date of the census, expressed in completed solar years. Every effort should be made to ascertain the precise age of each person, particularly of children under 15 years of age.

2.136.   Information on age may be secured either by obtaining the date (year, month and day) of birth or by asking directly for age at the person's last birthday.

2.137.   The first method yields more precise information and should be used whenever circumstances permit. If neither the exact day nor even the month of birth is known, an indication of the season of the year can be substituted. The question on date of birth is appropriate wherever people know their birth date, whether in accordance with the solar calendar or a lunar calendar, or whether years are numbered or identified in traditional folk culture by names within a regular cycle. It is extremely important, however, that there should be a clear understanding between the enumerator and the respondent about which calendar system the date of birth is based on. If there is a possibility that some respondents will reply with reference to a calendar system different than that of other respondents, provision must be made in the questionnaire for noting the calendar system that has been used. It is not advisable for the enumerator to attempt to convert the date from one system to another. The needed conversion can be best carried out as part of the computer editing work.

2.138.   The direct question on age is likely to yield less accurate responses for a number of reasons. Even if all responses are based on the same method of reckoning age, there is the possibility of a misunderstanding on the part of the respondent as to whether the age wanted is that at the last birthday, the next birthday or the nearest birthday. In addition, roundings to the nearest age ending in zero or five, estimates not identified as such and deliberate misstatements can occur with comparative ease. Difficulties may arise in the reporting or in the recording of the information for children under one year of age, which may be given erroneously as "one year of age" rather than "zero years of age". These difficulties may be mitigated by collecting information on the date of birth of all children reported as "one year of age", while using only the direct age question for the remainder of the population. Another possible approach is to obtain age in completed months for children under one year of age. This method, however, can give rise to another type of recording error, that is to say, the substitution of years for months, so that a three-month-old child, for example, might be entered in the questionnaire as being three years of age.

2.139. An additional complication may occur with the use of the direct question if more than one method of calculating age is in use in the country. In some countries, certain segments of the population may use an old traditional method whereby persons are considered to be one year of age at the time of birth and everyone advances one year in age at the same fixed date each year. Other segments of the population in the same countries may use the Western method, in which a person is not regarded as being one year of age until 12 months after the date of birth, and advances one year in age every succeeding 12 months. If there is a possibility of different methods of age calculation being used by respondents, provision must be made to ensure that the method used in each case is clearly indicated in the questionnaire and that the conversion is left to the editing stage.

2.140. In spite of its drawbacks, the direct question on age is the only one to be used when people cannot provide even a birth year. As regards persons for whom information on age is unavailable or appears to be unreliable, an estimated age may have to be entered. This may occur in isolated cases in societies where knowledge of age is widespread or in general in cultures where there is little awareness of individual age and no interest in it. In the latter circumstances, criteria for making estimates should be provided in the instructions for the enumerators.

2.141. One of the techniques that have been used to aid enumerators consists in providing them with calendars of historic events of national or local significance to be used either in probing questions or in identifying the earliest event the respondent recalls. Another technique consists in pre-identifying locally recognized age cohorts in the population and then asking about membership in the cohorts. Enumerators may also ask if the person in question was born before or after other persons whose ages have been roughly determined. Furthermore, use can be made of age norms for weaning, talking, marriage and so forth. Whatever techniques are used, enumerators should be impressed with the importance of securing age data that are as accurate as possible within the amount of time that they can devote to the topic.

2.142. In view of the possible difficulties in the collection of age data, census tests should be used, as appropriate, to determine the difference in results with the use of a question on age as compared with a question on date of birth, what calendar and/or method of age reckoning most people use, and in what parts of the country age will have to be estimated for the majority of the population and what techniques to use as an aid in estimation. Testing of the calendar and/or method of age reckoning that most people use is particularly important where an official change from one calendar and/or method of reckoning to another calendar and/or method has taken place recently enough so that the new calendar and/or method of reckoning may not yet be in popular use among some or all of the population.

2.143. Enumerators who are likely to be called upon to estimate age in a substantial number of cases should be given training in the applicable techniques as part of their general training.

(c)　Marital status (core topic)

Recommended tabulations:　3.1-A, 4.2-A

> 2.144.　**Marital status** is the personal status of each individual in relation to the marriage laws or customs of the country. The categories of marital status to be identified are at least the following:
>
> (*a*)　Single, in other words, never married;
>
> (*b*)　Married;
>
> (*c*)　Widowed and not remarried;
>
> (*d*)　Divorced and not remarried;
>
> (*e*)　Married but separated.

2.145.　In some countries, category (*b*) may require a subcategory of persons who are contractually married but not yet living as man and wife. In all countries, category (*e*) should comprise both the legally and the de facto separated, who may be shown as separate subcategories if desired. Regardless of the fact that couples who are separated may be considered to be still married (because they are not free to remarry), neither of the subcategories of (*e*) should be included in category (*b*).

2.146.　In some countries, it will be necessary to take into account customary unions, such as registered partnerships and consensual unions, which are legal and binding under law.

2.147.　The treatment of persons whose only or latest marriage has been annulled is dependent upon the relative size of this group in the country. Where its size is substantial, the group should constitute an additional category; if its size is insignificant, the individuals in the group should be classified according to their marital status before the (annulled) marriage took place.

2.148.　At times countries have experienced difficulties in distinguishing between (*a*) formal marriages and de facto unions and (*b*) persons legally separated and those legally divorced. If either of these circumstances necessitates a departure from the recommended classification of marital status, the composition of each category shown in the tabulations should be clearly stated.

2.149.　If complete information on marital status is needed, then this information should be collected and tabulated for persons of all ages, irrespective of the national minimum legal age, or the customary age for marriage, because the population may include persons who were married in another country with a different minimum marriage age; in most countries, there are also likely to be persons who were permitted to marry below the legal minimum age because of special circumstances. In order to permit international comparisons of data on marital status, however, any tabulations of marital status not cross-classified by detailed age should at least distinguish between persons under 15 years of age and those 15 years of age and over.

2.150.　The collection of additional information related to customs in particular countries (such as concubinage, polygamous or polyandrous marital status, inheritance of widows, and so on) may be useful in meeting national needs. For example, at times countries may wish to collect data on the number of spouses of each married person. Modifications of the tabulations to take account of such information should be made within the framework of the basic classification in order to maintain international comparability as far as possible.

2.151.　The concept of marital status and the marital status categories described above should not be confused with the concept of de facto union status which describes extralegal unions (including some consensual unions) of varying degrees of stability common in some countries. It should be recognized also that these marital status categories do not adequately describe the prevalence of formal legal marriage combined with the relatively stable de facto union which may exist outside the marriage. Information on these relationships is very useful in studies of fertility, but it is not possible to provide an international recommendation on this matter because of the different circumstances prevailing among countries. It is suggested, however, that countries wishing to investigate these relationships should consider the possibility of collecting separate data for each person, on de facto unions and on the duration of each type of union (see para. 2.192). Information on these relationships can also be derived from answers to the question on relationship to head/reference person.

(d) Religion

2.152. For census purposes, **religion** may be defined as either:

(a) Religious or spiritual belief of preference, regardless of whether or not this belief is represented by an organized group;

or

(b) Affiliation with an organized group having specific religious or spiritual tenets.

Each country that investigates religion in its census should use the definition most appropriate to its needs and should set forth, in the census publication, the definition that has been used.

2.153. The decision to collect and disseminate information on religion in a national census is dependent upon a number of considerations and national circumstances, including, for example, the national needs for such data, and the suitability and sensitivity of asking a religion question in a country's census. Owing to the sensitive nature of a question on religion, special care may be required to demonstrate to respondents that appropriate data protection and disclosure control measures are in place. It is important that the responding public be informed of the potential uses and needs for this information.

2.154. The amount of detail collected on this topic is dependent upon the requirements of the country. It may, for example, be sufficient to inquire only about the religion of each person; on the other hand, respondents may be asked to specify, if relevant, the particular sect to which they adhere within a religion.

2.155. For the benefit of users of the data who may not be familiar with all of the religions or sects within the country, as well as for purposes of international comparability, the classifications of the data should show each sect as a subcategory of the religion of which it forms a part. A brief statement of the tenets of religions or sects that are not likely to be known beyond the country or region would also be helpful.

(e) Language

2.156. There are three types of **language** data that can be collected in censuses, namely:

(a) Mother tongue, defined as the language usually spoken in the individual's home in his or her early childhood;

(b) Usual language, defined as the language currently spoken, or most often spoken, by the individual in his or her present home;

(c) Ability to speak one or more designated languages.

2.157.   Each of these types of information serves a very different analytical purpose. Each country should decide which, if any, of these types of information is applicable to its own needs. International comparability of tabulations is not a major factor in determining the form of the data to be collected on this topic.

2.158.   In compiling data on the usual language or on the mother tongue, it is desirable to show each language that is numerically important in the country and not merely the dominant language.

2.159.   Information on language should be collected for all persons. In the tabulated results, the criterion for determining language for children not yet able to speak should be clearly indicated.

(f)   Ethnicity

2.160.   The decision to collect and disseminate information on ethnic or national groups of a population in a census is dependent upon a number of considerations and national circumstances, including, for example, the national needs for such data, and the suitability and sensitivity of asking ethnicity questions in a country's census. Identification of the ethno-cultural characteristics of a country's population has increasing importance in the context of migration, integration and policies affecting minority groups. Owing to the sensitive nature of questions on ethnicity, special care may be required to demonstrate to respondents that appropriate data protection and disclosure control measures are in place. It is important that the responding public be informed of the potential uses and need for data pertaining to ethnicity, as this improves public support for the census exercise. Data on ethnicity provide information on the diversity of a population and can serve to identify subgroups of a population. Some areas of study that rely on such data include demographic trends, employment practices and opportunities, income distributions, educational levels, migration patterns and trends, family composition and structure, social support networks, and health conditions of a population.

2.161.   Broadly defined, **ethnicity** is based on a shared understanding of history and territorial origins (regional and national) of an ethnic group or community, as well as on particular cultural characteristics such as language and/or religion. Respondents' understanding or views about ethnicity, awareness of their family background, the number of generations they have spent in a country, and the length of time since immigration are all possible factors affecting the reporting of ethnicity in a census. Ethnicity is multidimensional and is more a process than a static concept, and so ethnic classification should be treated with movable boundaries.

2.162.   Ethnicity can be measured using a variety of concepts, including ethnic ancestry or origin, ethnic identity, cultural origins, nationality, race, colour, minority status, tribe, language, religion or various combinations of these concepts. Because of the interpretative difficulties that may occur with measuring ethnicity in a census, it is important that, where such an investigation is undertaken, the basic criteria used to measure the concept are clearly explained to respondents and in the dissemination of the resulting data. The method and the format of the question used to measure ethnicity can influence the choices that respondents make regarding their ethnic backgrounds and current ethnic identification. The subjective nature of the term (not to mention increasing intermarriage among various groups in some countries, for example) requires that information on ethnicity be acquired through self-declaration of a respondent and also that respondents have the option of indicating multiple ethnic affiliations. Data on ethnicity should not be derived from information on country of citizenship or country of birth. The classification of ethnic groups also requires the inclusion of the finest levels of ethnic groups, self-perceived groups, regional and local groups, as well as groups that are not usually considered to be ethnic groups, such as religious groups and those based on nationality. Countries collecting data on ethnicity should note that the pre-coding or the pre-classification of ethnic groups at the time of data capture may have a tendency to lose detailed information on the diversity of a population. Since countries collect data on ethnicity in different ways and for different reasons, and because the ethno-cultural composition of a country could vary widely from country to country, no internationally relevant criteria or classification can be recommended.

(g) Indigenous peoples

2.163.   Facilitating the collection of data on indigenous peoples for national and international needs can serve to improve socio-economic and active participation of indigenous peoples in the development process for many countries. The sensitive nature of questions pertaining to the indigenous population requires care in assuring the public that the appropriate disclosure and data protection methods are being enforced. The responding public should be informed on the potential uses and need for such data to improve public support for the census exercise.

2.164.   Dissemination of census data pertaining to indigenous peoples contributes to research in areas such as the socio-economic conditions of the indigenous population, trends, causes for inequities, and the effectiveness of existing policies and programmes. Availability of these data can also assist indigenous communities in assessing their conditions of living and give them the information they need to participate and advocate in the development of programmes and policies affecting their communities, such as those impacting health systems, models of economic production, environmental management and social organization. In addition, the development of indicators relevant to the indigenous population and the measurement of such indicators in the data-collection process can be used to monitor the human development of indigenous populations.

2.165.   Generally, **indigenous peoples** of a particular country are social groups with an identity that is distinct from the social and cultural identity of the dominant society in that country. Questions on indigenous identity should abide by the principle of self-identification. It is important that, where such an investigation is undertaken, multiple criteria are developed to accurately capture identity and socio-economic conditions of indigenous peoples. Defining the indigenous population can be done in many ways, such as through a question on ethnic origin (that is to say, ancestry) and/or on indigenous identity. Identifying the indigenous community also requires recognition of the diversity in this subpopulation, including nomadic, semi-nomadic and migrating peoples, peoples in transition, displaced persons, indigenous peoples in urban areas, and particularly vulnerable sects. It is important to point out that there is no single term among countries to describe the indigenous population. Consequently, countries tend to use their own national concepts to identify the indigenous population. For example, in Australia the terms "aboriginal" or "Torres Strait Islander" are used, while in New Zealand the term "Maori" is used.

2.166.   Differing national contexts also imply that enumerating the indigenous population can be done in multiple ways, for example, by way of specific questions on the census form, with specialized census forms for the indigenous population, and/or with follow-up or complementary surveys. In Canada, for example, identification of the indigenous population comes from not only a national census, but also a post-censal survey. In Australia, in addition to a national census, there is the National Aboriginal and Torres Strait Islander survey, while in Argentina there is a complementary survey after the census targeting indigenous peoples. In addition to a general census, Paraguay also administers a specific census in the same year to identify the indigenous population.

2.167. Involvement of the indigenous community in the data development and data-collection processes provides the arena for capacity-building and helps to ensure the relevance and accuracy of the data collection on indigenous peoples. Using local indigenous languages, employing local indigenous people (as interpreters, for example), and training and building the capacity of local indigenous people in data-collection processes can facilitate the collection and dissemination of this information. Non-indigenous professionals and technicians should also be informed of the culture and practices of indigenous peoples.

5. Fertility and mortality

2.168. The investigation of fertility and mortality in population censuses is particularly important in countries lacking a timely and reliable system of vital statistics because of the opportunity the data provide for estimating vital rates that would not otherwise be available. Even in countries with complete birth and death registration, some of the topics ("children born alive", "children living", and "age at marriage or union") are equally appropriate because they provide data that are not easily available from registration data. The population census provides an opportunity to collect data for estimating fertility and mortality at national and subnational levels in a cost-effective manner. The inclusion of these topics in population censuses for the purpose of estimating fertility and mortality rates and other related indicators is both prudent and cost-effective, particularly in countries where civil registration and vital statistics systems are weak, and costs of conducting large periodic demographic surveys are high. Nevertheless, it is important to note that census information is a poor substitute for complete and reliable vital registration data. If countries desire accurate and detailed estimates of fertility and mortality, they must maintain civil registration systems and ensure their universal coverage.

2.169. To obtain information on fertility, questions are posed on "children ever born", "date of last child born alive" and "age of mother at birth of first child born alive". In addition, questions on age, date or duration of marriage/union may improve fertility estimates based on children ever born (see para. 2.192). For the collection of reliable data, some of the topics may require a series of probing questions that, because they are time-consuming, are more suitable for use in sample surveys than in censuses.

2.170. The universe for which data should be collected for each of the topics included in this section consists of women 15 years of age[48] and over regardless of marital status. Information should be collected from all such women, regardless of marital status, unless from a cultural standpoint it is not feasible to collect information on childbearing from never-married women. In countries that do not use the data for women 50 years of age and over, it may be appropriate to limit data collection to women under the age of 50, allowing more concentrated effort on data collection for such women.

2.171. In addition to the topics indicated above that are used to estimate fertility, another useful topic that allows the estimation of fertility is the "own children" method.[49] The application of this method requires the identification of the "natural mother" of each child in the household when the natural mother appears in the same questionnaire as the child. In cases where it is difficult to ascertain the identity of the natural mother, one may use as a proxy the relationship to head of household or to

[48] It may be appropriate in some countries to reduce the lower age limit by several years.

[49] For methodological details, see *Manual X: Indirect Techniques for Demographic Estimation*, Population Studies, No. 81 (United Nations publication, Sales No. E.83.XIII.2), chap. VIII, sect. C.

reference person of household (see para. 2.114), or children living (see paras. 2.186 and 2.187) to establish the identity of the natural mother. In essence, information on the child's age and the mother's age are used to estimate a series of annual fertility rates for years prior to the census. The reliability of the estimates produced depends, among other things, on the proportion of mothers enumerated in the same questionnaire as their own children, the accuracy of age-reporting for both mothers and their children and the accuracy of available estimates of mortality for women and children.

2.172.   Mortality topics include infant and child mortality obtained from data on children ever born and children living, and adult mortality obtained from household deaths in the past 12 months and maternal or paternal orphanhood. The extent to which adult mortality can be adequately measured from population census data, particularly from the more innovative approaches to mortality estimation such as the orphanhood method, is still uncertain. Accurate responses to the questions described here are often difficult to obtain, thus resulting in faulty data. Nevertheless, it is often possible to derive useable adjusted estimates from this information.

2.173.   As far as possible, efforts should be made to obtain information on fertility, child mortality (or survival) and marriage directly from the woman or mother involved, because she is more likely to recall correctly the details of her fertility, the mortality of her offspring and her marital experiences than any other member of the household. Information on household deaths, by date, sex and age, in the 12-month period prior to the census should be collected from the head of the household (or reference person in the household). Information on maternal orphanhood and paternal orphanhood should be collected for each person in the household regardless of age. As with fertility, mortality questions may be limited to a sample of enumeration areas.

2.174.   A number of countries have restricted the collection of data from fertility and mortality questions in the census to a sample of enumeration areas,[50] entailing the introduction of more vigorous training and permitting the selection of more suitable field staff. When those items are included in the census, certain precautions to ensure accuracy and completeness should be observed. Every effort should be made to collect all relevant information directly from the woman concerned, because she is much more likely to correctly recall the details of her fertility, the mortality of her offspring and her marital experiences than any other member of the household. To reduce underreporting of events and to improve the accuracy of responses to questions on fertility and mortality, enumerators need to receive specific training on probing questions that highlight common errors and omissions. Enumerator manuals should also include the measures that are needed to minimize such errors.

2.175.   The limitations of the data collected and of the estimates based on them should be made clear in the census reports. Furthermore, since some of the estimation procedures are only suitable for use in certain circumstances, it is important that census data producers consult specialists and/or carefully evaluate the methodologies for estimating the indicators for their appropriateness in a given situation. In general, the data in the basic tabulations resulting from these questions should not be used for the direct calculation of fertility and mortality rates. Reliable estimation of fertility and mortality levels using census data requires adjustment based on methods of demographic analysis.[51]

2.176.   As a general guide, only one of the items discussed below is recommended for inclusion in all situations: "children ever born". Even in countries with reliable vital registration of births, census information on this topic can be useful for assessing the completeness of the registration system and for estimating levels of lifetime fertility for older cohorts.

[50] For the use of sampling in the enumeration, see chapter III.

[51] *Manual X: Indirect Techniques for Demographic Estimation*, Population Studies, No. 81 (United Nations publication, Sales No. E.83.XIII.2); National Academy of Sciences, Committee on Population and Demography, *Collecting Data for the Estimation of Fertility and Mortality*, Report No.6 (Washington D. C., National Academy Press, 1981), p.220; *Handbook of Population and Housing Censuses, Part II*, Studies in Methods, No. 54 (United Nations publication, Sales No. E.91.XVII.9), chaps. III and IV; *Step-by-Step Guide to the Estimation of Child Mortality*, Population Studies, No. 107 (United Nations publication, Sales No. E.89.XIII.9).

2.177.   In countries where vital registration of births and deaths is incomplete or unreliable, it is recommended that a subset of the remaining items should be included as well. Among these, one item is useful for the indirect estimation of current fertility levels: "date of birth of last child born alive". Two additional items are especially important, as they allow for the indirect estimation of mortality levels: "children living", and "household deaths in the past 12 months".

2.178.   The three remaining items have lower priority: "age, date or duration of first marriage/union"; "age of mother at birth of first child born alive"; and "maternal or paternal orphanhood". However, in situations where a country has included one of these items in consecutive previous censuses, it may be useful to collect comparable information for the sake of continuity and because cohort analysis, particularly of the prevalence of orphanhood, can be useful in assessing levels of mortality.

2.179.   It is worth emphasizing that all estimates of fertility and mortality derived from census data are approximate and subject to various sorts of error. Therefore, in the absence of complete and reliable civil registration data, it may be desirable to have more than one type of census information on each topic (for example, both household deaths in the past 12 months and maternal or paternal orphanhood for the purpose of estimating adult mortality). Lastly, it should also be born in mind that while fertility surveys can provide data on current fertility, they cannot provide the small area data that the census can. Therefore, a fertility question in the census can still be a priority for many countries.

(a)   Children ever born alive (core topic)

Recommended tabulations: 5.1-A

2.180.   Information on number of **children born alive** (lifetime fertility) should include all children born alive (that is to say, excluding foetal deaths) during the lifetime of the woman concerned up to the census date. The number recorded should include all live-born children, whether born in or out of marriage, whether born in the present or a prior marriage, or in a de facto union, or whether living or dead at the time of the census.

2.181.   Data on the total number of live-born children should preferably be collected for all women 15 years of age[52] and over, regardless of marital status. If, from a cultural standpoint, it is not feasible in some countries to obtain the information for single women, it should be collected at least for all women 15 years of age and over who are or have been married or in a union (in other words, all ever-married or ever-in-a union women), a group also including all widowed, divorced and separated women. In either case, the group of women for whom the data have been collected should be clearly described in the census report so as to avoid ambiguity in the analysis of the results. In some countries, there is substantial age-misreporting in the population census, which distorts fertility and mortality estimation based on children ever born and children living cross-tabulated by age of the woman.[53]

2.182.   In order to improve the completeness of coverage and to assist the respondent in recalling her children ever born alive, it is recommended that a sequence of questions be included in the following order: (*a*) "total number of sons ever born alive during the lifetime of the woman"; (*b*) "total number of sons living (surviving) at the time of the census"; (*c*) "total number of sons born alive who have died before the census date"; and (*d*) "total number of daughters ever born alive during the lifetime of the woman"; (*e*) "total number of daughters living (surviving) at the time of the census"; and (*f*) "total number of daughters born alive who have died before the census

[52] It may be appropriate in some countries to reduce the lower age limit by several years.

[53] The data on children ever born and children surviving at the time of the census become distorted by errors either in the reported number of children ever born and surviving or in the classification of women in particular age/duration-of-marriage groups. Such distributions (biases) result in gross underestimation of fertility and mortality levels, particularly when data are disaggregated for small geographical areas. See *Manual X: Indirect Techniques for Demographic Estimation*, Population Studies, No. 81 (United Nations publication, Sales No. E.83.XIII.2) chap. II, sect. A.2, and chap. III, sect. A.1. For additional methodological details on the uses of the data, see *Manual X*.

date". The responses to topics (*b*), (*c*), (*e*) and (*f*) allow for a checking of the responses to (*a*) and (*d*). Inconsistencies in the figures, if any, can sometimes be solved during the interview.

2.183.   The number of sons and daughters should comprise all children ever born alive whether born of the present or a prior marriage or union[54] and should exclude foetal deaths and adopted children. Also, the number of children, male and female, who are alive at the time of the census should include those living with the mother in the household and those living elsewhere, no matter where the latter may reside and regardless of their age and marital status.

2.184.   The collection of data on children ever born specified by sex not only improves accuracy of information but also provides data for indirect estimation of sex differentials in infant and child mortality, in combination with data on children living (surviving) by sex (see para. 2.186). If the information on "children ever born alive by sex" is collected for only a sample of women, the data on "children living by sex" should also be obtained for the same sample.

2.185.   Collecting data on the "total number of children ever born alive by sex" is desirable as it may improve the value of the information by providing a check on their quality, such as in ascertaining that sex ratios of births follow an expected pattern and do not behave oddly.

(b)   Children living[55] (core topic)

Recommended tabulation: 5.2-A

2.186.   Data on **children living**, in conjunction with those on children ever born are used in indirect estimation of infant and child mortality in situations where there are no reliable data from a civil registration. It is expected that improved coverage and quality of data on the total number of children ever born will be achieved if more detailed questions about the current residence of children ever born are asked, in terms of the following:

(*a*)   "Total number of sons living in the household";

(*b*)   "Total number of sons living elsewhere";

(*c*)   "Total number of sons born alive who have died before the census date";

(*d*)   "Total number of daughters living in the household";

(*e*)   "Total number of daughters living elsewhere";

(*f*)   "Total number of daughters born alive who have died before the census date".

These questions not only give a more complete and accurate reporting of children ever born alive specified by sex but also increase the questions' suitability for subsequent analysis.

2.187.   The identification of the natural mother of each child under 15 years of age in the same household, to be used in the " own children" method of estimating fertility, should be made by asking each woman who reports one or more of her children as being born alive and living in the household to identify these children in the census questionnaire. The section of the questionnaire on "relationship to the head of the household or to the reference person in the household" may be used for identifying the natural mother of each child living in the household.

(c) Date of birth of last child born alive (core topic)

Recommended tabulation: 5.3-A

2.188. Information on date of birth (day, month and year) of the last child born alive and on the sex of the child is used for estimating current fertility. This item can be useful as a means of deriving both national and subnational fertility estimates. In countries lacking adequate data from civil registration, sample surveys have become a major source of information for estimating national fertility levels, but surveys usually do not permit the derivation of reliable estimates at subnational levels.

2.189. At the processing stage, an estimate of the number of live births during the 12 months immediately preceding the census date can be derived from information on "date of birth of last child born alive." For estimating current age-specific fertility rates and other fertility measures, the data provided by this approach are more accurate than information from questions on the number of births to a woman during the 12 months immediately preceding the census. It should be noted, however, that information on the date of birth of the last child born alive does not produce complete data on the total number of children born alive during the 12-month period. Even if there are no errors in reported information on the last live-born child, this item ascertains the number of women who had at least one live-born child during the 12-month period, not the number of births, since a small proportion of women will have had more than one child in a year.

2.190. The information needs to be collected only for women between 15 and 50 years of age who have reported having at least one live birth during their lifetime. Also, the information should be collected for all the marital or union status categories of women for whom data on children ever born by sex (see para. 2.180) are collected. If the data on children ever born are collected for a sample of women, information on date of birth for the last child born alive should be collected for the same sample.

2.191. A census question on "date of birth of last child born alive" should always be paired with a simple follow-up question about whether the child is still alive, which yields data that can be used for studying child mortality. Although this pair of questions does not produce a valid estimate of the infant mortality rate (since the numerator excludes infant deaths occurring below age 1 in the past 12 months among children born 1-2 years before the census date), it can provide useful information on differences in child survival by age of mother or other socio-economic characteristics.

(d) Age, date or duration of first marriage

2.192. **Date of first marriage** comprises the day, month and year when the first marriage took place. In countries where date of first marriage is difficult to obtain, it is advisable to collect information on age at marriage or on how many years ago the marriage took place (duration of marriage). Include not only contractual first marriages and de facto unions but also customary marriages and religious marriages. For women who are widowed, separated or divorced at the time of the census, "date of/age at/ number of years since dissolution of first marriage" should be secured. Information on dissolution of first marriage (if pertinent) provides data necessary to calculate "duration of first marriage" as a derived topic at the processing stage. In countries in which duration of marriage is reported more reliably than age, tabulations of children ever born by duration of marriage yield better fertility estimates than those based on data on children born alive classified by age of the woman.[56] Data on duration of marriage can be obtained by subtracting the age at marriage from the current age, or directly from the number of years elapsed since the marriage took place.

[56] See *Manual X: Indirect Techniques for Demographic Estimation*, Population Studies, No. 81 (United Nations publication, Sales No. E.83.XIII.2), chap. II, sect. D.

[57] Ibid., chap. II, sect. B.3.

(e)   Age of mother at birth of first child born alive[57]

2.193.   Age of mother at the time of the birth of her first live-born child is used for the indirect estimation of fertility based on first births and to provide information on onset of childbearing and also for the indirect estimation of child mortality. If the topic is included in the census, information should be obtained for each woman who has had at least one child born alive.

(f)   Household deaths in the past 12 months[58] (core topic)

Recommended tabulation: 5.4-A

[58] See *Manual X: Indirect Techniques for Demographic Estimation*, Population Studies, No. 81 (United Nations publication, Sales No. E.83.XIII.2), chap. V, sects. A and B; *Data Bases for Mortality Measurement* (United Nations publication, Sales No. E.83.XIII.3); Ian M. Timaeus, "Measurement of adult mortality in less developed countries: a comparative review", *Population Index*, vol. 57, No. 4 (winter 1991), pp. 552-568.

2.194.   Information on household deaths in the past 12 months classified by sex of deceased and age at death is used to estimate the level and pattern of mortality in countries that lack satisfactory continuous death statistics from civil registration. In order for estimation derived from this item to be reliable, it is important that all deaths to household members occurring during the 12 months preceding enumeration be reported as completely and as accurately as possible. Typically, reports of deaths in censuses underestimate the overall number of deaths if only because some deaths result in the disintegration of households so that household survivors, if any, may not report their occurrence (in particular, deaths of persons living alone at the time of death are unlikely to be reported). Nevertheless, provided that there are no serious errors in the reporting of age at death, estimates of completeness of death reporting can be derived via indirect estimation and adequate mortality estimates obtained.

2.195.   Ideally, mortality should be sought for each household in terms of the total number of **deaths in the 12-month period** prior to the census date. For each deceased person reported, name, age, sex, date (day, month, and year) of death should also be collected. Care should be taken to clearly specify the reference period to the respondent so as to avoid errors due to its misinterpretation. For example, a precise reference period could be defined in terms of a festive or historic date for each country.

[59] It may be appropriate in some countries to reduce the lower age limit by several years.

[60] A few countries have collected information on maternal mortality in their censuses. See, Cynthia Stanton and others, "Every death counts: measurement of maternal mortality via census", World Health Organization, *Bulletin of the World Health Organization*, Vol. 79, July, 2001, pp. 657-664.

2.196.   When information is collected on household deaths in the past 12 months (or some other reference period), countries may wish to ask a pair of follow-up questions concerning cause of death. After ascertaining the name, age and sex of the deceased person and date of death, two additional questions could be asked: (*a*) Was the death due to an accident, violence, homicide or suicide?, and (*b*) If the deceased was a woman aged 15[59] to 49, did the death occur while she was pregnant or during childbirth or during the six weeks after the end of pregnancy?[60] Ideally, both of these questions should elicit a simple "yes/no" answer, although in some cases the only available answer may be "unknown" or "not sure."

2.197.   Data derived from such questions could be used to better understand trends in levels and some causes of adult mortality. At the processing stage, reported deaths would be tabulated according to broad categories of cause of death: external, pregnancy-related, other, and unknown. Ignoring the "unknown" responses, both external and pregnancy-related deaths could provide valuable information in countries where no other sources of information to systematically obtain causes of death are available. Of course, such information is approximate and must be interpreted with caution after careful evaluation and often adjustment. Nevertheless, using these simple questions should make it possible to derive some useful information about major trends in mortality that are otherwise difficult to obtain.

2.198.   There is no universal agreement about the feasibility of collecting reliable cause-of-death information as part of a population and housing census. The approach described here has been advocated by at least one group of experts[61] and has been incorporated into at least one national census (that of South Africa in 2001). A key motivating factor in both cases has been the desire to gain a better understanding of trends and levels of adult mortality, particularly in the context of HIV/AIDS. Although deaths due to AIDS would fall into the residual (or "other") category, major changes in this category between successive censuses (or between censuses and sample surveys) might be indicative of trends in AIDS mortality. Of course, such information would require careful interpretation, taking into account the overall epidemiological situation of a country. It is important to note that this general approach and the specific wording of the questions have not been tested systematically, and some of the analytical strategies described above remain speculative. As of July 2006, there has not been a thorough evaluation of the cause-of-death information collected as part of the 2001 census of South Africa. However, a preliminary investigation suggests that the South African data produced useful and mostly plausible estimates, although not fully consistent with information derived from other sources.[62] In sum, more research is needed on both the feasibility and methods of collecting cause-of-death information as part of a national census.

(g) Maternal or paternal orphanhood[63]

2.199.   Some countries may also wish to collect information on maternal or paternal orphanhood in another attempt to ascertain the level and patterns of mortality in the population. Census data from these two topics are intended for indirect estimation of mortality by sex. Estimates are based on the proportion of persons classified by age whose natural mothers or fathers are still alive at the time of the census.

2.200.   For the collection of information on orphanhood, two direct questions should be asked, namely (*a*) whether the natural mother of the person enumerated in the household is still alive at the time of the census, and (*b*) whether the natural father of the person enumerated in the household is still alive at the time of the census, regardless of whether or not the mother and father are enumerated in the same household. The investigation should secure information on biological parents. Thus, care should be taken to exclude adopting and fostering parents. It should be kept in mind, however, that overcounting may occur in the case of parents with more than one surviving child among the respondents, particularly in high fertility societies.

2.201.   It is preferable for these questions to be collected from every person in the household regardless of age.

6.   Educational characteristics

(a) Literacy (core topic)

Recommended tabulation: 6.3-A

2.202.   **Literacy** has historically been defined as the ability both to read and to write, distinguished between "literate" and "illiterate" people. A literate person is one who can both read and write a short, simple statement on his or her everyday life. An illiterate person is one who cannot, with understanding, both read and write such a statement. Hence, a person capable of reading and writing only figures and his or her own name should be considered illiterate, as should a person who can read but not write as well as one who can read and write only a ritual phrase that has been memorized. However, new understanding referring to a range of levels, of domains of application, and of functionality is now widely accepted.

[61] United Nations Population Division, Workshop on HIV/AIDS and adult mortality in developing countries, New York, 8-13 September 2003, http://www.un.org/esa/population/publications/adultmort/Adultmortality.htm

[62] Rob Dorrington, Tom A. Moultrie and Ian M. Timæus, "Estimation of mortality using the South African Census 2001 data", Centre for Actuarial Research, CARe Monograph No. 11, 2004.

[63] For methodological details on the uses of the data, see *Handbook of Population and Housing Censuses, Part II*, Studies in Methodology, No. 54 (United Nations publication, Sales No. E.91. XVII.9), chaps. III and IV, *Manual X: Indirect Techniques for Demographic Estimation*, Population Studies, No. 81 (United Nations publication, Sales No. E.83.XIII.2), chap. IV, sects A, B.1 and B.2; J. G. C. Blacker, "The estimates of adult mortality in Africa from data on orphanhood", *Population Studies*, vol. XXXI, No. 1 (March 1977), pp. 107-128; Kenneth H. Hill and T. James Trussel, "Further developments in indirect mortality estimation", *Population Studies*, vol. XXXI, No. 2 (July 1977), pp. 313-334; William Brass and K. Hill, "Estimating adult mortality from orphanhood", in *International Population Conference*, vol. 3 (Liège, Belgium, International Union for the Scientific Study of Population, 1973), pp.11-123; Ian Timaeus and Wendy Graham, "Measuring adult mortality in developing countries. A review and assessment of methods", World Bank Working Paper, No. 155 (Washington, D.C., World Bank, Population and Human Resources Department, April, 1989); Ian M. Timaeus, "Measurement of adult mortality in less developed countries: a comparative review", *Population Index*, vol. 57, No. 4 (winter 1991), pp. 552-568.

2.203.   The notion of literacy applies to any language insofar as it exists in written form. In multilingual countries, the census questionnaire may query the languages in which a person can read and write. Such information can be essential for the determination of educational policy. This item would, therefore, be a useful additional subject of inquiry.

2.204.   It is preferable that data on literacy be collected for all persons 10 years of age and over. In a number of countries, however, certain persons between 10 and 14 years of age may be about to become literate through schooling. The literacy rate for this age group may be misleading. Therefore, in an international comparison of literacy, data on literacy should be tabulated for all persons 15 years of age and over. Where countries collect the data for younger persons, the tabulations on literacy should at least distinguish between persons under 15 years of age and those 15 years of age and over.

2.205.   Straightforward operational criteria and instructions for collecting literacy statistics should be clearly established on the basis of the concept given in paragraph 2.202, and applied during census taking.[64] Accordingly, although data on literacy should be collected so as to distinguish between persons who are literate and those who are illiterate, consideration should be given to distinguishing broad levels of literacy skills. Simple questions with response categories that reflect different levels of literacy skills should be used. In addition, since literacy is an applied skill, it needs to be measured in relation to a particular task, such as reading, with understanding, personal letters and newspapers or magazines, or writing a personal letter or message. Respondents may be able to do so easily, with difficulty or not at all, reflecting the different levels of literacy skills. Reading and writing may be measured separately to simplify the questions.

2.206.   It would be preferable to use standardized questions, harmonized across countries to ensure comparability. The United Nations Educational, Scientific and Cultural Organization (UNESCO) has developed a reference database of model questions.[65] In addition, UNESCO recommends that literacy tests should be administered, in order to verify, as well as improve, the quality of literacy data. Nevertheless, administering a literacy test to all household members in the course of enumeration may prove impractical and affect participation, therefore limiting the utility of the results. Countries have regularly used simple self-assessment questions within a census to provide an indication of literacy rates at the small area level. An evaluation of the quality of statistics should be provided with census statistics on literacy.

2.207.   The collection and tabulation of statistics on literacy during the population census should not be based on any assumed linkages between literacy, school attendance and educational attainment. In operational terms, this means systematically inquiring about the literacy status of each household member irrespective of school attendance or highest grade or level completed.

2.208.   The literacy question currently varies across countries and, as a result, the data based on it are not always internationally comparable. Literacy should not be derived as an educational attainment proxy because although the two are related, there are substantial differences. For example, there are numerous cases where people leave school with only partial literacy skills, or lose them because of a lack of practice. Therefore educational attainment is not a good proxy measure of literacy skills.

(b)   School attendance (core topic)

Recommended tabulation: 6.1-A, 6.2-A

2.209.   **School attendance** is defined as regular attendance at any regular accredited educational institution or programme, public or private, for organized learning at

[64] Depending on the need for small area data and the circumstances in a country, literacy may best be measured through surveys.

[65] Census offices should consult the latest information on literacy assessment through the UNESCO Institute for Statistics website, www.uis.unesco.org to access an up-to-date source of information and guidance in this area for the census.

any level of education at the time of the census or, if the census is taken during the vacation period, at the end of the school year or during the last school year. According to the International Standard Classification of Education (ISCED), education is taken to comprise all deliberate and systematic activities designed to meet learning needs. Instruction in particular skills which is not part of the recognized educational structure of the country (for example, in-service training courses in factories) is not normally considered "school attendance" for census purposes.

2.210. Information on school attendance should, in principle, be collected for persons of all ages. It relates in particular to the population of official school age, which ranges in general from 5 to 29 years of age but can vary from country to country depending on the national education structure. In the case where data collection is extended to cover attendance in pre-primary education and/or other systematic educational and training programmes organized for adults in productive and service enterprises (such as the in-service training courses mentioned in paragraph 2.209), community-based organizations and other non-educational institutions, the age range may be adjusted as appropriate.

2.211. Data on school attendance should be cross-classified with data on educational attainment, according to the person's current level and grade (see para. 2.215). This cross-classification can provide useful information on the correspondence between age and level or grade of educational attainment for persons attending school.

2.212. The issue surrounding the number of out-of-school children has grown in importance within the last decade, particularly within the context of the UNESCO Education for All goal 2 with regard to achieving universal primary education. The census offers an opportunity to measure the number of "out-of-school" or "ever-in-school" children (reciprocal of attendance). There is a difference between "attending school" and "enrolled in school" thus results from censuses and administrative data may differ. The UNESCO Institute for Statistics and the United Nations Children's Fund (UNICEF) are jointly working on efforts to better measure the number of out-of-school children in the world.

2.213. School attendance is complementary to but must be distinguished from "school enrolment" which typically is obtained from administrative data. A child can be enrolled in school but not necessarily be attending. It is recommended that these concepts be clearly defined so that countries can determine which variable they wish to collect via the census.

2.214. It is also recommended that Member States consider the need for internationally harmonized question(s) in order to measure school attendance and school enrolment.

(c) Educational attainment (core topic)

Recommended tabulations: 6.1-A, 7.1-A, 8.2-A

2.215. The recommendations on "educational attainment" (see para. 2.216) and "educational qualifications" (see para. 2.229) make use of categories of the 1997 revision of ISCED, issued by UNESCO[66]. In accordance with national conditions and requirements, many countries can continue to apply national classifications of levels and grades of education and of fields of education in collecting and tabulating statistics from population censuses. Special attention needs to be paid to establishing appropriate level-grade equivalence for persons who have received education under a different or foreign educational system. These national classifications, however, should

[66] See annex II of document 29C/20 of the twenty-ninth session of the General Conference of UNESCO (8 August 1997).

be able to be converted or mapped to the ISCED97 classification system, this typically being achieved during post-census processing.

2.216. **Educational attainment** is defined as the highest grade completed within the most advanced level attended in the educational system of the country where the education was received. Some countries may also find it useful to present data on educational attainment in terms of highest grade attended. If required, data on educational attainment can take into account education and training received in all types of organized educational institutions and programmes, particularly those measurable in terms of grade and level of education or their equivalent, such as programmes in adult education, even if the education and training were provided outside of the regular school and university system. For international purposes, a "grade" is a stage of instruction usually covered in the course of a school year. Information on educational attainment should preferably be collected for all persons 5 years of age and over.

2.217. To produce statistics on educational attainment, a classification is needed that indicates the grades or years of education in primary, secondary and post-secondary school. Since the educational structure may have changed over time, it is necessary to make provisions for persons educated at a time when the national educational system differed from that in place at the time of the census. In addition to focusing attention on the collection of educational attainment data, enumerator instructions, coding and data processing need to be designed in a way that will take account of any changes in the educational system of a country over the years and of those educated in another country, as well as those educated in the current system.

2.218. Information collected on the highest grade of education completed by each individual facilitates flexible regrouping of the data according to various kinds of aggregation by level of education, for the purpose, for example, of distinguishing between persons who did and persons who did not complete each level of education.

2.219. For international comparison, data from the population census are needed for three levels of education: primary, secondary, and post-secondary. To the extent possible, countries can classify statistics on educational attainment by individual ISCED levels as given below (or by their equivalent as set forth according to the national classification of levels of education):

ISCED level 0:	Pre-primary education
ISCED level 1:	Primary education
ISCED level 2:	Lower secondary education
ISCED level 3:	(Upper) secondary education
ISCED level 4:	Post-secondary non-tertiary education
ISCED level 5a:	First stage of tertiary education (provides sufficient qualifications for gaining entry into advanced research programmes and professions with high skills requirements)
ISCED level 5b:	First stage of tertiary education (provides practical oriented/occupationally specific training, the successful completion of which usually provides the participants with a labour-market relevant qualification)
ISCED level 6:	Second stage of tertiary education (leading to an advanced research qualification)

Persons with no schooling should also be identified. Any differences between national and international definitions and classifications of education should be explained in the census publications in order to facilitate comparison and analysis.

2.220. Countries could consider asking a question which captures levels of education not successfully completed should this be of interest to policy. This could be in the form of a direct question asking if a person has some education at the relevant level or via a question asking the last grade/year completed from any given level of education.

2.221.   Data on school attendance, educational attainment and literacy status should be collected and tabulated separately and independently of each other, without (as elaborated in paragraph 2.207) any assumption of linkages between them.

2.222.   In order to ensure continued and improved international comparability of census data by level of education, it is recommended that Member States continue to ensure that the educational attainment variable is able to be mapped into the ISCED97 classification. This is typically achieved in post-census processing.

(d)   Field of education and educational qualifications

(i)   *Field of education*

2.223.   Information on persons by level of education and field of education is important for examining the match between the supply and demand for qualified manpower with specific specializations within the labour market. It is equally important for planning and regulating the production capacities of different levels, types and branches of educational institutions and training programmes.

2.224.   A question on field of education needs to be addressed to persons 15 years of age and over who attended at least one grade in secondary education or who attended other organized educational and training programmes at equivalent levels.

2.225.   The revised ISCED distinguishes between the following major fields (one-digit codes) and sub-fields (two- digit codes) of education:

Code

0   General programmes
   01   Basic programmes
   08   Literacy and numeracy
   09   Personal development

1   Education
   14   Teacher training and education science

2   Humanities and arts
   21   Arts
   22   Humanities

3   Social science, business and law
   31   Social and behavioural science
   32   Journalism and information
   34   Business and administration

4   Science
   42   Life sciences
   44   Physical sciences
   46   Mathematics and statistics
   48   Computing

5   Engineering, manufacturing and construction
   52   Engineering and engineering trades
   54   Manufacturing and processing
   58   Architecture and building

6   Agriculture
   62   Agriculture, forestry and fishery
   64   Veterinary
7   Health and welfare
   72   Health
   76   Social services
8   Services
   81   Personal services
   84   Transport services
   85   Environmental protection
   86   Security services
9   99   Not known or unspecified

2.226.   Countries may wish to consider collecting data on detailed fields of education, not only major ones. When coding field of education, countries should make use of an established national classification or, if this does not exist, adopt the classification and coding of fields of education of ISCED. Any difference between national and international definitions and classifications of fields of education should be explained in the census publications so as to facilitate international comparison and analysis.

2.227.   Countries coding field of education according to a national classification should also establish correspondence with ISCED, either through double-coding or through "conversion" from the detailed national classification to ISCED. A problem may arise in identifying the exact field(s) of education of persons with interdisciplinary or multidisciplinary fields of specialization. It is recommended that countries follow the procedure of identifying the major or principal field of education of those with multidisciplinary specialization.

2.228.   In order to ensure continued and improved international comparability of census data by field of education, it is recommended that the classification structure for the fields of education continue to be based on the ISCED97.

(ii)   *Educational qualifications*

2.229.   **Qualifications** are the degrees, diplomas, certificates, professional titles and so forth that an individual has acquired, whether by full-time study, part-time study or private study, whether conferred in the home country or abroad, and whether conferred by educational authorities, special examining bodies or professional bodies. The acquisition of an educational qualification therefore implies the successful completion of a course of study or training programme.

2.230.   According to national needs, information on qualifications may be collected from persons who have reached a certain minimum age or level of educational attainment. Such information should refer to the title of the highest certificate, diploma or degree received.

7.   Economic characteristics

(a)   Purpose of collecting data on the economic characteristics of persons

2.231.   Statistics on the economic characteristics of persons are needed from population censuses for many reasons. Information on the number and characteristics of the employed, unemployed and inactive persons are needed in detail at the same reference point of time that other demographic and social items are being measured so that a comprehensive picture of the socio-economic situation is available.

2.232.   Such statistics might be obtained from other sources, such as a household-based labour force survey or administrative records, but these other sources have certain limitations. Data obtained from sample surveys are constrained by sample precision and rarely provide reliable estimates for small areas, rare population groups, or for finely classified groups of industries and occupations. Administrative records may not have the same quality of occupational and industry coding nor the same comprehensiveness in population coverage as a population census.

2.233.   Other personal, household and dwelling characteristics that are included in the range of census topics (such as education, income level, type of dwelling, and so on) are strongly related to economic activity of the household members. It is therefore desirable to collect information on the economic characteristics of household members in the census so that cross-relationships between these data items can be examined.

2.234.   The population census provides benchmark information on economic characteristics to which statistics from other sources can be related. Population censuses also provide the sample frames for most household-based surveys, including labour force surveys. It is therefore useful to include as many data items as possible in the benchmark information or sample frames.

2.235.   There may, however, be problems in reconciling figures obtained from different sources owing to differences in scope and coverage, concepts and definitions, classifications, statistical units, reference periods, precision, measurement errors and so on. Household surveys, especially labour force surveys, have greater scope for generating quality statistics on economic characteristics at aggregate levels, such as national and broad regional groupings, while population censuses provide these statistics at lower levels of aggregation. When presenting census results, it is suggested that any such differences be highlighted and explained in footnotes to tables, in metadata as well as in textual analysis so that users are assisted to the extent possible in their work and the public has a better understanding of the use of these statistics. Countries that carry out regular labour force surveys may wish to designate these surveys as their official sources for statistics on the economically active population when reported at national level or for broad regional groupings.

2.236.   The census topics relating to economic characteristics of the population discussed below concentrate on the economically active population as defined in the recommendations of the International Conferences of Labour Statisticians (ICLS),[67] especially the resolution concerning statistics of the economically active population, employment, unemployment and underemployment adopted by the thirteenth ICLS.

(b)   Economic activity of persons

2.237.   The **economically active population** comprises all persons of either sex who provide the supply of labour during a specified time reference period, as employed or as unemployed, for the production of economic goods and services, where the concept of economic production is established with respect to the System of National Accounts (SNA)[68]. Activities are within the economic production boundary defined by the SNA[69] if they comprise:

(*a*)   Production of goods or services supplied, or intended to be supplied to units other than their producers, including the production of goods and services used up in the process of producing such goods or services (intermediate consumption);

(*b*)   Production of all goods retained by their producers for their own final use (own-account production of goods);

[67] International Labour Office, *Current International Recommendations on Labour Statistics* (Geneva, 2000).

[68] Commission of the European Communities/Eurostat, International Monetary Fund, Organization for Economic Cooperation and Development, United Nations and World Bank, *System of National Accounts 1993* (United Nations publication, Sales No. E.94.XVII.4).

[69] Ibid., para. 6.18.

[70] It should be noted that, although the own-account production of housing services by owner-occupiers is within the SNA economic production boundary, it has no labour input according to the SNA.

[71] *System of National Accounts 1993,* op.cit., paras. 6.24 and 6.25.

(*c*)　Production of housing services by owner-occupiers,[70]

(*d*)　Production of domestic and personal services produced by paid domestic staff (see figure 3).

2.238.　Own-account production of goods includes, for example, production of agricultural products and their subsequent storage; production of other primary products such as mining of salt, cutting of peat, supply of water; processing of agricultural products (the preparation of meals for own consumption is excluded); and other kinds of processing, such as weaving of cloth, dressmaking and tailoring; production of footwear, pottery, utensils or durables; making of furniture or furnishings; and major renovations, extensions to dwellings, replastering of walls or re-roofing by owners of owner-occupied dwellings.[71] It is advisable for countries to develop a more extensive list of such own-account production activities considered to be within the SNA production boundary, so as to ensure that those involved in such activities are correctly classified as economically active. In principle, the production of all goods falls within the SNA production boundary, irrespective of whether the goods are intended for supply to other units or for the producers' own final use. In practice, however, the production of a good for own final use within households should be recorded only if the amount of the good produced by households for their own final use is believed to be quantitatively important in relation to the total supply of that good in a country. According to the Thirteenth International Conference of Labour Statisticians, persons engaged in the production of goods for own final use within the same household should be considered as economically active only if such production comprises an important contribution to the total consumption of the household.

2.239.　Domestic or personal services provided by unpaid household members for final consumption within the same household are excluded from the economic production boundary and hence are not considered to be economic activities. (Examples are (*a*) the cleaning, decoration and maintenance of the dwelling occupied by the household, including small repairs of a kind usually carried out by tenants as well as owners; (*b*) the cleaning, servicing and repair of household durables or other goods, including vehicles used for household purposes; (*c*) the preparation and serving of meals; (*d*) the care, training and instruction of children; (*e*) the care of sick, infirm or old people; and (*f*) the transportation of members of the household or their goods.) Persons engaged in such activities may be included among "providers of non-paid social and personal services". (see paras. 2.293–2.295 below).

(*c*)　Activity status (core topic)

Recommended tabulations:　*7.1-A, 7.2-A, 7.3-A, 7.4-A, 7.5-A, 7.6-A, 7.7-A, 7.8-A, 8.3-A*

2.240.　The **activity status** of a person is determined over a short reference period such as a week or a day in terms of being economically active (employed or unemployed during the reference period as defined below in paragraphs 2.253–2.277) or economically inactive. Even within a short reference period, persons may have more than one economic activity status. So, to ascribe a single, unique activity status to each person, priority is given to the status of being economically active over being economically inactive and to being employed over being unemployed. In other words, a student who is seeking work should be classified as *unemployed* and economically active; and a person looking for work who also works for the minimum amount of time required by the census to count as being employed should be classified as *employed* and not as unemployed. This principle is referred to as the "priority rule". More details of the international standards are given in the resolution concerning statistics of the

Figure 3
Economic production as defined in the current System of National Accounts

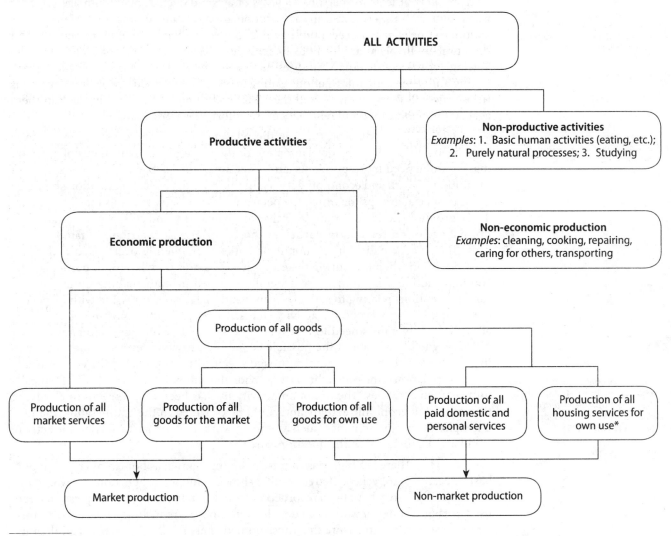

* No labour input.

2.241.   Information on activity status should in principle cover the entire population, but in practice it is collected for each person at or above a minimum age set in accordance with the conditions in each country. The minimum school-leaving age should not automatically be taken as the lower age-limit for the collection of information on activity status. Countries in which, normally, many children participate in agriculture or other types of economic activity (for example, mining, weaving and petty trade) will need to select a lower minimum age than that in countries where employment of young children is uncommon. In determining the lower limit, special note should be taken of the importance of statistics on the economic activities of children, especially with respect to child labour. Tabulations of economic characteristics should at least distinguish persons under 15 years of age and those 15 years of age and over; and countries where the minimum school-leaving age is higher than 15 years and where there are economically active children below this age should endeavour to collect data on the economic characteristics of these children with a view to achieving international comparability at least for persons 15 years of age and over. A maximum age limit for measurement of the economically active population is not recommended. Many people continue to be engaged in economic activities beyond their normal retirement age and the numbers involved are likely to increase as a result of factors associated with the "ageing" of the population. Countries may, however, wish to balance the cost of collecting and processing information relating to the economic activity of elderly persons (those aged 75 years or more) and the additional response burden imposed on them against the significance and reliability of the information provided.

2.242.   Depending on the way the relevant parts of the census questionnaire have been constructed, the determination of the economic activity status of a person may be influenced by respondents' and/or enumerators' subjective understanding of the notion of work and economic activity. In this regard, particular attention should be given to special groups for which the determination of activity status may be difficult. These groups include, for example, active youth, women, and elderly persons after the normal age of retirement, in particular those working as contributing family members. Their participation in economic activities is frequently overlooked and needs close attention when measuring the economically active population. In particular, the common notion that women are generally engaged in homemaking duties, or cultural perceptions relating to sex roles, can result in a serious omission with respect to measuring women's economic activity status. To reduce underreporting of economic activities, enumerators need to be explicitly instructed or the questionnaires specifically designed to ask about the possible economic activity of every woman and man in the household above the minimum age specified for measuring the economically active population. One possibility is to provide the enumerator with a list[72] of typically misclassified activities. The use of an activity list has been found useful in clarifying the concept of economic activity and could be provided in the enumerators' manual. Examples of specific activities, such as unpaid work, that are part of economic activity could also be included in the questionnaire.

2.243.   There is a high risk of misclassifying women as homemakers when only basic questions are asked. Better results, showing higher proportions of women as economically active, have been recorded in cases when further probing questions were used during an interview or more detailed questions were included in a self-administered questionnaire, to ensure that those homemakers involved in some typically misclassified economic activities were assigned to their correct economic activity status.

2.244.   The addition of probing questions in an interview or more detailed questions in a self-administered questionnaire may lengthen the time required to complete the questionnaire and increase the cost of the census. Accordingly, it will be necessary to balance the gains in terms of minimizing response errors when such questions are used against the added costs associated with their use. Given the importance of reliable data on activity status however, serious consideration should be given to minimizing classification errors. To this end, in the interview situation, as well as adding probing questions, improved training may help to reduce interviewers' bias and change their perceptions of what activities or types of production are economic. Training of enumerators should highlight likely sources of sex biases leading to underestimation of women's participation in economic activities as incomplete coverage of unpaid economic activities, failure of respondents and enumerators to take account of women's multiple activities, some economic and some non-economic, and the tendency to automatically enter women as homemakers, particularly if the women are married. Similar guidance could also be given in the instructions for a self-administered questionnaire.

[72] For an example of such a list and a basic principle to follow when drawing it up, see *System of National Accounts 1993*, op. cit., paras. 6.24 and 6.25.

(i)　*Economically active population*

2.245.　Two concepts of the **economically active population** can be distinguished:

(*a*)　The *usually active population*, measured in relation to a long reference period such as a year;

(*b*)　The *currently active population* (or, equivalently, the *labour force*), measured in relation to a short reference period such as one week or one day.

The choice between these measurement approaches should take into account the advantages and disadvantages of each approach, as well as national circumstances, the need for comparability with other national sources of data on economic characteristics (for example, labour force surveys, establishment surveys and administrative records) and other specific needs, such as the international comparability of economic statistics of countries and regions. It is, however, not advisable to use different concepts for different geographic regions in a country.

2.246.　A complete set of data compiled on both the usually active population and the currently active population has advantages for a number of important uses, but this may be difficult in a census because of expense, limitations of questionnaire space and the burden of coding and processing. To enhance the possibilities for the analysis of economic activity, countries using the labour-force concept (*current activity*) should endeavour to obtain supplementary data covering at least a count of persons who were *usually economically active* during a specified 12-month period, and countries using the concept of *usual activity* should endeavour to obtain supplementary data covering at least the size of the labour force during a one-week or one-day reference period.

2.247.　The "not economically active" population comprises all persons, irrespective of age, including those below the age specified for measuring the economically active population, who were not "economically active" as defined above in paragraphs 2.237–2.239.

(ii)　*Current activity status*

2.248.　**Current activity status** is the relationship of a person to economic activity, based on a brief reference period such as one week or one day.

2.249.　The use of the current activity concept is considered most appropriate for countries where the economic activity of people is not greatly influenced by seasonal or other factors causing variations over the year, that is to say where the results will not significantly depend on the timing of the reference period during the year. It may not, however, be equally appropriate for countries where the economic activity of people is carried out predominantly in sectors subject to significant seasonal variations, such as agriculture and tourism, and where people are therefore likely to be seasonally unemployed or engaged in more than one type of activity. Seasonal variations in employment and unemployment may be significant both in industrialized and in developing economies, but such variations tend to be less widespread in the former and are therefore generally measured through monthly or quarterly household surveys. Nevertheless, even for these countries, the census results will provide an important supplement, in particular for regions and small groups, as well as a source for benchmarking. Preferably, a time-reference period of one week rather than one day should be used, which may be either a specified recent fixed week (the preferred option), or the last complete calendar week, or the last seven days prior to enumeration. The "current activity" measure is the one used as the basis for international comparisons of the economically active population, employment and unemployment.

2.250.   One advantage of the use of a short reference period for measuring economic activity is that it requires information concerning only activities undertaken on the census reference date or immediately prior to that date. This minimizes the possibility for recall errors. Also, since the short reference period limits the possibility of having a large number of different activities undertaken and situations experienced, the construction of the questionnaire is simpler than when using a longer reference period.

a.   *Currently active population (the labour force)*

2.251.   The diagram in figure 4 depicts the labour force framework. The discussion below provides the relevant definitions, exceptions and clarifications for each of the boxes in the diagram.

2.252.   The **currently active population**, or the **labour force**, comprises all persons (above the stated minimum age) who are either employed or unemployed, as defined below.

b.   *Employed population*

2.253.   The *employed* population comprises all persons above the minimum age specified for measurement of the economically active population who, during a short reference period of either one week (preferred option) or one day (*a*) performed some work for pay, profit or family gain, in cash or in kind; or (*b*) were temporarily absent from a job in which they had already worked and to which they maintained a formal attachment or from a self-employment activity such as a business enterprise, a farm or a service undertaking.

2.254.   **Work** means engagement in economic activities as defined in paragraphs 2.237–2.239 above. The census documentation and tabulations should clearly describe the minimum time chosen for the purpose of considering persons to be at work. According to the present international recommendations, the notion of some work should be interpreted as work for at least one hour during the reference period. The one-hour criterion is an essential feature of the labour-force framework embedded in the international definitions of employment and unemployment, and a prerequisite for the consistency of employment statistics with national accounts data on production. It derives from the priority rules referred to in paragraph 2.240 above and ensures that one of the criteria in the definition of unemployment is a situation of total lack of work (zero hours of work). Countries concerned about the use of the one-hour criterion should collect information on the time worked variable, following the recommendations of paragraphs 2.322–2.325, so that employed persons can be classified by time worked.

2.255.   Special attention should be paid to homemakers, since some of their activities fall within the production boundary of the national accounts system and constitute employment (for example, production of agricultural products and their subsequent storage; production of other primary products, such as mining of salt, cutting of peat, supply of water; processing of agricultural products; and other kinds of processing such as weaving of cloth, dressmaking and tailoring) but may not be perceived as economic activity by those involved.

2.256.   Employees temporarily absent from work should be considered as in paid employment provided they maintained a formal job attachment. Such temporary absences might be because of illness or injury, holiday or vacation, strike or lockout, educational or training leave, maternity or parental leave, reduction in economic activity, temporary disorganization or suspension of work due to such reasons as bad

Figure 4
Labour force framework

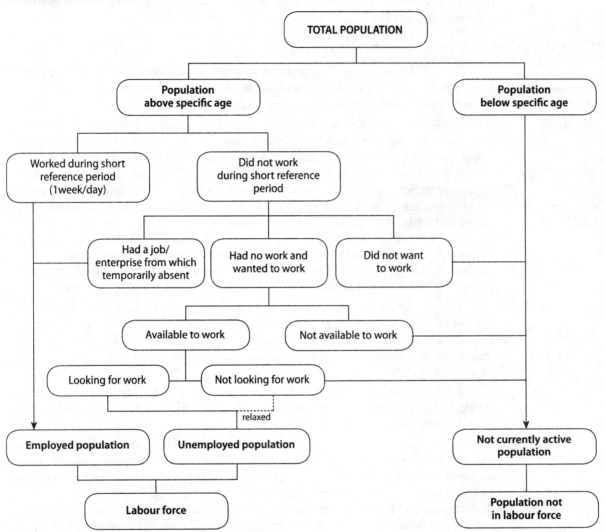

weather, mechanical or electrical breakdown, or shortage of raw materials or fuels, or characterized by other temporary absence with or without leave. A formal job attachment should be determined on the basis of one or more of the following criteria: a continued receipt of wage or salary; an assurance of return to work following the end of the contingency, an agreement as to the date of return; or the elapsed duration of absence from the job which, wherever relevant, may be that duration for which workers can receive compensation benefits without obligations to accept other jobs

2.257. Self-employed persons (excluding contributing family workers) should be considered "employed" and "with enterprise but not at work", if their absence from work is temporary and their enterprise meanwhile continues to exist, for example, because orders for work in the future are received.

2.258. Detailed information on the economic status classification of groups of persons on extended absence from work, such as women on maternity leave, employees on unpaid leave or other types of extended leave, seasonal employees and seasonal employers during the off-season, are available in the "Guidelines concerning treat-

[73] For further guidance, see "Guidelines concerning treatment in employment and unemployment statistics of persons on extended absences from work" in:
(i) International Labour Office, *Current International Recommendations on Labour Statistics*, Geneva, 2000, p.88;
(ii) http://www.ilo.org/public/english/bureau/stat/download/guidelines/exleave.pdf;
(iii) http://www.ilo.org/public/english/bureau/stat/download/16thicls/report4.pdf.

ment in employment and unemployment statistics of persons on extended absences from work", endorsed by the Sixteenth International Conference of Labour Statisticians in October 1998[73].

Treatment of specific groups

2.259. According to the standards adopted by the International Conference of Labour Statisticians in 1982, the following treatment of certain groups of individuals in paid employment or self-employment is recommended.

2.260. *Contributing family workers* should be considered to be at work on the same basis as other self-employed workers, that is to say, irrespective of the number of hours worked during the reference period. Countries that prefer for special reasons to set a minimum time criterion higher than one hour for the inclusion of contributing family workers among the employed should identify and separately classify those who worked less than the prescribed time, so as to be able to provide internationally comparable data. As contributing family members do not have an enterprise of their own, they cannot be "with an enterprise but not at work". Accordingly, contributing family workers who were not at work during the reference period should not be considered employed. They should be considered unemployed or not economically active depending on their current availability for work and recent job search activity.

2.261. Persons engaged in economic activities in the form of *own-account production* of goods for own final use within the same household should be considered to be in self-employment (and classified as own-account workers) if such production constitutes an important contribution to the total consumption of the household (see para. 2.238 above).

2.262. *Apprentices and trainees* who received pay in cash or in kind should be considered in paid employment and classified as at work or not at work on the same basis as other persons in paid employment.

2.263. Participation in *job training schemes* may be important in some countries and may generate particular forms of employment and intermediate situations on the borderlines of employment, unemployment and economic inactivity. Such participants are considered to be "employed" if the training takes place within the context of an enterprise and in connection with its production, or if the participants retain a formal job attachment to an enterprise in which they had formerly been employed, even if the training is outside the context of the enterprise or without connection to its production. Other participants in job training schemes are to be classified as unemployed or not economically active, depending upon their current availability for work and recent job-search activity. In particular, if the job training scheme implies a definite commitment to employment at the end of the training, participants who are currently available for work should be considered unemployed even when they are not actively seeking work (see para. 2.275).

2.264. In accordance with the priority rules of the labour force framework (para. 2.240), students, homemakers, pensioners, registered unemployed persons and others who were mainly engaged in non-economic activities during the reference period, but were at the same time in paid employment or self-employment as defined above should be considered employed on the same basis as other categories of employed persons.

2.265. All members of the armed forces should be included among persons in paid employment. The "armed forces" should include both regular and temporary members, as specified in the most recent revision of the International Standard Classification of Occupations (ISCO).

2.266.   "Requital" workers (that is persons who work for friends, neighbours and so on) within a mutual exchange of work as part of an exchange of work but not money) should be considered employed because the remuneration that they receive in exchange for their economic activity is the provision of labour input by someone else (barter of work).

2.267.   Persons who provide community work (building bus shelters, village administration and so on) for pay in cash or in kind should be considered as employed.

2.268.   Volunteers (without any pay in cash or in kind) who produce goods for any enterprise/institution/household or who produce services for a market enterprise should also be considered as employed. However, volunteers (without any pay in cash or in kind) who produce services for another household or for non-profit organizations are not considered to be employed. They should be considered as unemployed or not economically active depending on their current availability for work and recent job search activity.

2.269.   Similarly persons, including family members, who provide unpaid labour inputs to produce goods for any enterprise/institution/household or to produce services for a market enterprise should also be considered as employed. However, such persons who provide unpaid labour inputs to produce services for another household or for non-profit organizations are not considered to be employed (see paragraphs 2.293–2.295).

2.270.   Information should be given in the census reports describing how the above-mentioned groups and other relevant groups (for example, retired persons) were treated. Consideration should also be given to the desirability of identifying some of the groups (for example, apprentices and trainees) separately in tabulations.

c.   Unemployed population

2.271.   The *unemployed* population comprises all persons above the minimum age specified for measurement of the economically active population who during the reference period were:

(a)   *Without work*, in other words, were not in paid employment or self-employment, where work is as defined in paragraph 2.237 above;

(b)   *Currently available for work*, in other words, were available for paid employment or self-employment during the reference period;

(c)   *Seeking work*, in other words, had taken specific steps in a specified recent period to seek paid employment or self-employment. (The specific steps may have included registration at a public or private employment exchange; application to employers; checking at worksites, farms, factory gates, markets or other places of assembly; placing or answering newspaper or other forms of public advertisements; seeking assistance of friends and relatives; looking for land, building, machinery or equipment to establish one's own enterprise; arranging for financial resources; applying for permits and licences, and so forth.) It would be useful to distinguish first-time job seekers, who have never worked before, from other job seekers in the classification of the unemployed. Such a separation would be useful for policy purposes as well as in improving international comparability of employment statistics. To do so, however, may require an additional question regarding previous work experience, which may be too much for a population census.

2.272.   In general, to be classified as unemployed, a person must satisfy all three of the above criteria. However, in situations where the conventional means of seeking work are of limited relevance, where the labour market is largely unorganized or of limited scope, where labour absorption is, at the time, inadequate, or where the labour force is largely self-employed, the standard definition of unemployment may be applied by relaxing the criterion of seeking work. Such a relaxation is aimed primarily at those developing countries where the criterion does not capture the extent of unemployment in its totality. With this relaxation of the criterion of seeking work, which permits in extreme cases the criterion's complete suppression, the two basic criteria that remain applicable are "without work" and "currently available for work".

2.273.   In the application of the criterion of current availability for work, especially in situations where the seeking-work criterion is relaxed, appropriate tests should be developed to suit national circumstances. These tests may be based on notions such as present desire for work, previous work experience, willingness to take up work for wage or salary on locally prevailing terms, and readiness to undertake self-employment activity, given the necessary resources and facilities. These criteria are expected to ensure objectivity in the expression of current availability.

Treatment of specific groups

2.274.   As seen in paragraphs 2.253–2.258 above, in respect of *paid employment* or *self-employment*, some persons fall into borderline groups that require careful treatment to determine if their members are properly included in the category of unemployment. The following paragraphs discuss the treatment recommended in respect of such groups.

2.275.   Persons without work and currently available for work who had made arrangements to take up paid employment or undertake self-employment activity at a date subsequent to the reference period should be considered unemployed, irrespective of whether or not they recently sought work.

2.276.   Persons temporarily absent from their jobs, with no formal job attachment, who were currently available for work and were seeking work should be regarded as unemployed in accordance with the standard definition of unemployment. Countries may, however, depending on national circumstances and policies, prefer to relax the seeking-work criterion in the case of persons *temporarily laid off*. In such cases, persons temporarily laid off who were not seeking work but were classified as unemployed should be identified within a separate subcategory of unemployed persons.

2.277.   In accordance with the priority rules of the labour force framework, persons mainly engaged in non-economic activities during the reference period (for example, students, homemakers), who satisfy the criteria for unemployment laid down in paragraph 2.271 above should be regarded as unemployed on the same basis as other categories of unemployed persons and be identified separately, where possible. Information should be given in the census reports on how persons in these and any other specific groups were treated.

d.   Population not currently active (in other words, population not in the labour force)

2.278.   The population *not currently active* or, equivalently, persons not in the *labour force*, comprises all persons who were neither *employed* nor *unemployed* during the short reference period used to measure current activity, including persons below the minimum age specified for measurement of the economically active population.

2.279.   They may be classified, according to reason for not being *currently active*, in any of the following groups:

(*a*)   *Attending an educational institution* refers to persons not currently active, who attended any regular educational institution, public or private, for systematic instruction at any level of education, or temporary absence from the institution for relevant reasons corresponding to those specified for persons temporarily not at work; [74]

(*b*)   *Performing household duties* refers to persons not currently active, who engaged in household duties in their own home, such as spouses and other relatives responsible for the care of the home, children and elderly people. (Domestic and personal services produced by domestic employees working for pay in somebody else's home are considered as economic activities in line with paragraph 2.237 above.);

(*c*)   *Retiring on pension or capital income* refers to persons, not currently economically active who receive income from property or investments, interests, rents, royalties or pensions from former economic activities;

(*d*)   *Other reasons* refers to all persons, not currently economically active, who do not fall into any of the above categories (for example, children not attending school, those receiving public aid or private support and persons with disabilities).

2.280.   It is recommended that the population not in the labour force be classified at least according to the above-mentioned reasons for current inactivity. Some not currently economically active persons may be classifiable in more than one of the above categories. In such situations, priority should be given to the possible categories in the order above. Additional reasons for inactivity that are considered particularly important and included in the regional recommendations should also be taken into account in the classification of population not in the labour force. Information should be given in the census report on the minimum age for data on economic characteristics, the minimum school-leaving age and the typical age for the start of old-age retirement payments.

2.281.   Countries adopting the standard definition of unemployment may identify persons not classified as unemployed who were available for work but not seeking work during the reference period and classify them separately under the population not currently active.

(iii)   Usual activity status

2.282.   Usual activity status is the usual relationship of a person to economic activity based on a long reference period such as a specified 12-month period.

2.283.   A long reference period will provide information on the year as a whole, giving results that are much less dependent on the timing of the census date. Thus the census results will give data that are considered to represent a stable measure of the economically active population and its structural distribution for economic analysis, projections and development planning. Further, it provides an opportunity for collecting information needed not only on the principal activity of an individual but also on any secondary activity. It is also possible to obtain useful information on the intensity of activity over the year and relate it to household income for that period (if collected). The main drawback of the usual activity approach is that it is susceptible to recall errors. Another drawback is the problem of ascertaining the principal *occupation* and *industry* over a long period, such as a year, unless an appropriate question or series of questions are introduced to identify a main job, which may be defined in terms of time

[74] See also paragraphs 2.209 and 2.210 on school attendance.

worked or income earned. Resolving these complicates the construction of the census questionnaire. In countries where the economic activity of people varies widely over the year and where people are likely to be engaged in more than one type of economic activity during the year or to be seasonally unemployed, the "usual activity" concept is considered as appropriate. A specified 12-month period should be used as the reference period.

a.   *Usually active population*

2.284.   An illustration of the usually active population is presented in Figure 5. Formal definitions, exceptions and clarifications of each of the elements represented by the boxes in this diagram are given in the following paragraphs.

2.285.   The **usually active population** comprises all persons above a specified age whose main activity status, as determined in terms of the total number of weeks or days during a long specified period (such as the preceding 12 months or the preceding calendar year) was employed and/or unemployed, as defined within the labour force (current activity) framework in paragraphs 2.253–2.277 above.

2.286.   In applying the above definition of the usually active population, it is necessary to determine the main activity status of each person above the specified minimum age. For this purpose, the main activity status of a person is based on a summation of the variable activity statuses (active or inactive) of that person during the 52 weeks or the 365 days of the specified 12-month period. One procedure to determine the main activity status of a person is to classify the person as "usually active" if the number of weeks (or days) of active statuses (employed or unemployed) is greater than or equal to that of inactive statuses. This is referred to as the majority criterion. Another procedure is to classify a person as "usually active" if the number of weeks (or days) of active status is not less than some cut-off point (for example, duration of agriculture/tourist season).[75]

2.287.   The main activity status could be substantially different depending on whether it is based on weeks or days as the unit of measurement. In countries where employment is mostly of a regular and continuing nature and hence a week of employment generally means a week of full-time employment or, at any rate, employment for a major part of the working time, it is recommended to base the main activity status on weeks of employment or unemployment. However, in countries where employment is largely of an irregular nature and where a week of employment does not generally mean a week of full time employment or even employment for a major part of the working time, main activity status would better be based on days of employment or unemployment.

2.288.   The usually active population may be subdivided into usually employed and usually unemployed in accordance with the situation that prevailed most of the time. That is, usually active persons should be classified as usually employed if the number of weeks (or days) of employment is larger than or equal to the number of weeks (or days) of unemployment, and as usually unemployed if the number of weeks (or days) of employment is smaller than the number of weeks (or days) of unemployment. The subdivision into usually employed and usually unemployed is limited only to persons already determined to be usually active. Doing it the other way round, that is using the direct classification of all persons as usually employed or as usually unemployed in order to determine the usually active population, could lead to a different population group being classified as economically active than that derivable from the above definition. It is therefore recommended that the questionnaire be constructed in a way that makes it possible first to distinguish between usually active and usually

[75] R. Hussmanns, F. Mehran and V. Verma, *Surveys of the economically active population, employment, unemployment and underemployment: An ILO Manual on Concepts and Methods* (Geneva, International Labour Office, 1990), p. 51.

Figure 5
Usually active population*

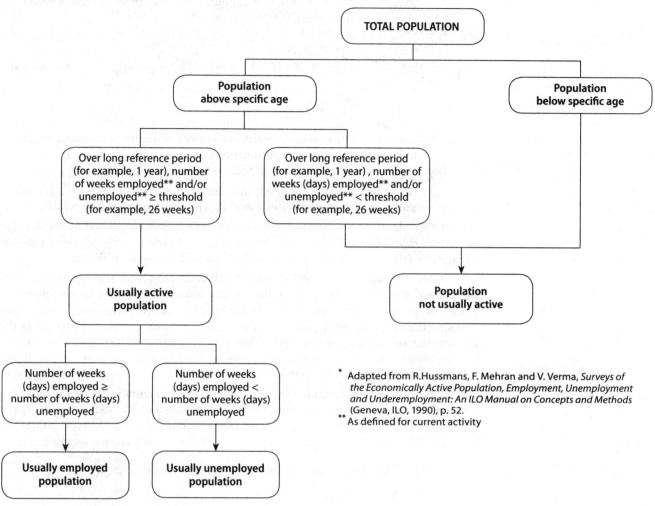

inactive persons, before making the distinction between usually employed and usually unemployed persons among the usually active persons.

2.289.   It is also worth noting that the usual activity status during a long reference period is not the same concept as the main activity during this period when comparing inactive, active employed and active unemployed. A person who spent 20 weeks inactive, 18 weeks unemployed and 14 weeks employed during the last year would be classified as active by usual activity status, for which the period of employment and the period of unemployment are summed. He/she would then be classified as usually unemployed, because the number of weeks unemployed exceeds the number of weeks employed. However, "inactivity" was the person's main activity as this occupied the largest spell among the three activities during the last year.

b.   *The population not usually active*

2.290.   The "population not usually active" comprises all persons, irrespective of age and of sex, whose main activity status during the long reference period used to measure usual activity was neither employed nor unemployed. It is recommended that this population be classified into the following four groups:

(*a*) *Students.* Persons not classified as usually economically active, who attended any regular educational institution, public or private, for systematic instruction at any level of education;

(*b*) *Homemakers.* Persons not classified as usually economically active, who were engaged in household duties in their own home, for example, spouses and other relatives responsible for the care of the home, children and the elderly (domestic employees, working for pay, however, are classified as economically active);

(*c*) *Pension or capital income recipients.* Persons not classified as usually economically active, who receive income from property or investments, interest, rent, royalties or pensions from former economic activities;

(*d*) *Others.* Persons not classified as usually economically active who are receiving public aid or private support, and all other persons not falling into any of the above categories (for example, children not attending school).

Where considered useful, separate subcategories may be introduced to identify (*a*) persons engaged in unpaid community and volunteer services, and (*b*) other persons engaged in activities that fall outside the boundary of economic activities.

2.291.   Since some individuals may be classifiable in more than one category of the not economically active population (for example, a person may be a student and a homemaker at the same time), the instructions for enumeration or self-completion should indicate the order of preference for recording persons in one or another of the categories. Consideration might also be given to presenting the categories in the census questionnaire in the preferred order because persons tend to answer according to the first category that applies to them.

2.292.   It is recommended that the census questionnaire be designed in such a way as to indicate for each person enumerated the total length of time in days, weeks or months over the long reference period that the person was engaged in economic activity (employed and/or unemployed) or in one of the four groups in paragraph 2.290.

(iv)   *Status of volunteers and other providers of non-paid social and personal services*

2.293.   Countries may wish to identify separately the persons who provide social and personal services to their own household, other households or to voluntary, non-profit organizations on an unpaid basis, either for a short reference period or for a longer one. Such persons may be subdivided either according to types of services provided or according to type of recipient.

2.294.   Unpaid services are a significant area of human activity. Information about unpaid services helps in understanding how individuals and families balance their paid work with other important aspects of their lives, such as family and community commitments. The information is important in measuring the characteristics of groups with special needs such as the elderly, children and people with disabilities. Areas covered may include unpaid domestic activities, unpaid care, unpaid care of children and unpaid voluntary work. Time use surveys are the key source of data on people's use of time, including activities such as unpaid work. However, being sample-based, information is not usually available at a small area level.

2.295.   It should be noted that the provision of non-paid services to other households and to voluntary, non-profit organizations is outside the production boundary as defined by the national accounts, and thus not considered as an economic activity. Such persons should be classified as unemployed or not economically active, depending upon their current availability for work and recent job-search activity. If classified as inactive, then separate subcategories of the inactive may be introduced to identify them, where considered useful.

(d) Selection of job to be classified by descriptive variables

2.296.   The descriptive variables "occupation", "industry", "status in employment" and "sector" should apply to either current or usual activity, depending on the choice of the main concept for the measurement of economic activity in the census. Individuals can be classified according to these variables only through their relationship with a job. This means that they must have been identified as being either employed or unemployed through the questions on economic activity. Whether economically active according to the *current activity (labour force)* concept or the usual activity concept, a person may have had more than one job during the reference period. For employed persons it is therefore recommended to first establish the main job held during the reference period and then, possibly the second job or (if more than two jobs) the second most important job and so on. It is recommended that each country should use the same criterion when ranking all jobs held in the reference periods. The criterion might be either on the basis of the hours usually worked (the preferred option) or on the basis of the highest income in cash and in kind. Hence, using the first criterion, the main job would be the job at which the person usually worked most of the time among all the jobs held during the reference period, the second (most important) job should be the job at which the person usually worked most of the time among any other jobs held during the same period and so on. When ranking jobs held during the reference period, it is important to consider also jobs from which the person is temporarily absent during the reference period.

2.297.   An unemployed person should be classified by "occupation", "industry", "status in employment" and "sector" on the basis of the last job which he/she had. The collection of data on characteristics of the last job (if any) of the unemployed is particularly important for users to have information on the characteristics of the unemployed in order to identify the specific areas of the economy or particular skills and occupations of unemployed people. The collection of these data is also relevant to countries applying ILO Convention No 160, known as the Labour Statistics Convention, 1985, which requires the preparation of statistics on the structure and distribution of the economically active population (that is, the employed and the unemployed) that are representative of the country as a whole.

2.298.   Such data, however, are of only limited relevance in respect of unemployed people who change jobs frequently or for the unemployed who last worked a long time ago. For the first group, it may be better to ask the characteristics of the type of job in which the person most frequently worked, and for the second group, it might be better to set a time limit for past work experience (for example, during the last 10 years) and only seek information on the characteristics of the last job if it was held within the time limit.

2.299.   It is important to design the census questionnaire or the census information taken from registers in a way that will ensure that the variables "occupation", "industry", "status in employment" and "sector" are measured for the same job. This should be a central concern also for countries that rely on the use of administrative registrations for the capturing of the correct values of these variables.

2.300.   Countries may want to describe in greater detail the type of secondary work carried out by respondents engaged in more than one job during the reference period, in particular if those countries wish to be able to describe the extent and structure of employment in the informal sector. In this case, the questionnaire should allow for the identification of a second, and perhaps even a third job for which information about occupation, industry, status in employment, sector and time worked can be collected and coded. The resources that would be required for collecting and processing this additional information should be taken into account.

(e)   Occupation (core topic)

Recommended tabulations: 2.4-A, 7.2-A, 7.6-A, 7.7-A

2.301.   **Occupation** refers to the type of work done in a job by the person employed (or the type of work done previously, if the person is unemployed), irrespective of the industry or the status in employment in which the person should be classified. Type of work is described by the main tasks and duties of the work.

2.302.   For purposes of international comparisons, it is recommended that countries make it possible to prepare tabulations involving occupations in accordance with the latest revision available of the International Standard Classification of Occupations (ISCO). At the time the present set of census recommendations was approved, an update to ISCO was in progress and was expected to be released in 2008. Hence, the latest revision available at this time (2006) was the one that was developed by the Fourteenth International Conference of Labour Statisticians in 1987 and adopted by the Governing Body of the International Labour Organization (ILO) in 1988.[76]

2.303.   Countries should code the collected occupational response at the lowest possible level supported by the information given. In order to facilitate detailed and accurate coding, it would be useful for the questionnaire to ask each active person for both the occupational title and a brief description of the main tasks and duties performed on the job.

2.304.   In preparation for the coding of the occupation responses, the organization responsible for the census should prepare a *coding index* reflecting the type of responses that will be given by the respondents.[77] The coding index should be constructed by occupational classification experts on the basis of responses to similar questions in other data collections, such as previous censuses, census tests and labour-force surveys, as well as input from job placement officers of the employment service and the content of newspaper advertisements of vacant jobs. The coding index should clearly distinguish between responses belonging to "not elsewhere classified" categories and responses that do not provide enough information to determine an occupational group.

2.305.   Countries coding *occupation* according to a national standard classification should establish a correspondence with ISCO either through double coding or through *mapping* from the detailed groups of the national classification to ISCO. Double coding can be achieved most easily when the coding index carries references both to the national classification and to ISCO, in which case coding should take the form of entering the line number of the selected index entry on the record for each response. Mapping means that, for each detailed group in the national classification, it is indicated to which ISCO group the (majority of) jobs in that national occupational group would be coded if coded directly to ISCO.

(f)   Industry (core topic)

Recommended tabulations: 7.3-A, 7.5-A, 7.7-A

2.306.   **Industry** (branch of economic activity) refers to the kind of production or activity of the establishment or similar unit in which the job(s) of the economically active person (whether employed or unemployed) was located during the time-reference period established for data on economic characteristics.[78]

[76] *International Standard Classification of Occupations (ISCO-88)* (Geneva, International Labour Office, 1990).

[77] The development and use of coding indexes, UNSD/ILO, *"Collection of economic characteristics in population censuses: technical report"* (New York and Geneva, 2002), chap. XII.

[78] For those persons who are recruited and employed by one enterprise but who actually work at the place of work of another enterprise (called "agency workers" or "seconded workers" in some countries), there would be user interest in gathering information about the industry of the employer as well as the industry of the place of work. However the collection of both would be more appropriate in a labour force survey rather than in a population census. The industry of the actual place of work may provide more reliable reporting of the "industry" variable in a population census. Any such choice should, however, be consistent with the treatment of this group in the SNA.

2.307.   For purposes of international comparisons, it is recommended that countries make it possible to prepare tabulations involving the industrial characteristics of economically active persons according to the most recent revision of the International Standard Industrial Classification of All Economic Activities (ISIC) available at the time of the census. At the time the present set of census recommendations was approved, the fourth edition of ISIC, adopted by the United Nations Statistical Commission at its thirty-seventh session in 2006, was the latest revision available.

2.308.   Countries should code the collected industry response at the lowest possible level supported by the information given. In order to facilitate detailed and accurate coding, the questionnaire should ask each active person the main products and services produced or the main functions carried out at the establishment or enterprise in which their job(s) was located. It is recommended that for those who work in fixed places the name and address of this place of work be collected. Countries with business registers that are complete and up-to-date can then use this response as a link to the register in order to obtain the industry code given there to the establishment. In preparation for the coding of the industry responses that cannot be matched to a pre-coded register the organization responsible for the census should create a *coding index* that reflects the type of responses that will be given on the census questionnaire. This coding index should be constructed by industry classification experts on the basis of available lists of enterprises, establishments, businesses and so forth, as well as from responses to similar questions in other data collections, including previous censuses, census tests and labour-force surveys. The coding index should clearly distinguish between responses belonging to "not elsewhere classified" categories and responses that do not provide enough information to allow for the coding of a detailed industry group.

2.309.   Countries coding *industry* according to a national standard classification should establish correspondence with ISIC either through double coding or through *mapping* from the detailed groups of the national classification to ISIC (see paragraph 2.305 for information about these techniques).

(g)   Status in employment (core topic)

Recommended tabulations: 7.4-A, 7.5-A, 7.6-A

2.310.   **Status in employment** refers to the type of explicit or implicit contract of employment with other persons or organizations that the economically active person has in his/her job. The basic criteria used to define the groups of the classification are the type of economic risk, an element of which is the strength of the attachment between the person and the job, and the type of authority over establishments and other workers that the person has or will have in the job. Care should be taken to ensure that an economically active person is classified by status in employment on the basis of the same job(s) as used for classifying the person by "*occupation*", "*industry*" and "*sector*".

2.311.   It is recommended that the economically active population be classified by status in employment as follows:[79]

- (a)   *Employees*, among whom it may be possible to distinguish between employees with stable contracts (including regular employees) and other employees;
- (b)   *Employers*;
- (c)   *Own-account workers*;
- (d)   *Contributing family workers*;

[79] For further details see the resolution concerning the International Classification of Status in Employment (ICSE) in International Labour Office, *Current International Recommendations on Labour Statistics* (Geneva, 2000); also in http://www.ilo.org/stat.

(e)   *Members of producers' cooperatives*;

(f)   *Persons not classifiable by status.*

It is also recommended to identify separately owner-managers of incorporated enterprises, who normally will be classified among employees, but whom one may prefer to group together with employers for certain descriptive and analytical purposes.

2.312.   An *employee* is a person who works in a *paid employment* job, that is to say, a job where the explicit or implicit contract of employment gives the incumbent a basic remuneration that is independent of the revenue of the unit for which he or she works (this unit can be a corporation, a non-profit institution, a government unit or a household). Persons in *paid employment* jobs are typically remunerated by wages and salaries, but may be paid by commission from sales, or through piece rates, bonuses or in-kind payment such as food, housing or training. Some or all of the tools, capital equipment, information systems and/or premises used by the incumbent may be owned by others, and the incumbent may work under the direct supervision of, or according to strict guidelines set by, the owner(s) or persons in the owner's employment. *Employees with stable contracts* are those employees who have had and who continue to have a contract, or a succession of contracts, with the same employer on a continuous basis. *Regular employees* are those employees with stable contracts for whom the employing organization is responsible for payment of relevant taxes and social security contributions and/or where the contractual relationship is subject to national labour legislation. *Owner-managers of incorporated enterprises* are workers who hold a job in an incorporated enterprise in which they (*a*) alone, or together with other members of their families or one or a few partners, hold controlling ownership of the enterprise and (*b*) have the authority to act on its behalf as regards contracts with other organizations and the hiring and dismissal of employees, subject only to national legislation regulating such matters and the rules established by the board of the enterprise.

2.313.   A *self-employment* job is a job where the remuneration is directly dependent upon the profits (or the potential for profits) derived from the goods and services produced (where own consumption is considered to be part of the profits).

2.314.   An *employer* is a person who, working on his or her own economic account or with one or a few partners, holds a *self-employment* job and, in this capacity, has engaged on a continuous basis (including the reference period) one or more persons to work for him/her as employees. The incumbent makes the operational decisions affecting the enterprise, or delegates such decisions while retaining responsibility for the welfare of the enterprise. In this context an *enterprise* includes one-person operations. Some countries may wish to distinguish among employers according to the number of persons they employ.

2.315.   An *own-account worker* is a person who, working on his own account or with one or a few partners, holds a *self-employment job*, and has not engaged on a continuous basis any employees. (Note, however, that during the reference period an own-account worker may have engaged one or more employees on a short-term and non-continuous basis without being thereby classifiable as an employer). Members of families belonging to a producers' cooperative whose only activity is the cultivation of privately owned ancillary plots or the care of privately owned livestock should be included in this category rather than the category "contributing family workers". It is recommended that in countries where the number of persons exclusively engaged in the own-account production of goods for own final use by their households is significant, such persons should be identified separately among own-account workers.

2.316.   A *contributing family worker* is a person who holds a self-employment job in a market-oriented establishment operated by a related person living in the same household, and who cannot be regarded as a partner (that is to say, an employer or own-account worker) because the degree of his or her commitment to the operation of the establishment, in terms of working time or other factors to be determined by national circumstances, is not at a level comparable with that of the head of the establishment. Where it is customary for young persons, in particular, to work without pay in an economic enterprise operated by a related person who does not live in the same household, the requirement that the person live in the same household may be relaxed.

2.317.   A *member of a producers' cooperative* is a person who holds a self-employment job in an establishment organized as a cooperative, in which each member takes part on an equal footing with other members in determining the organization of production, sales and/or other work, investments and the distribution of proceeds among the members. Note that employees of producers' cooperatives are not to be classified as in this group but should be classified as "employees". Members of informal cooperatives should be classified as "employers" or "own-account workers", depending on whether or not they employ any employees on a continuous basis.

2.318.   *Persons not classifiable by status* include those economically active persons for whom insufficient information is available, and/or who cannot be included in any of the preceding categories (for example, unpaid worker assisting a family member in the completion of a paid employment job).

2.319.   Countries that include members of the armed forces in the economically active population should show them in the category of employees. However, because of the wide range of national practices in the treatment of the armed forces, it is recommended that census tabulations and related notes provide an explicit indication of the *status-in-employment* category in which they are included.

2.320.   There are several groups of workers that are on the margin between employee and self-employed, such as owner-managers of incorporated enterprises, outworkers, contract workers and commission workers.[80] Consultations between national accountants and labour market analysts will be necessary to make decisions about the treatment of these groups in a consistent manner.

2.321.   In most census questionnaires, the information concerning status in employment will be captured through pre-coded alternatives where only a few words can be used to convey the intended meaning of each category. This may mean that classification of some of the situations on the borderline between two or more categories will be carried out according to the subjective understanding of the respondent rather than according to the intended distinctions. This should be kept in mind when presenting the resulting statistics. Countries which rely on the direct use of administrative records for the classification of persons according to status in employment may find that the group "contributing family workers" cannot be separately identified. Those who would have been classified as being in this group when using a questionnaire may either be excluded from the economically active population or classified as part of one of the other groups.

(h)   Time worked

2.322.   The number of employed persons provides only a very rough estimate of the volume of work performed, especially when such persons have non-standard working hours. Inclusion in the census of an item on *time worked* helps to ensure a

[80] For a discussion of the treatment of these groups, see the resolution concerning the International Classification of Status in Employment, para. 14, in International Labour Office, *Current International Recommendations on Labour Statistics* (Geneva, 2000). Also see http://www.ilo.org/stat.

more accurate measurement of the concept by capturing the full contribution of persons who were in and out of the workforce or who worked only for a brief time during the year (for example, women). This item is also particularly useful for countries concerned with the usefulness for some users of the one-hour criterion in the definition of employment when measuring current activity. Alternative lower limits for the definition of employment can then be applied when tabulating census results for such users. When employing the usual activity approach, information on time worked may be used to screen persons who did not have at least the minimum threshold of economic activity during the long reference period.

2.323. **Time worked** is the total time actually spent producing goods and services, within regular working hours and as overtime, during the reference period adopted for economic activity in the census[81]. It is recommended that if the reference period is short, for example, the week preceding the census, time worked should be measured in hours. In this case, time worked may be measured by requesting separate information for each day of the week. If the reference period is long, for example, the 12 months preceding the census, time worked should be measured in units of weeks, or in days where feasible, or in terms of larger time intervals. Time worked should also include time spent in activities that, while not leading directly to produced goods or services, are still defined as part of the tasks and duties of the job, such as preparing, repairing or maintaining the workplace or work instruments. In practice, it will also include inactive time spent in the course of performing these activities, such as time spent waiting or standing by, and in other short breaks. Longer meal breaks and time spent not working because of vacation, holidays, sickness or industrial disputes should be excluded.

2.324. It is recommended that, for persons who have had more than one job during the reference period, the questionnaire should ensure the recording both of *total time worked* (sum of *time worked* on all jobs) as well as time worked in the main job for which occupation and so forth is being registered.

2.325. The concept of time worked defined in the above paragraphs is that of "actual time worked" during the reference period. Thus, for current activity with a short reference period, it is possible that the value of time worked could be zero, for example for persons on vacation during the reference period, or reduced if any part of the reference period is taken off for sickness or holidays. Another time worked measure that could be used is that of *time usually worked*, defined as the time worked during a normal or typical week (or day), including overtime hours regularly worked, whether paid or unpaid. Days and hours not usually worked and unusual periods of overtime are excluded.

(*i*)   Time-related underemployment

2.326. When data are collected on time actually worked, it is possible to consider the measurement of time-related underemployment. The resolution concerning the measurement of underemployment and inadequate employment situations, adopted by the Sixteenth International Conference of Labour Statisticians (October 1998),[82] states that: **"Time-related underemployment** exists when the hours of work of an employed person are insufficient in relation to an alternative employment situation in which the person is willing and available to engage."

2.327. Time-related underemployment would be more appropriately measured by a labour force survey. However, for those countries without a labour force survey programme, it may be useful to include time-related underemployment as a population census topic.

[81] A detailed definition of hours actually worked is given in the resolution concerning statistics of hours of work, adopted by the Tenth International Conference of Labour Statisticians, October 1962; International Labour Office, in *Current International Recommendations on Labour Statistics* (Geneva, 2000). Also see http://www.ilo.org/stat. This definition may be revised by the resolution on working time that will be considered by the Eighteenth International Conference of Labour Statisticians, to be held in 2008.

[82] International Labour Office, *Current International Recommendations on Labour Statistics* (Geneva, 2000); also see http://www.ilo.org/stat.

2.328.   Persons in time-related underemployment comprise all persons in employment, as defined in paragraphs 2.253–2.270 above, who satisfy the following three criteria during the reference period used to define employment:

(a)   *Willing to work additional hours,* that is to say, persons who wanted another job (or jobs) in addition to their current job (or jobs) to increase their total hours of work; to replace any of their current jobs with another job (or jobs) with increased hours of work; to increase the hours of work in any of their current jobs; or a combination of the above. In order to show how willingness to work additional hours is expressed in terms of action that is meaningful under national circumstances, those who have actively sought to work additional hours should be distinguished from those who have not. Actively seeking to work additional hours is to be defined according to the criteria used in the definition of job search used for the measurement of the economically active population, also taking into account activities needed to increase the hours of work in the current job;

(b)   *Available to work additional hours,* that is to say, persons who are ready, within a specified subsequent period, to work additional hours, given opportunities for additional work. The subsequent period to be specified when determining workers' availability to work additional hours should be chosen in the light of national circumstances and comprise the period generally required for workers to leave one job in order to start another;

(c)   *Worked less than a threshold relating to working time,* namely, persons whose hours actually worked in all jobs during the reference period, as defined in paragraphs 2.322 and 2.323 above, were below a threshold, to be chosen according to national circumstances. This threshold may be determined by, for example, the boundary between full-time and part-time employment, median values, averages, or norms for hours of work as specified in relevant legislation, collective agreements, and agreements on working time arrangements or labour practices in countries.

2.329.   Among time-related underemployed persons, countries may want to identify separately the following two groups:

(a)   Persons who usually work part-time schedules and want to work additional hours;

(b)   Persons who during the reference period worked less than their normal hours of work and wanted to work additional hours.

(j)   Income

2.330.   Countries may wish to collect information on the amounts of income received by individual persons and/or households. If this topic is included in the census, it is recommended that data be obtained from all persons above a specified age, whether they are economically active or not. Income should be measured both for the individual and for the household of which he/she is a member.

2.331.   **Income** may be defined as:

(a)   Income, in cash or kind, received by each household member;

(b)   Total household income in cash and in kind from all sources.

The preferred reference period for income data should be the preceding 12 months or past year. The income could be classified as income from paid employment, self-employment, property and other investment, transfers from governments, other households and non-profit institutions.

2.332.   Collection of reliable data on income, especially income from self-employment and property income, is extremely difficult in general field inquiries, particularly population censuses. The inclusion of non-cash income further compounds the difficulties. Collection of income data in a population census, even when confined to cash income, presents special problems in terms of burden of work, response errors, and so forth. Therefore, this topic is generally considered more suitable in a sample survey of households. Depending on the national requirements, countries may nonetheless wish to obtain limited information on cash income. As thus defined, the information collected can provide some input into statistics that have many important uses.

2.333.   The income from employment of economically active persons should include wages and salaries of employees, income of members from producers' cooperatives and the entrepreneurial income of employers and own-account workers operating business and unincorporated enterprises. The wider concept of employment-related income includes in addition some transfer income from government and employers that is based on the current or past employment situation of the person.[83]

2.334.   In addition to the income from employment of its economically active members, the total income of the household should include, for example, the interest, dividends, rent, social security benefits, pensions and life insurance annuity benefits of all its members. The concepts involved in determining income are not simple to grasp and respondents may be unable or unwilling to provide exact information.[84] For example, income should include social security, pension fund contributions and direct taxes withheld from employees' salaries, but some persons will undoubtedly not include these amounts in reporting their salaries. Significant items of total household income may also be excluded or misstated. Despite instructions given to enumerators, the data collected can therefore be expected to be approximate. Accordingly, in the presentation of results it is usually appropriate to use broad income or earnings size-classes. As an aid to the interpretation of the results, tabulations of the data should be accompanied by a description of the items of income assumed to be included and, if possible, an estimate of the accuracy of the figures.

(k)   Institutional sector of employment

2.335.   The **institutional sector of employment**[85] relates to the legal organization and principal functions, behaviour and objectives of the enterprise with which a job is associated. Following the definitions provided in the System of National Accounts (SNA), it is recommended, if the census is to provide information on this topic, that the following institutional sectors be distinguished:

(a)   *Corporation,* comprising non-financial and financial corporations (in other words incorporated enterprises, private and public companies, joint-stock companies, limited liability companies, registered cooperatives, limited liability partnerships, and so forth) and quasi-corporations (that is to say, an unincorporated enterprise that is managed as if it were a corporation, in that a complete set of accounts is kept), as well as non-profit institutions, such as hospitals, schools and colleges that charge fees to cover their current production costs;

(b)   *General government,* comprising central, state and local government units together with social security funds imposed or controlled by those units, and non-profit institutions engaged in non-market production controlled and financed by government, or by social security funds;

[83] See the resolution on employment-related income, in International Labour Office, *Current International Recommendations on Labour Statistics* (Geneva, 2000).

[84] See the resolution on household income and expenditure statistics, and Report of the International Conference of Labour Statisticians (ILO, 2003), paras. 4-23, and http://www.ilo.org/stat.

[85] See United Nations Statistics Division/ILO, *"Collection of economic characteristics in population censuses: technical report",* (New York and Geneva, 2002); also available at http://unstats.un.org/unsd/demographic/sources/census/census3.htm.

> (c) *Non-profit institutions serving households* (for example, churches, professional societies, sports and cultural clubs, charitable institutions and aid agencies) that provide non-market goods and services for households (that is to say, free or at prices that are not economically significant) and whose main resources are from voluntary contributions;
>
> (d) *Households* (including unincorporated enterprises owned by households) comprising unincorporated enterprises directly owned and controlled by members of private and institutional households (made up of persons staying in hospitals, retirement homes, convents, prisons and so forth, for long periods of time), either individually or in partnership with others. Partners may be members of the same household or from different households.

2.336.   In most census questionnaires, the information concerning *institutional sector of employment* will be captured through pre-coded alternatives where only a few words can be used to convey the intended meaning of each category. This may mean that classification of some units on the borderline between two or more categories will be carried out according to the subjective understanding of the respondent rather than according to the intended distinctions. This should be kept in mind when presenting the resulting statistics.

(*l*)   Employment in the informal sector

2.337.   Where informal sector activities play an important role in employment creation and income generation, some countries may wish to consider collecting information on the number and characteristics of persons employed in the informal sector. However, given the complexity of the definition of the informal sector (it includes criteria such as the legal organization of the units as unincorporated enterprises, the lack of a complete set of accounts for them, the composition of their workforce, and so forth), it may be difficult to precisely apply some of its criteria in a population census.

2.338.   In brief, according to the ILO recommendation adopted by the International Conference of Labour Statisticians in 1993, concerning statistics of employment in the informal sector,[86] informal enterprises with regular employees (enterprises of informal employers) can be determined based on the small number of such employees, which should be determined according to national circumstances,[87] or on the non-registration of the enterprise under relevant forms of national legislation or on the non-registration of its employees, defined in accordance with the definition of regular employees in paragraph 2.312 above. Informal enterprises without regular employees (informal own-account enterprises) can be identified, depending on national circumstances, as either all own-account enterprises, or only those that are not registered under relevant forms of national legislation.

2.339.   The population employed in the **informal sector** comprises all persons who, during a given reference period, were employed (in the sense of para. 2.253 above) in at least one informal sector unit as defined in paragraphs 2.337 and 2.338 above, irrespective of their status in employment and whether it was their main or a secondary job.

2.340.   Surveys are in fact the most ideal method for collecting data on employment in the informal sector. However, countries still wishing to collect this information through their population census are encouraged to consult the United Nations Statistics Division/ILO "Collection of Economic Characteristics in Population Censuses: technical report"[88] where additional useful advice is given.

2.341.   It should be possible for many countries to derive from the census reasonably good estimates of the population employed in the informal sector by using information collected on the following topics: activity status, institutional sector of

[86] See the resolution on informal sector, in International Labour Office, *Current International Recommendations on Labour Statistics* (Geneva, 2000).

[87] The Delhi Group on Informal Sector Statistics recommends that for international reporting, a limit of "less than 5" should be used as the size cut-off; see http://mospi.nic.in/report_3.htm.

[88] See http://unstats.un.org/unsd/demographic/sources/census/census3.htm.

employment, occupation, status in employment and industry (and number of employees employed on a continuous basis or, alternatively, total number of employees or total number of persons, including the enterprise owner(s) and contributing family workers employed in the enterprise during the reference period (this topic is not covered in these recommendations)).

(*m*) Informal employment

2.342. The Seventeenth International Conference of Labour Statisticians, in November 2003, considered the related concept of informal employment[89] and established a set of "Guidelines concerning a statistical definition of informal employment". Under these guidelines, informal employment comprises all informal jobs as defined below, whether carried out in formal sector enterprises, informal sector enterprises or households, during a given reference period.

2.343. **Informal employment** includes the following types of jobs:

(*a*) Own-account workers employed in their own informal sector enterprises;

(*b*) Employers employed in their own informal sector enterprises;

(*c*) Contributing family workers, irrespective of whether they work in formal or informal sector enterprises;

(*d*) Members of informal producers' cooperatives (producers' cooperatives are considered informal if they are not formally established as legal entities and also meet the other criteria of informal sector enterprises specified in the resolution concerning statistics of employment in the informal sector adopted by the Fifteenth International Conference of Labour Statisticians);

(*e*) Employees holding informal jobs[90] (that is, jobs in which their employment relationship is, in law or in practice, not subject to national labour legislation, income taxation, social protection or entitlement to certain employment benefits such as advance notice of dismissal, severance pay, paid annual or sick leave and others) in formal sector enterprises, informal sector enterprises, or as paid domestic workers employed by households;

(*f*) Own-account workers engaged in the production of goods exclusively for own final use by their household, if considered employed as defined in para. 2.253.

2.344. Countries that exclude agricultural activities from the scope of their informal sector statistics should develop suitable definitions of informal jobs in agriculture, especially with respect to jobs held by own-account workers, employers and members of producers' cooperatives.

2.345. It should be noted that the informal employment concept is complex and therefore accurate data on it can only be collected through household surveys.

(*n*) Place of work

2.346. **Place of work** is the location in which a currently employed person performed his or her main job, and where a usually employed person performed the main job used to determine his/her other economic characteristics such as occupation, industry and status in employment (see paras. 2.301–2.321). Type of place of work refers to the nature of the workplace and distinguishes between the home and other workplaces, whether fixed or otherwise.

[89] See http://www.ilo.org/public/english/bureau/stat/download/guidelines/defempl.pdf.

[90] The operational criteria for defining informal jobs of employees are to be determined in accordance with national circumstances and data availability.

2.347.   The following response categories, or a variation thereof necessitated by national circumstances, are recommended for classifying type of place of work:

(a)   *Work at home.* This category includes those whose economic activities are conducted from within the home, such as farmers who work and live on their farms, homeworkers, self-employed persons operating (work)shops or offices inside their own homes, and persons working and living at work camps;

(b)   *No fixed place of work.* This category should be restricted to persons whose work involves travel in different areas and who do not report daily in person to a fixed address, for example, travelling salesmen, taxi drivers and long-distance lorry drivers. It also includes ambulant vendors, operators of street or market stalls which are removed at the end of the workday, construction workers working at different sites during the reference period and push-cart operators, and so forth.

(c)   *With a fixed place of work outside the home.* This category will include the remaining employed population. To this group should also be classified persons who do not have a fixed place of work but who report to a fixed address at the beginning of their work period (for example, bus drivers, airline pilots and stewards), as well as operators of street or market stalls which are not removed at the end of the work day. This group may also include individuals who travel to work, on a regular basis, across the border to a neighbouring country. Persons working at changing sites, for example, in construction, should give the location of their current worksite rather than the address of their employer's place of business, if appearance at this site will be required for at least one week.

2.348.   Selection of the last response category in paragraph 2.347 should lead to a request for the precise location (for example, street address and locality) of the place of work or the reporting place during the reference period. Coordination with the name (and address if given) of the enterprise or establishment collected for the industry variable is recommended. To devise an appropriate coding procedure for places of work abroad to which respondents travel regularly, it is recommended to use geographic reference files from the neighbouring countries. While information on the geographic location of the place of work can be used to develop area profiles in terms of the employed labour force (as opposed to demographic profiles by place of residence), the primary objective is to link the place of work information to the place of residence. Therefore, the geographic location of the place of work should be coded to the smallest civil division in which the economic activity is performed in order to establish accurate commuter flows from the place of usual residence to the place of work.

2.349.   It is likely that for some activities or jobs, performance is at more than one location (for example, at home some of the time/season and in a fixed location outside the home at other times) or the category cannot be clearly distinguished. One approach, in the case of the former, would be to select the place where the individual spends/spent a major part of his or her working time. Where the distinction between categories is blurred, as is the case for work done, for example, on a rented plot of land adjacent to one's home, it would be useful to identify borderline cases, according to national circumstances. Specific instructions should be given to the enumerators on how to select between two or three possible responses or to classify borderline cases.

8. Disability characteristics

2.350. A census can provide valuable information on disability and human functioning in a country. For countries that do not have regular special population-based disability surveys or disability modules in ongoing surveys, the census can be the only source of information on the frequency and distribution of disability and functioning in the population at national, regional and local levels. Countries that have a registration system providing regular data on persons with the most severe types of impairments may use the census to complement these data with information related to selected aspects of the broader concept of disability and functioning based on the International Classification of Functioning Disability and Health as described below. Census data can be utilized for general planning programmes and services (prevention and rehabilitation), monitoring selected aspects of disability trends in the country, evaluation of national programmes and services concerning the equalization of opportunities, and for international comparison of selected aspects of disability prevalence in countries.

(a) Disability status (core topic)

Recommended tabulations: 8.1-A, 8.2-A, 8.3-A

2.351. **Disability status** characterizes the population into those with and without a disability. The International Classification of Functioning, Disability and Health defines disability as "an umbrella term for impairments, activity limitations and participation restrictions. It denotes the negative aspects of the interaction between an individual (with a health condition) and that individual's contextual factors (environmental and personal factors)." For the purpose of determining disability status using census data, persons with disabilities are defined as those persons who are at greater risk than the general population for experiencing restrictions in performing specific tasks or participating in role activities. This group would include persons who experience limitations in basic activity functioning, such as walking or hearing, even if such limitations were ameliorated by the use of assistive devices, a supportive environment or plentiful resources. Such persons may not experience limitations in the specifically measured tasks, such as bathing or dressing, or participation activities, such as working or going to church, because the necessary adaptations have been made at the person or environmental levels. These persons would still, however, be considered to be at greater risk for restrictions in activities and/or participation than the general population because of the presence of limitations in basic activity functioning and because the absence of the current level of accommodation would jeopardize their current levels of participation.

2.352. It is recommended that the following four domains be considered essential in determining disability status in a way that can be reasonably measured using a census and that would be appropriate for international comparison:

(*a*) Walking;

(*b*) Seeing;

(*c*) Hearing;

(*d*) Cognition.

A comprehensive measure would include all domains (see para. 2.367). Two other domains, self care and communication, have been identified for inclusion, if possible. Another domain that should be considered for inclusion is upper body functioning.

(b) Disability framework and terminology

2.353.　In 2001 the World Health Organization (WHO) issued the International Classification of Functioning, Disability and Health (ICF)[91] which is the successor of the International Classification of Impairments, Disabilities and Handicaps (ICIDH), issued in 1980.[92] ICF is a classification system offering a conceptual framework with terminology and definitions of the terms, and classifications of the contextual components associated with disability including both participation and environmental factors.

2.354.　ICF distinguishes multiple dimensions that can be used to monitor the situation of individuals with disability. The system is divided into two parts each with two components;

　(1.0)　Functioning and disability, which include the components:

　(1.1)　Body functions and body structures (impairments)

　(1.2)　Activities (limitations) and participation (restrictions)

　(2.0)　Contextual factors which include the components:

　(2.1)　Environmental factors

　(2.2)　Personal factors

2.355.　ICF provides classification schemes for all these elements except for personal factors.

(i) *Interactions between components of the International Classification of Functioning, Disability and Health*

2.356.　The interactions between the parts and components of ICF are shown in figure 6 below.

Figure 6
Interactions between the components of ICF

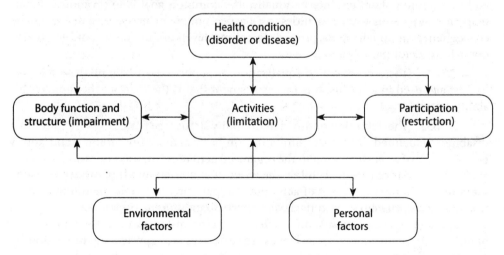

2.357.　The main structure of the classification is reported in annex 1.

(ii) *Use of the census to measure disability at the aggregate level*

2.358.　A census format offers only limited space and time for questions on any one topic such as disability. Since ICF offers several dimensions for use to develop a

[91] Geneva, World Health Organization, 2001.

[92] Geneva, World Health Organization, 1980.

[93] The Washington Group on Disability Statistics, a United Nations city group which focuses on proposing international measures of disability is developing these questions. See www.cdc.gov/nchs/citygroup.htm for updates on the questions.

[94] The World Programme of Action concerning Disabled Persons was adopted by the United Nations General Assembly at its 37th regular session on 3 December 1982, by its resolution 37/52.

census measure, it is best to focus on a few of those dimensions, leaving the remaining dimensions for use in more extensive household surveys. Short sets of disability questions, which can be included in censuses and extended sets to be recommended for inclusion in population-based surveys are being developed and tested.[93] The aim of the recommended sets is to improve comparability of disability and functioning data across countries.

2.359.   The World Programme of Action concerning Disabled Persons[94] provides a valuable guide for conceptualizing the uses of data on disability. The three major goals of the World Programme of Action are equalization of opportunities, rehabilitation and prevention.

2.360.   Three major classes of purposes for measuring disability in a census are:

(*a*)   To provide services, including the development of specific programs and policies for service provision and the evaluation of these programs and services. The provision of services at the population level includes, but is not limited to, addressing needs for housing, transportation, assistive technology, vocational or educational rehabilitation, and long-term care;

(*b*)   To monitor the level of functioning in the population. Monitoring levels of functioning includes estimating rates and analyzing trends. The level of functioning in the population is considered a primary health and social indicator, which characterizes the status of the population in a society;

(*c*)   To assess equalization of opportunities. The assessment of equalization of opportunity involves monitoring and evaluating outcomes of anti-discrimination laws and policies, and service and rehabilitation programmes designed to improve and equalize the participation of persons with disabilities in all aspects of life.

2.361.   The intent of these purposes for measurement is consistent with that of the World Programme of Action, which outlines major goals for policy formulation and programme planning, internationally. The common goal is to promote the participation of persons with disabilities in all aspects of life by preventing the onset and consequences of impairments, promoting optimal levels of functioning and equalizing opportunities for participation.

2.362.   The assessment of equalization of opportunity is the purpose that can be best achieved in a census. It is this assessment that is the focus of the topic of disability status.

2.363.   The definition outlined in disability status (see para. 2.351) requires that disability be defined in terms of limitations in basic activity functioning, and not by performance of or participation in the organized activities (such as educational attendance or work participation) While assessment of equalization of opportunities might seem to require measurement of activities and participation, such an approach does not help to identify changes in the level of participation in the population in response to changes in opportunities. It only reflects the circumstances of those who because of unfriendly environments or lack of assistive devices are experiencing restrictions in participation. Approaching the assessment of equalization of opportunity by recognizing the link between a basic level of activity and subsequent participation can reduce some of the methodological problems.

2.364.   Disentangling the conceptual dimensions of basic activity limitations from the more complex activities associated with participation provides the opportunity to determine the intervening mechanisms that facilitate or interfere with performance of tasks and organized activity. At the analysis stage, people who are identified with and without disabilities on the basis of their ability to perform basic activities can be compared in relation to their participation in organized activities (such as school and work). This comparison can assess the level of equalization of opportunities. The separation between activities and performance differentiates approaches for the purpose of monitoring functioning in the population and for the purpose of assessing equalization of opportunity. When assessing opportunity equalization, the connection between the conceptual elements is made during analysis, whereas for monitoring functioning the connection is done during data collection.

2.365. Within the framework of the ICF model and its four major dimensions (body structure and function, activity, participation and environment), an activity-oriented set of questions, located at the simplest and most basic level, should be used to capture the basic activity elements required for comparison and analysis. This will also provide a good measure for analysis in conjunction with data on participation restrictions.

2.366. Given the sensitivity and the complexity of disability and functioning, it is recommended that, rather than enquire about a general disability status, several activity domains be identified where people can be asked about their ability to perform in such domains.

(iii) *Essential domains*

2.367. The set of domains should capture the definition of disability that is being operationalized. It is suggested that only those domains that have satisfied a set of selection criteria be eligible for inclusion in a short set of questions recommended for use in censuses. Criteria for inclusion include cross-population or cross-cultural comparability, suitability for self-reporting and space on the census form. Other suggested criteria include the importance of the domain in terms of public health problems. Based on these criteria, four basic domains are considered to be essential: the areas of walking, seeing, hearing and cognition. If space permits, two other domains have been identified for inclusion, self-care and communication.

2.368. *Walking* fulfils the criteria of cross-cultural applicability and space requirements for comparable data since walking is a good indicator of a central physical function and is a major cause of limitation in participation. It is also a basic area of activity functioning that can be self-reported.

2.369. While *seeing* also represents a public health problem, self-reporting of seeing limitation is more problematic, particularly when individuals use glasses to correct visual impairments. Similar difficulties are associated with asking about *hearing* activity. The most direct way to deal with assistive devices like glasses and hearing aids without contributing to confusion over answering such questions is to ask the questions about difficulty hearing or seeing without any devices or assistance.

2.370. However, devices, such as glasses, provide almost complete accommodation for large proportions of those with impaired functioning and the numbers with the impairment can be very high. It is often argued that asking about seeing without the use of glasses greatly increases the number of persons with disabilities and makes the group too heterogeneous, that is, the group would include persons at very little risk of participation problems along with those at great risk. An alternative is to ask questions on difficulty seeing even with the use of glasses if they are usually worn and difficulty hearing with the use of hearing aids if these devices are used.

2.371. Of the four essential domains, *cognition* is the most difficult to operationalize. Cognition includes many functions such as remembering, concentrating, decision-making, understanding spoken and written language, finding one's way or following a map, doing mathematical calculations, reading and thinking. Deciding on a cross-culturally similar function that would represent even one aspect of cognition is difficult. However, remembering and concentrating or making decisions would probably serve the cultural compatibility aspects the best. Reading and doing mathematical calculations or other learned capacities are very dependent on educational systems within a culture.

(iv)   *Additional domains*

2.372.   There are additional physical functioning domains that could be included in a set of census questions depending on the space available, such as upper body functioning of the arms, hands and fingers. Another domain that could be incorporated is psychological functioning. While identifying problems with psychological functioning in the population is a very important element of measuring disability for the stated objective, questions that attempt to represent mental/psychological functioning would run into difficulty because of the levels of stigmatization of such problems within a culture. This could jeopardize the whole set of questions.

(v)   *Census questions*

2.373.   It is recommended that special attention be paid in designing census questions to measure disability. The wording and the construct of questions greatly affect the precision in identifying people with disabilities. Each domain should be asked through a separate question.[95] The language used should be clear, unambiguous and simple. Negative terms should always be avoided. The disability questions should be addressed to each single household member and general questions on the presence of persons with disabilities in the household should be avoided. If necessary, a proxy respondent can be used to report for the family member who is incapacitated. The important thing is to account for each family member individually rather than ask a blanket question. Scaled response categories can also improve the reporting of disability.

2.374.   The information that results from measuring disability status (see para. 2.351) is expected to:

(*a*)   Represent a large proportion, but not all persons with limitation in basic activity functioning in any one country (only the use of a wider set of domains would potentially cover close to all such persons, but as stated this would not be possible in a census context);

(*b*)   Represent the most commonly occurring basic activity limitations within any country;

(*c*)   Capture persons with similar problems across countries.

2.375.   The questions identify the population with limitations in basic activities that have the potential to limit independent participation in society. The intended use of these data would be to compare levels of participation in employment, education, or family life for those with disability as measured by the question set versus those without disability to see if persons with disability have achieved social inclusion. In addition, the data could be used to monitor prevalence trends for persons with limitations in the particular basic activity domains selected. It would not represent the total population with limitations nor would it necessarily represent the 'true' population with disability, which would require measuring limitation in all domains.

2.376.   Because disability is a complex concept, it is necessary to adopt an explicit definition based on the ICF domains used when developing census or survey questions

[95] When domains are combined, such as asking a question about seeing or hearing, respondents frequently are confused and think they need to have difficulty in both domains in order to answer yes. In addition, having the numbers with specific limitations is useful for both internal planning and for cross-national comparisons.

that will be used to identify disability status. The recommended set of questions for censuses is based on such an explicit definition (as described above). It is essential that estimates or tabulations based on the recommended set be accompanied by information on how disability is defined and how the questions are asked. This information should be included as part of the metadata associated with the questions and data set and it should be included as a footnote to tables that include these estimates.

(c)　Use of census to screen for disability and follow-up with other surveys

2.377.　Countries that are planning specialized surveys on disability may want to use the census to develop a sampling frame for these surveys and include a screening instrument to identify persons who will be interviewed subsequently. The definitions and the instruments used for this purpose are very different from the ones used to assess equal opportunities. The main purpose of a screening is to be the most inclusive as possible in order to identify the largest group of people who could be further studied. The screening question should be designed so that false negatives[96] are minimized, while false positives[97] should be less of a concern.

2.378.　Within the framework of ICF, the census screening may include all of the three main dimensions of body structure and function, activity, and participation. This will allow for keeping a broad approach to the follow-up survey where the different aspects of disability can be better studied.

2.379.　The same recommendations highlighted in paragraphs 2.373–2.376 should also be considered when a screening module is designed.

2.380.　Before embarking on using the census to develop a frame for a follow-up survey, it is important that the legal implications of using the census data for this purpose are fully considered. Respondents should be informed that the data may be used for follow-up studies and national authorities responsible for ensuring the privacy rights of the population may need to be consulted in order to obtain their approval.

[96] Persons who have disabilities but are not identified in the census as having disabilities.

[97] Persons who are identified with disabilities in the census but in reality do not have disabilities (as assessed in the largest instrument used in the follow-up survey).

9.　Agriculture

(a)　Introduction

2.381.　In this chapter two non-core topics on agriculture are presented. These two alternative topics could be considered by countries that would like to collect in the population and housing census information that would facilitate the preparation of the frame of agricultural holdings in the household sector, for a subsequent agricultural census (see also para. 1.44–1.50).

2.382.　With the first topic, at the household level, information is collected on whether any member of the household is engaged in own-account agricultural production activities at their place of usual residence or elsewhere. With the second topic, at the individual person level, information is collected to identify persons involved in agricultural activities during a longer period, such as a year.

(b)　Own-account agriculture production

2.383.　Some countries may want to use the population census to identify households engaged in own-account agricultural production to provide additional data for agriculture related analysis of the population census and for use as a frame for a subsequent agricultural census or other surveys. In this case, information should be collected for all households on whether any member of the household is engaged in any form of own-account agricultural production activities.

2.384. Where possible, information should be collected separately on the type of activity under the broad headings of crop production and livestock production. For countries where household level agriculture is particularly important, additional information on the size (area) of the agricultural holding and the numbers of livestock by type may also be collected in the population census.

2.385. Where aquacultural production is important at the household level, information can also be collected on whether any member of the household is engaged in any form of own-account aquacultural production activities. Agricultural production activities refer to groups 011, 012 and 013 of ISIC (Rev 3.1) namely:

Group 011:   Growing of crops; market gardening; horticulture.

Group 012:   Farming of animals.

Group 013:   Growing of crops combined with farming of animals (mixed farming).

Aquacultural production activities refer to Class 0502 of ISIC (Rev 3.1), namely:

Class 0502:   Aquaculture

2.386. An own-account worker in agricultural production (agricultural holder) is a person who is working on his/her own account (self-employed), or with one or more partners, and where that person has overall responsibility for the management of the agricultural production unit.

(c) Characteristics of all agricultural jobs during the last year

2.387. The population census normally collects employment data in respect of a person's main activity during a short reference period, which may not cover all persons working in agriculture because of the seasonality of many agricultural activities. To overcome this problem, information should be collected for all economically active persons on all agricultural jobs carried out during the year preceding the population census day. The information to be collected should normally be limited to occupation and status of employment, but can be expanded to identify main or secondary occupation and time worked.

2.388. Information on occupation and status in employment of all agricultural jobs can be used as an alternative way of identifying households engaged in own-account agricultural production activities (topic reference code), for use as a frame for an agricultural census. It can also provide additional data for agriculture-related analysis of the population census.

2.389. Where aquacultural production is important in a country, an additional topic on occupation and status in employment of all aquacultural jobs carried out during the year preceding the population census day can also be included and expanded to identify main or secondary occupation and time worked, as required.

2.390. An agricultural job is defined as a job in the agricultural industry as defined by groups 011, 012 and 013 of ISIC (Rev 3.1); namely:

Group 011:   Growing of crops; market gardening; horticulture.

Group 012:   Farming of animals.

Group 013:   Growing of crops combined with farming of animals (mixed farming).

An aquacultural job is defined as a job in the aquacultural industry as defined by

Class 0502:   Aquaculture of ISIC (Rev 3.1).

Chapter VII
Topics to be investigated in housing censuses

A. Factors determining the selection of topics

2.391. In line with the overall approach of revision 2 of *Principles and Recommendations for Population and Housing Censuses*, the selection of housing census topics is based on outputs expected to be produced by the housing census. Thus, the first step involves clear identification of expected outputs, and then the core and additional topics are decided on that basis. For each of the core topics there is a recommended tabulation.

2.392. Also with reference to the selection of topics to be included in a housing census, limiting statistical inquiries to the collection of data that can be processed and published within a reasonable period of time was deemed important. Such admonitions are especially applicable in connection with a housing census, since it is customary to conduct a housing and a population census as simultaneous or consecutive operations and there is a high probability that the amount of data requested in the questionnaires may be beyond the capacity of enumerators and data-processing facilities. It may be sufficient in some developing countries, for example, to ascertain only the number of housing units and other sets of living quarters of various types, the number and characteristics of the occupants thereof and the availability of a water supply system. Indeed, it might be neither feasible nor desirable in some cases to do more; if more were attempted, the success and quality of the census could be jeopardized.

2.393. In this context, it is false economy to collect housing data that are so incomplete that they fail to serve the principal purposes for which they are required. In this connection, it is important for census takers to consult closely with the principal users at an early stage in the preparations for a housing census in order to concentrate on collecting the data most urgently required and supplying them in their most useful formats.

2.394. The topics, therefore, to be covered in the questionnaire (that is to say, the subjects regarding which information is to be collected for living quarters, households and buildings) should be determined upon balanced consideration of (*a*) the needs of the country (national as well as local) to be served by the census data; (*b*) the achievement of international comparability, both within regions and on a worldwide basis; (*c*) the probable willingness and ability of the public to give adequate information on the topics; (*d*) the technical competence of the enumerators in regard to obtaining information on the topics by direct observation; and (*e*) the total national resources available for conducting the census.

2.395. Such a balanced consideration will need to take into account the advantages and limitations of alternative methods of obtaining data on a given topic within the context of an integrated national programme for gathering housing statistics.

2.396.   In making the selection of topics, due regard should be paid to the usefulness of historical continuity which provides the opportunity for measuring changes over time. Census takers should avoid, however, collecting information no longer required. Information should not be collected simply because it was traditionally collected in the past. It becomes necessary, therefore, to review periodically the topics traditionally investigated and to re-evaluate the need for the series to which they contribute.

1.   Priority of national needs

2.397.   Priority must be given to the fact that housing censuses should be designed to meet national needs. Should any discrepancy exist among national needs, regional recommendations and global recommendations, national needs should take precedence followed by regional recommendations and finally by global recommendations. The first consideration is that the census should provide information on the topics of greatest value to the country, with questions framed in such a way as to elicit data of maximum use to that country. Experience has shown that national needs will best be served if the census includes topics generally recognized as being of basic value and defined in accordance with regional and global standards.

2.398.   It is recognized that many countries will find it necessary to include in the census topics of national or local interest in addition to the topics included in the recommendations, and that the census data may need to be supplemented by data from housing surveys in order to obtain information on topics that cannot be included in the census either because they would overburden the enumerator or because they require specially trained interviewers. It is also possible that some countries may omit from the census certain recommended topics because it may be assumed with a high degree of confidence that a particular facility, such as electricity, for example, is available in virtually all sets of living quarters in the country. Conversely, some topics may not be investigated because of the almost total absence of certain facilities, particularly in the rural areas of some developing countries.

2.399.   In all cases, the importance of involving stakeholders in the process of identifying priorities and policy needs has to be taken into consideration early in the process of designing the housing census. The topics that are of particular interest to the policymakers need to be carefully assessed in terms of applicability, reliability of data and census limitations (number of questions, and so forth). More detailed information on involvement of stakeholders is presented in part one, in the section on "Census communication activities: user consultations, census publicity and promotion of census products" (paras. 1.112–1.116), and also in the *Handbook on Census Management for Population and Housing Censuses.*[98]

[98] United Nations publication, Sales No. E.00.XVII.15 Rev.1.

2.   Importance of international comparability

2.400.   The desirability of achieving regional and worldwide comparability should be another major consideration in the selection and formulation of topics for the census schedule. National and international objectives are usually compatible, since international recommendations are based on broad studies of country experiences and practices.

2.401.   If particular circumstances within a country necessitate departures from international standards, every effort should be made to explain these departures in the census publications and to indicate how the national presentation can be adapted to the international standards.

3. Suitability of topics

2.402. The topics investigated should be such that the respondents will be willing and able to provide adequate information on them. Those for which information is to be obtained through direct observation by the enumerator should be within his or her technical competence. Thus, it may be necessary to avoid topics that are likely to arouse fear, local prejudice or superstition, and questions that are too complicated and difficult for the average respondent or enumerator to answer easily. The exact phrasing for each question that is needed in order to obtain the most reliable responses will of necessity depend on national circumstances and, as described in part one, such formulations should be well tested prior to the census (see para. 1.186).

4. Resources available for the census

2.403. The selection of topics should be carefully considered in relation to the total resources available for the census. An accurate and efficient collection of data for a limited number of topics, followed by prompt tabulation and publication, is more useful than the collection of data for an overambitious list of topics that cannot be properly investigated, tabulated or stored in the database. In balancing the need for data against resources available, the extent to which questions can be pre-coded should be considered. This may be an important factor in determining whether or not it is economically feasible to investigate certain topics in the census.

B. List of topics

2.404. The units of enumeration for housing censuses are buildings, living quarters, households and occupants. The building is regarded as an indirect but important unit of enumeration for housing censuses since the information concerning the building (building type, material of construction of external walls and certain other characteristics) is required to describe properly the living quarters located within the building and for the formulation of housing programmes. In a housing census, the questions on building characteristics are normally framed in terms of the building in which sets of living quarters being enumerated are located, and the information is recorded for each of the housing units or other sets of living quarters located within it.

2.405. The principal direct units of enumeration in a housing census are the sets of living quarters. Only by recognizing them as such can data be obtained that will provide a meaningful description of the housing situation and a suitable basis for the formulation of housing programmes.

2.406. The second, direct, units of enumeration are households occupying living quarters. For each household, it is often useful to collect information on characteristics of the head or reference person, tenure in the housing unit and other relevant characteristics.

2.407. The final units of enumeration are individuals or members of household. Characteristics of each individual are collected in a population census and are covered in chapter VI.

2.408. The list presented below is based on the global and regional census experience of the last several decades. The topics included in the list are those on which there is considerable agreement in regard to their importance and feasibility in respect of measuring and evaluating housing conditions and formulating housing programmes: a study of housing census experiences indicates the feasibility of collecting information on those topics by means of a housing census. Those that are likely to present difficulties and require time-consuming questioning can probably best be investigated in a sample of sets of living quarters.

2.409.   Core topics are those of common interest and value to countries or areas and also of importance in enabling comprehensive comparison of statistics at the international level. Additional topics refer to topics that need to be collected in order to allow for preparation of tabulations that would meet most of the needs of the users (also referred to as "optimum set of census tabulations").

2.410.   It should be emphasized that the topics or variables on housing contained herein are for tabulation and production of outputs as this is the overall orientation of these guidelines. Issues that pertain to data collection are addressed in other parts of the *Principles and Recommendations for Population and Housing Censuses* and other relevant United Nations handbooks.

Legend:

◆ Core topic
☐ Core topic, derived
○ Additional topic

Table 2
Housing census topics by unit of enumeration

| | | Living quarters | | | |
| | | Housing units | Collective living quarters | Buildings | Households |
No.	Topic				
1.	Living quarters—type of	☐	◆		
2.	Location	☐	◆	☐	☐
3.	Occupancy status	◆			
4.	Ownership—type of	◆			☐
5.	Rooms—number of	◆			☐
6.	Bedrooms—number of	○			○
7.	Useful floor space	○	○		○
8.	Water supply system	◆	○		☐
9.	Drinking water—main source of	◆	○		☐
10.	Toilet—type of	◆	○		☐
11.	Sewage disposal	◆			☐
12.	Bathing facilities	◆	○		☐
13.	Kitchen—availability of	◆	○		☐
14.	Fuel used for cooking	◆			☐
15.	Lighting and/or electricity—type of	◆	○		☐
16.	Solid waste disposal—main type of	◆			☐
17.	Heating—type and energy used for	○			○
18.	Hot water—availability of	○			○
19.	Piped gas—availability of	○			○
20.	Use of housing unit	○			○
21.	Occupancy by one or more households	☐			◆
22.	Occupants—number of	◆	◆		☐
23.	Building—type of			☐	
24.	Construction material of outer walls	☐		☐	
25.	Year or period of construction	○		○	
26.	Dwellings in the building—number of	○		○	
27.	Construction material of floors, roof	○		○	
28.	Elevator—availability of	○		○	

| No. | Topic | Living quarters | | Buildings | Households |
		Housing units	Collective living quarters		
29.	Farm building	O		O	
30.	State of repair	O		O	
31.	Age and sex of head or other reference member of household				◆
32.	Tenure				◆
33.	Rental and owner-occupied housing costs				O
34.	Furnished/unfurnished	O			O
35.	Information and communication technology (ICT) devices—availability of				◆
36.	Cars—number of				O
37.	Durable household appliances—availability of				O
38.	Available outdoor space				O

C. Definitions and specifications of topics

2.411. Paragraphs 2.412–2.553 below contain the recommended definitions. It is important that census data be accompanied by the definitions used in carrying out the census. It is also important that any changes in definitions that might have been made since the previous census be indicated and, if possible, accompanied by estimates of the effect of such changes on the relevant data. In this way, users will not confuse valid changes over time with increases or decreases that have occurred as the result of changed definitions.

1. Living quarters—type of (core topic)

Recommended tabulations: H1-R–H18-R

(a)   Definition of living quarters

2.412.   **Living quarters** are structurally separate and independent places of abode. They may:

(a)   Have been constructed, built, converted or arranged for human habitation, provided that they are not at the time of the census used wholly for other purposes and that, in the case of non-conventional housing units and collective living quarters, they are occupied at the time of the census; or

(b)   Although not intended for habitation, actually be in use for such a purpose at the time of the census.

2.413.   Instructions should be issued so that it is clearly understood at what stage of completion sets of living quarters should be included in the housing census. They may be included in the housing census as soon as construction has begun, at various stages of construction or when construction has been completed. Living quarters being demolished or awaiting demolition should normally be excluded. The system used should be consistent with that employed for the system of current housing statistics and should avoid double counting where construction statistics are used to bring the census data up to date. Special instructions will need to be issued concerning "core dwellings" in countries where these are provided within a preliminary phase of dwelling construction.

(*b*)   Classification of living quarters

2.414.   Living quarters are either housing units or collective living quarters. Normally, the collection of information concerning housing units will be considered of first importance in a housing census, since it is in housing units that the majority of the population permanently lives. Furthermore, housing units are intended for occupancy, or are occupied, by households, and it is with the provision of accommodation for households that housing programmes and policies are mainly concerned. However, certain types of "collective living quarters" are also of significance with respect to the housing conditions of households; these include hotels, rooming houses and other lodging houses and camps occupied by households. Housing units should be classified so as to distinguish at least conventional dwellings from other types of housing units. It should be emphasized that without an adequate classification of living quarters, no meaningful analysis of housing conditions based on housing census data is possible.

2.415.   The classification outlined below (see also figure 7) and a system of three-digit codes have been designed to group in broad classes housing units and collective living quarters with similar structural characteristics. The distribution of occupants (population) among the various groups supplies valuable information about the housing accommodation available at the time of the census. The classification also affords a useful basis of stratification for sample surveys. The living quarters may be divided into the following categories:

1   Housing units
    1.1   Conventional dwellings
        1.1.1   Has all basic facilities
        1.1.2   Does not have all basic facilities
    1.2   Other housing units
        1.2.1   Semi-permanent housing units
        1.2.2   Mobile housing units
        1.2.3   Improvised housing units
        1.2.4   Housing units in permanent buildings not intended for human habitation
        1.2.5   Other premises not intended for human habitation
2   Collective living quarters
    2.1   Hotels, rooming houses and other lodging houses
    2.2   Institutions
        2.2.1   Hospitals
        2.2.2   Correctional institutions (prisons, penitentiaries)
        2.2.3   Military institutions
        2.2.4   Religious institutions (monasteries, convents, and so forth)
        2.2.5   Retirement homes, homes for elderly
        2.2.6   Student dormitories and similar
        2.2.7   Staff quarters (for example, hostels and nurses' homes)
        2.2.8   Orphanages
        2.2.9   Other
    2.3   Camps and workers' quarters
        2.3.1   Military camps
        2.3.2   Worker camps
        2.3.3   Refugee camps
        2.3.4   Camps for internally displaced people
        2.3.5   Other
    2.4   Other

Figure 7
Classification of living quarters

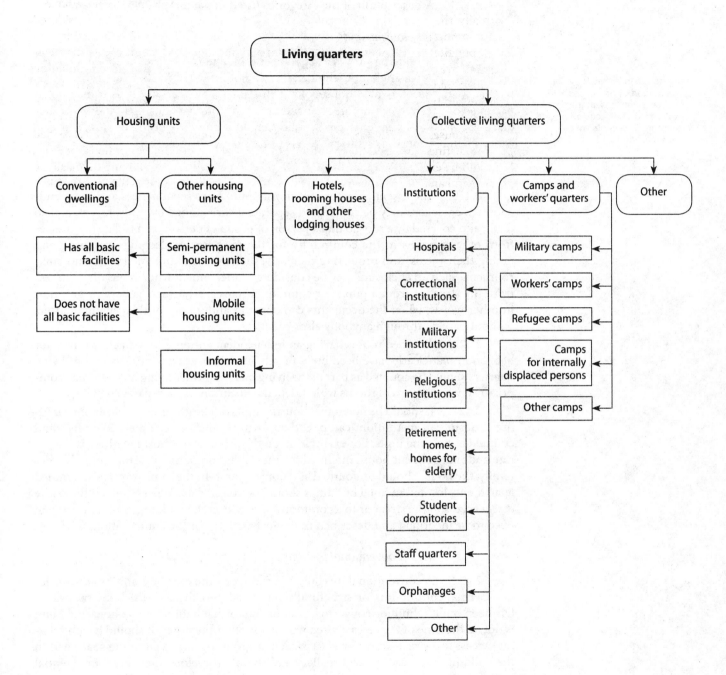

2.416.   Not all the categories in the above classification are of importance under all circumstances. For example, in some countries certain of the groups may not need to be considered separately, while in others it will be convenient to subdivide them. However, some of the categories are of special significance for assessing the housing situation and should be distinguished even where a simplified classification is employed. Yet, the distinction between conventional and informal housing units is referred to particularly.

(c)   Definitions of each type of living quarters

2.417.   A description of the categories listed in paragraph 2.415 is given below.

1   *Housing units*

2.418.   **A housing unit** is a separate and independent place of abode intended for habitation by a single household,[99] or one not intended for habitation but occupied as living quarters by a household at the time of the census. Thus it may be an occupied or vacant dwelling, an occupied non-conventional housing unit or any other place occupied as living quarters by a household at the time of the census. This category includes housing of various levels of permanency and acceptability and therefore requires further classification in order to provide for a meaningful assessment of housing conditions.

[99] Although intended for habitation by one household, a housing unit may, at the time of the census, be occupied by one or more households or by a part of a household.

2.419.   The essential features of housing units are separateness and independence. An enclosure may be considered separate if surrounded by walls, fences, and so forth, and covered by a roof so that a person or group of persons can isolate themselves from other persons in the community for the purposes of sleeping, preparing and taking their meals, and protecting themselves from the hazards of climate and environment. Such an enclosure may be considered independent when it has direct access from the street or from a public or communal staircase, passage, gallery or grounds, in other words, when the occupants can come in and go out of their living quarters without passing through anybody else's premises.

2.420.   Attached rooms having an independent entrance, or detached rooms for habitation that clearly have been built, or rebuilt or converted for use as part of living quarters should be counted as part of the living quarters. Thus, living quarters may comprise rooms or groups of rooms with independent entrances, or separate buildings.

2.421.   It should be noted that housing units on the grounds or within the buildings housing an institution, camp, and so forth should be separately identified and counted as housing units. For example, if, on the grounds of a hospital, there is a separate and independent house intended for the habitation of the director and his or her family, the house should be counted as a housing unit. In the same way, self-contained apartments located in hotel buildings should be counted as housing units if they have direct access to the street or to a common space within the building. Similar cases will need to be identified and described in the instructions for the enumeration.

1.1   *Conventional dwellings*

2.422.   A conventional dwelling is a room or suite of rooms and its accessories in a permanent building or structurally separated part thereof which, by the way it has been built, rebuilt or converted, is intended for habitation by one household and is not, at the time of the census, used wholly for other purposes. It should have a separate access to a street (direct or via a garden or grounds) or to a common space within the building (staircase, passage, gallery and so on). Therefore, there are four essential features of a conventional dwelling:

(*a*)   It is a room or suite of rooms;

(*b*)   It is located in a permanent building;

(*c*)   It has separate access to a street or to a common space;

(*d*)   It was intended to be occupied by one household.

2.423.   Examples of conventional dwellings are houses, flats, suites of rooms, apartments and so forth. Although a conventional dwelling is a housing unit intended, that is to say, constructed or converted, for habitation by one household, it may, at the time of the census, be vacant or occupied by one or more households. It may be noted that the terms dwelling, dwelling unit, dwelling house, residential dwelling unit, family dwelling, house, *logement, vivienda, unidad de vivienda* and so forth have been used indiscriminately to refer to housing units of any type. The referent of the term "dwelling" is here limited to a housing unit located in a permanent building and designed for occupancy by one household.

2.424.   A permanent building is understood to be a structure not intended to be moved and that may be expected to maintain its stability for 15 years or more, depending on the way countries define durability. It is recognized that the criterion of permanency or durability is difficult for the census enumerators to apply and that its adaptation to local conditions would require considerable study and experimentation by the national offices with respect to the significance of materials and methods of construction. In some cases, it may be of greater significance nationally to apply the criteria of construction materials and methods of construction directly in order to establish whether or not the building containing the housing unit is of permanent construction, rather than to translate these criteria into a time period.

1.1.1   *Conventional dwelling—has all basic facilities*

2.425.   A conventional dwelling that has all basic facilities refers to a unit that meets all the needs of the household within its confines, such as protection from elements, cooking, maintaining hygiene and so forth Thus, in addition to the four essential features of a conventional dwelling described in paragraph 2.422, all of the following facilities must be available for a dwelling to fall in this category:

(*a*)   Piped water within dwelling;

(*b*)   Toilet within dwelling;

(*c*)   Fixed bath or shower within dwelling;

(*d*)   Kitchen or other space for cooking within dwelling.

1.1.2   *Conventional dwelling—does not have all basic facilities*

2.426.   The conventional dwellings that fall in this category are dwellings that have the essential features of a conventional dwelling (see para. 2.422) and some, but not all, of the basic facilities described in paragraph 2.425. Thus, it is a permanent structure or a part of a permanent structure, and will be a room or a suite of rooms in a permanent building, but it is without some or all of the conventional dwelling facilities such as kitchen, fixed bath or shower, piped water or toilet. In a number of countries or areas, a certain proportion of the housing inventory comprises such dwellings, which possess some but not all the basic facilities.

2.427.   With increased urbanization, the need for building low-cost housing units within the city limit has been developed. This housing most frequently consists of buildings containing a number of separate rooms whose occupants share some or all facilities (bathing, toilet or cooking facilities). Those units do not meet all the criteria of a conventional dwelling with all basic facilities available within the dwelling, especially from the point of view of maintaining health standards and privacy. For example, these units are known as *casa de palomar* in Latin America.

1.2   *Other housing units*

1.2.1   *Semi-permanent housing unit*

2.428.   The term "semi-permanent housing unit" refers to a structure that, by the way it has been built, is not expected to maintain its durability for as long a period of time as a conventional dwelling, but has some of the main features and facilities of a conventional dwelling. As discussed earlier, durability needs to be specifically defined on the basis of national standards and practices. The number of these units in some countries and areas may be substantial. Semi-permanent housing is not to be confused with informal housing units.

2.429.   For example, in some countries "core" or "nuclear" dwellings around which a dwelling will eventually be constructed are provided as part of the housing programmes. In others, a significant proportion of the housing inventory is composed of dwellings that are constructed of locally available raw materials and may be less durable than conventional dwellings.

2.430.   Many countries with insufficient resources to meet their housing needs have attempted to alleviate the housing conditions of the population living in squatter areas by providing core or nuclear dwellings. Under these programmes, the households move their improvised shacks from the squatter area to a new location, the idea being that gradually, and generally with government assistance, the households with core or nuclear dwellings will keep adding to the nucleus until they can abandon their shacks entirely.

2.431.   A core dwelling is sometimes only a sanitary unit containing bathing and toilet facilities, to which may be added, in subsequent phases, the other elements that will finally make up the completed dwelling. Such units do not fall within the definition of a conventional dwelling. However, although the household obviously continues to occupy its original shelter (which would probably be classified as an "improvised housing unit"), its housing situation is a vast improvement over that of households remaining in the squatter areas and the provision of the cores is a significant step towards the alleviation of housing shortages.

2.432.   The problem is thus one of reflecting in the statistics the improvements brought about by programmes such as those described above without distorting the data that refer to fully constructed conventional dwellings. It is recommended, therefore, that core dwellings should be counted as dwellings in the census if at least one room[100] in addition to the sanitary facilities, is completed, and also that those dwellings that have not reached this stage of completion should be recorded as cores. Arrangements should be made so that the facilities available in the core can be related during data processing to the households for whose use they have been provided.

[100] For the definition of "room", see paragraph 2.472.

2.433.   In still other countries and areas, the population has developed, over time, a traditional and typical type of housing unit that does not have all the characteristics of conventional dwellings but is considered somewhat suitable from the point of view of climate and tradition. This is especially the case in many tropical and subtropical rural areas where housing units have been constructed or built with locally available raw materials such as bamboo, palm, straw or any similar materials. Such units often have mud walls, thatched roofs and so forth, and may be expected to last only for a limited time (from a few months to several years), although occasionally they may last for longer periods. This category is intended to cover housing units that are typical and traditional in many tropical rural areas. Such units may be known, for example, as cabins, *ranchos* or *bohíos* (Latin America), *barastis* (Bahrain), or *bahay kubo* (the Philippines).

1.2.2   *Mobile housing units*

2.434.   A mobile housing unit is any type of living accommodation that has been produced to be transported (such as a tent) or is a moving unit (such as a ship, boat, barge, vessel, railroad car, caravan, trailer, yacht and so on) occupied as living quarters at the time of the census. Trailers and tents used as permanent living quarters are of special interest.

2.435. Although mobile housing units are significantly different from other housing units in that they can be readily moved or transported, mobility in itself is not necessarily an indictor of low quality. For the assessment of housing conditions in countries with a substantial number of mobile units, it may be useful to classify them further, as tents, wagons, boats, trailers, and so forth.

1.2.3 Informal housing units

2.436. The term "informal housing unit" refers to those units that do not have many of the features of a conventional dwelling and are generally characterized as unfit for human habitation, but that are used for that purpose at the time of the census. Therefore, it is neither a permanent structure nor one equipped with any of the essential facilities. Depending on national circumstances, countries should develop detailed instructions to distinguish between informal and semi-temporary housing units.

2.437. Informal housing units comprise three subgroups, namely, "improvised housing units", "housing units in permanent buildings not intended for human habitation" and "other informal housing units". These units are characterized by the fact that they are either makeshift shelters constructed of waste materials and generally considered unfit for habitation (squatters' huts, for example) or places that are not intended for human habitation although in use for that purpose at the time of the census (barns, warehouses, natural shelters and so on). Under almost all circumstances, such places of abode represent unacceptable housing and they may be usefully grouped together in order to analyse the housing conditions of the population and to estimate housing needs. Each subgroup is defined below.

1.2.3.1 Improvised housing units

2.438. An improvised housing unit is an independent, makeshift shelter or structure, built of waste materials and without a predetermined plan for the purpose of habitation by one household, which is being used as living quarters at the time of the census. Included in this category are areas of squatters' huts, *poblaciones callampas* (Chile), *hongos* (Peru), *favelas* (Brazil), *sarifas* (Iraq), *jhuggis* (India and Pakistan), *gubuks* (Indonesia), *gecekondula* (Turkey), *barong barong* (the Philippines) and any similar premises arranged and used as living quarters, though they may not comply with generally accepted standards for habitation, and not having many of the characteristics of conventional dwellings. This type of housing unit is usually found in urban and suburban areas, particularly at the peripheries of the principal cities.

2.439. There is a wide variation in the procedures and criteria used in classifying these units. There are many borderline cases, and countries will need to make decisions and issue detailed instruction on how to enumerate and classify improvised housing units.

1.2.3.2 Housing units in permanent buildings not intended for human habitation

2.440. Included in this category are housing units (in permanent buildings) that have not been built, constructed, converted or arranged for human habitation but that are actually in use as living quarters at the time of the census. These include housing units in stables, barns, mills, garages, warehouses, offices, booths and so forth.

2.441.   This category also may cover units and their occupants in buildings initially built for human habitation but later abandoned with all services cut because of deterioration. These dilapidated buildings can be found, especially in large cities, still standing, although marked for demolition. They should be included in this category if inhabited.

2.442.   Premises that have been converted for human habitation, although not initially designed or constructed for this purpose, should not be included in this category.

1.2.3.3   *Other informal housing units*

2.443.   This category refers to living quarters that are not intended for human habitation or located in permanent buildings but that are nevertheless being used as living quarters at the time of the census. Caves and other natural shelters fall within this category.

2   *Collective living quarters*

2.444.   **Collective living quarters** include structurally separate and independent places of abode intended for habitation by large groups of individuals or several households and occupied at the time of the census. Such quarters usually have certain common facilities, such as cooking and toilet installations, baths, lounge rooms or dormitories, which are shared by the occupants. They may be further classified into hotels, rooming houses and other lodging houses, institutions and camps.

2.445.   Housing units on the grounds or within the building housing an institution, camp, hotel and so forth should be separately identified and counted as housing units.

2.446.   The criteria established for the identification of collective living quarters are not always easy to apply and it is sometimes difficult for an enumerator to decide whether living quarters should be classified as a housing unit or not. This is particularly true in the case of a building occupied by a number of households. Enumerators should be given clear instructions as to when the premises occupied by a group of people living together are to be considered a housing unit and when collective living quarters.

2.1   *Hotels, rooming houses and other lodging houses*

2.447.   This group comprises permanent structures that provide lodging on a fee basis and in which the number of borders or lodgers exceed five. Hotels, motels, inns, boarding houses, pensions, lodging houses and so forth fall within this category.

2.2   *Institutions*

2.448.   This group covers any set of premises in a permanent structure or structures designed to house (usually large) groups of persons who are bound by either a common public objective or a common personal interest. Such sets of living quarters usually have certain common facilities shared by the occupants (baths, lounges, dormitories and so forth). Hospitals, military barracks, boarding schools, convents, prisons and so forth fall within this category (see the categories in para. 2.415).

2.449.   It may be useful, depending on national needs, to require that an institution be used as the principle usual residence of at least one person at the time of the census.

2.3 Camps

2.450.   Camps are sets of premises originally intended for the temporary accommodation of persons with common activities or interests. Included in this category are military camps, refugee camps and camps established for the housing of workers in mining, agriculture, public works or other types of enterprises.

2.4 Other

2.451.   This is a residual category for collective living quarters which may not conform to the definitions of those included in groups 2.1 through 2.3. It should be used only when the number of units in question is small. Where the number is substantial, additional groups of living quarters having characteristics that are similar and of significance for an appraisal of housing conditions should be established.

2.452.   In some countries, it seems that certain types of multi-household living quarters have emerged in response to the particular needs of the population and that the characteristics of these quarters enable them to be readily identified by an enumerator. It may be useful in these countries to provide a separate subgroup for any such special types. An example of such a subgroup, multi-household living quarters (living quarters intended for habitation by more than one household), includes buildings and enclosures intended for communal habitation by several households.

2.453.   In this example, structurally separate and independent sets of living quarters for occupancy by individual households are not provided. This category would include housing arrangements peculiar to certain countries, such as the Malaysian long house (*sarawak*) and the *kibbutz* (Israel).

2.454.   It should be noted that the types of living quarters to be included in this category are those intended for communal habitation by several households, that is to say, constructed or converted for this purpose. Housing units intended for occupancy by one household, but those at the time of the census are occupied by several households, are not to be included as collective living quarters because this obscures the identification of households doubling up in dwellings (an important element in estimating housing needs). It is suggested that, in carrying out the census, a strict distinction be maintained between a housing unit occupied by more than one household and living quarters constructed or converted for communal habitation by several households.

2.   Location of living quarters (core topic)

Recommended tabulations: H1-R–H18-R

2.455.   A great deal of information relevant to the location of living quarters is contained under the definition of "locality" and "urban and rural". It is important for those concerned with carrying out housing censuses to study this information, because the geographical concepts used in carrying out a housing census to describe the location of living quarters are extremely important both for the execution of the census and for the subsequent tabulation of the census results. When the housing census is combined with, or closely related to, a population census, these concepts need to be carefully considered and coordinated so that the geographical areas recognized in carrying out the two censuses are of optimum value for both operations.

2.456.   Information on location should be collected in sufficient detail to enable tabulations to be made for the smallest geographical subdivisions required by the tabulation plan. To satisfy the requirements of the geographical classifications recommended in the tabulations in this publication, information is needed on whether the living quarters are located in an urban or rural area, the major civil division, the minor civil division and, for living quarters located in principal localities, the name of the locality.

2.457.   Where a permanent system of house or building numbers does not already exist, it is essential for the census to establish a numbering system so that the location of each set of living quarters can be adequately described. Similarly, in cases where streets do not have names or numbers properly displayed, such identification should be provided as one of the pre-census operations. Adequate identification provides the basis for the preparation of census control lists (see also "living quarters and household listing" in paras. 1.173–1.176); it is required in order to monitor and control the enumeration, and to identify living quarters for possible call-backs and post-enumeration evaluation surveys as well as for other post-censal inquiries that use the census as a sampling frame or other point of departure. Ideally, each building or other inhabited structure should be provided with a number, as should each set of living quarters within buildings or structures. In preparing a census control listing, it is the practice to identify further each household within the living quarters.

2.458.   Living quarters that are not located in areas with a conventional pattern of streets, such as those in squatter areas or in some places not intended for habitation, may require special identification. Since it may not be possible to describe the location of these units in terms of a formal address, it may be necessary to describe them in terms of their proximity to natural or created landmarks of various kinds or in relation to buildings that are located in areas where a formal address is possible.

2.459.   The various geographical designations that together define the location of living quarters are discussed below.

(a)   Address

2.460.   Information that describes the place where the living quarters are to be found and distinguishes them from other living quarters in the same locality falls within this category. As a rule, the information includes the name or number of the street and the number of the living quarters; in the case of apartments, the building number and the apartment number are required.

(b)   Locality

2.461.   For the definition of "locality", see paragraphs 2.78–2.80 of the current revision of the *Principles and Recommendations for Population and Housing Censuses*.

(c)   Urban and rural

2.462.   For the definition of "urban and rural", see paragraphs 2.81–2.84 of the current revision of the *Principles and Recommendations for Population and Housing Censuses*.

3.   Occupancy status (core topic)

Recommended tabulation: H4-R

2.463.   Information should be obtained for each conventional dwelling to show whether the dwelling is occupied or vacant at the time of the census. For vacant units intended for year-round occupancy, the type of vacancy (for rent, for sale, and so forth) should be reported. Occupancy status applies only to conventional dwellings, since all other types of living quarters are required by definition to be occupied in order to fall within the scope of the census.

2.464.　　The enumeration of vacant conventional dwellings is likely to pose difficult problems, but at least a total count should be made for purposes of controlling the enumeration. The type of vacancy is frequently indicated by "for sale" or "for rent" signs posted on the dwelling. Although it may not be feasible to investigate all of the topics included in the census for vacant units, as much information as possible should be collected, including information on whether the living quarters are vacant seasonally or non-seasonally.

2.465.　　Vacant units intended for seasonal occupancy may represent a substantial proportion of the housing inventory in resort areas and in areas where large numbers of seasonal workers are employed. The separate identification of such a category may be necessary for the correct interpretation of the overall vacancy rate, as well as for an evaluation of the housing situation in the area concerned. Vacant units may be further distinguished according to the type of occupancy for which they are intended, for example, as holiday home, seasonal workers' quarters and so forth.

2.466.　　Whether living quarters whose occupants are temporarily absent or temporarily present should be recorded as occupied or vacant will need to be considered in relation to whether a de jure or de facto population census is being carried out. In either case, it would seem useful to distinguish as far as possible conventional dwellings that are used as a second residence. This is particularly important if the second residence has markedly different characteristics from the primary residence, as is the case, for example, when agricultural households move during certain seasons of the year from their permanent living quarters in a village to rudimentary structures located on agricultural holdings. The recommended classification of occupancy status for conventional dwellings is as follows:

1　Occupied
2　Vacant
　　2.1　Seasonally vacant
　　　　2.1.1　Holiday homes
　　　　2.1.2　Seasonal workers' quarters
　　　　2.1.3　Other
　　2.2　Non-seasonally vacant
　　　　2.2.1　Secondary residences
　　　　2.2.2　For rent
　　　　2.2.3　For sale
　　　　2.2.4　For demolition
　　　　2.2.5　Other

4.　Ownership—type of (core topic)

Recommended tabulation:　H5-R

2.467.　　This topic refers to the type of ownership of the housing unit itself and not of that of the land on which it stands. Type of ownership should not be confused with tenure. Information should be obtained to show:

(*a*)　Whether the housing unit is owned by the public sector (central government, local government, public corporations);

(*b*)　Whether the housing unit is privately owned (by households, private corporations, cooperatives, housing associations and so on). The question is sometimes expanded to show whether the housing units are fully paid for, being purchased in installments or mortgaged. The classification of housing units by type of ownership is as follows:

1   Owner-occupied

2   Non owner-occupied

   2.1   Publicly owned

   2.2   Privately owned

   2.3   Communally owned

   2.4   Cooperatively owned

   2.5   Other

2.468.   Housing units are defined as owner-occupied if used wholly or partly for own occupation by the owner. In principle, if a housing unit is being purchased in instalments or mortgaged according to national legal systems and practices, it should be enumerated as being owned. Instructions should also cover other arrangements, such as housing units in cooperatives, housing associations and so forth.

2.469.   The information on ownership may be classified, as a minimum, into two main groups, namely "private ownership" and "other ownership". Depending upon the prevalence of various types of ownership and their significance with respect to housing conditions and the formulation of housing programmes, it may be useful to dissect the category "other ownership" into the relevant examples of the subgroups shown. The categories used should be consistent with those employed in the system of national accounts of the country concerned and in accordance with the recommendations contained in the *System of National Accounts, 1993.*[101]

[101] United Nations publication, Sales No. E.94.XVII.4.

2.470.   It has been observed that the collection of information on type of ownership in a general census may be hampered by the fact that the occupants might not know who the owner of the property is and that the owners or their representatives may be situated outside the enumeration zone. Furthermore, there are numerous cases of borderline and mixed ownership, which make the topic difficult for nationwide enumeration. This is one of the topics for which more accurate information might be obtained through a housing survey.

2.471.   In countries where there is a substantial amount of employer-issued housing, it would be useful to include the subcategories "issued by the employer" and "not issued by the employer" under the category "privately owned" (or publicly owned where the employer is a public sector entity). It is important that such information be known from the point of view of assessing the impact of job loss, in order to gauge the magnitude of the population whose loss of a job would include loss of housing as well.

5.   Rooms—number of (core topic)

Recommended tabulation: H6-R

2.472.   A **room** is defined as a space in a housing unit or other living quarters enclosed by walls reaching from the floor to the ceiling or roof covering, or to a height of at least two meters, of an area large enough to hold a bed for an adult, that is, at least four square meters. The total number of types of rooms therefore includes bedrooms, dining rooms, living rooms, studies, habitable attics, servants' rooms, kitchens, rooms used for professional or business purposes, and other separate spaces used or intended for dwelling purposes, so long as they meet the criteria concerning walls and floor space. Passageways, verandas, lobbies, bathrooms and toilet rooms should not be counted as rooms, even if they meet the criteria. Separate information may be collected for national purposes on spaces of less than four square meters that conform in other respects to the definition of "room" if it is considered that their number warrants such a procedure.

2.473.   Rooms used exclusively for business or professional purposes should be counted separately, as it is desirable to include them when calculating the number of rooms in a dwelling but to exclude them when calculating the number of persons per room. This procedure allows density levels to be studied according to the number of rooms available for living purposes in relation to the number of occupants. In any event, each country should indicate the procedure that has been followed.

2.474.   It is recommended that kitchens be included in the count of rooms provided they meet the criteria concerning walls and floor space. Kitchens or kitchenettes that have an area smaller than four square meters or that have other characteristics that disqualify them should be excluded. For national purposes, countries may wish to identify and count kitchens within a separate group that may be analysed with respect to size and utilization, and to consider separately those used exclusively for cooking.

6.   Bedrooms—number of

2.475.   In addition to enumerating the number of rooms, a number of national censuses collect information on the number of bedrooms in a housing unit, which is the unit of enumeration for this topic. A **bedroom** is defined as a room equipped with a bed and used for night rest.

7.   Useful floor space

2.476.   This topic refers to the useful floor space in housing units, that is to say, the floor space measured inside the outer walls of housing units, excluding non-habitable cellars and attics. In multiple-dwelling buildings, all common spaces should be excluded. The approach for housing units and collective living quarters should differ.

2.477.   For collective living quarters, it would be more useful to collect information on the useful floor space per occupant of the set of collective living quarters. Data should be derived by dividing the total useful floor space by the number of occupants who are living in the space.

2.478.   Collecting information on the floor space available to occupants of housing units may prove to be difficult; occupants often may not know the exact or even the approximate area of the housing unit they occupy; training enumerators to calculate the floor space would be complicated and costly, and would result in inaccuracies. In this context, and taking into account the importance of the information concerned, countries should take into consideration developing detailed instructions on proper procedures for assessing these data (for example, a request for information on floor space from the official documents available to the occupants, such as the rental agreement and the title, that are supposed to include such information).

8.   Water supply system (core topic)

Recommended tabulation: H7-R

2.479.   Basic information to be obtained in the census is whether housing units have or do not have a piped water installation, in other words, whether or not water is provided to the housing unit by pipes from a community-wide system or a private installation, such as a pressure tank or pump. The unit of enumeration for this topic is a housing unit. It is also necessary to indicate whether the unit has tap water inside or, if not, whether it is within a certain distance from the door. The recommended distance is 200 metres, assuming that access to piped water within that distance allows occupants of the housing unit to obtain water for household needs without being subjected to extreme efforts. Besides the location of the tap water relative to the housing unit, the source of water available to households is also of interest. Therefore, the recommended classification of housing unit by water supply system is as follows:

1 Piped water inside the unit
    1.1 From the community scheme
    1.2 From an individual source
2 Piped water outside the unit but within 200 metres
    2.1 From the community scheme
        2.1.1 For exclusive use
        2.1.2 Shared
    2.2 From an individual source
        2.2.1 For exclusive use
        2.2.2 Shared
3 Other (see category 3 of the classification in para. 2.484 for more details)

2.480.   A community scheme is one that is subject to inspection and control by public authorities. Such schemes are generally operated by a public body but, in some cases, they are operated by a cooperative or private enterprise.

2.481.   For collective living quarters, it may be useful to collect information on the availability of piped water for the use of occupants. Such living quarters are usually equipped with multi-facilities for the use of large groups, and information on the water supply system in relation to the number of occupants would be significant in respect of analysing housing conditions. The water supply system in collective living quarters constitutes an additional topic.

2.482.   The most significant information from a health point of view is whether the living quarters have piped water within the premises. However, a category may be added to distinguish cases where the piped water supply is not within the living quarters but rather within the building in which the living quarters are situated. It may also be useful to collect information that would show whether the water supply is for the sole use of the occupants of the living quarters being enumerated or whether it is for the use of the occupants of several sets of living quarters, as indicated in the above classification at the three-digit level. Where there is a large proportion of housing units with no piped water, this category may be expanded to specify sources commonly used in a country. Additional information may be sought on the availability of hot as well as cold water and on the kind of equipment used for heating water.

9.   Drinking water—main source of (core topic)

Recommended tabulation: H8-R

2.483.   Having enough water for drinking and personal hygiene is essential, but quantity by itself is not sufficient. The quality of the water is also a crucial health issue. Consequently, one of the targets of the Millennium Development Goals is "sustainable access to safe drinking water and basic sanitation", assessed in part by having access to an improved water supply source. Sustainable access to an improved water source as defined in the guidelines for monitoring the Millennium Development Goals refers to the following types of water supply: piped water, public tap, borehole, protected dug well, protected spring, properly collected rainwater and bottled water.[102] Improved water sources do not include vendor-provided water, tanker truck water, unprotected wells and springs, or surface water (river, stream, dam, lake, pond, canal, and irrigation channel).

[102] Bottled water is considered an "improved" source of drinking water only where there is a secondary source of improved water for other uses such as personal hygiene and cooking. Source: *Water for life: making it happen* (World Health Organization and UNICEF, 2005).

2.484. Countries are encouraged to collect the information on the main source of drinking water for the household, particularly where there is considerable difference between sources of water for general household use and for drinking. For those countries wishing to collect this information, the following categories of main source of drinking water are recommended:

1 Piped water inside the unit
    1.1   From the community scheme
    1.2   From an individual source
2 Piped water outside the unit but within 200 metres
    2.1   From the community scheme
        2.1.1   For exclusive use
        2.1.2   Shared
    2.2   From an individual source
        2.2.1   For exclusive use
        2.2.2   Shared
3 Other
    3.1   Borehole
    3.2   Protected dug well
    3.3   Protected spring
    3.4   Rainwater collection tank
    3.5   Vendor-provided water
    3.6   Bottled water
    3.7   Tanker trucks
    3.8   Unprotected dug well/spring/river/stream/lake/pond/dam

10. Toilet—type of (core topic)[103]

Recommended tabulation: H9-R

2.485. A **toilet** may be defined as an installation for the disposal of human excreta. A flush toilet is an installation provided with piped water that permits humans to discharge their wastes and from which the wastes are flushed by water. The unit of enumeration for this topic is a housing unit.

2.486. For housing units reported as having a toilet, additional information may be sought to determine whether the toilet is used exclusively by the occupants of the living quarters being enumerated or whether it is shared with the occupants of other living quarters. For living quarters reported as having no toilet, it would be useful to know whether the occupants have the use of a communal facility and the type of facility, whether they have the use of the toilet of other living quarters and the type, or whether there is no toilet of any kind available for the use of the occupants.

2.487. Some countries have found it useful to expand the classification for non-flush toilets so as to distinguish certain types that are widely used and indicate a certain level of sanitation. The recommended classification of housing unit by toilet facilities is as follows:

1 With toilet within housing unit
    1.1   Flush/pour flush[104] toilet
    1.2   Other
2 With toilet outside housing unit

[103] Also necessary to distinguish between conventional dwellings with all main facilities and other conventional dwellings.

[104] A pour flush toilet uses a water seal, but unlike a flush toilet, a pour flush toilet uses water poured by hand for flushing (no cistern is used).

[105] A ventilated improved pit latrine (VIP) is a dry pit latrine that uses a hole in the ground to collect the excreta and a squatting slab or platform that is firmly supported on all sides, easy to clean and raised above the surrounding ground level to prevent surface water from entering the pit. The platform has a squatting hole, or is fitted with a seat.

2.1   For exclusive use

    2.1.1   Flush/pour flush toilet

    2.1.2   Ventilated improved pit latrine[105]

    2.1.3   Pit latrine without ventilation with covering

    2.1.4   Holes or dug pits with temporary coverings or without shelter

    2.1.5   Other

2.2   Shared

    2.2.1   Flush/pour flush toilet

    2.2.2   Ventilated improved pit latrine

    2.2.3   Pit latrine without ventilation with covering

    2.2.4   Holes or dug pits with temporary coverings or without shelter

    2.2.5   Other

3   No toilet available

    3.1   Service or bucket facility (excreta manually removed)

    3.2   Use of natural environment, for example, bush, river, stream, and so forth

2.488.   For housing units occupied by more than a certain number of households (more than two, for example) and for collective living quarters, particularly those of the multi- household and hotel/boarding-house type, it may be useful to gather information on the number and type of toilets available to the occupants. Living quarters of this type are usually equipped with multi-facilities for the use of large groups, and information on the number and type of toilets in relation to the number of occupants would be significant in terms of analysing housing conditions. The availability of toilets for collective living quarters represents an additional topic.

11.   Sewage disposal (core topic)

Recommended tabulation: H9-R

2.489.   Information on toilets should be combined with the sewage disposal system to which they are connected in order to determine the adequacy of sanitation facilities of the housing unit. To be considered adequate sanitation, toilets or latrines have to be connected to non-clogged sewage disposal systems. The information on housing units by type of sewage disposal system may be classified as follows:

1   Empties into a piped system connected to a public sewage disposal plant

2   Empties into a piped system connected to an individual sewage disposal system (septic tank, cesspool)

3   Other—toilet empties into an open ditch, a pit, a river, the sea, and so forth

4   No disposal system

[106] Also necessary to distinguish between conventional dwellings with all main facilities and other conventional dwellings.

12.   Bathing facilities (core topic)[106]

Recommended tabulation: H10-R

2.490.   Information should be obtained on whether or not there is a fixed bath or shower installation within the premises of each set of housing units. The unit of enumeration for this topic is a housing unit. Additional information may be collected to show whether or not the facilities are for the exclusive use of the occupants of the living quarters and where there is a supply of hot water for bathing purposes or cold water only. In some areas of the world the distinction proposed above may not be the most appropriate for national needs. It may be important, for example, to distinguish in terms of availability among a separate room for bathing in the living quarters, a separate room for bathing in the building, an open cubicle for bathing in the building and a public bathhouse. The recommended classification of housing units by availability and type of bathing facilities is as follows:

1 With fixed bath or shower within housing unit
2 Without fixed bath or shower within housing unit
    2.1 Fixed bath or shower available outside housing unit
        2.1.1 For exclusive use
        2.1.2 Shared
    2.2 No fixed bath or shower available

2.491. For housing units occupied by more than a certain number of households (more than two, for example) and for collective living quarters, particularly those of the multi- household and hotel/boarding-house type, it may be useful to gather information on the number of fixed baths or showers available to the occupants. Living quarters of this type are usually equipped with multi-facilities for the use of large groups, and information on the number of fixed baths or showers in relation to the number of occupants would be significant in terms of analysing housing conditions. The number of fixed baths or showers in collective living quarters would represent an additional topic.

13. Kitchen—availability of (core topic)[107]

[107] Ibid.

Recommended tabulation: H11-R

2.492. Information should be obtained on whether the housing unit has a kitchen, whether some other space is set aside for cooking, such as a kitchenette, or whether there is no special place set aside for cooking. The unit of enumeration for this topic is a housing unit.

2.493. A **kitchen** is defined as a space that conforms in all respects to the criteria for a room, and is equipped for the preparation of the principal meals of the day and intended primarily for that purpose.

2.494. Any other space reserved for cooking, such as a kitchenette, will fall short in respect of possessing the attributes of a room, although it may be equipped for the preparation of the principal meals of the day and is intended primarily for that purpose. The collection of data on the availability of a kitchen may provide a convenient opportunity to gather information on the kind of equipment that is used for cooking, for example, a stove, hotplate, or open fire, and on the availability of a kitchen sink and a space for food storage so as to prevent spoilage. The recommended classification of housing units by availability of a kitchen or other space reserved for cooking is as follows:

1 With kitchen within housing unit
    1.1 For exclusive use
    1.2 Shared
2 With other space for cooking within housing unit, such as kitchenette
    2.1 For exclusive use
    2.2 Shared
3 Without kitchen or other space for cooking within housing unit
    3.1 Kitchen or other space for cooking available outside housing unit
        3.1.1 For exclusive use
        3.1.2 Shared
    3.2 No kitchen or other space for cooking available

2.495. For housing units occupied by more than a certain number of households (more than two, for example) and for collective living quarters, particularly those of the multi-household and hotel/boarding-house type, it may be useful to gather information on the number of kitchens available for the occupants. Living quarters of this type are usually equipped with multi-facilities for the use of large groups, and information on the number of kitchens or kitchenettes in relation to the number of occupants would be significant in terms of analysing housing conditions. It represents an additional topic.

14. Fuel used for cooking (core topic)

Recommended tabulation: *H11-R*

2.496. The proportion of households using solid fuels is one of the indicators for monitoring the Millennium Development Goals. There are important linkages between household solid fuel use, indoor air pollution, deforestation and soil erosion and greenhouse gas emissions. The type of fuel and participation in cooking tasks are important predictors of exposure to indoor air pollution. It is thus recommended to collect information on the fuel used for cooking by each housing unit. Fuel used for cooking refers to the fuel used predominantly for preparation of principal meals. If two fuels (for example, electricity and gas) are used, the one used most often should be enumerated. The classification of fuels used for cooking depends on national circumstances and may include electricity, gas, oil, coal, firewood, animal dung and so forth. It would also be useful to collect this information for collective living quarters as well, especially if the number of sets of collective living quarters in the country is significant. The classification of fuel used for cooking is as follows:

1   Gas
2   Electricity
3   Liquefied petroleum gas (LPG)
4   Kerosene/paraffin (petroleum-based)
5   Oil (including vegetable oils used as fuel)
6   Coal
7   Firewood
8   Charcoal
9   Animal dung
10   Crop residues (for example, cereal straw from maize, wheat, paddy rice, rice hulls, coconut husks, groundnut shells)
11   Other

15. Lighting and/or electricity—type of (core topic)

Recommended tabulation: *H12-R*

2.497. Information should be collected on the type of lighting in the housing unit, such as electricity, gas, oil lamp and so forth. If the source of energy for lighting is electricity, some countries may wish to collect information showing whether the electricity mainly comes from a community supply, private generating plant or some other source (industrial plant, mine and so on). In addition to the type of lighting, countries may assess the information on the availability of electricity for purposes other than lighting (such as cooking, heating water, heating the premises and so forth). If housing conditions in the country allow this information to be derived from the type of lighting, there would be no need for additional inquiry.

2.498.   For collective living quarters, it may be useful to collect information on availability of electricity to the occupants. Such living quarters are usually equipped with multi-facilities for the use of large groups, and information on electricity would be significant in terms of analysing housing conditions. The availability of electricity in collective living quarters is defined as an additional topic.

16. Solid waste disposal—main type of (core topic)

Recommended tabulation: H13-R

2.499.   Securing sustainable development and, in this context, the usual manner of treatment of solid waste (garbage) generated by the household, prompted the incorporation of this topic in a number of national housing censuses.

2.500.   This topic refers to the usual manner of collection and disposal of solid waste/garbage generated by occupants of the housing unit. The unit of enumeration is a housing unit. The classification of housing units by type of solid waste disposal is according to the following guidelines:

1   Solid waste collected on a regular basis by authorized collectors
2   Solid waste collected on an irregular basis by authorized collectors
3   Solid waste collected by self-appointed collectors
4   Occupants dispose of solid waste in a local dump supervised by authorities
5   Occupants dispose of solid waste in a local dump not supervised by authorities
6   Occupants burn solid waste
7   Occupants bury solid waste
8   Occupants dispose solid waste into river/sea/creek/pond
9   Occupants compost solid waste
10   Other arrangement

17.   Heating—type and energy used for

2.501.   This topic refers to the type of heating of housing units and the energy used for that purpose. The units of enumeration are all housing units. This topic is irrelevant for a number of countries where, owing to their geographical position and climate, there is no need to provide heating. Type of heating refers to the kind of system used to provide heating for most of the space: it may be central heating serving all the sets of living quarters or serving a set of living quarters, or it may not be central in which case the heating will be provided separately within the living quarters by a stove, fireplace or some other heating body. As for the energy used for heating, it is closely related to the type of heating and refers to the predominant source of energy, such as solid fuels (coal, lignite and products of coal and lignite, wood), oils, gaseous fuels (natural or liquefied gas), electricity and so forth.

18.   Hot water—availability of

2.502.   This topic refers to the availability of hot water in housing units. Hot water denotes water heated to a certain temperature and conducted through pipes and tap to occupants. The information collected may indicate whether there is hot water available within the housing units, or outside the living quarters for exclusive or shared use, or not at all.

19. Piped gas—availability of

2.503.   This topic refers to whether piped gas is available in the housing unit or not. Piped gas is usually defined as natural or manufactured gas that is distributed by pipeline and whose consumption is recorded. This topic may be irrelevant for a number of countries where there is either a lack of sources of natural gas or no developed pipeline system.

20. Use of housing unit

2.504.   **Use of housing unit** refers to whether the housing unit is being used wholly for habitation (residential) purposes or not. The housing unit can be used for habitation and for commercial, manufacturing or some other purposes. In a number of countries, houses are used simultaneously for more than one purpose. For example, the lower floor is used as a store or workshop, and the upper floors for habitation. The recommended classification of use of housing unit is as follows:

1 Used solely for habitation

2 Used for habitation and economic activity

21.   Occupancy by one or more households (core topic)

Recommended tabulation: H14-R

2.505.   For the definitions of "household", "household head" and "persons living in institutions", see paragraphs 2.107–2.132 and 1.454–1.455 in the current revision of the *Principles and Recommendations for Population and Housing Censuses.*

2.506.   For the purpose of a housing census, each household must be identified separately. With respect to housing programmes, the use of the separate concepts of household and living quarters in carrying out housing censuses permits the identification of the persons or groups of persons in need of their own dwellings. If the household is defined as a group of persons occupying a set of living quarters, the number of households in the living quarters and the number of sets of occupied living quarters will always be equal and there will be no apparent housing need as reflected by doubled-up households requiring separate sets of living quarters. If living quarters are defined as the space occupied by a household, the number of households in living quarters will again be equal to the number of sets of living quarters, with the added disadvantage that there will be no record of the number of structurally separate living quarters.

2.507.   Occupancy by more than one household is a useful topic for assessing the current housing situation and measuring the need for housing. For countries relying on the housekeeping concept, the number of households will yield this information. For countries relying on the dwelling unit concept of households, information on the type of households occupying a housing unit is needed to supplement this since the household is equivalent to the dwelling unit.

2.508.   In countries where it is traditional to count families, the family in the broad sense of the term may be adopted as an additional unit of enumeration; in the great majority of cases the composition of this unit will coincide with that of the household.

2.509.   A household should be defined in the same way for housing census purposes as for population censuses.

22. Occupants—number of (core topic)

Recommended tabulations:　H3-R and H6-R

2.510.　Each person usually resident in a housing unit or set of collective living quarters should be counted as an occupant. Therefore, the units of enumeration for this topic are living quarters. However, since housing censuses are usually carried out simultaneously with population censuses, the applicability of this definition depends upon whether the information collected and recorded for each person in the population census indicates where he or she was on the day of the census or whether it refers to the usual residence (see paras. 2.46-2.56). Care should be exercised in distinguishing persons occupying mobile units, such as boats, caravans and trailers, as living quarters from persons using these units as a means of transportation.

23. Building—type of (core topic)

Recommended tabulation:　H15-R

(a) Definition of building

2.511.　A **building** is any independent free-standing structure comprising one or more rooms[108] or other spaces, covered by a roof and usually enclosed within external walls or dividing walls[109] that extend from the foundations to the roof. However, in tropical areas, a building may consist of a roof with supports only, that is to say, without constructed walls; in some cases, a roofless structure consisting of a space enclosed by walls may be considered a "building" (see also "compound" in para. 2.518).

2.512.　A building may be used or intended for residential, commercial or industrial purposes or for the provision of services. It may therefore be a factory, shop, detached dwelling, apartment building, warehouse, garage, barn and so forth. In some exceptional cases, facilities usually provided by a set of living quarters are located in two or more separate detached structures, as when a kitchen is in a separate structure. In the case of living quarters with detached rooms, these rooms should be considered separate buildings. A building may therefore contain several sets of living quarters, as is the case for an apartment building or duplex; it may be coextensive with a single detached set of living quarters; or it may be only part of a set of living quarters, as is the case, for example, for living quarters with detached rooms, which are clearly intended to be used as part of the living quarters.

2.513.　The concept of a building should be clearly defined and the instructions for the housing census should indicate whether all buildings are to be listed and enumerated or only those used in whole or in part for residential purposes. Instructions should also indicate whether buildings under construction are to be recorded and, if so, at what stage of completion they are to be considered eligible for inclusion. Buildings being demolished or awaiting demolition should normally be excluded.

(b) Classification of buildings by type

2.514.　The following classification by type is recommended for buildings in which some space is used for residential purposes.

  1　Buildings containing a single housing unit
  　　1.1　Detached
  　　1.2　Attached
  2　Buildings containing more than one housing unit

[108] For the definition of "room", see para. 2.472.

[109] The term "dividing walls" refers to the walls of adjoining buildings that have been so constructed as to be contiguous, for example, the dividing walls of "row" houses.

2.1   Up to 2 floors

2.2   From 3 to 4 floors

2.3   From 5 to 10 floors

2.3   Eleven floors or more

3   Buildings for persons living in institutions

4   All others

2.515.   It should be noted that, for the purpose of the housing census, the above classification refers to the building in which the sets of enumerated living quarters are located and that sets of living quarters, not buildings, will be tabulated according to the classification, since information concerning the building is required to describe the sets of living quarters within it.

2.516.   Category 1 provides separate subgroupings for "detached" and "attached" buildings because, although most single-unit buildings (suburban homes, villas, and so forth) are detached, in some countries a substantial number may be attached (row houses, for example) and in such cases it may be useful to identify these separately. According to the definition of building in paragraph 2.511 above, a group of, for example, three row houses that are attached is considered to be three separate buildings if their "external walls or dividing walls" extend from "the foundations to the roof". Buildings containing more than one housing unit (category 2) will usually be apartment buildings, but they may also be other types of buildings, for example, buildings that are structurally subdivided so as to contain more than one housing unit. Buildings under the latter category should be subdivided into the following: up to two floors, from 3 to 10 floors and 11 floors or more. Category 3, "Buildings for persons living in institutions", includes hospital buildings, prisons, military establishments, and so on. On the other hand, a structurally separate housing unit (a house or apartment intended for the occupancy of staff of the institution) or one that is either within a building of the institution or detached but within the grounds, belongs in category 1; if the housing unit is coextensive with a building, it belongs in category 2.

2.517.   In addition to the above, and for subsequent analysis of housing conditions, each country will find it useful to provide for separate identification of the special types of buildings that are characteristic of the country concerned. These can be classified as category 4.

(c)   Compound

2.518.   In some countries, it may be appropriate to use the "compound" as a unit of enumeration. In some areas of the world, housing units are traditionally located within compounds and the grouping of sets of housing units in this way has economic and social implications that need to be studied. A compound, in these circumstances, becomes a distinct unit of enumeration, at par with a housing unit. For purposes of international comparability, a compound should be classified according to the main features and facilities it displays and classified with housing units.

24.   Year or period of construction

2.519.   This topic refers to the age of the building in which the sets of living quarters are located. It is recommended that the exact year of construction be sought for buildings constructed during the intercensal period immediately preceding if it does not exceed 10 years. Where the intercensal period exceeds 10 years or where no previous census has been carried out, the exact year of construction should be sought for buildings constructed during the preceding 10 years. For buildings constructed before that time, the information should be collected in terms of periods that will provide a useful means of assessing the age of the housing stock. Difficulty may be experienced in collecting data on this topic because in some cases the occupants may not know the date of construction.

2.520.   The collection of data for single years during the intercensal period is seen as a method of checking construction statistics for deficient coverage and of more closely integrating the housing census with current housing statistics.

2.521.   The periods should be defined in terms of events that have some special significance in the country concerned; examples would be the period since the Second World War, the period between the First World War and the Second World War; the period before the earthquake, flood and so forth. Three age groups may be regarded as constituting a minimum classification. The total period covered by the age groups and the number of groups distinguished will depend upon the materials and methods of construction used in the country concerned and the number of years that buildings normally last.

2.522.   Where parts of buildings have been constructed at different time, the year or period of construction should refer to the major part. Where living quarters comprise more than one building (living quarters with detached rooms, for example), the age of the building that contains the major part of the living quarters should be recorded.

2.523.   In countries where a significant number of households construct their own living quarters (countries with large non-monetary sectors, for example), it may be useful to include an additional question that will distinguish the living quarters according to whether or not they were constructed by the household(s) occupying them. The information should refer only to living quarters constructed during the preceding intercensal or 10-year period, and it should be made clear in formulating the question that it refers to living quarters constructed mainly by households (with or without the help of other households in the community) and not to construction executed by enterprises on behalf of households.

25.   Dwellings in the building—number of

2.524.   This topic refers to the number of conventional dwellings in the building. This topic is applicable in cases where there is a possibility to have unique identifier for the building itself. If a census established such an identifier (building number, for example, linked to the address) then it would be possible to introduce this topic.

26.   Construction material of outer walls (core topic)

Recommended tabulations: H15-R and H16-R

2.525.   This topic refers to the construction material of external (outer) walls of the building in which the sets of living quarters are located. If the walls are constructed of more than one type of material, the predominant type of material should be reported. The types distinguished (brick, concrete, wood, adobe and so on) will depend upon the materials most frequently used in the country concerned and on their significance from the point of view of permanency of construction or assessment of durability.

2.526. In some countries, the material used for the construction of roofs or of floors may be of special significance for the assessment of durability and, in such cases, it may be necessary to collect information on this as well as on the material of the walls. Durability refers to the period of time for which the structure remains habitable, subject to regular maintenance. A durable structure is one expected to remain sound for a considerable period of time. Countries may wish to define the length of the period, for example, 15 or 20 years. Durability does not depend solely on the materials used in construction, since it is also affected by the way the building was erected, that is to say, the consideration whether it was built according to construction standards and regulations. Recently, technological developments in treating traditional building materials, such as bamboo, have extended the durability of those materials for several decades. Construction material of outer walls may be considered an indicator of the building's durability. Therefore, in order to assess quality of the national housing stock, durability may be measured in terms of material used together with adherence to construction standards. Specific instructions for enumerators at the national level should be developed on the basis of national building construction practice.

2.527. While the material of construction is a useful addition to data collected on the type of living quarters, it should not be considered a substitute for the latter type of information. Wood, for example, may be the material of a poorly constructed squatter's hut or of a durable and well-constructed dwelling. In these cases, information on the type of unit adds significantly to the possibility of quality appraisal.

27. Construction material of floor, roof

2.528. In some cases the material used for the construction of roofs and floors may be of special interest and can be used to further assess the quality of dwellings in the building. This topic refers to the material used for roof and/or floor (although, depending on the specific needs of a country, it may refer to other parts of the building as well, such as the frame or the foundation). Only the predominant material is enumerated and, in the case of a roof, it may be tile, concrete, metal sheets, palm, straw, bamboo or similar vegetation material, mud, plastic sheets and so forth.

28. Elevator—availability of

2.529. This topic refers to the availability of an elevator (an enclosed platform raised and lowered to transport people and freight) in a multi-storey building (categories 2.2 and 2.3 of the classification of buildings). The information is collected on the availability of an elevator for most of the time, in other words, one that is operational for most of the time, subject to regular maintenance.

2.530. This topic should be looked upon as one indicating accessibility to the building or the housing unit, as this is of utmost importance especially for older persons and people with disabilities. The census can include other additional topics in regard to accessibility, such as ramp, steps, and so forth.

29. Farm building

2.531. A number of national censuses found it necessary to specify whether the enumerated building was a farm building or not. A farm building is one that is part of an agricultural holding and used for agricultural and/or housing purposes.

30. State of repair

2.532.   This topic refers to whether the building is in need of repair and to the kind of repair needed. This topic is applicable in cases where there is a possibility to have a unique identifier for the building itself. If a census established such an identifier (building number, for example, linked to the address) then it would be possible to introduce this topic. The classification of buildings according to the state of repair may include: repair not needed, in need of minor, moderate or serious repair and irreparable. Minor repairs refer mostly to the regular maintenance of the building and its components, such as repair of a cracked window. Moderate repairs refer to the correcting of moderate defects such as missing gutters on the roof, large areas of broken plaster, stairways with no secure handrails and so forth. Serious repairs are needed in the case of serious structural defects of the building, such as missing shingles or tiles on the roof, cracks and holes in the exterior walls, missing stairways and so forth. The term "irreparable" refers to buildings that are beyond repair, that is to say, with so many serious structural defects that it is deemed more appropriate to tear the buildings down than to undertake repairs; most usually this term is used for buildings with only the frame left standing, without complete external walls and/or roof and so forth.

31. Age and sex of head or other reference member of household (core topic)

Recommended tabulation: H17-R

2.533.   From among the topics recommended for inclusion in the population census, age has been selected as being of most significance in relation to housing conditions. For the housing census, the data usually relate only to the head or other reference member of the household, although in some cases (for a detailed study of overcrowding, for example), it may be necessary to tabulate information (age and sex, in this instance) for the other members of the household.

2.534.   In some cases, the characteristics of the person identified as the head or other reference member of the household might not be of significance in connection with the housing conditions of the household. To provide a basis for valid assumptions concerning this relationship, the circumstances likely to affect it should be carefully considered and provided for in carrying out census tests and in analysing the results of those tests. Post-enumeration evaluation surveys will provide a further opportunity to examine the relationship between the characteristics (para. 2.535) of those identified as heads or other reference members of the household and the housing conditions of the household in question.

2.535.   If the population and housing censuses are conducted simultaneously, as is the practice in the majority of countries, then information on age of the head or other reference member of the household will be collected together with other relevant demographic characteristics in the population part of the census. If, however, the housing census is collected independently of the population census, then there must be a provision for collecting this information.

32. Tenure (core topic)

Recommended tabulation: H18-R

2.536.   Tenure refers to the arrangements under which the household occupies all or part of a housing unit. The unit of enumeration is a household occupying a housing unit. The classification of households by tenure is as follows:

1   Member of household owns housing unit

2   Member of household rents all or a part of housing unit

    2.1   Member of household rents all or a part of housing unit as a main tenant

    2.2   Member of household rents a part of housing unit as a subtenant

3   Occupied free of rent

4   Other arrangement

2.537.   National circumstances can dictate the need to assess the number of households occupying the housing unit free of rent (category 3 in para. 2.536) and to further distinguish whether such arrangement is with or without the consent of the owner. However, this information regarding the consent of the owner is subject to special scrutiny in terms of reliability. Furthermore, in countries where communal ownership is significantly represented, this topic on tenure should be further elaborated in order to capture tenure arrangements of communally owned housing. Likewise, the category "Other arrangements" can be further elaborated to capture forms of tenure specific to some countries.

2.538.   The question of tenure needs to be clearly distinguished in the questionnaire as one to be asked of all households; otherwise there is a danger that it may be omitted in cases where more than one household occupies a single housing unit. Tenure information collected for living quarters shows very clearly the distinction between rented units and units that are owner-occupied, but it fails to distinguish the various forms of sub-tenancy that exist in many areas, information regarding which could be obtained from a question directed at households,[110] nor does it allow for an investigation of the relationship between tenure and socio-economic characteristics of heads of the household. Under some circumstances, it may be useful to indicate separately households that, although not subtenants in the sense that they rent from another occupant who is a main tenant or owner-occupant, rent part of a housing unit from a landlord who lives elsewhere. These households and subtenant households may be of special significance in formulating housing programmes. On the contrary, in countries where subtenancy is not usual, information on subtenants may not be collected in the census or, if collected, may be tabulated only for selected areas.

2.539.   In countries where the land and the living quarters are frequently occupied under separate tenure, the topic may be expanded to show separate information for the tenure under which the household or households occupy the living quarters and for the tenure of the land upon which those living quarters are located.

33. Rental and owner-occupant housing costs

2.540.   Rent is the amount paid periodically (weekly, monthly, and so forth) for the space occupied by a household. Information may be obtained on the basis of a scale of rents rather than on that of the exact amount paid. The data may be considered in relation either to household characteristics or to the characteristics of the living quarters. In the latter case, where more than one household occupies a single set of living quarters, the rents paid by all the households will need to be summed in order to obtain the total rent for the living quarters. In the case of living quarters that are partly rented and partly owner-occupied, it may be necessary to impute the rent for the owner-occupied portion.

2.541.   In addition to the amount of rent paid by renting households, it may be useful to collect information on the housing costs of the owner-occupants. Such costs could include information on monthly mortgage payments, taxes, cost of utilities and so forth.

[110] Some indication of the number of households occupying their living quarters as subtenants could be obtained from a comparison of the number of sets of living quarters of various types with the number of occupant households.

34. Furnished/unfurnished

2.542. Provision must be made for indicating whether the housing units covered by the rent are furnished or unfurnished and whether utilities such as gas, electricity, heat, water and so forth are included. Provision also needs to be made for recording households that occupy their premises rent-free or pay only part of the economic rent. In countries where rent for the housing unit is paid separately from rent for the land upon which the housing unit stands, separate information may need to be collected reflecting the amount of ground rent paid.

35. Information and communication technology devices—availability of (core topic)

Recommended tabulation: H19-R

2.543. The importance of availability of information communication technology (ICT) devices is increasing significantly in contemporary society. These devices provide a set of services that are changing the structure and pattern of major social and economic phenomena. The housing census provides an outstanding opportunity to assess the availability of these devices to the household. The choice of topics should be sufficient for understanding the place of ICTs in the household, as well as for use for planning purposes by government and private sector to enable wider and improved delivery of services, and to assess their impact on the society. The recommended classification is:

1   Household having radio
2   Household having television set
3   Household having fixed-line telephone
4   Household having mobile cellular telephone(s)
5   Household having personal computer(s)
6   Household accessing the Internet from home
7   Household accessing the Internet from elsewhere other than home
8   Household without access to the Internet

2.544. In the case of ICT topics, census designers have many options to consider. A sensible approach for presenting questions in a census is to group topics into categories by technology, theme, and/or objective, in order to give census designers the utmost flexibility in choosing the set of questions that best matches their national policy plans. For instance, a category on the "Internet and personal computers (PCs)" would be concerned with determining the status of access to the Internet and PCs by households for a country, in relation to other socio-economic or geographic classificatory variables, while a category on "access path and devices" would be concerned with determining the households with the means for electronic communication (fixed-line and mobile cellular telephones) and the equipment that provides the interface between the user and the network (PCs), in relation to other socio-economic or geographic classificatory variables.

2.545. In designing the questions, census designers should differentiate between two distinct viewpoints, namely (*a*) the availability of ICTs to the households, and (*b*) access to, and use of, ICTs by the household members. The distinction is important, since households need not own, but may still have access to personal computers and the Internet through school/university, public access centres, and/or other households. It also means that countries interested in collecting information on ICT use, particularly of the Internet, would need to include a relevant question topic in their census individual form. The rational for adopting either viewpoint, or even a combination of both, is not necessarily only technical, but rests more on the prevailing conditions in the society, and/or on how the information will be used to characterize the socio-economic profile of households of a country. The recommended tabulation H19 tabulates statistics concerned with the availability of ICT devices. Usage statistics, including the intensity (frequency) of use and the range of activities performed, are preferably obtained using household surveys.

2.546.   Radio and television are the most widespread ICTs in the world. They are also the reliable and useful ICTs for many parts of the world where modern, Internet-based ICTs are not affordable, or not yet available. In hindsight, radio and television are the narrowband and broadband ICTs of old. Few countries collect the number of radio and television sets, and thus most data are estimates. A radio set is a device capable of receiving broadcast radio signals, using popular frequencies in the FM, AM, LW and SW ranges. A radio set may be a standalone device, or it may be integrated into another device, such as a Walkman, a car, or an alarm clock. A television set is a device capable of receiving broadcast television signals, using popular access means such as over-the-air, cable and satellite. A television set is typically a standalone device, but it may also be integrated into another device, such as a computer or a mobile device.

2.547.   Fixed-line telephones refer to telephone lines, typically copper wires, which connect a customer's terminal equipment, for example, a telephone set or facsimile machine, to a public switched telephone network (PSTN), and have a dedicated port on a telephone exchange. Although fixed telephone lines have now been surpassed by mobile telephony globally, they are still an important affordable communication medium. Furthermore, they provide a basis for Internet access in most economies, whether through dial-up, Integrated Services Digital Networks (ISDNs), or Digital Subscriber Line (DSL) services.

2.548.   Mobile cellular telephones are becoming the predominant method of communications in many countries. Indicators related to mobile telephony are therefore fundamental indicators of the information society. Mobile cellular telephones refer to portable telephones using cellular technology that provides access to PSTN. Mobile cellular subscribers refer to users of such telephones with either post-paid subscriptions or pre-paid accounts.

2.549.   The personal computer (PC) is a generic term that refers to any computer designed primarily for use by one person at a time at home, office, or school. PCs, whether desktops or notebooks, comprise any combination of processors, input/output devices, storage drives and network interface cards; are run by a variety of operating systems; and may be connected to other PCs or to the Internet. They exclude terminals connected to mainframe computers for data processing, and midrange multi-user systems that are primarily intended for shared use. Devices such as handheld personal digital assistants (PDAs) and smart telephones are usually not considered PCs, as they have only some, but not all, of the components of the PC, such as, for instance, standard keyboard and large screen. Internet-enabled telephones, which essentially perform a similar service as the PC but for mobile networks, are also not considered PCs.

2.550.   Internet access from home refers to the ability of the household to connect to the public Internet using TCP/IP protocols. Internet connections may be classified according to the technology employed, devices used, communication medium, and/or connection bandwidth (speed). Internet access at home is meant to include both narrowband and broadband connections. Broadband may be defined loosely as transmission capacity with sufficient bandwidth to permit combined provision of voice, data and video. The International Telecommunication Union has set a lower limit of broadband access at 256 Kbit/sec, as the sum of the connection uploading and downloading capacities. Broadband is implemented mainly through xDSL, cable, (wireless) local area network ([W]LAN), satellite broadband Internet, or fibre-to-the-home Internet access. Narrowband access is typically carried out through dial-up modems, ISDNs, and most second-generation (2G) mobile cellular telephones. Access to the Internet is measured irrespective of the type of access, device used to access the Internet, or the method of payment.

36. Cars—number of

2.551.   This topic refers to the number of cars and vans normally available for use by members of the household. The term "normally available" refers to cars and vans that are either owned by occupants or are under some other more or less permanent agreement, such as a lease, and those provided by an employer if available for use by the household, but excludes vans used solely for carrying goods.

37. Durable household appliances—availability of

2.552.   The unit of enumeration is a household occupying a housing unit and information may be collected on the availability within the housing unit of durable appliances such as laundry washing machines, dishwashing machines, refrigerators, deep freezes and so forth, depending on national circumstances.

38. Outdoor space—availability of

2.553.   This topic refers to the availability of outdoor space intended for the recreational activities of the members of a household occupying a housing unit. The classification can refer to the outdoor space available as part of a housing unit (for example, the backyard in the case of a detached house), the outdoor space available adjacent to the building (for example, backyards and playgrounds placed next to the apartment building), the outdoor space available as part of common recreational areas within a 10-minute walk from the housing unit (for example, parks, sports centres and similar sites) or outdoor space not available within a 10-minute walk.

PART THREE

Census Products and Data Utilization

Chapter VIII
Census products and services

3.1.	The population and housing census represents one of the pillars for the data collection on the number and characteristics of the population of a country. The population and housing census is part of an integrated national statistical system, which may include other censuses (for example, agriculture), surveys, registers and administrative files. It provides at regular intervals the benchmark for the population counting at national and local levels. For small geographical areas or sub-population it may represent the only source of information for certain social, demographic and economic characteristics. For many countries the census also provides a unique source for a solid framework to develop sampling frames.

3.2.	The role of the census to provide information in support of government programmes and policies should be carefully discussed with census stakeholders early in the planning stages. For some countries, the census is the only source of this information. When a country's national statistical system also includes other well developed sources of statistical information, such as registers and surveys, the consultations with stakeholders should consider which of these vehicles can best serve their particular data needs.

3.3.	With the rapid development of technology, census data users have an increasing interest in a broad range of products and services from the census organization. The types of output that census offices may produce and disseminate have been covered in part one (see paras. 1.206–1.209). With the availability of microcomputers, some data users may prefer to obtain census products in computer media rather than in printed form. However, there are still many users who would prefer to receive census results in printed form. Since the cost of producing census products in various formats, for example, printed, in computer media or online, can be high, it is recommended that countries consider very carefully the forms in which the census results are disseminated. If a cost-recovery scheme is being planned from the dissemination programme, early study and analysis of the potential data users and their requirements are particularly important.

3.4.	Some data users will need specialized products that the census organization is not planning to produce as part of the general census programme. In such cases, it is recommended that the census organization establish a service to meet such specialized requests, usually on a cost reimbursement basis. Consultation with data users is recommended prior to deciding the type of services that may be required by the data users (see also para. 1.113). Consultation will also assist the census organization in determining the cost that the users are prepared to pay for the services required. For example, if the third level of administrative area is the lowest unit of aggregation for the dissemination of certain characteristics, users who require more detailed disaggregation may be charged for the services required to produce these tabulations. Sometimes a major user or user group may contract prior to the census for a specific census product. Such an advance contracting will greatly facilitate census planning and may mean, as a result, that the census organization can provide the product at reduced cost. However, it is important for the creditability of the census organization that the authorities continue to give priority to general census products funded by general government funding over such specially funded outputs.

3.5.   Processed material can be made accessible in a number of ways. Tabulations required by only a few users, such as certain government offices or specialized research organizations, can be supplied in unpublished form (that is to say, unpublished hard copy tables or tabulations in machine-readable format). Some data may not be tabulated until they are required. Computers provide the opportunity to produce a greater number and a wider variety of tabulations than was the case with previous tabulation procedures. The data stored in the census database represent a rich source of information, which allows fast and relatively inexpensive production of additional tables as they are requested. Online access or dissemination of such micro- and/or macro-databases on computer media can greatly contribute to an enlarging of the user base and thus to the demand for census data. Two cautionary notes are important to keep in mind, however. First, certain cross-tabulations may be of questionable value from a substantive viewpoint because of response, sampling or processing errors or because of processing or imputation procedures. The census authorities will have to establish procedures for warning potential users about such problems to help safeguard the credibility of the entire census. Some census organizations refuse to permit the release of certain cross-tabulations for reasons related to substantive quality, although such a policy may alienate users. Other organizations will release such cross-tabulations only where there is a clear policy that takes into account both substantive and technical considerations. Second, some detailed cross-tabulations and all files with individual records potentially pose problems in respect of disclosing information about identifiable individual respondents in violation of the rules on census confidentiality. This issue is more fully discussed in part one (see paras. 1.376 and 1.377). Both the substantive quality and confidentiality issues need to be addressed and appropriate safeguards established. On the other hand, neither issue should pose any problem with respect to the dissemination of a wide range of census products.

3.6.   An increasing number of statistical organizations make a clear distinction between delivering basic information to the public and delivering information to specific users. In the case where cost recovery is applied, census product users requiring customized information or a copy of a product are charged. The prices of the products and services are generally established to cover all expenses related to production costs, marketing costs and standard agency overhead, including support. Production costs do not include costs of collecting and processing the data since these activities are performed in the conduct of surveys and censuses driven primarily by public policy needs.

A.   Publication of census results

1.   Provisional results

3.7.   The initial release of population counts is generally awaited with anticipation, from the general public to programme and policy administrations. Thus, some countries release provisional results very soon after enumeration is completed. Subject to change once the full data-processing and verification operations have been completed, they nevertheless provide a general picture of population trends. Data users should be made aware of implications of using provisional population counts. The schedule and description of upcoming releases of final results and products should be made public early in the process to maintain interest by the public in the census.

The releases can be staggered, from simple, descriptive one-page summary fact sheets covering a country's major geographical divisions initially, to more comprehensive tabulations and descriptive reports later on.

2. Tabulations

3.8.   Every effort should be made to publish the principal results of a population census (such as those on age, sex and geographical distribution of the population) and of a housing census (such as a geographical distribution of sets of living quarters, households and population by type of living quarters) as soon as possible after the enumeration, otherwise their usefulness and the extent of their interest to the public will be diminished. With the almost universal use of modern computer equipment for the processing of census data, the time required for processing has been greatly reduced in comparison with that for older forms of processing, and the processing cost of each tabulation and the relative cost of processing additional tabulations represent a much smaller fraction of the total census cost than in the past. As a result, collection restrictions, in terms of cost and accuracy of the data, have a greater relative weight in determining the number and complexity of the tabulations that can be produced and disseminated.

3.9.   The population and housing census tabulations shown below and illustrated in annex II and annex III are intended to provide, in published form, the most important census information needed as a basis for programmes of economic and social development and to be used for research purposes. They do not in any way represent all of the tabulations that a given country may publish and certainly not all of the tabulations that may eventually be prepared for special purposes. The tabulations do not take into account the form in which information may be entered into a database, which may be more detailed than that required for these illustrative census tabulations.

3.10.   While the census is the main source of information for the tabulations in annex II and annex III, other sources may include registers, surveys and civil registration. This is particularly the case for countries with well developed vital statistics registers that provide input to the tabulations on fertility and mortality. Conversely, the United Nations publishes other tables that are not based primarily on census data.

3.11.   A major goal of these recommendations is to provide a set of tabulations that need to be produced at the lowest geographical level pertaining to the same point in time so that a country or area is able to meet its data needs for evidence-based socio-economic development planning and monitoring. While the majority of national statistical authorities use a population and housing census as the single most comprehensive vehicle to collect these necessary statistics, others use sample surveys, registers of population and vital events, and other administrative sources or a combination of these methods to derive them.

3.12.   Unlike *Principles and Recommendations for Population and Housing Censuses, Revision 1*,[111] revision 2 contains three categories of tabulations: (*a*) basic/essential, (*b*) recommended, and (*c*) optimum tabulations as described below.

[111] Statistical Papers, No. 67/Rev.1 (United Nations publication, Sales No. E.98.XVII.8).

(*a*)   Basic/essential tabulations

3.13.   These are tabulations that are deemed of top priority for production by countries. They are also regarded as essential for countries in difficult circumstances, such as those that have emerged from a conflict or those that have not carried out a census in a long time, in terms of providing minimum statistics to meet their basic data needs.

3.14.   There are 20 basic/essential tabulations on population and 7 on housing characteristics. They are marked with an asterisk in the list below.

(b)   Recommended tabulations

3.15.   Recommended tabulations are those that are considered adequate for meeting the essential data needs for evidence-based planning, monitoring and implementation of national policies because of their perceived relevance at both the national and the international levels. These tabulations are also designed with the potential for producing statistics at the lowest geographical level and are expected to be produced by each country at least once in the census decade.

3.16.   The recommended set of tabulations also includes the basic/essential tabulations discussed above and includes 33 tabulations on population (see annex II) and 19 on housing characteristics (see annex III).

3.17.   Associated with the recommended tabulations are the core topics that go into their production. Core topics are therefore the main variables for the recommended tabulations. There are 31 core topics on population with 25 of them direct topics and 6 indirect (for a more detailed discussion of direct and indirect topics, see para. 2.14).

3.18.   As stated in paragraph 2.1, the aim of the recommended tabulations is to permit national and international comparability of data due to use of common concepts and definitions of the core topics. For each of the recommended tabulations, the core topics that it represents are listed as part of the metadata. Other metadata that are presented for each of the recommended tabulations include: (*a*) the source of statistics, that is to say, whether from a (i) traditional census, (ii) register-based census, (iii) survey, or (iv) rolling survey; (*b*) the type of population count, that is to say, whether a de jure or de facto population or a combination of these; and (*c*) the definition of urban and rural areas used.

(c)   Additional tabulations

3.19.   The optimum set of tabulations includes the basic/essential and the recommended tabulations discussed above, as well as additional tabulations, and is designed to meet the needs of most of the users at the national and the international levels. This set can be viewed as being equivalent to the complete set of tabulations contained in the *Principles and Recommendations for Population and Housing Censuses, Revision 1.*[112] Annex IV and annex V present the list of additional tabulations for population and housing censuses, respectively.

[112] Ibid.

[113] Recommended tabulations are identified by an "R" as part of the table number.

[114] An asterisk (*) represents a basic/essential tabulation.

List of recommended tabulations for population censuses[113,114]

Group 1.   Tabulations on geographical and internal migration characteristics

P1.1-R   Total population and population of major and minor civil divisions, by urban/rural distribution and by sex*

P1.2-R   Population by size-class of locality and by sex*

P1.3-R   Population of principal localities and of their urban agglomerations, by sex

P1.4-R   Native and foreign-born population, by age and sex*

P1.5-R   Population, by duration of residence in locality and major civil division, age and sex*

P 1.6a-R   Population by place of usual residence, duration of residence, place of previous residence and sex

P.1.6b-R   Population ... years of age and over, by place of usual residence, place of residence at a specified date in the past, age and sex

Group 2.   Tabulations on international migration and immigrant stock

P2.1-R   Foreign-born population, by country of birth, age and sex
P2.2-R   Foreign-born population, by year or period of arrival, country of birth, age and sex*
P2.3-R   Population, by country of birth and citizenship, age and sex
P2.4-R   Economically active foreign-born population ... years of age and over, by year or period of arrival, main occupation and sex

Group 3.   Tabulations on household and family characteristics

P3.1-R   Population in households, by relationship to head or other reference member of household, marital status and sex, and size of institutional population
P3.2-R   Head or other reference member of household, by age and sex; and other household members, by age and relationship to head or other reference member*
P3.3-R   Households, population in households and number of family nuclei, by size of household*

Group 4.   Tabulations on demographic and social characteristics

P4.1-R   Population, by single years of age and sex*
P4.2-R   Population, by marital status, age and sex*

Group 5.   Tabulation on fertility and mortality

P5.1-R   Female population 10 years of age and over, by age and number of children ever born alive by sex*
P5.2-R   Female population 10 years of age and over, by age and number of children living (or dead) by sex*
P5.3-R   Female population ... to 49 years of age, by age, number of live births, by sex within the 12 months preceding the census, and deaths among these live births, by sex
P5.4-R   Household deaths, by sex and age within the 12 months preceding the census; and total population, by age and sex

Group 6.   Tabulations on educational characteristics

P6.1-R   Population ... years of age and over by school attendance, educational attainment, age and sex*
P6.2-R   Population 5 to 29 years of age, by school attendance, single years of age and sex*
P6.3-R   Population 10 years of age and over, by literacy, age and sex

Group 7.   Tabulations on economic characteristics

P7.1-R   Population ... years of age and over, by current (or usual) activity status, educational attainment, age and sex*
P7.2-R   Currently (or usually) active population by activity status, main occupation, age and sex*

P7.3-R   Currently (or usually) active population by activity status, main **industry**, age and sex*

P7.4-R   Currently (or usually) active population by activity status, main status in employment, age and sex*

P7.5-R   Currently (or usually) active population by activity status, main status in employment, main industry and sex

P7.6-R   Currently (or usually) active population by activity status, main status in employment, main occupation and sex

P7.7-R   Currently (or usually) active population by activity status, main **industry**, main occupation and sex*

P7.8-R   Population not currently (or usually) active, by functional category, **age and sex***

Group 8.   *Tabulations on disability characteristics*

P8.1-R   Population with and without disabilities by age and sex*

P 8.2-R   Population 5 years of age and over, by disability status, educational attainment, age and sex

P 8.3-R   Population 15 years of age and over, by disability status, current (or usual) activity status, age and sex

Group 9.   *Tabulations on housing characteristics*

H1-R   Persons, by broad types of living quarters and number of roofless*

H2-R   Persons in collective living quarters by type

H3-R   Households in occupied housing units, by type of housing unit*

H4-R   Conventional dwellings by occupancy status

H5-R   Occupied housing units, by type of housing unit, cross-classified by type of ownership of the housing units

H6-R   Housing units, by number of rooms, cross-classified by type of housing unit and number of occupants per housing unit

H7-R   Occupied housing units, by type of housing unit, cross-classified by water supply system*

H8-R   Occupied housing units, by type of housing unit, cross-classified by main source of drinking water*

H9-R   Occupied housing units, by type of housing unit, cross-classified by type of toilet and type of sewage disposal*

H10-R   Occupied housing units, by type of housing unit, cross-classified by type of bathing facilities

H11-R   Occupied housing units, by type of housing unit, cross-classified by availability of kitchen and fuel used for cooking

H12-R   Occupied housing units, by type of housing unit, cross-classified by type of lighting and/or use of electricity

H13-R   Occupied housing units, by type of housing unit, cross-classified by main type of solid waste disposal

H14-R   Households in housing units, by type of housing unit occupied, cross-classified by number of households per housing unit

H15-R   Conventional dwellings by type of building, and construction material of outer walls

H16-R   Housing units by type and construction material of outer walls

H17-R   Households, by type of living quarters, cross-classified by sex and age of head or other reference member of household*

H18-R   Households in housing units, by type of housing unit, cross-classified by tenure of household and, for tenant households, ownership of housing unit occupied*

H19-R   Households in housing units, by type of housing unit, cross-classified by information and communication technology devices and access to Internet

3.20.   In order to avoid producing census tabulations that are overly voluminous or that contain a large number of empty cells, some countries may find it necessary to employ a more restricted geographical classification than that suggested in the illustrations. For example, basic facilities such as piped water or electricity may be almost completely lacking for large areas of some countries. Under these circumstances, tabulation of the relevant data for small geographical areas would not be appropriate. The geographical classification to be utilized needs to be carefully considered, taking into account the type of information being tabulated, its probable frequency distribution and the uses to which the data are likely to be put.

3.21.   Some countries may also collect data on additional topics in the census questionnaire to address specific concerns. For example, whether or not the birth of an individual is registered, the age a woman first marries, or vocational and technical skills. In other cases, detailed tabulations for special population may be required for use in planning or evaluation of programmes. Tabulations for the non-core topics may be done after the basic tabulations are completed. Consultations with user groups both at the national and at the local levels may be helpful in determining the most suitable tabulation plan and method of dissemination.

3.22.   Metadata is a key element of census dissemination to ensure that the underlying concepts are well understood and that the results are well interpreted. All tabulations should include the following metadata or references to where this information can be obtained. Census questions; reasons why they are asked; conceptual definitions (census dictionary); geographic hierarchies used; changes since the previous census with regard to content, operational methods or geographic boundaries; and quality indicators such as coverage rates and item non-response. If a long-form sample is used in the census, metadata should also provide information on the sampling variability of the results. When the census tabulations include suppressed data cells due to small numbers, the metadata should also include a methodological note on the rules and methods of suppression.

3.   Thematic statistical or analytical reports

3.23.   Many countries prepare different types of thematic or analytical reports. These may range from volumes presenting extensive and detailed statistical tabulations, particularly cross-tabulations, to more analytical reports that combine tabular materials with some interpretative or analytical text. This latter group of reports might include, for example, *volumes of regional analysis* on such subjects as population or housing conditions of urban areas, major metropolitan areas or big cities, and regional distributions; and comparisons of key social indicators such as education, living arrangements, housing conditions, sanitation and economic activities. Other such reports might include *community profile analysis*, of, for example, the indigenous population, and so forth and *profiles of specific population groups*, such as families, children, youth and the elderly population. Reports on *population growth and dis-*

tribution that examine changes in the demographic characteristics of the country's population with breakdowns by two or three levels of administrative areas would be very useful. Such reports might focus on the growth, location and mobility of the population at the national and regional levels, and administrative areas. Partnership and external cooperation with academic institutions and other specialists in subject matter, which can facilitate such work and strengthen collaborations, should be sought whenever possible.

3.24.   Other published reports may include the census methodology, encompassing, if applicable, sampling design and methodology and a census evaluation report, which may include estimates of census coverage and the methodology used for their preparation.

4.   Other reports

3.25.   It is important that users of census products be provided on a timely basis with as much relevant information regarding the census as possible. A publication that contains information on all types of products that will be available following the census is very useful to users. A brief description of each product should be provided including the estimated timing of release, the level of geographical detail that each product carries and, for products released periodically, the frequency of release. In the case of large census operations, several such documents tailored to the needs of different sets of users (for example, users in education, health or local government) may be useful.

3.26.   Many countries publish a *census dictionary*, which contains comprehensive definitions of terms and concepts and detailed classifications used to present census outputs. Some countries also publish geographical classifications and codes and the definitions of areas used in the census and their relationships with the administrative areas. Explanations of user-defined areas for specific census tabulations and the type of format available (printed or electronic) may be provided.

5.   Procedural report

3.27.   One of the most important reports in the publication programme is the *administrative report,* which is a record of the entire census undertaking, including problems encountered and their solutions. The report may include the following topics: a brief history of the census in the country, legal basis for conducting the census, budget requirements and control, census committees and their activities, census organization and personnel structure, quality control procedures, census calendar, census cartographic work, development and design of the questionnaires, enumeration methodology of each census, field organization, manual editing and coding, data-processing development and organization, data capture, computer editing and imputation procedure, computer hardware and software used, census evaluation, publication and data dissemination programme. The census administrative report is very useful both for the users and for the census organization itself. Given the long lapse of time between censuses and the likelihood of changes in personnel, particularly in the upper echelon, the administrative report is an essential product for the planning of future censuses (see also paras. 1.406 and 1.407).

3.28.   With developments in information technology, the census data files and publications have become increasingly available in computer media. A description of the procedure in the development of these data files may also be included in the procedural report. Consideration of a separate volume of the procedural report for the processing and dissemination phases may be considered to ensure the completion of the planning and field operations phases immediately after the census enumeration.

B. Census mapping

1. Basic mapping

3.29.   Published analogous and digital maps are tools that make the census results more understandable and easier to use. The provision of maps serves two purposes: first, census area identification maps locate and show the boundaries of all administrative areas for which data are reported in census publications and, second, statistical or thematic maps present the significant results of the census, thus allowing the general user to visualize the geographical distributions and patterns inherent in the data. Well-designed and attractive maps will interest the users of census reports, and may raise questions that send them to the statistical tables for further details.

3.30.   A comprehensive map publication programme should be developed as part of the overall population and housing census publication programme in order that the needed resources may be provided within the budget at the initial planning stages. In addition to preparing maps for the census tables and reports, many countries have also found it useful to produce a population atlas as a census output. Collaboration with other departments and interested agencies should be sought to facilitate the production of an atlas volume. The atlas would include maps depicting population and housing characteristics, as well as other data influencing the growth, composition and distribution pattern of population and housing (see paras. 1.143–1.148).

3.31.   There are three major types of area identification maps that are commonly used in most census publications: (*a*) national maps showing the boundaries of the first- and second-order geographical divisions and of the major cities or metropolitan areas; (*b*) maps of each first-order division showing the boundaries of the second- and third-order divisions for which statistical tables will be prepared; and (*c*) urban or metropolitan maps showing small sub-area boundaries as well as general streets, roads and rivers.

3.32.   The purpose of statistical maps is to present the results in terms of their geographical distribution. There is special interest in the current pattern of the distribution and also in changes in the patterns that have occurred over time, particularly since the last census.

2. Thematic mapping

3.33.   As regards *thematic maps*, priority indicators for a population and housing census are total population and its distribution by sub-areas, population density, urban and rural population or metropolitan and non-metropolitan population, and changes in the population totals since the last census. Other important indicators include age, sex, fertility, mortality, migration, educational attainment, employment, household size, type of housing, ownership, number of rooms, and sanitary facilities, with a growing demand also for data on communication (telephones, television, computers and Internet access), transport (vehicles), a broad range of household amenities, and recently also population-based development indicators such as household access to safe water, household waste management, and multiple sources of household incomes, such as the incidence of remittances. This list of indicators is merely an illustration of the type of thematic maps individual countries might find useful to produce.

Producing maps using the same set of indicators enables countries to meaningfully compare their results over time and with international or regional norms.

3.34.   Maps are an invaluable aid in meaningfully comparing subnational results with national values or with other international and regional norms. Desktop mapping and desktop publishing software provides great flexibility in composing informative and visually appealing maps. Often several maps can be combined on a single page to show one indicator, for example, for the urban and the rural population. Also, combining maps and statistical charts is an effective means of presenting census information. On the other hand, some care should be exercised in respect of producing complex printed maps involving several variables, as such maps are often difficult to reproduce clearly and the general user may find them difficult to understand.

3.35.   By having associated graphing and mapping capabilities, databases will greatly increase their usefulness. Ideally users should be able to generate the graphs and/or maps required by themselves, and then print or plot them, paste them into a report or make the images available for other uses. Several census organizations have produced this kind of product, sometimes in cooperation with a commercial company. Many users require small area data concerning such matters as home ownership, educational profiles, the labour market, and so on. While the database may be for one census, some historical information can be included to allow users to observe prevailing trends over time. As with all time-series type data, it is important to maintain consistency in both definition and spatial representations to ensure comparability.

3.36.   Both micro- and macro-data can be at the basis of these dissemination products. However, owing to the need to maintain confidentiality, and in order to increase processing speed, some form of prior aggregation is usually applied, for example by using summary data. Such summary data could also be combined with the general purpose graphing and mapping software. However, this would result in a reduction of the user community to those able to handle rather more complicated processing jobs. Making available a census database with tightly integrated graphing and mapping capabilities (which usually implies a tabulation function) is an excellent way to improve the effectiveness of census information dissemination. If it is to be commercially successful, the product must be easy to use.

3.37.   The following list presents some suggested topics for census maps. The list is not exhaustive: most topics that appear in the questionnaire as well as derived topics covered in part two can be presented in cartographic form. In some countries, special topics such as population distribution by ethnic or language group may be appropriate. Conversely, some of the listed maps present information on the same topic in somewhat different form, so that a statistical agency may wish to select the most suitable indicator for the needs of the country.

Illustrative list of thematic census maps

- *Population dynamics and distribution*
    - Percentage population change during intercensal period(s)
    - Average annual growth rate
    - Population density (persons per square kilometre)
    - Urban population as percentage of total population
    - Distribution and size of major cities and towns
    - In-migration, out-migration and net migration rates
    - Born in country and foreign-born
    - Born in another division of the country

- *Demographic characteristics*
  - › Sex ratio (males per 100 females), possibly by age groups
  - › Percentage of population age 0-14
  - › Percentage of population age 15-64
  - › Percentage of population age 65 and over
  - › Percentage female population in childbearing ages 15-49
  - › Total dependency ratio (population age 0-14, and 65 and over, as percentage of population age 15-64)
  - › Marital status
  - › Birth rate
  - › Total fertility rate
  - › Mean age at first marriage
  - › Death rate
  - › Infant mortality rate
  - › Life expectancy at birth
  - › Percentage of people with disabilities
- *Socio-economic characteristics*
  - › Percentage of children not in primary school
  - › Adult literacy rate (age 15 and over)
  - › Mean years of schooling (age 25 and over)
  - › Illiteracy rate of population age 15 and over
  - › Illiterate population age 15 and over (total number)
  - › Educational level of population age 10 and over
  - › Labour force as percentage of total population
  - › Women's share of adult labour force
  - › Percentage of labour force by economic sector, type of occupation and status in employment
- *Households and housing*
  - › Average number of persons per household
  - › Percentage of households headed by women
  - › Average number of dwelling rooms per household
  - › Tenure status (owned, rented, and so forth)
  - › Type of construction material
  - › Percentage of population with access to adequate shelter
  - › Percentage of population with access to safe water
  - › Percentage of population with access to electricity
  - › Percentage of population with access to sanitation
  - › Percentage of population with access to health services

3.38.   Where appropriate, the indicators can be presented disaggregated by gender as well as by urban/rural areas (for example, where the rural population is greater than about 25 per cent of the total population). If information about an indicator is also available from a previous census, it is often very informative to produce change maps or to present maps for both time periods.

3.39.   The development of village population size maps by region is of particular value. These maps combine two types of information: village population statistics and village locations in each region or subnational area. More information can be presented on, for example, the village location within the district and the region, habitable and non-habitable areas, densely populated villages, areas with no villages, and the proximity of villages. Village population size maps can also be used as base maps for additional information on village services and activities, and on location and distribution of villages without specific services, such as primary schools, dispensaries, piped water, and so forth.

C.   Interactive digital outputs

1.   Overview

3.40.   It is of paramount importance that census data and information produced are widely disseminated and communicated, and that agencies involved in this process have a pronounced customer/client and stakeholder focus, place more emphasis on providing a service than merely providing products, and be guided by user-relevance and user-friendliness in all its operations, rather than by tradition in producing tables, graphs and reports that they have always produced.

3.41.   While statistical tables or census reports, printed or digital maps and atlases, including the provision of some dynamic mapping capability, can be conveniently disseminated through various forms, including different types of computer media, growing demand by users for an ever-growing variety of census data outputs is most effectively and efficiently met by enabling and empowering census data users to access census data themselves, and build their own customized tables or spatially configure data outputs according to varying spatial requirements. Analytical tools like population geographic information systems are good illustrations of recent developments that make census data accessible on national statistical office websites and through CD ROMs.

2.   Geographic information systems

3.42.   Geographic information systems (GIS) embody hardware and software configurations designed to support the capture, management, analysis and dissemination of spatially referenced data. Applied to census activities and outputs, such systems facilitate census cartography and data capture, and by linking population data (demographic, social and socio-economic) to geographical areas, GIS provides very powerful data management functionalities in allowing users to explore, analyse, describe and communicate population census information according to their own data and information demands.

3.43.   In practical terms, such systems may range from simple desktop mapping facilities to complete GIS systems capable of solving complex planning and management problems or producing detailed geo-referenced inventories. The ability to use space to integrate and manipulate data sets from heterogeneous sources can make its application relevant to planning and managing the census process itself. For example, GIS provides functions for the aerial interpolation of statistical data in cases where the boundaries of aerial units have changed between censuses. However, the development and implementation of such a repository of geo-referenced data are not easy tasks to accomplish, and simple desktop mapping systems generating thematic maps from a database of base maps and indicators will satisfy the needs of most census organizations.

3.44. GIS technology should be considered only at a level appropriate to the skills and resources available, and constitute an integral part of the overall work of a national statistical organization. Collaborative arrangements with other agencies, such as national mapping and survey agencies, should be pursued particularly with regard to the acquisition and maintenance of base maps and digital databases, which should not become a responsibility of national statistical organizations. Along similar lines, any GIS development by statistical organizations should be compatible with systems that might already exist in other public sector agencies, and where the role of the statistical agency would consist in primarily supplying census data and other important statistics useful for policymakers across a broad range of sectoral applications, at levels and in formats compatible with such systems. National statistical offices should only proceed with their own GIS development and applications when it is feasible to maintain such systems and applications during the intercensal years, where there is no dependence on continued external technical support, and where there are explicit demands from users in the public and private sectors for such developments and outputs.

3.45. Statistical offices may nevertheless develop GIS applications with population data and other geo-referenced data from other sources for more advanced forms of spatial analysis. The task could be shared with other institutions, or be delegated completely to specialists elsewhere. The role of the census office would then consist in supplying census data at the right level and in the right format for such a system. Census offices provide vital information on current demographic conditions and future trends for policymakers in a range of sectors, such as health care, education, infrastructure planning, agriculture and natural resources management; and the provision of spatially referenced census databases is an essential prerequisite of the facilitation of the use of demographic data in these fields.

3.46. To achieve maximum efficiency gains, GIS applications should also be capable of generating additional geographical delimitations beyond those used in the census, such as school and health districts, water and other biophysical catchment areas, and power and utility service units. These entities will have to be constructed from the smallest geographically identified units available in the census, such as census blocks, grid squares, or enumeration areas (EAs). If, as is the case in most developing countries, EAs are the smallest units, this will have important implications for the establishment of EA boundaries. This requires close collaboration between national statistical organizations and national mapping and survey agencies on one side, and school, health, water and power authorities on the other, when EA boundaries are drawn or modified, to avoid potential problems later on.

3.47. Being a rather complex technology and requiring some specialized technical resources, national statistical organizations, particularly in developing countries, ought to approach the introduction of GIS systems gradually and with care, and at all times ensuring compatibility with other systems possibly in circulation elsewhere. As an alternative to immediately launching full-scale GIS applications, countries may start with a simple and robust design that is likely to be understood and maintained by a wide array of users, transferable to a wide range of software packages and independent of any hardware platform. GIS implementation in a developing country may follow a hierarchical strategy, with the national statistical office employing a high-end commercial GIS with extensive capabilities for handling and analysing large amounts of spatial data. Widespread dissemination of databases can then be achieved by creating a version of the finished databases using a lower-end mapping software format for distribution at low cost, as is currently developed in some countries.

3.48.   Apart from providing national statistical organizations with a very effective means to disseminate and increase the utilization of census data, geographic information systems, more than any other data management system, provide easy and user-friendly access to census data in user-relevant formats. This allows analysts and planners to undertake policy analysis, planning and research that can more readily identify thematic and geographic priority areas and thus contribute to evidence-based and better-informed policy and decision-making at different levels of geography; it allows governments to effectively monitor development progress across different sectors at village, municipality and subregional levels; it raises awareness about the importance of census and other socio-economic data; and it increases the institutional capacity of national statistical offices and social/economic planning agencies to engage in more in-depth analyses of social and economic data and deliver information products in even more user-friendly formats.

D.   Customized products and services

3.49.   The increasing activity in the field of economic and social planning and the attention of such planning to subnational areas are placing new demands on statistical information in general and on population and housing censuses in particular. There is an increasing need for tabulations and mapping not only by major and minor civil divisions and by other units of analysis such as metropolitan areas but even, beyond these, by small local areas.

3.50.   Therefore, it is useful to establish an *"on request"* service for users who require aggregates not available through other means. This will be especially relevant in situations where outsiders cannot obtain census micro-databases. In essence, the service would require that users provide the census office with the details of the tables or other aggregates requested so that the census office could fulfil the request, normally against payment of a certain compensation fee. Offering and promoting this service would place the statistical service in a more desirable proactive position, rather than a static one, and could be a strong catalyst for closer cooperation with census product users.

3.51.   The cost of such special-purpose tabulations, which require computer programming, could be high, especially for academic institutions and other users who do not have access to a large budget. Some statistical organizations allow the users to do the necessary work using a user-friendly kind of software. A clearly written manual is required to guide the users in using the software, including the contents of the census data dictionary and other relevant information. The resulting tables are checked for any possible breach of confidentiality, in particular table cells with very small values.

3.52.   Many census organizations provide services for special requests for census products, such as thematic databases, tables, and graphic and mapping outputs that can be designed for small, medium and large businesses, communities or special interest groups. These services are normally provided to meet the increasing demand of data users for a wide range of applications, such as monitoring trends, analysing unmet needs, identifying market potentials, segmenting markets, identifying service areas and priority zones, determining optimum site locations, designing and advertising new products and services, and so forth. Each category of products should also be made available on various media (namely, paper, disk or online) for dissemination according to the users' requirements (see paras. 1.358–1.375).

3.53.   Once the databases are created and have served the policy needs, they can serve other data users if they have market value. Since the national statistical organization is normally the only source of many geographical databases related to census data applications, market demand for these products is increasing, particularly in the geographical and population-related areas. In such cases, census products could be governed by a licence. The licence permits the users to use the product without a transferring of the ownership, since the ownership remains with the government agency. Either of two different licensing arrangements may be applied. The first is offered to organizations that use the data for their own needs and the other is offered to organizations that redistribute data or provide analytical services using census data to other persons or organizations for a fee.

3.54. Customized services of data on computer media are differentiated in terms of the forms of the data. Census products may be distributed in their original form, with or without other related information, or they can be distributed after making certain value-added modifications to meet the need of the users. Examples of such value-added activities include converting the data into another format (for use by other software packages), making the data more useful by correcting errors, adding missing information, creating subsets of the original data sets, merging the data from other sources, and bundling with software. In cases where copyright laws protect census data ownership, some royalty fees and data usage fees may be charged to the distributors to ensure a minimum return. However, if prices are too high such charges can also be a barrier to the use of the census data.

E. General interest products and special audience reports

3.55. The traditional approach to the publication of census information is through release of cross-classified tabulations. This is not, however, easy for non-expert users to access. As these traditional forms of data on population and housing censuses are being published, there are many ways to disseminate census data in a more accessible format and thus increase the utilization of the information collected.

3.56. It should be noted that the following material can only be effective in encouraging the use of census information if it is prepared in a timely and professional manner. This will require specialist skills from people used to writing for these audiences, the use of high quality materials and considerable planning. As such resources are often expensive, any country planning to undertake such campaigns must allow for the costs of such activities when planning their budget.

1. Posters

3.57. One of the most common ways to disseminate census information consists of publishing posters highlighting key facts such as: How many are we? Where do we live? and summarizing a profile for the major civil divisions of a country. Posters might also be prepared addressing issues relevant to special population segments: teenagers, adults, indigenous populations, seniors, and women's groups.

3.58. Since the objective of a poster is to catch the eye at a distance, relatively few facts should be presented in a way so that the key message is immediately visible. Posters can be greatly enhanced by the addition of a well-designed graph and the use of fonts to increase the readability and comprehensibility of the key message.

2. Brochures

3.59. Professionally designed brochures are another way to disseminate basic census data. These brochures should be written in a very easy and comprehensible language indicating the demographic profile of the country illustrated with suitable graphics and explanatory material. In some countries these brochures might be addressed to specific relevant issues on population. They are particularly suitable for preparation as give-aways for people attending events, such as the launch of more traditional materials, or for inclusion on display racks in libraries of government offices.

3. Special audience reports

3.60. Information generated by a census is by definition of use to a wide range of users with a wide range of statistical expertise.

3.61. Owing to these attributes, national statistical offices may wish to prepare specific analytical reports for special audiences. While these reports may not require the attention attracting features of the posters and brochures, they will need to incorporate a high level of very sound analysis undertaken by staff who have a solid foundation in analytical techniques as well as the topic being analysed. In some cases it might be seen as desirable or necessary to undertake the analysis as collaboration with academic institutions or other specialists.

3.62. The target audience might be any part of the census user audience interested in the topic. Criteria used in establishing the topics chosen will have to be set by the country concerned but could include such factors as the importance of the topic to the country; particularly interesting facts shown by the census data (perhaps confirming or rebutting conventional theories; confronting census data with material from other sources; or responding to issues raised by the public during user consultations of the collection.

4. Videos

3.63. The use of graphics such as charts or maps included on videotape; compact disc (CD) or digital video disc (DVD) format are media useful to promote the story behind the numbers and thus increase use of census data. These might indicate how census data can assist policymakers, planners and people in general to understand their societies and how census data can assist in identifying the main problems and assist with evaluation of solutions.

5. Instructional materials

3.64. Instructional materials in an easy to understand form can be prepared for the general public, indicating the advantages and limitations of census data. Such material can often form the basis of information campaigns as part of the advocacy material for the next census.

3.65. A particular implementation of instructional materials can be the preparation of a kit for use in schools. Not only will this provide high quality information for the students but, by including exposure to the use of statistical materials in the school process, it will encourage the use of evidence based analysis throughout society. It should be noted that professional assistance should be sought in ensuring that these materials follow sound educational practices and can be accommodated within the appropriate curriculum.

Chapter IX
Census data utilization

A. General uses of population and housing censuses

3.66. Population censuses are traditionally used for public and private sector policymaking, planning, and administrative and research purposes. One of the most basic of the administrative uses of census data is in the demarcation of constituencies and the allocation of representation on governing bodies. Certain aspects of the legal or administrative status of territorial divisions may also depend on the size of their populations. Housing censuses are used to develop benchmark housing statistics and to formulate housing policy and programmes, and in the private sector to assist in site selection for industrial, retail and service facilities, as well as for the commercial development of residential housing.

3.67. Information on the size, distribution and characteristics of a country's population is essential to describing and assessing its economic, social and demographic circumstances and to developing sound policies and programmes aimed at fostering the welfare of a country and its population. The population and housing census, by providing comparable basic statistics for a country as a whole and for each administrative unit and locality therein, can make an important contribution to the overall planning process and the management of national development. The availability of information at the lowest levels of administrative units is valuable for the management and evaluation of such programmes as education and literacy, employment and human resources, reproductive health and family planning, housing and environment, maternal and child health, rural development, transportation and highway planning, urbanization and welfare. Population and housing censuses are also unique sources of data for producing relevant social indicators to monitor the impact of these government policies and programmes (see paras. 3.86-3.88).

1. Uses of population censuses

3.68. The uses of population census results and the associated tabulations described in this volume are listed according to the topics presented in paragraph 2.16. Detailed general descriptions of the uses of tabulations in all eight subject groups may be obtained in the following United Nations publications: *General Principles for National Programmes of Population Projections as Aids to Development Planning*;[115] manuals on methods of estimating population: *Manual I: Methods of Estimating Total Population for Current Dates*;[116] and *Manual X: Indirect Techniques for Demographic Estimation*;[117] *Projection Methods for Integrating Population Variables into Development Planning*, vol. I: *Methods for Comprehensive Planning, Module One: Conceptual issues and methods for preparing demographic projections*, and *Module Two: Methods for preparing school enrolment, labour force and employment projections*;[118]

[115] United Nations publication, Sales No. E.65.XIII.2.

[116] United Nations publication, Sales No. E.52.XIII.5.

[117] Population Studies, No. 81 (United Nations publication, Sales No. E.83.XIII.2).

[118] ST/ESA/SER.R/90 and Add.1.

[119] United Nations publication, Sales No. E.96.II.A.16.

[120] United Nations publication, Sales No. E.01.XVII.10).

[121] Studies in Methods, No. 54 (United Nations publication, Sales No. E.91.XVII.9).

[122] United Nations publication, Sales No. E.70.XIII.3.

[123] United Nations publication, Sales No. E.94.XIII.3.

[124] Statistical Papers, Series M, No. 58, Rev.1 (United Nations publication, Sales No. E.98. XVII.14).

[125] United Nations publication, Sales No. E.73.XIII.2.

[126] Studies in Methods, No. 54 (United Nations publication, Sales No. E.91.XVII.9).

[127] United Nations publication, Sales No. E.05.XVII.7.

[128] Studies in Methods, No. 32 (United Nations publication, Sales No. E.84.XVII.2).

[129] United Nations publication, Sales No. E.56.XIII.2.

[130] Studies in Methods, No. 49 (United Nations publication, Sales No. E.89.XVII.6).

[131] United Nations Development Programme, New York, 2004.

[132] Studies in Methods, No. 54 (United Nations publication, Sales No. E.91.XVII.9).

[133] United Nations publication, Sales No. E.56.XIII.3.

[134] ST/ESA/SER.R/76.

Indicators of Sustainable Development Framework and Methodologies;[119] and *Principles and Recommendations for a Vital Statistics System, Revision 2.*[120]

3.69. The total population, as defined in paragraph 2.71, and its distribution among major and minor territorial divisions and localities are frequently a legal requirement of the census because these results are used for determining the apportionment of representation in legislative bodies, for administrative purposes and for planning the location of economic and social facilities. Internal migration, one of the major sources of population change, frequently affects the trends in population distribution. Data on internal and international migration, together with fertility and mortality, are needed to prepare population estimates for planning purposes and for determining policies on migration and assessing their effectiveness. For more detailed descriptions, see the following United Nations publications: *Handbook of Population and Housing Censuses, Part II: Demographic and Social Characteristics;*[121] *Manual VI: Methods of Measuring Internal Migration*[122] (manuals on methods of estimating population); *Internal Migration of Women in Developing Countries;*[123] and *Recommendations on Statistics of International Migration, Revision 1.*[124]

3.70. The household, a basic socio-economic unit in all countries, is often central to the study of social and economic development. The number, size and structure of households and changes in the rate of household formation are useful for planning and for developing special policies formulated for selected groups of the population, such as children, the elderly and persons with disabilities. Therefore, the distribution of individuals within households is used to determine the living arrangements of families, the patterns of family structure observed, the time when new families are formed and changes in family structure due to death, divorce, migration or the departure of children to form their own households. The relationship among household members can be used to determine family structure and the existence of households composed, partially or completely, of unrelated persons, as indicated in the following manuals on methods of estimating population: *Manual VII: Methods of Projecting Households and Families;*[125] and *Handbook of Population and Housing Censuses, Part II : Demographic and Social Characteristics.*[126]

3.71. Traditionally defined demographic and social characteristics collected from the population census include sex, age, marital status, religion, language, and national and/or ethnic group. Sex and age are fundamental to the majority of the characteristics collected in the census. Census data provide more data than any other single source on gender differences, as indicated in the following United Nations publications: *The World's Women 2005: Progress in Statistics;*[127] *Compiling Social Indicators on the Situation of Women*[128]; *Manual II: Methods of Appraisal of Quality of Basic Data for Population Estimates;*[129] and *Handbook on Social Indicators.*[130]

3.72. Depending on national circumstances, cultural diversity may be measured by language spoken in the home or community, religion and national and/or ethnic group. For countries that are not homogeneous in terms of one or more of these variables, linguistic, religious and national and/or ethnic groups provide the basic information for a quantitative assessment of the relative size and age-sex distribution of this diversity. For more detailed descriptions of the uses of the data in the tabulations, see the following United Nations publications: *Human Development Report 2004;*[131] *Handbook of Population and Housing Censuses, Part II: Demographic and Social Characteristics;*[132] *Manual III: Methods for Population Projections by Sex and Age;*[133] and *First Marriage: Patterns and Determinants, 1988.*[134]

3.73. Although census data on fertility and mortality cannot serve as a substitute for reliable birth and death statistics from registers, they are particularly valuable for countries where birth or death registration is lacking or incomplete and vital statistics are therefore unavailable. Even in countries with complete registration of these events, the population census is useful as a supplement to satisfactory registration data because the fertility questions provide data for calculating lifetime fertility of the female population or cohort fertility. For more detailed descriptions of the uses of the data in tabulations dealing with fertility and mortality, see the following United Nations publications: *Step-by-Step Guide to the Estimation of Child Mortality*;[135] *Handbook of Population and Housing Censuses, Part II: Demographic and Social Characteristics*;[136] "Assessing the effects of mortality reduction of population ageing";[137] and *Socio-economic Differentials in Child Mortality in Developing Countries*.[138]

3.74.　Education has historically been one of the key factors determining the quality of life, and interest in education continues today in most countries of the world, with emphasis on improving access to education and the quality of education, as well as broadening the scope of basic education.[139] Education is also considered a major tool in closing the gap between women and men in respect of socio-economic opportunities. Benchmark data obtained from national population censuses will therefore be of considerable importance towards fulfilling this objective. Census data reveal the disparity in educational opportunities between the sexes, age cohorts or generations, urban/rural populations and so forth, and provide important indications of the capacity of the nation for economic and social development. They furnish material for the comparison of the present educational equipment of the adult population with the present and anticipated requirements of educated human resources for various types of economic activities. Such a comparison may serve as a guide both for national policy in terms of the development of the educational system, and for the planning of the economic development programmes that it will be feasible to undertake in view of human resource requirements. For more details, see the following United Nations publications: *Human Development Report, 1996*;[140] *Report on the World Social Situation, 2005*;[141] and *Education For All: Global Monitoring Report, 2006*.[142]

3.75.　Census information on the economic characteristics of the population focuses on enumerating the economically active population so as to provide benchmark data for current studies of employment, unemployment and underemployment. It provides information on the growth, composition and distribution of the economically active population for use in policy formulation and the appraisal of human resource utilization. Economic data from censuses can also provide some input into statistics on the distribution of income, consumption and accumulation of households, on participation in agriculture and non-agricultural activities, and on participation in the informal sector. Furthermore, the data on the economically active population may give an approximate indication of the number of workers who are responsible for the support of dependants.

3.76.　Statistics obtained from different sources (for example, labour-force surveys, agriculture surveys, establishment surveys and administrative records) rely on the census for sampling frames, and the use of common concepts in the different sources helps in securing comparability when multiple sources for changing patterns of economic activity are being relied upon. See the following United Nations publications: "Collection of economic characteristics in population censuses";[143] *Methods of Analysing Census Data on Economic Activities of the Population*;[144] *Handbook of Household Surveys (Revised Edition)*;[145] and *Handbook of Population and Housing Censuses, Part IV: Economic Activity Status*.[146]

3.77.　As interest in the movement of people across national boundaries, in other words, international migration, has grown steadily among countries, census items and tabulations relative to international migration have grown in importance.

[135] United Nations publication, Sales No. E.89.XIII.9.

[136] Studies in Methods, No. 54 (United Nations publication, Sales No. E.91.XVII.9).

[137] Article by Shiro Horiuchi in Population Bulletin of the United Nations (New York), Nos. 31/32 (1991). Sales No. E.91.XIII.18.

[138] United Nations publication, Sales No. E.85.XIII.7.

[139] Education for All Summit of Nine High-Population Countries, New Delhi, 12-16 December 1993: Final Report (Paris, UNESCO, 1994).

[140] New York, Oxford University Press, 1996.

[141] United Nations publication, Sales No. E. 05.IV.5.

[142] Paris, United Nations Educational, Scientific and Cultural Organization, 2005.

[143] Technical Report by the United Nations Statistics Division and International Labour Office, 2002 (ST/ESA/STAT/119).

[144] United Nations publication, Sales No. E.69.XIII.2.

[145] Studies in Methods, No. 31 (United Nations publication, Sales No. E.83.XVII.13).

[146] Studies in Methods, No. 54 (Part IV) (United Nations publications, Sales No. E.96.XVII.13).

[147] Economic and Social Commission for Asia and the Pacific, *Comparative Study on Migration, Urbanization and Development in ESCAP Region. National Migration Surveys,* Manuals I-IX (Bangkok, 1984).

[148] Statistical Papers, No. 58, Rev.1 (United Nations publication, Sales No. E.98.XVII.14).

[149] The Standard Rules on the Equalization of Opportunities for Persons with Disabilities were adopted by the United Nations General Assembly at its 48th session on 20 December 1993 (Resolution 48/96).

[150] The World Programme of Action concerning Disabled Persons was adopted by the United Nations General Assembly at its 37th regular session on 3 December 1982, by its resolution 37/52.

[151] Statistics on Special Population Groups, No. 8 (United Nations publication, Sales No. E.96. XVII.4 and Corr.1).

Such tabulations are designed to assess the impact of migration on receiving countries, to understand patterns of diversity and develop programmes for the adaptation of migrants to new countries, and to serve as a source of information on emigration from sending countries. For further details, see the following United Nations publications: *National Migration Surveys,* Manuals I-IX[147] and *Recommendations on Statistics of International Migration, Revision 1.*[148]

3.78. The census is also an important source of data on persons with disabilities. Census data help to monitor the social and living conditions of persons with disabilities in terms of school attendance, educational attainment, employment, marital status and living arrangements. The data also provide a basis for developing policies to meet the needs of persons with disabilities and for evaluating the effectiveness of these policies, as demonstrated in the following: *Standard Rules on the Equalization of Opportunities for Persons with Disabilities*[149]; *World Programme of Action Concerning Disabled Persons;*[150] *Manual for the Development of Statistical Information for Disability Programmes and Policies.*[151]

2. Uses of housing censuses

3.79. The primary uses of information from housing censuses include development of a basis for planning housing and human settlement programmes and policies, public and private sector studies of urban and other non-agricultural land use, evaluation of the adequacy of housing stock and assessment of the need and market for new housing, and studies of the living conditions of the homeless and those living in temporary or substandard housing. Information collected on the number of sets, type and characteristics of living quarters and their occupants is crucial from the point of view of monitoring housing conditions and needs of the population. Combined with the information collected by regular annual statistical programmes on housing construction, data from the housing census provide a basis for identifying national, regional and local housing patterns which are needed for the development of a rational housing market aimed at stimulating various types of housing construction. The type and quality of shelter in which people are housed, that is to say, the space, degree of crowding, facilities, surroundings and available transport, affect their economic activity, health, social intercourse and general outlook. The supply, characteristics and costs of housing are therefore subjects for which the housing census is an important source of information.

B. Uses of small area data

3.80. Censuses provide data from the highest to the lowest geographical levels of aggregation. Tabulations from census results yield the relevant statistics for any reasonable combination of characteristics for the country as a whole, regions or provinces, down to small areas such as localities, villages, and even enumeration areas. This important feature of the census makes the data amenable to the development of estimates of variables of interest for small/local areas in two major ways: directly from the production of tables from the micro-level data for the required characteristics, and indirectly from applying estimation techniques by combining other sources, such as sample surveys and administrative statistics to the population and housing census results.

3.81. Census data are typically aggregations of data for many individual small areas, and may commonly be used to study large regions or entire nations. Data for small areas enable the user to obtain statistical information about any number of local areas of interest, in addition to showing variations among small areas in individual parts of the country. Modern computer technology greatly facilitates the utilization of census results for analysing the information for small areas, limited only by issues of confidentiality and collection design when cell entries in cross-tabulations become very small. For example, the analysis of whether population programmes have affected the level of fertility at a regional level may be carried out by analysing data from the smallest administrative units so as to observe local variation and produce more accurate assessments of cause and effect.

3.82.   Implementation of various national social and economic development programmes is a function of the state, province or lower levels of government in many countries. Results of population and housing censuses are useful for planning and monitoring development at the local area, small town level or small area. Small area data are also important for private businesses in developing their distribution and marketing strategies. For example, information on housing demand from the population and housing census may be used by local authorities, local real estate companies, building and housing development contractors, and manufacturers of construction materials, among others.

3.83.   Census data have been traditionally aggregated by various types of administrative units (for example, towns, villages, provinces, electoral units and so forth). In addition, other types of small areas are sometimes used in the census that are essentially statistical in nature (for example, census tracts and grid squares which do not change from census to census, and very small units such as city blocks or block faces). There have also been increasing demands for small area data that cut across the local administrative boundaries. Population and housing censuses provide a powerful tool for assessing the impact of population on the environment, for example, on drainage basins and on water resource management systems. The spatial units for such a study may combine a group of local administrative areas. In this situation the availability of census databases with mapping capability (see paras. 1.126–1.128) is of great importance.

3.84.   Tabulations for small areas may be prepared on the basis of the resident population of each area or on the basis of the population present in each area at the time of the census. Tabulations relating to the resident population are produced for the apportionment of representation in legislative bodies, the measurement of internal migration, the computation of measures of fertility and mortality by place of residence, and the planning and administration of such services as schools and housing, which have relevance only to the resident population. Tabulations based on the population present in the area at the time of the census are useful where this population is considerably larger than the resident population and thus raises the demand for products and services above the level required by the resident population alone. The combined population and housing census may also be used to make comparisons of resident and daytime populations in specific localities, if an item on place of work is included in the population census. As indicated in part one (see paras. 1.14–1.19), users need to express their needs for particular data disseminated in a given format, based on the usual residence or place of enumeration, at an early stage of census preparations.

3.85.   It was mentioned in chapter 1 how the census plays an essential role in the economic and social components of the national statistical system and serves as a sampling frame for sample surveys. Another significant way in which the census results complement survey statistics is in small area estimation, whereby models constructed from survey data are applied to census results for any specified geographical area. This estimation approach may be used for generating such indicators as employ-

[152] Technical report on "Collection of economic characteristics in population censuses: technical report" (ST/ESA/STAT/119), chap. XVII.

ment, poverty and other economic indicators, for which measurement is required at the local area level.[152] The application of small area estimation technique to poverty measurement and mapping is an important extension in the use of census results. If such use is contemplated, it would need to be taken into account during the planning stages of the census exercise, when decisions about topics to be included in the census are being made.

C. Cross-cutting and emerging social issues

3.86.   Reflecting the concerns and priorities among countries around the world, the United Nations convened, between 1990 and 1996, a series of global conferences: on children, education, environment, human rights, population, social development, women and human settlements. Each of these conferences recognized the importance of adequate information in formulating policy and monitoring progress in the achievement of conference goals, and called on countries and international organizations to develop and improve the requisite statistics and indicators. These recommendations are reflected for example in the Vienna Declaration and Programme of Action of the World Conference on Human Rights;[153] the Programme of Action of the International Conference on Population and Development;[154] the Copenhagen Declaration on Social Development and the Programme of Action of the World Summit for Social Development;[155] and the Platform for Action[156] adopted by the Fourth World Conference on Women. The programmes of action adopted by these international conferences targeted many interrelated areas of concern, and called for improved statistics to monitor progress. In deciding which social groups merit monitoring in regard to measuring the disadvantages suffered by particular groups of people, each country should determine which groups within it need special attention. Some of the common factors leading to social disadvantage are gender, age, physical or mental impairment, race, creed, and so forth. The disadvantaged are not necessarily small in number; they may constitute the majority of the population.[157]

[153] A/CONF.157/24 (Part I), chap. III.

[154] *Report of the International Conference on Population and Development, Cairo, 5-13 September 1994* (United Nations publication, Sales No. E.95.XIII.18), chap. I, resolution 1, annex.

[155] *Report of the World Summit for Social Development, Copenhagen, 6-12 March 1995* (United Nations publication, Sales No. E.96.IV.8), chap. I, resolution 1, annexes I and II.

[156] *Report of the Fourth World Conference on Women, Beijing, 4-15 September 1995* (United Nations publication, Sales No. E.96.IV.13), chap. I, resolution I, annex II.

[157] Note by the Secretary-General transmitting the report of the Expert Group on the Statistical Implications of Recent Major United Nations Conferences (E/CN.3/AC.1/1996/R.4), annex, paras. 68-69. Presented to the Working Group on International Statistical Programmes and Coordination at its eighteenth session, New York, 16-19 April 1996.

3.87.   To meet the need for statistics on gender, many activities have been undertaken during the last two decades at the national and international levels to improve concepts, definitions and classifications for collection of statistics related to women and men. In the present publication, the importance of the population and housing census as a data source has often been stressed. The population and housing census is also the principal or sometimes the only comprehensive national data source with respect to meeting the need for statistics on children, youth, the elderly and the disabled in the development of policies and programmes at the national and the international levels. Therefore, it is important that countries identify data requirements concerning various population groups of particular interest when planning their censuses and ensure that the definitions and classification to be followed in censuses are appropriate and also consistent with those in use for the entire population.

3.88.   Furthermore, the census tabulation plan should ensure in advance the inclusion of all relevant details about special population groups and a range of cross-classifications for each group, with a view to analysing its social and economic conditions. Concepts and methods for the census and the tabulation plan should be reviewed with users concerned with statistics for each special population group. In the case of some groups, for example, people with disability, a special set of questions is required to identify members of the group. In the case of others, standard questions, for example, on age, are sufficient to identify groups such as children, youth and the elderly. In both cases, most variables needed for cross-tabulations are already provided for in the international recommendations and many national censuses. In the census operations, however, attention will often need to be given to improvement of coverage, quality-of-data issues and avoidance of stereotypic treatment. The present section deals with gender, a few special population categories such as children and youth, the elderly, and persons with disabilities, so as to assist in the preparing of detailed tabulations and databases according to international standards.

1. Statistics on gender

3.89.   The global conferences on women have contributed to an increased awareness of the importance of statistics not only on women but, more broadly, on gender issues. For example, in developing census plans in a number of countries, efforts have been made to review and assess the adequacy of statistics for understanding the diversity of both women's and men's lives. It is now recognized that biases in statistics extend, in the case of women, to their economic roles and in the case of men, to their roles in the family as husband and father and their roles in the household. Improvement of statistics and statistical methods related to gender should be an important priority at all stages of work on the census, in planning, data collection, analysis and dissemination, and in all topics.

3.90.   In addition to the more general problems of the quality of census data, two other types of problem that apply particularly to women and stem from sex-based stereotypes and sex biases have been noted. The first type is based, for example, on the idea that women are simply homemakers and therefore not part of the economically active population. Similarly, the notion that only men can be heads of the household affects the way questions have been designed and asked in censuses. Such stereotypes also affect the way respondents reply to the questions. If, for example, the gardening and poultry-raising done by many rural women are not perceived as work, such women may not be reported as economically active even though those activities may be the main source of family livelihood.

3.91.   The second type of problem relates to biases in the collection, processing, compilation and presentation of data. For example, when census tabulations are prepared for the employed by occupation, they may be prepared either for males only or for both sexes, but only on the assumption that information on the occupational pattern of women is not of much use.

3.92.   During the past few decades, considerable effort has been devoted, on the one hand, to reviewing such bias and its impact on statistics concerning the situation of women and, on the other hand, to improving the concepts and methods involved in the collection of data in censuses and surveys. Related improvements in the revised System of National Accounts (SNA) and the International Labour Organization (IL0) recommendations concerning statistics of the economically active population are also of importance to the population census. They are intended to overcome the above-mentioned conceptual deficiencies and to identify all women active in agriculture and in the informal sector. Similarly, efforts at the national level have been focused, for example, on eliminating biases in concepts, classifications and definitions of head of the household. For more information on these developments and their application in censuses for the improvement of statistics on women, see *Improving Concepts and Methods for Statistics and Indicators on the Situation of Women*[158] and *Methods of Measuring Women's Economic Activity: Technical Report.*[159]

3.93.   Important statistical series and measures on the status of women can be readily obtained based on the topics in paragraph 2.16 and recommended tabulations for preparation from censuses. Furthermore, in the case of most topics, the primary

[158] Studies in Methods, No. 33 (United Nations publication, Sales No. E.84.XVII.3).

[159] Studies in Methods, No. 59 (United Nations publication, Sales No. E.93.XVII.6).

unit of classification is the individual and therefore a vast array of indicators may be obtained by devising appropriate additional cross-classifications for the female and male populations separately. For an illustration of census topics and tabulations that are useful for developing comprehensive statistics on women, see "Statistics and indicators on women and men"[160] and *Handbook for the Development of National Statistical Data Bases on Women and Development.*[161] The household and family status classifications presented in paragraph 2.132 are appropriate for analysing the living situation of women and men, with specific reference to single mothers and fathers and elderly women and men living alone.

3.94.   It should be emphasized that while all data collected at the individual level can be presented by sex, this is not always done. Cross-classifications by sex tend to be suppressed when cross-tabulations become complex with multiple-variable tables. In order to satisfy one basic condition for gender statistics, which is that all statistics on individuals should be presented by sex, sex should be considered the overriding variable in all tables, irrespective of the medium of storage or dissemination. This disaggregation by gender should be provided in all publications, databases and computer printouts of census tables on individuals.

3.95.   Another important consideration is to broaden the target of dissemination and use of census data by popularizing the statistics that are published. One approach to achieving this wide outreach is to present statistics in the form of charts and simplified tables, with a simple and clear interpretation of the data. Countries planning to issue an analytical report might wish to consider using such innovative techniques and formats as those presented in *The World's Women 2005: Progress in Statistics*[162] in order to highlight the census findings and to make the statistics more readily accessible to a wide group of users. The analytical publication could cover the main census topics or alternatively a few areas that are especially important to understanding the relative position of women and men in the country. Guidelines on preparing an analytical publication on gender statistics at the national level are provided in *Handbook for Producing National Statistical Reports on Women and Men.*[163]

2.   Statistics on children and youth

3.96.   Extensive data on children and youth are available in censuses but may need improvements in terms of coverage and quality of information on specific characteristics, and on their presentation.

3.97.   For statistical purposes, "children" are defined as persons under 15 years of age and "youth" are defined as those aged 15-24. However, it is useful to further divide these special groups by five-year age groups (or nationally, by groups of specific school ages) because of the rapid changes in characteristics in this age range, such as in school attendance, marital status and activity status. Also, because of differences by sex in the age at marriage, family or household status and entry into the labour market, data should be classified not only by age but also by sex. To this end, the distribution by single years of age and sex is useful. If single-year age distribution is not feasible for young children under age 5, it would be desirable to distinguish between those under one year of age (infants) and those aged 1-4. For youth aged 15-19, it would be desirable to distinguish between those 15-17 years of age and those 18-19 years of age, or to have a distinction corresponding to the age below which the country considers an individual to be a minor.

3.98.   For the purpose of developing statistics on children, the principal topics in census recommendations include, inter alia, (*a*) sex, (*b*) age, (*c*) school attendance

[160]   Available at: http://unstats. un.org/unsd/demographic/ products/indwm/indwm2.htm.

[161]   Social Statistics and Indicators, No. 6 (United Nations publication, Sales No. E.89. XVII.9).

[162]   United Nations publication, Sales No. E.05.XVII.7.

[163]   See note by the Secretary-General transmitting the report of the Expert Group on the Statistical Implications of Recent Major United Nations Conferences (E/CN.3/AC.1/1996/R.4) annex.

(for school-age children) and (*d*) relationship to head or other reference member of the household.

3.99. Children under five years of age are generally underenumerated in censuses and all efforts should be made to achieve complete coverage of this group. Further improvement of age data should be striven for in censuses, including an in-depth evaluation of the accuracy of age data.

3.100. Given the priority on the girl child highlighted by the World Summit for Children (1990), the International Conference on Population and Development (1994) and the Fourth World Conference on Women (1995), special attention needs to be given to improving and disseminating statistics on children. Of particular concern is the situation of the girl child with respect to school attendance, mortality, early marriage and so forth A basic problem with statistics on the girl child is that data on children ever born and children surviving tend not to be disaggregated by sex at either the questionnaire design or the tabulation stage. These data are used for indirect estimates of child mortality.

3.101. The principal topics of investigation identified for children apply also to youth, with the following additions: (*a*) marital status, (*b*) literacy, (*c*) educational attainment, (*d*) economic activity status, (*e*) number of children born alive and (*f*) age at marriage.

3.102. Some of the useful statistics and measures can be readily compiled based on the above-mentioned topics, while any additional indicators can also be obtained based on more detailed cross-classifications using the existing recommended census topics and/or tabulations. For an illustrative set of indicators on youth, see *Statistical Indicators on Youth*.[164]

3. Statistics on the elderly

3.103. For the elderly also, extensive data are available in population and housing censuses but may need detailed age-sex classification, as described below.

3.104. The elderly are defined as all persons aged 60 years and over. For purposes of classification, depending on the national situation, it is useful to tabulate data by five-year age groups up to age 100, instead of including them in the single broad age category 60 and over.

3.105. For the purpose of developing statistics and indicators on the elderly, the principal topics in census recommendations include, inter alia, (*a*) sex, (*b*) age, (*c*) marital status, (*d*) economic activity status, (*e*) income, (*f*) household (or family) composition, (*g*) type of living quarters and (*h*) institutional population.

3.106. The statistics needed for studies of the elderly are disparate, depending as they do on national policies and circumstances. Internationally, no illustrative list of indicators is available to ensure appropriate tabulations from the censuses. For some guidance in this area, see *Handbook on Social Indicators*[165] and consult regional recommendations, where available.

4. Statistics on persons with disabilities

3.107. The census can provide a valuable source of information on the frequency and distribution of disability in the population, at national, regional and local levels. Experience shows that although an increasing number of countries ask questions about disability in their censuses, the presentation of disability data has often been limited to tabulations showing the number of specific severe disabilities present

[164] Statistics on Special Population Groups, No. 1 (United Nations publication, Sales No. E.85. XVII.12).

[165] Studies in Methods, No. 49 (United Nations publication, Sales No. E.89.XVII.6).

in the population. Unfortunately, cross tabulations with other characteristics are not usually made.

3.108. A great deal of work on concepts, classifications and development of statistics on persons with disabilities has been undertaken in recent years, particularly through the work of the Washington Group on Disability Statistics,[166] and increasing numbers of countries are including disability as a topic in their censuses. For the second time, recommendations on including disability questions in a population census are included in these guidelines (see paras. 2.350-2.380). A brief treatment of this topic is given below to highlight issues involved in preparing detailed census tabulations on people with disability.

3.109. For the purpose of developing statistics on the situation of persons with disabilities the principal topics in census recommendations that would be necessary for the assessment of equalization of opportunities include, inter alia (*a*) sex, (*b*) age, (*c*) place of residence, (*d*) type of household, (*e*) marital status, (*f*) educational attainment and school attendance, (*g*) activity status, (*h*) status of employment, (*i*) industry and (*j*) occupation.

3.110. Not only should the tabulation plan for the disability data include prevalence rates by sex and age, but it is also very important that tabulations comparing persons with and without disabilities on key social and economic characteristics be presented. Tabulations based on the topics listed above provide information on prevalence of disability and on the situation of persons with disabilities. In addition, tabulations should be presented in a way that facilitates comparisons of persons with disabilities and those without. For further discussion on the development and use of concepts, definitions and indicators related to disability statistics, see the *Guidelines and Principles for the Development of Disability Statistics*[167] and *Manual for the Development of Statistical Information for Disability Programmes and Policies*.[168]

5.   Ethno-cultural characteristics

3.111. Collecting information about ethnic composition of population allows for deeper studying of the ethnic background of a country's population, especially with respect to indigenous population, international migrants and other specific groups of population (for example nomads).

3.112. There are some difficulties in collecting this information since some population groups may name their ethnic identification based on its local meaning and in order to correctly allocate these persons to their particular ethnic group it is necessary to compile a list of ethnos, sub-ethnos and local definitions of small ethnic population groups. This will allow for obtaining accurate data about the ethnic composition of population. It would also be useful if scientists and specialists in the field of ethnography, as well as organizations dealing with indigenous people, would be involved in creating such a list.

3.113. In order to obtain comprehensive information characterizing ethnic composition of population, it would be useful to tabulate data by (*a*) sex, (*b*) age, (c) place of residence, (*d*) marital status, (*e*) birth, (*f*) death, (*g*) education, (*h*) economic activity, (*i*) employment status, (*j*) industry, (*k*) occupation, and (*l*) type and size of household.

3.114. It is important to obtain comprehensive information on indigenous populations in order to have statistics on the number as well as the demographic and socio-economic structure of the given population group. These data would be valuable information to support the development of programmes for social support of indigenous peoples.

[166] For more information on the Washington Group on Disability Statistics, go to: http://www.cdc.gov/nchs/citygroup.htm.

[167] Statistics on Special Population Groups, No. 10 (United Nations publication, Sales No. E.01. XVII.15).

[168] Statistics on Special Population Groups, No. 8 (United Nations publication, Sales No. E.96. XVII.4 and Corr.1).

3.115. Statistics about the ethnic composition of international migrants together with information about country of birth and citizenship will help to more precisely determine the flows and volume of international migration.

3.116. Population censuses are also a source of information about religious identification of the population. It would be useful to obtain this information by (*a*) sex, (*b*) age, (*c*) ethnic group, (*d*) place of residence, and (*d*) place of birth. This information would be useful to study distribution of confessions.

3.117. Information about knowledge of languages is widely used. Countries find it useful to study the official language of the country as well as mother tongues or some other languages. In any case it would be useful to have this information by (*a*) sex, (*b*) age, (*c*) ethnic group, (*d*) place of residence, and (*d*) place of birth.

3.118. Information about knowledge of the official language of the country would be very useful for studying the integration of international migrants and may be used, for example, for development of programmes to learn the language.

3.119. Information about knowledge of the mother tongue of indigenous population is very important. This information could allow obtaining statistics of "indigenous" languages and would be very useful for development programmes to support the development of those languages.

D. Development indicators

3.120. Major United Nations conferences and summits held in the 1990s[169] generated much focus on statistical implications of the outcomes of these conferences. These conferences recognized the importance of adequate information in formulating policy and monitoring progress in the achievement of conference goals, and called on countries and international organizations to develop and improve the necessary statistics and indicators. The demand for indicators by these conferences, which covered a wide range of issues and concerns, necessitated multiple sets of indicators and a great burden on statistical agencies to provide the statistics to meet the reporting requirements of the conferences. A lot of effort was therefore devoted to rationalizing and harmonizing the various sets of conference indicators with the ultimate aim of strengthening national capacity to produce relevant indicators for policy decision-making. Consequently, at its thirty-second session (New York, 6-9 March 2001), the Statistical Commission recommended the formation of the Friends of the Chair Adviser Group to, among other things, "technically validate conference indicators and elaborate recommendations for a limited list of indicators".[170] The work carried out by the Friends of the Chair as well as their recommended set of indicators was presented to the Statistical Commission at its thirty-third session (New York, 5-8 March 2002).[171]

3.121. In recent years, however, the focus has shifted to the Millennium Development Indicators as a framework for assessing and monitoring progress towards a set of internationally agreed development goals and targets.[172] This followed the adoption by the General Assembly, in 2000, of the United Nations Millennium Declaration committing to a global partnership to make the right to development a reality for everyone. The objective of the Millennium Declaration was to promote "a comprehensive approach and a coordinated strategy, tackling many problems simultaneously across a broad front".[173] Embedded in the Declaration were the Millennium Development Goals, a set of time-bound targets aimed at improving human well-being and lifting peoples and nations out of poverty by the year 2015. The framework subsequently developed for monitoring and reporting on progress towards the achievement of these

[169] The major conferences include the International Conference on Population and Development (Cairo, 5-13 September 1994), the World Summit for Social Development (Copenhagen, 6-12 March 1995), and the Fourth World Conference on Women (Beijing, 4-15 September 1995).

[170] *Report of the Statistical Commission on its thirty-second session, 6-9 March 2001, Official Records of the Economic and Social Council, Supplement No.4* (E/2001/24-E/CN.3/2001/25).

[171] Report of the Friends of the Chair of the Statistical Commission on an assessment of the statistical indicators derived from United Nations summit meetings: Note by the Secretary-General (E/CN.3/2002/26), available at http://unstats.un.org/unsd/statcom/sc2002.htm.

[172] More information on the Millennium Indicators can be found at http://unstats.un.org/unsd/mi/mi_goals.asp, and on the Millennium Development Goals at http://www.un.org/millenniumgoals/.

[173] Road map towards the implementation of the United Nations Millennium Declaration: Report of the Secretary-General (A/56/326).

[174] Harmonization of indicators and reporting on progress towards the millennium development goals: Report of the Secretary General (E/CN.3/2003/21).

goals and targets and indicators comprises 48 indicators, as shown in table 3. The indicators provide an agreed starting point for global monitoring of targets and goals that have been universally endorsed at the highest level.[174]

3.122.   At the global level, monitoring is based on data series compiled by specialized international organizations responsible for the different areas covered by the Millennium Development Goals. The work is undertaken through the Inter-agency and Expert Group on Millennium Development Goals Indicators, coordinated by the United Nations Statistics Division of the Department of Economic and Social Affairs of the United Nations Secretariat. The data are contained in the Millennium Indicators Database maintained by the United Nations Statistics Division and available at http://millenniumindicators.un.org/unsd/mdg. At the national level, the Millennium Development Goals framework is adapted to national circumstances and policy priorities and is used to track progress made within the country.

3.123.   It should be emphasized that both global and national reporting and monitoring require reliable and comparable national data for the compilation of the Millennium Indicators. In this regard, it is of paramount importance that countries have the statistical capacity to produce, analyse and disseminate the requisite data for the Millennium Indicators. The availability of reliable statistics and the capacity of the governments to systematically measure and monitor indicators is a critical success factor for the achievement of the Millennium Development Goals. The lack of statistical capabilities in some developing countries makes it difficult to obtain good and reliable data. Many countries do not have a sustainable, coherent programme of household surveys, or administrative data systems which can be used to produce basic statistics routinely.[175] Where basic statistical systems are not available, the global monitoring may have to rely on national and international estimates of widely varying quality and reliability. This may lead to misjudgements regarding progress and may undermine the effectiveness of policy interventions at national and subnational levels.

[175] See, for example, the case studies and international study of the PARIS21 Task Team on Improved Statistical Support for Monitoring Development Goals, available from http://www.paris21.org/pages/task-teams/teams/introduction/index.asp?id_team=2.

3.124.   It is therefore to the advantage of all concerned when countries have the required data in order to avoid reliance on estimates of national Millennium Development Goal Indicators. It should be noted, however, all the sources of data (census, sample surveys and administrative records) are required to fulfil the data requirements for the Millennium Development Goals. By their nature, however, most of the Indicators cannot be computed from data that are typically collected through population and housing censuses, but would require data from either household sample surveys or vital statistics. There are some, however, that can potentially be computed from census data, as shown in table 4. Even when not collected directly by the population and housing census, however, statistics needed for producing Indicators is dependent on the censuses in quite a few ways. For example, the population census provides the total population figure, which is a denominator for most Indicators. Also, the population and housing census provides the sample frame without which the design of necessary and accurate household surveys would be adversely affected. For these reasons, therefore, a functional national integrated statistical system is of fundamental importance for the generation of data for the Millennium Development Goal Indicators, and to support other national reporting requirements such as those in regard to the goals of the Convention on the Elimination of All Forms of Discrimination against Women and the 1994 International Conference on Population and Development.

Table 3

Millennium Development Goals, targets and indicators (effective as of 8 September 2003)

Goals and targets (from the Millennium Declaration)	Indicators for monitoring progress

Goal 1.   Eradicate extreme poverty and hunger

Target 1. Halve, between 1990 and 2015, the proportion of people whose income is less than one dollar a day.	1. Proportion of population below $1 (PPP) per day[a] 2. Poverty gap ratio [incidence x depth of poverty] 3. Share of poorest quintile in national consumption
Target 2. Halve, between 1990 and 2015, the proportion of people who suffer from hunger.	4. Prevalence of underweight children under-five years of age 5. Proportion of population below minimum level of dietary energy consumption

Goal 2.   Achieve universal primary education

Target 3. Ensure that, by 2015, children everywhere, boys and girls alike, will be able to complete a full course of primary schooling.	6. Net enrolment ratio in primary education 7. Proportion of pupils starting grade 1 who reach grade 5[b] 8. Literacy rate of 15-24 year-olds

Goal 3.   Promote gender equality and empower women

Target 4. Eliminate gender disparity in primary and secondary education, preferably by 2005, and in all levels of education no later than 2015.	9. Ratios of girls to boys in primary, secondary and tertiary education 10. Ratio of literate women to men, 15-24 years old 11. Share of women in wage employment in the non-agricultural sector 12. Proportion of seats held by women in national parliament

Goal 4.   Reduce child mortality

Target 5. Reduce by two thirds, between 1990 and 2015, the under-five mortality rate.	13. Under-five mortality rate 14. Infant mortality rate 15. Proportion of 1 year-old children immunized against measles

Goal 5.   Improve maternal health

Target 6. Reduce by three quarters, between 1990 and 2015, the maternal mortality ratio.	16. Maternal mortality ratio 17. Proportion of births attended by skilled health personnel

Goal 6.   Combat HIV/AIDS, malaria and other diseases

Target 7. Have halted by 2015 and begun to reverse the spread of HIV/AIDS.	18. HIV prevalence among pregnant women aged 5-24 years 19. Condom use rate of the contraceptive prevalence rate[c] 19a. Condom use at last high-risk sex 19b. Percentage of population aged 15-24 years with comprehensive correct knowledge of HIV/AIDS[d] 19c. Contraceptive prevalence rate 20. Ratio of school attendance of orphans to school attendance of non-orphans aged 10-14 years
Target 8. Have halted by 2015 and begun to reverse the incidence of malaria and other major diseases.	21. Prevalence and death rates associated with malaria 22. Proportion of population in malaria-risk areas using effective malaria prevention and treatment measures[e] 23. Prevalence and death rates associated with tuberculosis 24. Proportion of tuberculosis cases detected and cured under directly observed treatment short course (internationally recommended TB control strategy)

[a]   For monitoring country poverty trends, indicators based on national poverty lines should be used, where available.

[b]   An alternative indicator under development is "primary completion rate".

[c]   Amongst contraceptive methods, only condoms are effective in preventing HIV transmission. Since the condom use rate is only measured among women in union, it is supplemented by an indicator on condom use in high-risk situations (indicator 19a) and an indicator on HIV/AIDS knowledge (indicator 19b). Indicator 19c (contraceptive prevalence rate) is also useful in tracking progress in other health, gender and poverty goals.

[d]   This indicator is defined as the percentage of population aged 15-24 who correctly identify the two major ways of preventing the sexual transmission of HIV (using condoms and limiting sex to one faithful, uninfected partner), who reject the two most common local misconceptions about HIV transmission, and who know that a healthy-looking person can transmit HIV. However, since there are currently not a sufficient number of surveys to be able to calculate the indicator as defined above, UNICEF, in collaboration with UNAIDS and WHO, produced two proxy indicators that represent two components

Continued on the next page

Goals and targets (from the Millennium Declaration)	Indicators for monitoring progress

Goal 7. Ensure environmental sustainability

Target 9.	Integrate the principles of sustainable development into country policies and programmes and reverse the loss of environmental resources.	25. Proportion of land area covered by forest 26. Ratio of area protected to maintain biological diversity to surface area 27. Energy use (kg oil equivalent) per $1 gross domestic product (GDP) (PPP) 28. Carbon dioxide emissions per capita and consumption of ozone-depleting chlorofluorocarbons (CFCs) (ODP tons) 29. Proportion of population using solid fuels
Target 10.	Halve, by 2015, the proportion of people without sustainable access to safe drinking water and basic sanitation.	30. Proportion of population with sustainable access to an improved water source, urban and rural 31. Proportion of population with access to improved sanitation, urban and rural
Target 11.	By 2020, to have achieved a significant improvement in the lives of at least 100 million slum dwellers.	32. Proportion of households with access to secure tenure

Goal 8. Develop a global partnership for development

Target 12.	Develop further an open, rule-based, predictable, non-discriminatory trading and financial system. *Includes a commitment to good governance, development and poverty reduction, both nationally and internationally.*	*Some of the indicators listed below are monitored separately for the least developed countries, Africa, landlocked developing countries and small island developing States.* *Official development assistance (ODA)* 33. Net ODA, total and to the least developed countries, as percentage of OECD/DAC donors' gross national income
Target 13.	Address the special needs of the least developed countries. *Includes tariff and quota free access for the least developed countries' exports; enhanced programme of debt relief for heavily indebted poor countries (HIPC) and cancellation of official bilateral debt; and more generous Official Development Assistance (ODA) for countries committed to poverty reduction.*	34. Proportion of total bilateral, sector-allocable ODA of OECD/DAC donors to basic social services (basic education, primary health care, nutrition, safe water and sanitation). 35. Proportion of bilateral official development assistance of OECD/DAC donors that is untied 36. ODA received in landlocked developing countries as a proportion of their gross national incomes
Target 14.	Address the special needs of landlocked developing countries and small island developing States (through the Programme of Action for the Sustainable Development of Small Island Developing States and the outcome of the twenty-second special session of the General Assembly).	37. ODA received in small island developing States as a proportion of their gross national incomes *Market access* 38. Proportion of total developed country imports (by value and excluding arms) from developing countries and least developed countries, admitted free of duty
Target 15.	Deal comprehensively with the debt problems of developing countries through national and international measures in order to make debt sustainable in the long term.	39. Average tariffs imposed by developed countries on agricultural products and textiles and clothing from developing countries 40. Agricultural support estimate for OECD countries as a percentage of their gross domestic product 41. Proportion of ODA provided to help build trade capacity *Debt sustainability* 42. Total number of countries that have reached their HIPC decision points and number that have reached their HIPC completion points (cumulative) 43. Debt relief committed under HIPC Initiative 44. Debt service as a percentage of exports of goods and services
Target 16.	In cooperation with developing countries, develop and implement strategies for decent and productive work for youth.	45. Unemployment rate of young people aged 15-24 years, each sex and total[f]
Target 17.	In cooperation with pharmaceutical companies, provide access to affordable essential drugs in developing countries.	46. Proportion of population with access to affordable essential drugs on a sustainable basis
Target 18.	In cooperation with the private sector, make available the benefits of new technologies, especially information and communications.	47. Telephone lines and cellular subscribers per 100 population 48. Personal computers in use per 100 population and Internet users per 100 population

of the actual indicator. They are the following: (*a*) percentage of women and men 15-24 who know that a person can protect herself/himself from HIV infection by "consistent use of condom"; (*b*) percentage of women and men 15-24 who know a healthy-looking person can transmit HIV.

[e] Prevention to be measured by the percentage of children under 5 sleeping under insecticide-treated bednets; treatment to be measured by percentage of children under 5 who are appropriately treated.

[f] An improved measure of the target for future years is under development by the International Labour Organization.

Table 4
Millennium Development Goal Indicators that could be produced from population and housing censuses

No.	Indicator
8	Literacy rate of 15-24 years old
10	Ratio of literate women to men, 15-24 years old
11	Share of women in wage employment in the non-agricultural sector
13	Under five mortality rate (potential)
14	Infant mortality rate (potential)
16	Maternal mortality ratio (potential)
21	Death rates associated with malaria (potential)
23	Death rates associated with tuberculosis (potential)
45	Unemployment rate of young people aged 15-24 years, each sex and total
29	Proportion of the population using solid fuels
30	Proportion of population with sustainable access to an improved water source, urban and rural
31	Proportion of population with access to improved sanitation, urban and rural
32	Proportion of households with access to secure tenure
47	Telephone lines and cellular subscribers per 100 population (potential)
48	Personal computer in use in 100 population and Internet use per 100 population (potential)

E. Promotion of, and training on, uses of census data

3.125.　The main purpose of a census is to collect, process and disseminate information that will be used as the basis of informed, evidence-based decision-making. The benefits of this approach to decisions are not always apparent to users, especially in situations where other approaches may have been used in the past. It is therefore important to promote such uses of census results among users.

3.126.　In other cases, users may be willing to use the information but require additional training to more fully understand the data. Such training may be usefully combined with training in statistical dissemination techniques and/or uses of more advanced data products. At a very basic level, some users may require training in such mundane issues as how to contact the national statistical office and/or how to find the information they require within the systems of that office.

3.127.　Whichever approach is taken to enhancing promotion and training in the use of statistical data, a number of strategic issues need to be addressed. These include:

(*a*)　Ensuring that the needs for training are identified early in the census planning process and that required funds are included in the census budget. In this regard it should be noted that in many cases the courses requested by users will be specific to those users: in such a case it may be desirable to request the user to provide funds to cover the marginal (or full) costs of the course;

(*b*)　The proposed courses or materials should be fully integrated into the overall census advocacy or training programme. It is essential that messages about the use of data fully reflect the message(s) given when initially advocating taking the census and/or seeking public cooperation with and participation in the collection phase;

(c)   If the training facility is itself promoted properly, it is highly likely that the demand for training will far outstrip the ability of the statistical office to deliver it. In this case it will be necessary for the statistical office to have prepared transparent strategies that (a) identify those areas in which the statistical office wishes to participate (for example, dealing with lifeline clients; and topics on which the statistical office has particular knowledge or expertise); (b) establish partnerships with other bodies to provide training in other cases; (c) use approaches other than classroom training to provide learning-at-a-distance opportunities (for example, use of self-help facilities on CD-ROM); and (d) have a pricing regime to cover costs where this is seen as desirable.

3.128.   The possible list of target audiences and topics for such training is very much a matter for decision by countries. It should be noted, however, that basic training in the use and interpretation of the results of one census is a very strong method of advocating support for future censuses. It is thus recommended that countries consider development of a basic course in (a) potential uses of census data; (b) how to access census data and (c) interpretation of census data at the broadest level, including the interpretation of its completeness and level of accuracy. The target audience for such training should be key decision makers in the political and administrative hierarchy of the country. It should be outlined that the uses of census data at the local level (small areas) offer substantial potential for constructive use of census data: spatial distribution of population by age and sex, for example, provides an ideal framework for local officials to address the most pressing issues of their constituents, such as location of schools, utilities and so forth.

3.129.   A second group of key importance are members of the mass media, such as print, radio and TV journalists. A focus on training such personalities is important because they can carry the message to many other people. This will assist in the general raising of awareness in the population at large, as well as in generating an awareness of the census among the government, academic and business users who may not have contact with the statistical office on a regular basis. Obviously such training should be completely integrated with the overall public relations and advocacy work.

ANNEXES

Annex I
International Classification of Functioning, Disability and Health model

Interactions between components of the International Classification of Functioning, Disability and Health

The interactions between the parts and components are reflected in the following model:

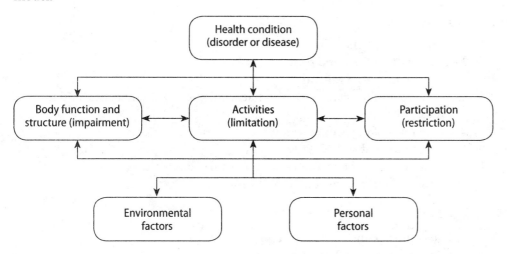

Main concepts, terms and definitions

The main concepts, terms and definitions of the ICF are:

Body functions are the physiological functions of body systems (including psychological functions).

Body structures are anatomical parts of the body such as organs, limbs and their components.

Impairments are problems in body function or structure such as a significant deviation or loss.

Activity is the execution of a task or action by an individual.

Activity limitations are difficulties an individual may have in executing activities.

Participation is involvement in a life situation.

Participation restrictions are problems an individual may experience in involvement in life situations.

Functioning is the umbrella term for body function, structure, activity and participation.

Disability is the umbrella term for impairment, activity limitation and participation restriction.

Environmental factors make up the physical, social and attitudinal environment in which people live and conduct their life.

Personal factors are the particular background of an individual's life and living and comprise features of the individual that are not part of a health condition or health states, such as gender, race, age, fitness, lifestyle habits, coping styles, social background, education, profession, and so forth. ICF does not include a classification of personal factors.

Contextual factors represent the complete background of an individual's life and living including two components, being environmental factors and personal factors which may have an impact on the individual with a health condition and that individual's health and health-related states.

The content of ICF is illustrated by the first-level or parent categories (chapter headings) of each of the classifications included in ICF.

Body functions:

1. Mental functions
2. Sensory functions and pain
3. Voice and speech functions
4. Functions of the cardiovascular, haematological, immunological and respiratory systems
5. Functions of digestive, metabolic and endocrine systems
6. Genitoury and reproductive functions
7. Neuromusculoskeletal and movement-related structures
8. Functions of the skin and related structures

Body structures:

1. Structures of the nervous system
2. The eye, ear and related structures
3. Structures involved in voice and speech
4. Structures of the cardiovascular, immunological and respiratory systems
5. Structures related to the digestive, metabolic and endocrine systems
6. Structures related to the genitourinary and reproductive systems
7. Structures related to movement
8. Skin and related structures

Activity and participation:[a]

1. Learning and applying knowledge
2. General tasks and demands
3. Communication
4. Mobility
5. Self-care
6. Domestic life
7. Interpersonal interactions and relationships
8. Major life areas (such as education, work and employment, economic life)
9. Community, social and civic life

[a] At the time the revision process of the ICIDH was in a final stage it seemed to be possible to distinguish activity and participation at the level of definitions. However it was not possible to reach agreement about the related classifications. For this reason there is one classification for activity and participation (domains) with four suggestions on how to use this in an activity or participation mode.

Environmental factors

1. Products and technology
2. Natural environment and human-made changes to environment
3. Support and relationships
4. Attitudes
5. Services, systems and policies

Personal factors are mentioned as important factors but are not classified in ICF. For health conditions (disorder, disease, injuries and congenital causes of disability) reference is made to the International Statistical Classification of Diseases and Related Health Problems, 10th Revision (ICD-10)[b] and the International Classification of External Causes of Injury (ICECI).[c]

In order to specify the functioning and disability situation of a person, qualifiers are available to indicate the extent and level of functioning/disability and the environmental factors as being facilitators or barriers. The advantage of the ICF is the broad spectrum offered from the body function/structure (impairment) point of view up to the participation one including the influence of environmental factors. It is recommended to use this broad spectrum as often as possible.

[b] http://www.who.int/classifications/icd/en/.

[c] http://www.who.int/classifications/icd/adaptations/iceci/en/index.html.

Annex II
Recommended Tabulations for Population Censuses

List of recommended tabulations for population censuses[a],[b]

[a] Recommended tabulations are identified by an "R" as part of the table number.
[b] An asterisk (*) represents a basic/essential tabulation.

Group 1. Tabulations on geographical and internal migration characteristics

P1.1-R Total population and population of major and minor civil divisions, by urban/rural distribution and by sex*

P1.2-R Population by size-class of locality and by sex*

P1.3-R Population of principal localities and of their urban agglomerations, by sex

P1.4-R Native and foreign-born population, by age and sex*

P1.5-R Population, by duration of residence in locality and major civil division, age and sex*

P 1.6a-R Population by place of usual residence, duration of residence, place of previous residence and sex

P.1.6b-R Population ... years of age and over, by place of usual residence, place of residence at a specified date in the past, age and sex

Group 2. Tabulations on international migration and immigrant stock

P2.1-R Foreign-born population, by country of birth, age and sex

P2.2-R Foreign-born population, by year or period of arrival, country of birth, age and sex*

P2.3-R Population, by country of birth and citizenship, age and sex

P2.4-R Economically active foreign-born population ... years of age and over, by year or period of arrival, main occupation and sex

Group 3. Tabulations on household and family characteristics

P3.1-R Population in households, by relationship to head or other reference member of household, marital status and sex, and size of institutional population

P3.2-R Head or other reference member of household, by age and sex; and other household members, by age and relationship to head or other reference member*

P3.3-R Households, population in households and number of family nuclei, by size of household*

Group 4.   Tabulations on demographic and social characteristics

P4.1-R   Population, by single years of age and sex*

P4.2-R   Population, by marital status, age and sex*

Group 5.   Tabulations on fertility and mortality

P5.1-R   Female population 10 years of age and over, by age and number of children ever born alive by sex*

P5.2-R   Female population 10 years of age and over, by age and number of children living (or dead) by sex*

P5.3-R   Female population … to 49 years of age, by age, number of live births, by sex within the 12 months preceding the census, and deaths among these live births, by sex

P5.4-R   Household deaths, by sex and age within the 12 months preceding the census; and total population, by age and sex

Group 6.   Tabulations on educational characteristics

P6.1-R   Population … years of age and over by school attendance, educational attainment, age and sex*

P6.2-R   Population 5 to 29 years of age, by school attendance, single years of age and sex*

P6.3-R   Population 10 years of age and over, by literacy, age and sex

Group 7.   Tabulations on economic characteristics

P7.1-R   Population … years of age and over, by current (or usual) activity status, educational attainment, age and sex*

P7.2-R   Currently (or usually) active population by activity status, main occupation, age and sex*

P7.3-R   Currently (or usually) active population by activity status, main industry, age and sex*

P7.4-R   Currently (or usually) active population by activity status, main status in employment, age and sex*

P7.5-R   Currently (or usually) active population by activity status, main status in employment, main industry and sex

P7.6-R   Currently (or usually) active population by activity status, main status in employment, main occupation and sex

P7.7-R   Currently (or usually) active population by activity status, main industry, main occupation and sex*

P7.8-R   Population not currently (or usually) active, by functional category, age and sex*

Group 8.   Tabulations on disability characteristics

P8.1-R   Population with and without disabilities by age and sex*

P 8.2-R   Population 5 years of age and over, by disability status, educational attainment, age and sex

P 8.3-R   Population … years of age and over, by disability status, current (or usual) activity status, age and sex

Group 1.　Tabulations on geographical and internal migration characteristics

P1.1-R.　Total population and population of major and minor civil divisions, by urban/rural distribution and by sex

Geographical division and urban/rural distribution	Number of localities	Population by sex		
		Both sexes	Male	Female
Total				
Urban				
Rural				
Major civil division A*				
Urban				
Rural				
Minor civil division A1*				
Urban				
Rural				
Minor civil division A2*				
Major civil division B*				
Urban				
Rural				
Minor civil division B1*				
Urban				
Rural				
Minor civil division B2*				
Urban				
Rural				
.				
.				
.				
Major civil division Z*				
Urban				
Rural				
Minor civil division Z1*				
Urban				
Rural				
Minor civil division Z2*				
Urban				
Rural				
(etc.)				

Population included:　total population

Classifications:

(a)　Geographical division: (i) total country; (ii) each major civil division; (iii) each minor civil division and separately, the number of localities of each geographical division. Distinguish between urban and rural for (i), (ii), and (iii)

(b)　Sex: both sexes; male; female

Metadata for this tabulation:

(a)　Source of statistics:
  - Traditional population census
  - Register-based population census
  - Registers/Surveys systems
  - Rolling surveys
  - Civil registration

(b)　De jure or de facto population or a combination with detailed description

(c)　Definition of urban and rural areas

Core topics:
  - Place of usual residence or Place where present at time of census
  - Sex

Note:

Total population distributed among major and minor civil divisions is frequently a legal requirement of the census, because the results are used for apportionment of representation in legislatures and for various administrative purposes. The tabulation provides data needed for studies and policy analysis with regard to economic and social development of each part of the country, for the location of economic development projects as well as of health facilities. These data are also required for the computation of vital statistics rates usually used in projections of future population of civil divisions.

* Name of major or minor civil division.

P1.2-R. Population by size-class of locality and by sex

Geographical division and size-class of locality	Number of localities	Population by sex		
		Both sexes	Male	Female
Total country				
Total				
All localities				
5,000,000 or more inhabitants				
1,000,000-4,999,999 inhabitants				
500,000-999,999 inhabitants				
100,000-499,999 inhabitants				
50,000-99,999 inhabitants				
20,000-49,999 inhabitants				
10,000-19,999 inhabitants				
5,000-9,999 inhabitants				
2,000-4,999 inhabitants				
1,000-1,999 inhabitants				
500-999 inhabitants				
200-499 inhabitants				
Less than 200 inhabitants				
Population not in localities				
Major civil divisions (as for "Total country")				

Population included: total population

Classifications:
(*a*)   Geographical division: (i) total country; (ii) each major civil division.
(*b*)   Size-class of locality: 5,000,000 or more inhabitants; 1,000,000-4,999,999 inhabitants; 500,000-999,999 inhabitants; 100,000-499,999 inhabitants; 50,000-99,999 inhabitants; 20,000-49,999 inhabitants; 10,000-19,999 inhabitants; 5,000-9,999 inhabitants; 2,000-4,999 inhabitants; 1,000-1,999 inhabitants; 500-999 inhabitants; 200-499 inhabitants; less than 200 inhabitants; and, separately, the number of localities of each size-class
(*c*)   Population not in localities: total
(*d*)   Sex: both sexes; male; female

Metadata for this tabulation:
(*a*)   Source of statistics:
  ➤ Traditional population census
  ➤ Register-based population census
  ➤ Registers/Surveys systems
  ➤ Rolling surveys
  ➤ Civil registration
(*b*)   De jure or de facto population or a combination with detailed description
(*c*)   Definition of locality

Core topics:
  ➤ Place of usual residence or Place where present at time of census
  ➤ Sex

Note:
This tabulation provides data on national patterns of concentration or dispersion of population, which will afford a reasonable degree of international comparability, provided that the unit of classification is the locality as defined in paragraph 2.78. In those countries where the distinction between urban and rural population can be based on size of locality, these data provide the basis for the urban/rural classification and also for the calculation of rates of urbanization. Use of data from successive censuses is possible to assess the rate of change, over given periods, in the number of localities in each size-class and the proportion of the population in each size-class of locality.

P1.3-R. Population of principal localities and of their urban agglomerations, by sex

Locality	Population by sex					
	Both sexes		Male		Female	
	City proper	Urban agglomeration	City proper	Urban agglomeration	City proper	Urban agglomeration
City or town A*						
City or town B*						
City or town C*						
City or town D*						
.						
.						
.						
City or town Z*						

Population included: population of localities above a specified size and the urban agglomeration of each such locality

Classifications:
(a) Geographical division: total country
(b) Principal localities and their urban agglomeration): each specified city or town, the urban agglomeration of each specified city or town (when an urban agglomeration comprises more than one specified city or town, each specified city or town should be clearly distinguished)
(c) Sex: both sexes; male; female

Metadata for this tabulation:
(a) Source of statistics:
  ➢ Traditional population census
  ➢ Register-based population census
  ➢ Registers/Surveys systems
  ➢ Rolling surveys
  ➢ Civil registration
(b) De jure or de facto population or a combination with detailed description
(c) Definition of city proper
(d) Definition of urban agglomeration

Core topics:
  ➢ Place of usual residence or Place where present at time of census
  ➢ Sex

Note:
Information on the population size of the principal cities or towns and of the urban agglomerations of which these cities or towns are a part is needed for the study of the growth of the largest clusters of population within a country. The results of such study are useful in planning the local services (such as utilities, roads, schools, hospitals and so forth) that are required in proportion to population size.

The use of figures for urban agglomerations, in addition to those for the city proper, gives a more adequate indication of the size of the concentration of population, which often extends beyond the legal borders of the city. These figures may in fact reveal the need to redraw the city boundaries. For the most effective use of the data, figures are needed both for the city proper and for the urban agglomeration, because cities usually have some form of local government that does not extend over to the surrounding densely settled fringe. Responsibility for the determination of policy and subsequent action may therefore have to be shared by several minor administrative divisions, each of which requires information on the population within its own borders.

* Name of city or town.

P1.4-R.   Native and foreign-born population, by age and sex

Geographical division, sex and age (in years)	Total	Native	Foreign-born	Not Stated

Total country

Both sexes

All ages
- Under 1 year
- 1-4
- 5-9
- 10-14
- 15-19
- 20-24
- 25-29
- 30-34
- 35-39
- 40-44
- 45-49
- 50-54
- 55-59
- 60-64
- 65-69
- 70-74
- 75-79
- 80-84
- 85-89
- 90-94
- 95-99
- 100 and over
- Not stated

Male
(Age groups as above)

Female
(Age groups as above)

Major civil division
(as for "Total country")

Principal locality
(as for "Total country")

Population included: total population

Classifications:
(a)   Geographical divisions: (i) total country; (ii) each major civil division; (iii) each principal locality. Distinguish between urban and rural for (i), (ii) and (iii)
(b)   Place/country of birth: native; foreign-born
(c)   Age: all ages; under 1 year; 1-4 years; 5-9 years; 10-14 years; 15-19 years; 20-24 years; 25-29 years; 30-34 years; 35-39 years; 40-44 years; 45-49 years; 50-54 years; 55-59 years; 60-64 years; 65-69 years; 70-74 years; 75-79 years; 80-84 years; 85-89 years; 90-94 years; 95-99 years; and 100 years and over; not stated
(d)   Sex: both sexes; male; female

Metadata for this tabulation:
(a)   Source of statistics:
- Traditional population census
- Register-based population census
- Registers/Surveys systems
- Rolling surveys
- Civil registration

(b)   De jure or de facto population or a combination with detailed description
(c)   Definition of urban and rural areas
(d)   Definition of age

Core topics:
- Place of usual residence or Place where present at time of census
- Sex
- Age
- Place of birth/country of birth

Note:
These data are the basis for assessing the net contribution of immigration to the age and sex structure of the population. In countries where immigration has occurred on a large scale, it is very useful to tabulate the data on age-sex structure separately for the native and the foreign-born population. Thus the effects of immigration on the growth and structure of the population can be examined and estimates of future mortality and fertility can be improved by taking into account differentials between native and foreign-born population. The provision of the category of infants under one year of age is useful for studying relative underenumeration of foreign-born and native infants.

P1.5-R. Population, by duration of residence in locality and major civil division, age and sex

Geographical division, sex and duration of residence	Age (in years)										
	All ages	Under 1	1-4	5-9	10-14	15-19	20-24	...	95-99	100 and over	Not stated
Both sexes											
Total											
Resident*											
Resident in major civil division since birth											
Resident in locality since birth											
Not resident in locality since birth											
Resident in locality 10 years or more											
Resident in locality 5-9 years											
Resident in locality 1-4 years											
Resident in locality less than 1 year											
Duration of residence in locality not stated											
Not stated whether resident in locality since birth											
Not resident in major civil division since birth											
Resident in major civil division 10 or more years											
Resident in locality 10 or more years											
Resident in locality 5-9 years											
Resident in locality 1-4 years											
Resident in locality less than 1 year											
Duration of residence in locality not stated											
Resident in major civil division 5-9 years											
Resident in locality 5-9 years											
Resident in locality 1-4 years											
Resident in locality less than 1year											
Duration of residence in locality not stated											
Resident in major civil division 1-4 years											
Resident in locality 1-4 years											
Resident in locality less than 1 year											
Duration of residence in locality not stated											
Resident in major civil division less than 1 year											
Duration of residence in major civil division not stated											
Resident in locality 10 or more years											
Resident in locality 5-9 years											
Resident in locality 1-4 years											
Resident in locality less than 1 year											
Duration of residence in locality not stated											
Not stated whether resident in major civil division since birth											
Resident in locality 10 or more years											
Resident in locality 5-9 years											
Resident in locality 1-4 years											
Resident in locality less than 1 year											
Duration of residence in locality not stated											
Transient or visitor*											
Not stated whether resident, transient or visitor*											
Males (as for "Both sexes")											
Females (as for "Both sexes")											

Population included: total population

Classifications:

(a) Geographical division: (i) total country; (ii) each major civil division. Distinguish between urban and rural for (i) and (ii)

(b) Duration of residence in locality: since birth; not since birth—resident for: less than 1 year, 1-4 years, 5-9 years, 10 or more years, number of years not stated; not stated whether resident in locality since birth (for additional categories needed if tabulation is prepared on the basis of the population present in each area at the time of the census, see illustration)

(c) Duration of residence in major civil division): same as for (b)

(d) Age: all ages; under 1 year; 1-4 years; 5-9 years; 10-14 years; 15-19 years; 20-24 years; 25-29 years; 30-34 years; 35-39 years; 40-44 years; 45-49 years; 50-54 years; 55-59 years; 60-64 years; 65-69 years; 70-74 years; 75-79 years; 80-84 years; 85-89 years; 90-94 years; 95-99 years; and 100 years and over; not stated

(e) Sex: both sexes; male; female

Metadata for this tabulation:

(a) Source of statistics:
> Traditional population census
> Register-based population census
> Registers/Surveys systems
> Rolling surveys
> Civil registration

(b) De jure or de facto population or a combination with detailed description

(c) Definition of urban and rural areas

(d) Definition of age

(e) Definition of duration of residence

Core topics:
> Place of usual residence or Place where present at time of census
> Sex
> Age
> Duration of residence

Note:

Data on levels of net migration also show the direction of in-migration (on the basis of information on duration of residence in locality and major division), in terms of major civil divisions of the country and the most important localities. Such data are useful for preparing estimates of the future population of specific areas of the country. These estimates are used both for planning in areas of anticipated growth and for the determination of policy on internal migration and possible measures that can be employed to affect trends in migration.

---

* This category is needed only if the tabulation is prepared on the basis of the population present in each area at the time of the census; it is not required if the tabulation is based on the resident population of each area.

P1.6a-R. Population by place of usual residence, duration of residence, place of previous residence, and sex

Geographical division, place of usual residence, duration of residence and sex	Total population	Place of previous residence*					
		Major or other civil division A*	Major or other civil division B*	...	Major or other civil division Z*	Foreign country	Not stated
Both sexes							
Total							
Major or other civil division A**							
Resident since birth							
Not resident since birth							
Resident less than 1 year							
Resident 1-4 years							
Resident 5-9 years							
Resident 10 or more years							
Duration of residence not stated							
Whether residence since birth not stated							
Major or other civil division B** (as for "Major or other civil division A")							
.							
.							
Major or other civil division Z** (as for "Major or other civil division A")							
Male (as for "Both sexes")							
Female (as for "Both sexes")							

Population included: total population

Classifications:

(a)   Geographical division: (i) total country; (ii) each major or other civil division

(b)   Place of usual residence: each major or other civil division of the country

(c)   Duration of residence in the major or other civil division: since birth; not since birth—resident for: less than 1 year, 1-4 years, 5-9 years, 10 or more years, number of years not stated, not stated whether resident in major or other civil division since birth (for additional categories needed if tabulation is prepared on the basis of the population present in each area at the time of the census, see outline of tabulation P1.5-R above)

(d)   Place of previous residence: each major or other civil division of the country; foreign country; not stated

(e)   Sex: both sexes; male; female

Metadata for this tabulation:

(a)   Source of statistics:
  - Traditional population census
  - Register-based population census
  - Registers/Surveys systems
  - Rolling surveys
  - Civil registration

(b)   De jure or de facto population or a combination with detailed description

(c)   Definition of urban and rural areas

(d)   Definition of age

(e)   Definition of duration of residence

Core topics:
  - Place of usual residence
  - Duration of residence
  - Place of previous residence
  - Sex

Note:
Data from a series of censuses on the sources and direction of migration between civil divisions during a specified period, and on the age composition of the migrants, make it possible to assess changes in migration over time. It is therefore useful for preparing estimates of the future population of civil divisions, which are needed for the purposes stated in respect of the use of recommended tabulation P1.5-R. Unit of observation and classifications are the same as in the above-mentioned table.

  * Place of previous residence does not apply to those who have been residing in the same civil division since birth.

 ** Name of major or other civil division.

P1.6b-R. Population ... years of age and over, by place of usual residence, place of residence at a specified date in the past, age and sex

Geographical division, place of usual residence, age (in years) and sex	Population* ... years of age and over	Place of residence at a specified date in the past						
		Major or other civil division A**	Major or other civil division B**	...	Major or other civil division Z**	Foreign country	Not stated
Both sexes							
Total		**Population included:** population ... years of age and over					
Major or other civil division A**		**Classifications:**					
All ages		(a) Geographical division: (i) total country; (ii) each major or other civil division					
1-4 years		(b) Place of usual residence: each major or other civil division of the country					
5-9		(c) Place of residence at a specified date in the past: each major or other civil division of the country; foreign					
10-14		country; not stated (for persons who have always resided in the same civil division, the place of previous					
15-19		residence will be the same as the place of usual residence)					
20-24		(d) Age: all ages; 1-4 years; 5-9 years; 10-14 years; 15-19 years; 20-24 years; 25-29 years; 30-34 years; 35-39					
25-29		years; 40-44 years; 45-49 years; 50-54 years; 55-59 years; 60-64 years; 65-69 years; 70-74 years; 75-79					
30-34		years; 80-84 years; 85-89 years; 90-94 years; 95-99 years;100 years and over;					
35-39		(e) Sex: both sexes; male; female					
40-44							
45-49		**Metadata for this tabulation:**					
50-54		(a) Source of statistics:					
55-59		➤ Traditional population census					
60-64		➤ Register-based population census					
65-69		➤ Registers/Surveys systems					
70-74		➤ Rolling surveys					
75-79		➤ Civil registration					
80-84		(b) De jure or de facto population or a combination with detailed description					
85-89		(c) Definition of urban and rural areas					
90-94		(d) Definition of age					
95-99							
100 years and over		**Core topics:**					
Not stated		➤ Place of usual residence					
		➤ Place of residence at a specified date in the past					
Major or other civil division B**		➤ Age					
(Age groups as above)		➤ Sex					
.							
Major or other civil division Z**		**Note:**					
(Age groups as above)		Data on the sources and direction of migration between civil divisions during a specified period and on the					
		age composition of the migrants from a series of censuses make it possible to assess changes in the phe-					
Male		nomena measured for comparable lengths of time. It is therefore useful for preparing estimates of the future					
(Age groups as above)		population of civil divisions, which are needed for the purposes stated in the use of recommended tabulation					
Female		P1.5-R. Unit of observation and classifications are the same as in the above-mentioned table.					
(Age groups as above)							

* The lower age-limit depends on the specified date in the past adopted by the country. The age classification in this illustration is appropriate when the specified date in the past is one year prior to the enumeration.
** Name of major or other civil division.

Group 2.   Tabulations on international migration and immigrant stock

P2.1-R.   Foreign-born population, by country of birth, age and sex

Geographical division, continent and country of birth, and sex	All ages	Age (in years)								
		Under 5	5-9	10-14	15-19	20-24	...	95-99	100 and over	Not stated

Both sexes
  All countries
    Africa
      Country A*
      Country B*
      .
      .
      .
      Country Z*
      All other countries
      Country not stated

    America, North (as for "Africa")

    America, South (as for "Africa")

    Asia (as for "Africa")

    Europe (as for "Africa")

    Oceania (as for "Africa")

    Continent not stated

Male
  (as for "Both sexes")
Female
  (as for "Both sexes")

Population included: foreign-born population

Classifications:

(a)   Geographical division: (i) total country; (ii) each major civil division;

(b)   Country/place of birth: each continent (Africa; America, North; America, South; Asia; Europe; Oceania); each country within the continent that is the birthplace of a significant number of foreign-born persons; all other countries (combined) in each continent; country not stated; continent not stated

(c)   Age: all ages; under 5 years; 5-9 yeas; 10-14 yeas; 15-19 years; 20-24 years; 25-29 years; 30-34 years; 35-39 years; 40-44 years; 45-49 years; 50-54 years; 55-59 years; 60-64 years; 65-69 years; 70-74 years; 75-79 years; 80-84 years; 90-94 years; 95-99 years; 100 years and over; not stated.

(d)   Sex: both sexes; male; female

Metadata for this tabulation:

(a)   Source of statistics:
> Traditional population census
> Register-based population census
> Registers/Surveys systems
> Rolling surveys
> Civil registration

(b)   De jure or de facto population or a combination with detailed description

Core topics:
> Place of usual residence or Place where present at time of census
> Sex
> Age
> Country of birth

Note:

These data provide the basis for assessing the age and sex structure of the population and the contribution of immigration from specified countries. Thus the effects of immigration from specific countries on the growth and structure of the population can be estimated. As indicated in recommended tabulation P1.4-R, the differences in future fertility and mortality between immigrants from specific countries can also be improved.

*   Name of country.

P2.2-R. Foreign-born population, by year or period of arrival, country of birth, age and sex

Sex, country of birth and age (in years)	All periods	Year or period of arrival prior to the census date*			
		1-4 years	5-9 years	10 years and more	Not stated
Both sexes					
All countries					
Africa					
Country A**					
Total 1 year and over					
1-4					
5-9					
10-14					
15-19					
20-24					
...					
40-44					
45-49					
50-54					
...					
90-94					
95-99					
100 and over					
Age not stated					
Country B** (as for "Country A")					
.					
.					
Country Z** (as for "Country A")					
All other countries (as for "Country A")					
Country not stated (as for "Country A")					
America, North (as for "Africa")					
America, South (as for "Africa")					
Asia (as for "Africa")					
Europe (as for "Africa")					
Oceania (as for "Africa")					
Continent not stated (as for "Country A")					
Male (as for "Both sexes")					
Female (as for "Both sexes")					

Population included: all foreign-born persons in the country for more than one year

Classifications:
(a) Year or period of arrival: all periods; 1-4 years prior to the date of inquiry; 5-9 years; 10 years or more; not stated
(b) Place or country of birth: each continent (Africa; America, North; America, South; Asia; Europe; Oceania); each country within the continent that is the birthplace of a significant number of foreign-born persons; all other countries (combined) in each continent; country not stated; continent not stated
(c) Age: total 1 year and over; 1-4 years; 5-9 years; 10-14 years; 15-19 years; 20-24 years; 25-29 years; 30-34 years; 35-39 years; 40-44 years; 45-49 years; 50-54 years; 55-59 years; 60-64 years; 65-69 years; 70-74 years; 75-79 years; 80-84 years; 85-89 years; 90-94 years; 95-99 years; and 100 years over; and age not stated
(d) Sex: both sexes; male, female

Metadata for this tabulation:
(a) Source of statistics:
   ‣ Traditional population census
   ‣ Register-based population census
   ‣ Registers/Surveys systems
   ‣ Rolling surveys
   ‣ Civil registration
(b) De jure or de facto population or a combination with detailed description

Core topics:
   ‣ Place of usual residence or Place where present at time of census
   ‣ Sex
   ‣ Age
   ‣ Year or period of arrival
   ‣ Country of birth

Note:
This tabulation furnishes data to assess the cumulative effect of annual flows of migration and, in particular, the proportion of the total population that is of foreign origin and its demographic characteristics. In the absence of migration flow statistics, it provides information on the sources of immigration and their relative contributions over the years for use in preparing population estimates and projections. Cross-classification by year or period of arrival provides information on the changes in the relative size of population originating from specified countries and their composition by age and sex over recent years. An indication of return migration can be obtained based on similar tabulation from successive censuses.

* In actual published tables, the period of arrival may be shown in calendar years.
** Name of country.

P2.3-R. Population, by country of birth and citizenship, age and sex

Sex, continent, country of birth and citizenship	All ages	Age (in years)								No stated
		Under 5	5-9	10-14	15-19	20-24	...	95-99	100 and over	
Both sexes										
Total										
Africa										
Country A (*Country A is country of birth*)*										
Country of enumeration (*Those born in country A who have citizenship of country of enumeration*)										
Country of birth (*Those born in country A and are still citizens of country A*)										
Other country (*Those born in country A who have citizenship of other countries, excluding country A and country of enumeration*)										
Country B (*Country B is country of birth*)*										
Country of enumeration (*Those born in country B who have citizenship of country of enumeration*)										
Country of birth (*Those born in country B and are still citizens of country B*)										
Other country (*Those born in country B who have citizenship of other countries, excluding country B and country of enumeration*)										
America, North (as for "Africa")										
America, South (as for "Africa")										
Asia (as for "Africa")										
Europe (as for "Africa")										
Oceania (as for "Africa")										
Continent not stated										
Male (as for "Both sexes")										
Female (as for "Both sexes")										

Population included: total population

Classifications:

(a) Geographical division: total country

(b) Name of country

(c) Country/place of birth: each continent (Africa; America, North; America, South; Asia; Europe; Oceania); each country within the continent that is the birthplace of a significant number of foreign-born persons; all other countries (combined) in each continent; country not stated; continent not stated

(d) Country of citizenship: country of tabulation (for example, if this tabulation is generated for Canada, it would be Canadian citizenship), country of birth and other country

(e) Age: all ages; under 5 years;5-9 years; 10-14 years; 15-19 years; 20-24 years; 25-29 years; 30-34 years; 35-39 years; 40-44 years; 45-49 years; 50-54 years; 55-59 years; 60-64 years; 65-69 years; 70-74 years; 75-79 years; 80-84 years; 90-94 years; 95-99 years; 100 years and over; not stated.

(f) Sex: both sexes; male; female

Metadata for this tabulation:

(a) Source of statistics:
> Traditional population census
> Register-based population census
> Registers/Surveys systems
> Rolling surveys
> Civil registration

(b) De jure or de facto population or a combination with detailed description

Core topics:
> Place of usual residence or Place where present at time of census
> Sex
> Age
> Country of birth
> Citizenship

Note:
This tabulation is useful in identifying the country of birth and citizenship of the population according to age and sex. It is possible to determine the frequency with which persons become citizens and the place of birth of citizens in each country. Data can also be of use in the study of the rate of assimilation of the foreign-born population.

---

* Country of birth.

P2.4-R. Economically active* foreign-born population ...** years of age and over, by year or period of arrival, main occupation and sex

Sex and main occupation	All periods	Year or period of arrival prior to the census date***			
		1-4 years	5-9 years	10 years or more	Not stated

Both sexes

Sub-major group 11
  Minor group 111
  Minor group 112
  (etc.)
Sub-major group 21
  Minor group 211
  Minor group 212
  (etc.)
.
.
.
Sub-major group 91
  Minor group 911
  Minor group 912
  (etc)
Sub-major group 01
  Minor group 011

Male (as for "Both sexes")

Female (as for "Both sexes")

Population included: foreign-born persons above the specified minimum age in the country who are economically active according to current (or usual) activity status

Classifications:

(a) Year or period of arrival: all periods; 1-4 years prior to the date of inquiry; 5-9 years: 10 years or more; not stated

(b) Main occupation: according to, or convertible to, the latest revision of the International Standard Classification of Occupations (ISCO-88), at least to the minor group (in other words, three-digit) level

(c) Sex: both sexes; male; female

Metadata for this tabulation:

(a) Source of statistics:
> Traditional population census
> Register-based population census
> Registers/Surveys systems
> Rolling surveys
> Civil registration

(b) De jure or de facto population or a combination with detailed description

Core topics:
> Place of usual residence or Place where present at time of census
> Sex
> Occupation
> Year or period of arrival

Note:

These data provide information on the occupations of the foreign-born population needed to study immigrant workers, particularly their economic integration and mobility in the country of immigration. Together with a similar tabulation for the native population, the data constitute the basis for undertaking an in-depth analysis of occupational patterns and making occupational forecasts for the economy. From the cross-classification by year or period of arrival, one can observe the pattern of inflow of skilled migrants during previous years. When classification is also by country of birth, data are provided for countries that are losing a large volume of highly qualified migrants; such data are useful in the formulation of employment and educational policies in the countries of origin for dealing with the impact of the outflow of skilled personnel.

*The treatment of unemployed immigrants (including those who never worked before) should be clearly stated.

**The minimum age adopted by the country for enumerating the economically active population.

***In actual published tables, the period of arrival can be shown in calendar years.

Group 3. Tabulations on household and family characteristics

P3.1-R. Population in households, by relationship to head or other reference member of household, marital status and sex, and size of institutional population

Geographical division, relationship to head or other reference member of household, sex and institutional population	Total	Marital status					
		Single (never married)	Married	Widowed	Divorced	Separated	Not stated
TOTAL POPULATION							
Male							
Female							
All households							
Male							
Female							
Head or other reference member							
Male							
Female							
Spouse							
Male							
Female							
Child							
Male							
Female							
Spouse of child							
Male							
Female							
Grandchild or great-grandchild							
Male							
Female							
Parent or parent of spouse							
Male							
Female							
Other relative							
Male							
Female							
Domestic employee							
Male							
Female							
Other person not related to the head or other reference member							
Male							
Female							
Not stated							
Male							
Female							
Institutional population							
Male							
Female							
Not stated whether or not living in a household/ institutions							

Population included: total population, including persons living alone (one-person households)

Classifications:

(a)   Geographical division: (i) total country; (ii) each major civil division; (iii) each minor civil division; (iv) each principal locality. Distinguish between urban and rural for (i), (ii) and (iii)

(b)   Relationship to head or other reference member of household: head or other reference member; spouse; child; spouse of child; grandchild or great-grandchild; parent or parent of spouse; other relative; domestic employee; other person not related to the head or other reference member; not stated

(c)   Institutional population: total number

(d)   Marital status: total; single (never married), married, widowed, divorced, separated, not stated

(e)   Sex: both sexes; male; female

Metadata for this tabulation:

(a)   Source of statistics:
  > Traditional population census
  > Register-based population census
  > Registers/Surveys systems
  > Rolling surveys
  > Civil registration

(b)   De jure or de facto population or a combination with detailed description

(c)   Definition of urban and rural areas

(d)   Definition of institutional population

Core topics:
  > Place of usual residence or Place where present at time of census
  > Relationship to head or other reference member of household
  > Sex
  > Marital status

Note:
Data for the study of the distribution of individuals within households serve to indicate the relationship among members of households, particularly for information on the prevalence of multigenerational households and of households consisting of unrelated individuals. Marital status is also useful in the study of family living arrangements. Comparison of these data with similar data from an earlier census can provide information on changing patterns of household composition and of some of the characteristics of members of the household, and for the preparation of projections of the number of households.

P3.2-R. Head or other reference member of household, by age and sex; and other household members, by age and relationship to head or other reference member

Geographical division, age and sex of head or other reference member, and age of other household members	Head or other reference member*	Relationship of other household members								
		Total	Spouse	Child	Spouse of child	Grandchild or great-grandchild	Parent or parent of spouse	Other relative	Person not related	Not stated

Both sexes

  Total

    Under 25 years
      Age of other household members
      Under 15
      15-19
      20-24
      ...
      95-99
      100 and over
      Not stated

    25-29 years
      (age of other household members as for "Under 25 years")

    30-34 years
      (age of other household members as for "Under 25 years")

    ...

    95-99 years
      (age of other household members as for "Under 25 years")

    100 years and over
      (age of other household members as for "Under 25 years")

    Age not stated
      (age of other household members as for "Under 25 years")

Male
  (as for "Both sexes")

Female
  (as for "Both sexes")

Population included: all members of households

Classifications:

(a) Geographical division: (i) total country; (ii) each major civil division; (iii) each minor civil division; (iv) each principal locality. Distinguish between urban and rural for (i), (ii) and (iii)

(b) Relationship to head or other reference member of household: head or other reference member; spouse; child; spouse of child; grandchild or great-grandchild; parent or parent of spouse; other relative; domestic employee; other person not related to the head or other reference member; not stated

(c) Age of head or other reference member of household: under 25 years; 25-29; 30-34; ...; 95-99;100 and over; not stated

(d) Age of other household members: under 15 years; 15-19; 20-24; 25-29; 30-34; ... ; 95-99; 100 and over; not stated

(e) Sex: both sexes; male; female

Metadata for this tabulation:

(a) Source of statistics:
- Traditional population census
- Register-based population census
- Registers/Surveys systems
- Rolling surveys
- Civil registration

(b) De jure or de facto population or a combination with detailed description

(c) Definition of urban and rural areas

Core topics:
- Place of usual residence or Place where present at time of census
- Relationship to head or other reference member of household
- Age
- Sex

Note:

Data on the age of the head or other reference member of the household and of other household members, classified by their relationship to the head or other reference member, provide additional information for the purposes stated in the use of tabulation P3.1-R and for the study of the prevalence of multigenerational households.

---

* Including persons living alone (one-person households).

P3.3-R.　Households, population in households and number of family nuclei, by size of household

Geographical division and size of household	Total		Households with indicated number of family nuclei						Number of family nuclei
	Households	Population	0	1	2	3	4 or more	Not stated	
All households									
Households consisting of									
1 person									
2 persons									
3 persons									
4 persons									
5 persons									
6 persons									
7 persons									
8 persons									
9 persons									
10 persons or more									
Not stated									

Population included:　all members of households

Classifications:

(a)　Geographical division: (i) total country; (ii) each major civil division; (iii) each minor civil division; (iv) each principal locality. Distinguish between urban and rural for (i), (ii) and (iii)

(b)　Size of household: 1 person; 2 persons; 3 persons; 4 persons; 5 persons; 6 persons; 7 persons; 8 persons; 9 persons; 10 persons or more; not stated; and separately, the number of households of each size and the aggregate population by size of household

(c)　Number of family nuclei: none; one; two; three; four or more; not stated; and separately, the aggregate number of family nuclei

Metadata for this tabulation:

(a)　Source of statistics:

- ➤ Traditional population census
- ➤ Register-based population census
- ➤ Registers/Surveys systems
- ➤ Rolling surveys
- ➤ Civil registration

(b)　De jure or de facto population or a combination with detailed description

(c)　Definition of urban and rural areas

(d)　Definition of family nucleus

Core topics:

- ➤ Place of usual residence or Place where present at time of census
- ➤ Relationship to head or other reference member of household
- ➤ Household and family composition

Note:

Information on the number and size of households and on changes in the rate of household formation is needed by the planners for, and suppliers of, many goods and services, for which the demand is related to households rather than to individuals. Agencies dealing with housing problems need these data for the determination of current and projected rates of household formation, on the basis of which the number and size of new housing units required can be estimated. This tabulation can provide information needed to plan new sample surveys, and to design the sample that will be used, as well as comparative data for estimating the accuracy of some of the survey results. Information on household structure in terms of number of family nuclei in the household is needed for studies of household formation, projections of numbers of households and estimates of potential housing needs. Information from a series of censuses is very useful for the study of the disintegration of the households consisting of several family nuclei in countries where this pattern of living is changing.

Group 4.   Tabulations on demographic and social characteristics

P4.1-R.   Population, by single years of age and sex

Geographical division and age (in years)	Both sexes	Male	Female
All ages			
Under 1			
1			
2			
3			
4			
1-4			
5			
6			
7			
8			
9			
5-9			
.			
.			
.			
99			
100 and over			
Not stated			

Population included: total population

Classifications:

(a)   Geographical division: (i) total country; (ii) each major civil division; (iii) each minor civil division; (iv) each principal locality. Distinguish between urban and rural for (i), (ii) and (iii). (If it is considered inadvisable to present the single-year classification for any particular geographical division, at least the age categories "under 1", "1-4" and the five-year age groups should be shown for that division.)

(b)   Age: all ages; under 1 year; 2 years; 3 years; 4 years; 5 years; 6 years; 7 years; … single years to 99; 100 years and over; not stated (distinguish between subtotals: 1-4 years, five-year age groups 5-9, 10-14, … 95-99, and 100 and over)

(c)   Sex: both sexes; male; female

Metadata for this tabulation:

(a)   Source of statistics:
  ➤ Traditional population census
  ➤ Register-based population census
  ➤ Registers/Surveys systems
  ➤ Rolling surveys
  ➤ Civil registration

(b)   De jure or de facto population or a combination with detailed description

(c)   Definition of urban and rural areas

(d)   Definition of age

Core topics:
  ➤ Place of usual residence or Place where present at time of census
  ➤ Sex
  ➤ Age

Note:

Information on the detailed age and sex structure of the population is needed for actuarial analysis of the probability of survival and of related life-table functions. As populations age, the probability of survival to advanced age increases and the proportion of persons at older ages expands; thus it is important to present detailed age data up to 100 years. It is also essential for the evaluation of the accuracy of census age data for the population. From this tabulation, it is possible to reconstitute any selected age grouping (for example, the school-age population and the population of voting age or groups used in the calculation of food requirements) without interpolating from population classified by five-year age groups.

The five-year age groups are essential for many purposes, including the analysis of the factors of population change, the preparation of current population estimates and of projections, the calculation of age-specific vital rates, analysis of the factors of labour supply and the study of problems of dependency. The grouped age classification is recommended because it is appropriate to cross-classification by other variables. The tabulation provides a convenient summary of the total, urban and rural population by the various geographical areas according to the age groups used in most of the other recommended tabulations. The tabulation should present reported rather than adjusted age data.

P4.2-R. Population, by marital status, age and sex

Geographical division, sex and marital status	All ages	Age (in years)									
		Under 15	15	16	...	29	30-34	...	95-99	100 and over	Not stated
Both sexes											
Total											
Single (never married)											
Married											
Widowed											
Divorced											
Separated											
Not stated											
Male (as for "Both sexes")											
Female (as for "Both sexes")											

Population included: total population

Classifications:

(a) Geographical division: (i) total country; (ii) each major civil division; (iii) each principal locality. Distinguish between urban and rural for (i) and (ii)

(b) Marital status: single (never married); married; widowed; divorced; separated; not stated. (Persons whose only, or latest marriage, has been annulled may be classified in a separate category or classified according to their marital status before the annulled marriage took place.)

(c) Age: all ages; under 15 years; 15 years; 16 years; ... single years up to 29; 30-34 years; 35-39 years; 40-44 years; 45-49 years; 50-54 years; 55-59 years; 60-64 years; 65-69 years; 70-74 years; 75-79 years;80-84 years; 85-89 years; 90-94 years; 95-99 years; and 100 years and over; not stated

(d) Sex: both sexes; male; female

Metadata for this tabulation:

(a) Source of statistics:

> Traditional population census
> Register-based population census
> Registers/Surveys systems
> Rolling surveys
> Civil registration

(b) De jure or de facto population or a combination with detailed description

(c) Definition of urban and rural areas

Core topics:

> Place of usual residence or Place where present at time of census
> Sex
> Age
> Marital status

Note:

This tabulation provides material for the study of age at marriage, of the frequency of celibacy, widowhood and divorce and of the effect of these factors on population growth through their influence on fertility. A simple measure of the influence of nuptiality on fertility is the comparison of the ratio of children to all women of childbearing age with the ratio of children to those women who have ever been married. The data are also required for the preparation of nuptiality tables. A refinement of this tabulation, showing heads or other reference members of households by marital status, age and sex, can be used together with the present tabulation to obtain age-sex marital status-specific rates for the head or other reference member. Application of these rates to the projected population by age, sex and marital status provides projected numbers of households.

Group 5.   Tabulations on fertility and mortality

P5.1-R.   Female population 10 years of age and over, by age and number of children ever born alive by sex

Geographical division, age of females (in years) and sex of child	Total	Female population with indicated number of children born alive						Total number of children ever born alive
		0	1	2	...	12 or more	Not stated	
Total country								
Children, both sexes								
Total 10 years and over								
10-14								
15-19								
20-24								
25-29								
30-34								
35-39								
40-44								
45-49								
50-54								
55-59								
60-64								
65-69								
70-74								
75-79								
80-84								
85-89								
90-94								
95-99								
100 and over								
Not stated								
Children, males (age groups as above)								
Children, females (age groups as above)								

Population included: female population 15 years of age and over. (If the population included is restricted to ever-married females, this fact should be clearly stated.)

Classifications:
(a)   Geographical division: (i) total country; (ii) each major civil division; (iii) each principal locality. Distinguish between urban and rural for (i), (ii) and (iii)
(b)   Age: total 10 years and over; 10-14 years; 15-19 years; 20-24 years; 25-29 years; 30-34 years; 35-39 years; 40-44 years; 45-49 years; 50-54 years; 55-59 years; 60-64 years; 65-69 years; 70-74 years; 75-79 years; 80-84 years;85-89 years; 90-94 years; 95-99 years; and 100 years and over; not stated
(c)   Sex: both sexes; male and female children ever born alive
(d)   Number of children ever born alive: none; 1 child; 2 children; 3 children; 4 children; 5 children; 6 children; 7 children; 8 children; 9 children; 10 children; 11 children; 12 or more children; not stated; and, separately, the aggregate number of children ever born alive to women in each age category

Metadata for this tabulation:
(a)   Source of statistics:
  ➤ Traditional population census
  ➤ Register-based population census
  ➤ Registers/Surveys systems
  ➤ Rolling surveys
  ➤ Civil registration
(b)   De jure or de facto population or a combination with detailed description
(c)   Definition of urban and rural areas

Core topics:
  ➤ Place of usual residence or Place where present at time of census
  ➤ Sex
  ➤ Age
  ➤ Children ever born

Note:
Census data on fertility are particularly valuable for countries where birth registration statistics are lacking or deficient, because they can be used to estimate age-specific fertility rates, the total fertility rate, the crude incidence of births in the total population and other fertility indicators. In addition, they are useful as a supplement to satisfactory registration data, because they provide a summary of the lifetime fertility of the female population. The principal measures of fertility that can be derived from this tabulation are (a) the gross fertility ratio (average number of children ever born alive to women of childbearing age and over), (b) the average number of children ever born alive by sex to women who have reached the end of the childbearing period (in other words, 50 years of age and over), (c) the proportion of women who have had no children by the end of their reproductive life, (d) the average number of children born per woman who has already borne at least one child specified by sex and (e) cumulative average gross fertility ratios by age groups. The data also provide the base for the computation of birth rates specific for parity by sex. The use of information from a series of censuses makes it possible to identify cohorts of women and to study their reproductive patterns as they advance from one age group to another.

P5.2-R.   Female population 10 years of age and over, by age and number of children living (or dead) by sex

Geographical division, age of females (in years) and sex of child	Total	Female population with indicated number of children living (or dead)						Total number of children living (or dead)
		0	1	2	...	12 or more	Not stated	
Total country								
Children, both sexes								
TOTAL 10 years and over								
10-14								
15-19								
20-24								
25-29								
30-34								
35-39								
40-44								
45-49								
50-54								
55-59								
60-64								
65-69								
70-74								
75-79								
80-84								
85-89								
90-94								
95-99								
100 and over								
Not stated								
Children, males (age groups as above)								
Children, females (age groups as above)								

Population included: female population 10 years of age and over. (If the population included is restricted to ever-married females, this fact should be clearly stated.)

Classifications:

(a)   Geographical division: (i) total country; (ii) each major civil division; (iii) each principal locality. Distinguish between urban and rural for (i), (ii) and (iii)

(b)   Age: total 10 years and over; 10-14 years; 15-19 years; 20-24 years; 25-29 years; 30-34 years; 35-39 years; 40-44 years; 45-49 years; 50-54 years; 55-59 years; 60-64 years; 65-69 years; 70-74 years; 75-79 years; 80-84 years; 90-94 years; 95-99 years; and 100 years and over; not stated

(c)   Sex: both sexes; male and female children ever born alive

(d)   Number of children living (or dead): none; 1 child; 2 children; 3 children; 4 children; 5 children; 6 children; 7 children; 8 children; 9 children; 10 children; 11 children; 12 or more children; not stated; and, separately, the aggregate number of children living (or dead) to women in each age category

Metadata for this tabulation:

(a)   Source of statistics:
- Traditional population census
- Register-based population census
- Registers/Surveys systems
- Rolling surveys
- Civil registration

(b)   De jure or de facto population or a combination with detailed description

(c)   Definition of urban and rural areas

Core topics:
- Place of usual residence or Place where present at time of census
- Sex
- Age
- Children living

Note:

These data are most useful for countries where death registration statistics are lacking or deficient. Census estimates of fertility and mortality can be derived directly or using generally more reliable indirect techniques. Two measures of fertility can be derived from the tabulations. These are (*a*) the net fertility ratio (average number of children surviving to women of childbearing age and over) and (*b*) cumulative average net fertility ratios by age groups. Child mortality rates can be estimated for each sex. Some measure of mortality in a generation can also be obtained by comparison of the net fertility ratio derived from this tabulation with the gross fertility ratio, which can be derived from recommended tabulation P5.1-R. This measure is particularly valuable where death rates estimated from civil registration data are not available or are defective. In addition to the above-mentioned measures of fertility and mortality, the tabulation also provides information for the analysis of family composition by number of living offspring by sex. These data cannot be obtained from birth registration statistics; neither can they be obtained from the census information on relationship to head of household because census families comprise only those persons who live and are enumerated within the same household; thus they do not necessarily include all the living (or dead) children of the woman enumerated.

P5.3-R.   Female population …* to 49 years of age, by age, number of live births, by sex within the 12 months preceding the census, and deaths among these live births, by sex

Geographical division, age of females (in years) and sex of children	Total females …* to 49 years of age	Live births in past 12 months	
		Total	Number of which have died

Total country

Births, both sexes

  Total
    Under 10**
    10-14
    15-19
    20-24
    25-29
    30-34
    35-39
    40-44
    45-49
    Not stated

Births, males
  (age groups as above)

Births, females
  (age groups as above)

Population included: female population between the minimum age limit adopted by the country for collecting information on current fertility and 49 years of age (If the population is restricted to ever-married females, this fact should be clearly stated.)

Classifications:
(a)   Geographical division: (i) total country; (ii) each major civil division; (iii) each principal locality. Distinguish between urban and rural for (i), (ii) and (iii)
(b)   Live births by sex within the 12 months preceding the census and children who have died among them by sex: total number of births of both sexes; total number of male births; total number of female births
(c)   Age: Total; under 10 years; 10-14 years; 15-19 years; 20-24 years; 25-29 years; 30-34 years; 35-39 years; 40-44 years; 45-49 years; not stated
(e)   Sex: both sexes; male; female

Metadata for this tabulation:
(a)   Source of statistics:
  ➤ Traditional population census
  ➤ Register-based population census
  ➤ Registers/Surveys systems
  ➤ Rolling surveys
  ➤ Civil registration
(b)   De jure or de facto population or a combination with detailed description
(c)   Definition of urban and rural areas

Core topics:
  ➤ Place of usual residence or Place where present at time of census
  ➤ Sex
  ➤ Age
  ➤ Births in the past 12 months
  ➤ Deaths among children born in the past 12 months

Note:
This tabulation refers to female population between the minimum age limit adopted by the country for collecting information on current fertility and 49 years of age distributed among geographical divisions. It also provides data to estimate current age specific fertility rates and current infant mortality rates by sex, particularly as a supplement to vital rates or as an estimation for these rates where birth and death registration is defective or inadequate.

* The minimum age adopted by the country for census questions on current fertility
** All ages between the minimum age adopted by the country for census questions on current fertility if the minimum age is under 10 years.

P5.4-R. Household deaths*, by sex and age within the 12 months preceding the census; and total population, by age and sex

Geographical division, sex and age (in years)	Household deaths in the past 12 months			Total population		
	Both sexes	Male	Female	Both sexes	Male	Female
Total country						
Both sexes						
All ages						
Under 1 year						
1-4						
5-9						
10-14						
15-19						
20-24						
25-29						
30-34						
35-39						
40-44						
45-49						
50-54						
55-59						
60-64						
65-69						
70-74						
75-79						
80-84						
85-89						
90-94						
95-99						
100 and over						
Not stated						
Males (as for "Both sexes")						
Females (as for "Both sexes")						

Population included: total population

Classifications:

(a) Geographical division: (i) total country; (ii) each major civil division; (iii) each principal locality. Distinguish between urban and rural for (i), (ii) and (iii)

(b) Household deaths by sex within the 12 months preceding the census: total number of deaths; male deaths; female deaths

(c) Sex: both sexes; male; female

(d) Age: All ages; under 1 year; 1-4 years; 5-9 years; 10-14 years; 15-19 years; 20-24 years; 25-29 years; 30-34 years; 35-39 years; 40-44 years; 45-49 years; 50-54 years; 55-59 years; 60-64 years; 65-69 years; 70-74 years; 75-79 years; 80-84 years; 85-89 years; 90-94 years; 95-99 years; 100 years and over; not stated

Metadata for this tabulation:

(a) Source of statistics:
  - Traditional population census
  - Register-based population census
  - Registers/Surveys systems
  - Rolling surveys
  - Civil registration

(b) De jure or de facto population or a combination with detailed description

(c) Definition of urban and rural areas

Core topics:
  - Place of usual residence or Place where present at time of census
  - Sex
  - Age
  - Total population
  - Household deaths in the past 12 months

Note:
These data are used to estimate levels and patterns of recent mortality in combination with data on the population by age and sex.

---

* Collected from the head of the household or reference person in the household.

Group 6. Tabulations on educational characteristics

P6.1-R. Population ...* years of age and over by school attendance, educational attainment, age and sex

		Age (in years)					
Geographical division, sex, school attendance and educational attainment	Total population ...* years of age and over	Single years of age up to 14 years*	15-19	20-24	....	100 and over	Not stated

ATTENDING AND NOT ATTENDING SCHOOL

Both sexes

   No schooling

   ISCED level 1: Primary education

   ISCED level 2: Lower secondary education

   ISCED level 3: Upper secondary education

   ISCED level 4: Post-secondary education

   ISCED level 5: First stage of tertiary education (not leading directly to an advanced research qualification)

   ISCED level 6: Second stage of tertiary education (leading to an advanced research qualification)

   Level of education not stated

Male (classification of educational attainment as above)

Female (classification of educational attainment as above)

ATTENDING SCHOOL

Both sexes

   (classification of educational attainment as above)

Male (classification of educational attainment as above)

Female (classification of educational attainment as above)

NOT ATTENDING SCHOOL

Both sexes (classification of educational attainment as above)

Male (classification of educational attainment as above)

Female (classification of educational attainment as above)

Population included: all persons at or above the usual age for entrance into school who are attending and not attending school

Classifications:

(a)   Geographical division: (i) total country; (ii) each major civil division; (iii) each principal locality. Distinguish between urban and rural for (i) and (ii)

(b)   Educational attainment: no schooling; ISCED level 1: Primary education; ISCED level 2: Lower secondary education; ISCED level 3: Upper secondary education; ISCED level 4: Post-secondary education; ISCED level 5: First stage of tertiary education (not leading directly to an advanced research classification); ISCED level 6: Second stage of tertiary education (leading to an advanced research qualification); level of education not stated

(c)   Age: total; single years up to 14 years; 15-19 years; 20-24 years; 25-29 years; 30-34 years; 35-39 years; 40-44 years; 45-49 years; 50-54 years; 55-59 years; 60-64 years; 65-69 years; 70-74 years; 75-79 years; 80-84 years; 85-89 year; 90-94 years; 95-99 years; 100 years and over; not stated

(d)   Sex: both sexes; male; female

Metadata for this tabulation:

(a)   Source of statistics:

   ➤ Traditional population census

   ➤ Register-based population census

   ➤ Registers/Surveys systems

   ➤ Rolling surveys

   ➤ Civil registration

(b)   De jure or de facto population or a combination with detailed description

(c)   Definition of urban and rural areas

(d)   Definition of school attendance

Core topics:

   ➤ Place of usual residence or Place where present at time of census

   ➤ Sex

   ➤ Age

   ➤ School attendance

   ➤ Educational attainment

Note:

By showing the distribution of human resources by educational attainment in a country, this tabulation provides an important indication of the capacity and potential of the nation for economic, social and cultural development. When compared with current and anticipated needs for educated manpower by various sectors, types and levels of economic activities, it can guide the making of more effective policies and coordinated plans for the development of different levels/categories of education in close relation to development programmes.

---

*   The lower age limit should be the usual age for entrance into school.

P6.2-R. Population 5 to 29 years of age, by school attendance, single years of age and sex

Geographical division, sex and age (in years)	Total	School attendance		
		Attending school	Not attending school	Not stated
Total country				
Both sexes				
Total				
5*				
6				
7				
8				
9				
10				
11				
12				
13				
14				
.				
.				
.				
29**				
Male (as for "Both sexes")				
Female (as for "Both sexes")				

Population included: all persons between the usual age for entering the first level of school and 29 years of age

Classifications:

(a) Geographical division: (i) total country; (ii) each major civil division; (iii) each principal locality. Distinguish between urban and rural for (i), (ii) and (iii)

(b) School attendance: total; attending school; not attending school; not stated

(c) Age: total; 5 years; 6 years; 7 years; 8 years; 9 years; 10 years; 11 years; 12 years; 13 years; 14 years; 15 years; 16 years; 17 years; 18 years; 19 years; 20 years; 21 years; 22 years; 23 years; 24 years; 25 years; 26 years; 27 years; 28 years; 29 years

(d) Sex: both sexes; male; female

Metadata for this tabulation:

(a) Source of statistics:
  › Traditional population census
  › Register-based population census
  › Registers/Surveys systems
  › Rolling surveys
  › Civil registration

(b) De jure or de facto population or a combination with detailed description

(c) Definition of urban and rural areas

(d) Definition of school attendance

Core topics:
  › Place of usual residence or Place where present at time of census
  › Sex
  › Age
  › School attendance

Note:

Data on the classification of young persons attending and not attending school, by single years of age and sex, are essential for studies of the numerical relationship between the population of school age and the population actually in school. The proportion of the school-age population that is able to take advantage of the educational system is one of the first types of information required for the assessment of the adequacy of the educational system of a country. School enrolment statistics derived from institutional records are not adequate, in many countries, for providing an exact measure of total attendance or data on important characteristics of the school-going population, particularly age. Even countries with detailed, comprehensive statistics compiled from records of educational institutions can benefit from a periodic assessment of the accuracy of these statistics by comparison with the census information on net school attendance.

* The lower age limit should be the usual age for entrance into school.

** If it is desired to include older persons attending school, the upper age-limit should be extended as appropriate and the necessary additional categories should be added to the age classification.

P6.3-R.   Population 10 years of age and over, by literacy, age and sex

Geographical division, sex and age (in years)	Total	Literacy		
		Literate	Illiterate	Not stated

Both sexes

Total 10* years and over

10-14*

Total 15 years and over

15-19

20-24

25-29

30-34

35-39

40-44

45-49

50-54

55-59

60-64

65-69

70-74

75-79

80-84

85-89

90-94

95-99

100 and over

Not stated

Male
(as for "Both sexes")

Female
(as for "Both sexes")

Population included: all persons 10 years of age and over

Classifications:

(*a*)   Geographical division: (i) total country; (ii) each major civil division; (iii) each principal locality. Distinguish between urban and rural for (i) , (ii) and (iii)

(*b*)   Literacy: total; literate; illiterate; not stated

(*c*)   Sex: both sexes; male; female

(*d*)   Age: total 10 years and over; 10-14 years; total 15 years and over; 15-19 years; 20-24 years; 25-29 years; 30-34 years; 35-39 years; 40-44 years; 45-49 years; 50-54 years; 55-59 years; 60-64 years; 65-69 years; 70-74 years; 75-79 years; 80-84 years; 85-89 years; 90-94 years; 95-99 years; 100 years and over; not stated

Metadata for this tabulation:

(*a*)   Source of statistics:

> Traditional population census

> Register-based population census

> Registers/Surveys systems

> Rolling surveys

> Civil registration

(*b*)   De jure or de facto population or a combination with detailed description

(*c*)   Definition of urban and rural areas

(*d*)   Definition of literacy

Core topics:

> Place of usual residence or Place where present at time of census

> Sex

> Age

> Literacy

Note:

Data on literacy provide one of the indicators of national levels of living and a measure of one of the factors in the national capacity for technological and cultural development; they are needed for tracing the progress in educational development of past generations and projecting future trends. In countries where the adult population is largely illiterate, the tabulation is of immediate use in planning for adult literacy, particularly if the data are tabulated for local areas. In addition, these data serve as the denominator in the computation of vital rates differentiated by literacy used as a socio-economic variable, such as birth rates by literacy of mother, and marriage and divorce rates by literacy of husband and wife.

* Where it is felt that the literacy rate for the age group 10-14 years may be misleading in international comparison, the lower age-limit for the tabulation may be 15 years.

Group 7. Tabulations on economic characteristics

P7.1-R. Population ...* years of age and over, by current (or usual) activity status, educational attainment, age and sex

Geographical division, sex, educational attainment, and age (in years)	Total ...* years of age and over	Current (or usual) activity status					
			Unemployed			Not economically active	Not stated
		Employed	Total	Worked before	Never worked before		

Both sexes
All levels of education
  All ages
    Under 15**
    15-19
    20-24
    25-29
    30-34
    35-39
    40-44
    45-49
    50-54
    55-59
    60-64
    65-69
    70-74
    75-79
    80-84
    85-89
    90-94
    95-99
    100 and over
    Not stated
No schooling
  (as for "All levels of education")
ISCED level 1: Primary education (as for "All levels of education")
ISCED level 2: Lower secondary education (as for "All levels of education")
ISCED level 3: Upper secondary education (as for "All levels of education")
ISCED level 4: Post-secondary education (as for "All levels of education")
ISCED level 5: First stage of tertiary education (as for "All levels of education")
ISCED level 6: Second stage of tertiary education (as for "All levels of education")
Level of education not stated (as for "All levels of education")
Male (as for "Both sexes")
Female (as for "Both sexes")

Population included: population at or above the minimum age adopted for enumerating the economically active population

Classifications:
(a) Geographical division: (i) total country; (ii) each major civil division; (iii) each minor civil division; (iv) each principal locality. Distinguish between urban and rural for (i), (ii) and (iii)
(b) Activity status: total; employed; unemployed (distinguishing persons who ever and never worked before); not economically active; not stated
(c) Age: all ages; under 15 years; 15-19 years; 20-24 years; 25-29 years; 30-34 years; 35-39 years; 40-44 years; 45-49 years; 50-54 years; 55-59 years; 60-64 years; 65-69 years; 70-74 years; 75-79 years; 80-84 years; 85-89 years; 90-94 years; 95-99 years; 100 years and over; not stated.
(d) Educational attainment: all levels of education; no schooling; ISCED level 1: Primary education; ISCED level 2: Lower secondary education; ISCED level 3: Upper secondary education; ISCED level 4: Post-secondary education; ISCED level 5: First stage of tertiary education (not leading directly to an advanced research classification); ISCED level 6: Second stage of tertiary education (leading to an advanced research qualification); level of education not stated
(e) Sex: both sexes; male; female

Metadata for this tabulation:
(a) Source of statistics:
  ‣ Traditional population census
  ‣ Register-based population census
  ‣ Registers/Surveys systems
  ‣ Rolling surveys
  ‣ Civil registration
(b) De jure or de facto population or a combination with detailed description
(c) Definition of urban and rural areas

Core topics:
  ‣ Place of usual residence or Place where present at time of census
  ‣ Sex
  ‣ Age
  ‣ Activity status
  ‣ Educational attainment

Note: This tabulation provides the data needed for computing crude and age-specific participation rates, that is to say, the percentages of economically active persons, which are fundamental for studies of factors determining the size and structure of the economically active population, and for making projections, in conjunction with life-table functions, to calculate the working life expectancy, entry into and retirement from economic activity. Information on the employed and the unemployed furnishes part of the data needed for the appraisal of human resources utilization for policy formulation. It can provide some of the benchmark data for more current studies of employment, unemployment and underemployment. The level of education attained is a major attribute in explaining the ability to participate in the labour market and to find employment. Hence the table will provide useful information on the effects that education has on labour force participation rates and unemployment rates. Skills acquired through formal education may be expected to improve a person's chance of employment. The information is also important in manpower planning and planning for vocational training that relies on certain formal education standards. Consequently the table will be useful in understanding the relationship between the level of formal education reached and the extent to which a person is employed or unemployed or economically inactive. This is especially important for studies of youth (males and females separately) in urban areas, and in aggregate.

---

* The minimum age adopted by the country for enumerating the economically active population.
** The category "Under 15 years" should include all ages between the minimum age-limit adopted by the country for census questions on economic activity and 14 years, if the minimum is below 15 years.

P7.2-R. Currently (or usually) active population by activity status, main occupation, age and sex

Geographical division, activity status, sex and main occupation	Age (in years)								
	All ages	Under 15*	15-19	20-24	25-29	...	95-99	100 and over	Not stated

TOTAL ECONOMICALLY ACTIVE POPULATION

Both sexes

    Sub-major group 11
       Minor group 111
       Minor group 112
       (etc.)

    Sub-major group 21
       Minor group 211
       Minor group 212
       (etc.)
    ...
    Sub-major group 91
       Minor group 911
       Minor group 912
       (etc.)
    Sub-major group 01
       Minor group 011

Male (as for "Both sexes")

Female (as for "Both sexes")

EMPLOYED (as for "Total economically active population")

UNEMPLOYED, TOTAL (as for "Total economically active population")

UNEMPLOYED, WORKED BEFORE (as for "Total economically active population")

UNEMPLOYED, NEVER WORKED BEFORE
    Both sexes
    Male
    Female
    (by definition, the occupational classification above does not apply to this category; this category is required only as total for ensuring the consistency of the figure for total economically active population)

NOT STATED
(as for "Unemployed, never worked before")

Population included: currently (or usually) active population at or above the minimum age adopted for enumerating the economically active population

Classifications:
(a)   Geographical division: (i) total country; (ii) each major civil division; (iii) each minor civil division; (iv) each principal locality. Distinguish between urban and rural for (i), (ii) and (iii)

(b)   Occupation: according to, or convertible to, the latest revision of the International Standard Classification of Occupations (ISCO-88), at least to the minor group (in other words, three-digit) level

(c)   Activity status: total economically active population; employed; unemployed (distinguishing persons who ever and never worked before); not stated

(d)   Age: all ages; under 15 years; 15-19 years; 20-24 years; 25-29 years; 30-34 years; 35-39 years; 40-44 years; 45-49 years; 50-54 years; 55-59 years; 60-64 years; 65-69 years; 70-74 years; 75-79 years; 80-84 years; 85-89 years; 90-94 years; 95-99 years; 100 years and over; not stated

(e)   Sex: both sexes; male; female

Metadata for this tabulation:
(a)   Source of statistics:
> Traditional population census
> Register-based population census
> Registers/Surveys systems
> Rolling surveys
> Civil registration

(b)   De jure or de facto population or a combination with detailed description
(c)   Definition of urban and rural areas

Core topics:
> Place of usual residence or Place where present at time of census
> Sex
> Age
> Activity status
> Occupation

Note:
These data make it possible to carry out prospective studies of the number of workers likely to be attached to various occupations which serve as the basis for projections of the national economy and the total economically active population. The tabulation provides the basis for analysis of differential fertility and mortality according to occupation. It also makes available useful data for the planning of social welfare schemes, health insurance programmes and so forth, which frequently pertain only to the employed population. A classification of unpaid family workers by sex and age is needed for international analysis of activity rates for females, in view of the different practices followed in defining and enumerating this group of workers in different countries.

---

*   The category "Under 15 years" should include all ages between the minimum age limit adopted by the country for census questions on economic activity and 14 years, if the minimum is below 15 years.

P7.3-R.   Currently (or usually) active population by activity status, main industry, age and sex

Geographical division, activity status, sex and main industry	Age (in years)								
	All ages	Under 15*	15-19	20-24	25-29	...	95-99	100 and over	Not stated

TOTAL ECONOMICALLY ACTIVE POPULATION

Both sexes

  Division 01
    Group 011
    Group 012
    (etc.)

  Division 02
    Group 020
    Group 021
    (etc.)
  ...

  Division 99
    Group 990

Male
(as for "Both sexes")

Female
(as for "Both sexes")

EMPLOYED
(as for "Total economically active population")

UNEMPLOYED, TOTAL
(as for "Total economically active population")

UNEMPLOYED, WORKED BEFORE
(as for "Total economically active population")

UNEMPLOYED, NEVER WORKED BEFORE
  Both sexes
  Male
  Female
(by definition, the industrial classification above does not apply to this category; this category is required only as total for ensuring the consistency of the figure for total economically active population)

NOT STATED
(as for "Unemployed, never worked before")

Population included: currently (or usually) active population at or above the minimum age adopted for enumerating the economically active population

Classifications:
(a)   Geographical division: (i) total country; (ii) each major civil division; (iii) each minor civil division; (iv) each principal locality. Distinguish between urban and rural for (i), (ii) and (iii)
(b)   Industry: according to, or convertible to, the latest revision of the International Standard Industrial Classification of All Economic Activities (ISIC, Rev.3) at least to the level of groups (three-digit)
(c)   Activity status: total economically active population; employed; unemployed (distinguishing persons who ever and never worked before); not stated
(d)   Age: all ages; under 15 years; 15-19 years; 20-24 years; 25-29 years; 30-34 years; 35-39 years; 40-44 years; 45-49 years; 50-54 years; 55-59 years; 60-64 years; 65-69 years; 70-74 years; 75-79 years; 80-84 years; 85-89 years; 90-94 years; 95-99 years; 100 years and over; not stated.
(e)   Sex: both sexes; male; female

Metadata for this tabulation:
(a)   Source of statistics:
  ➤ Traditional population census
  ➤ Register-based population census
  ➤ Registers/Surveys systems
  ➤ Rolling surveys
  ➤ Civil registration
(b)   De jure or de facto population or a combination with detailed description
(c)   Definition of urban and rural areas

Core topics:
  ➤ Place of usual residence or Place where present at time of census
  ➤ Sex
  ➤ Age
  ➤ Activity status
  ➤ Industry

Note:
These data furnish material for analyses of structural types of economic activities and may serve as a first indicator of socio-economic status. These data make it possible to carry out prospective studies of the number of workers likely to be attached to various industries in order to prepare projections of the national economy and the total economically active population. The tabulation also provides the basis for analysis of differential fertility and mortality according to industry. It also makes available useful data for the planning of social welfare schemes, health insurance programmes and so forth, which frequently pertain only to the employed population. A classification of unpaid family workers by sex and age is needed for international analysis of activity rates for females, in view of the different practices followed in defining and enumerating this group of workers in different countries.

---

*   The category "Under 15 years" should include all ages between the minimum age limit adopted by the country for census questions on economic activity and 14 years, if the minimum is below 15 years.

P7.4-R.   Currently (or usually) active population by activity status, main status in employment, age and sex

Geographical division, activity status, sex and age (in years)	Main status in employment						
	Total	Employer	Own-account worker	Employee	Contributing family worker	Member of producers' cooperative	Persons not classifiable by status

TOTAL ECONOMICALLY ACTIVE POPULATION

Both sexes

  All ages
    Under 15*
    15-19
    20-24
    25-29
    30-34
    ...
    85-89
    90-94
    95-99
    100 and over
    Not stated

Male
  (as for "Both sexes")

Female
  (as for "Both sexes")

EMPLOYED
  (as for "Total economically active population")

UNEMPLOYED, TOTAL
  (as for "Total economically active population")

UNEMPLOYED, WORKED BEFORE
  (as for "Total economically active population")

UNEMPLOYED, NEVER WORKED BEFORE
  Both sexes
  Male
  Female
  (by definition, the main ststus in employment classification above does not apply to this category; this category is required only as total for ensuring the consistency of the figure for total economically active population)

NOT STATED
  (as for "Unemployed, never worked before")

Population included: currently (or usually) active population at or above the minimum age adopted for enumerating the economically active population

Classifications:
(a)   Geographical division: (i) total country; (ii) each major civil division; (iii) each minor civil division; (iv) each principal locality. Distinguish between urban and rural for (i), (ii) and (iii)
(b)   Status in employment: total; employer; own-account worker; employee; contributing family worker; member of producers' cooperative; persons not classifiable by status
(c)   Activity status: total economically active: employed; unemployed (distinguishing persons who ever and never worked before); not stated
(d)   Age: all ages; under 15 years; 15-19 years; 20-24 years; 25-29 years; 30-34 years; 35-39 years; 40-44 years; 45-49 years; 50-54 years; 55-59 years; 60-64 years; 65-69 years; 70-74 years; 75-79 years; 80-84 years; 90-94 years; 95-99 years; 100 years and over; not stated.
(e)   Sex: both sexes; male; female

Metadata for this tabulation:
(a)   Source of statistics:
  ➤ Traditional population census
  ➤ Register-based population census
  ➤ Registers/Surveys systems
  ➤ Rolling surveys
  ➤ Civil registration
(b)   De jure or de facto population or a combination with detailed description
(c)   Definition of urban and rural areas

Core topics:
  ➤ Place of usual residence or Place where present at time of census
  ➤ Sex
  ➤ Age
  ➤ Activity status
  ➤ Status in employment

Note:
These data make it possible to carry out prospective studies of the number of workers by status in employment in order to prepare projections of the national economy and the total economically active population. The tabulations also provide the basis for analysis of differential fertility and mortality according to status in employment. It also makes available useful data for the planning of social welfare schemes, health insurance programmes and so forth, which frequently pertain only to the employee group. A classification of unpaid family workers by sex and age is needed for international analysis of activity rates for females, in view of the different practices followed in defining and enumerating this group of workers in different countries.

---

*   The category "Under 15 years" should include all ages between the minimum age limit adopted by the country for census questions on economic activity and 14 years, if the minimum is below 15 years.

P7.5-R. Currently (or usually) active population by activity status, main status in employment, main industry and sex

Geographical division, activity status, sex and main industry	Main status in employment						
	Total	Employer	Own-account worker	Employee	Contributing family worker	Member of producers' cooperative	Persons not classifiable by status

TOTAL ECONOMICALLY ACTIVE POPULATION

Both sexes

  Division 01
    Group 011
    Group 012
    (etc.)
  Division 02
    Group 020
    Group 021
    (etc.)
  ...
  Division 99
    Group 990

Male
(as for "Both sexes")

Female
(as for "Both sexes")

EMPLOYED
(as for "Total economically active population")

UNEMPLOYED, TOTAL
(as for "Total economically active population")

UNEMPLOYED, WORKED BEFORE
(as for "Total economically active population")

UNEMPLOYED, NEVER WORKED BEFORE

  Both sexes

  Male

  Female

(by definition, the industrial and main status in employment classifications above do not apply to this category; this category is required only as total for ensuring the consistency of the figure for total economically active population)

NOT STATED
(as for "Unemployed, never worked before")

Population included: currently (or usually) active population at or above the minimum age adopted for enumerating the economically active population

Classifications:
(*a*) Geographical division: (i) total country; (ii) each major civil division; (iii) each minor civil division; (iv) each principal locality. Distinguish between urban and rural for (i), (ii) and (iii)
(*b*) Status in employment: total; employer; own-account worker; employee; contributing family worker; member of producers' cooperative; persons not classifiable by status
(*c*) Activity status: total economically active population; employed; unemployed (distinguishing persons who ever and never worked before); not stated
(*d*) Sex: both sexes; male; female
(*e*) Industry: according to, or convertible to, the latest revision of the International Standard Industrial Classification of All Economic Activities (ISIC, Rev.3) to the level of groups (three-digit)

Metadata for this tabulation:
(*a*) Source of statistics:
  ➤ Traditional population census
  ➤ Register-based population census
  ➤ Registers/Surveys systems
  ➤ Rolling surveys
  ➤ Civil registration
(*b*) De jure or de facto population or a combination with detailed description
(*c*) Definition of urban and rural areas

Core topics:
  ➤ Place of usual residence or Place where present at time of census
  ➤ Sex
  ➤ Activity status
  ➤ Status in employment
  ➤ Industry

Note:
These tabulations furnish an inventory of a country's economically active population and its structure used in formulating economic policy and planning developmental programmes. Such tabulations play an essential part in analyses of national product and national income. Studies of the proportion of the economically active population in each industrial sector of the economy and of the shifts from one sector to another, give information on the level and trend of industrialization and on important aspects of the country's potential for economic development. Studies of migration from rural areas to cities require analysis of the industrial structure of employment in the cities and often of the major areas of out-migration, as an aid to assessment of economic aspects of internal migration. Studies of these types are also relevant to programmes of resettlement and to the formulation of policy with respect to internal migration.

P7.6-R. Currently (or usually) active population by activity status, main status in employment, main occupation and sex

Geographical division, activity status, sex and main occupation	Main status in employment						
	Total	Employer	Own-account worker	Employee	Contributing family worker	Member of producers' cooperative	Persons not classifiable by status
TOTAL ECONOMICALLY ACTIVE POPULATION							
Both sexes							
Sub-major group 11							
Minor group 111							
Minor group 112							
(etc.)							
Sub-major group 21							
Minor group 211							
Minor group 212							
(etc.)							
...							
Sub-major group 01							
Minor group 011							
Male (as for "Both sexes")							
Female (as for "Both sexes")							
EMPLOYED (as for "Total economically active population")							
UNEMPLOYED, TOTAL (as for "Total economically active population")							
UNEMPLOYED, WORKED BEFORE (as for "Total economically active population")							
UNEMPLOYED, NEVER WORKED BEFORE							
Both sexes							
Male							
Female							
(by definition, the occupational and main status in employment classifications above do not apply to this category; this category is required only as total for ensuring the consistency of the figure for total economically active population)							
NOT STATED (as for "Unemployed, never worked before")							

Population included: currently (or usually) active population at or above the minimum age adopted for enumerating the economically active population

Classifications:
(a) Geographical division: (i) total country; (ii) each major civil division; (iii) each minor civil division; (iv) each principal locality. Distinguish between urban and rural for (i), (ii) and (iii)
(b) Status in employment: total; employer; own-account worker; employee; contributing family worker; member of producers' cooperative; persons not classifiable by status
(c) Activity status: total economically active population; employed; unemployed (distinguishing persons who ever and never worked before); not stated
(d) Sex: both sexes; male; female
(e) Occupation: according to, or convertible to, the latest revision of the International Standard Classification of Occupations (ISCO-88), at least to the minor group (in other words, three-digit) level

Metadata for this tabulation:
(a) Source of statistics:
  › Traditional population census
  › Register-based population census
  › Registers/Surveys systems
  › Rolling surveys
  › Civil registration
(b) De jure or de facto population or a combination with detailed description
(c) Definition of urban and rural areas

Core topics:
  › Place of usual residence or Place where present at time of census
  › Sex
  › Activity status
  › Status in employment
  › Occupation

Note:
This tabulation provides an inventory of a country's economically active population and its structure, used in formulating economic policy and planning developmental programmes. Together with recommended tabulations P7.5-R and P7.7-R, it provides information for analysing national product and national income. Studies of migration from rural areas to cities require analysis of the occupational structure of employment in the cities and often of the major areas of out-migration, as an aid to assessment of economic aspects of internal migration. Also, decisions concerning possible sites for industrial establishments and vocational schools require information on the occupational structure of the labour force in various localities and regions of the country.

P7.7-R.   Currently (or usually) active population by activity status, main industry, main occupation and sex

Geographical division, activity status, sex and main occupation	Total	Main industry			Division 99
		Division 01		… … … … … …	Group
		Group			
		011	021		990

TOTAL ECONOMICALLY ACTIVE POPULATION

Both sexes

    Sub-major group 11

       Minor group 111

       Minor group 112 (etc.)

    Sub-major group 21

       Minor group 211

       Minor group 212

       (etc.)

    …

    Sub-major group 01

       Minor group 011

Male
(as for "Both sexes")

Female
(as for "Both sexes")

EMPLOYED
(as for "Total economically active population")

UNEMPLOYED, TOTAL
(as for "Total economically active population")

UNEMPLOYED, WORKED BEFORE
(as for "Total economically active population")

UNEMPLOYED, NEVER WORKED BEFORE

Both sexes

Male

Female

(by definition, the occupational and industrial classifications above do not apply to this category; this category is required only as total for ensuring the consistency of the figure for total economically active population)

NOT STATED
(as for "Unemployed, never worked before")

Population included: currently (or usually) active population at or above the minimum age adopted for enumerating the economically active population

Classifications:

(a) Geographical division: (i) total country; (ii) each major civil division; (iii) each minor civil division; (iv) each principal locality. Distinguish between urban and rural for (i), (ii) and (iii)

(b) Industry: according to, or convertible to, the latest revision of the International Standard Industrial Classification of All Economic Activities (ISIC, Rev.3) to the level of groups (three-digit)

(c) Activity status: total economically active population; employed; unemployed (distinguishing persons who ever and never worked before); not stated

(d) Occupation: according to, or convertible to, the latest revision of the International Standard Classification of Occupations (ISCO-88), at least to the minor group (in other words, three-digit) level

(e) Sex: both sexes; male; female

Metadata for this tabulation:

(a) Source of statistics:
- Traditional population census
- Register-based population census
- Registers/Surveys systems
- Rolling surveys
- Civil registration

(b) De jure or de facto population or a combination with detailed description

(c) Definition of urban and rural areas

Core topics:
- Place of usual residence or Place where present at time of census
- Sex
- Activity status
- Industry
- Occupation

Note:
This tabulation provides an inventory of a country's economically active population and its structure in formulating economic policy and planning developmental programmes. In planning for the development and expansion of an educational system and efficient utilization of human resources, studies are needed that assess requirements of labour in different industries and occupations.

P7.8-R. Population not currently (or usually) active, by functional category, age and sex

Geographical division, sex and age (in years)	Total not currently (or usually) active	Functional category				
		Homemaker	Student	Income recipient	Other	Not stated
Both sexes						
All ages						
Under 15*						
15-19						
20-24						
25-29						
30-34						
35-39						
40-44						
45-49						
50-54						
55-59						
60-64						
65-69						
70-74						
75-79						
80-84						
85-89						
90-94						
95-99						
100 and over						
Not stated						
Male (as for "Both sexes")						
Female (as for "Both sexes")						

Population included: population not currently (or usually) active at or above the minimum age adopted for enumerating the economically active population

Classifications:

(*a*) Geographical division: (i) total country; (ii) each major civil division; (iii) each minor civil division; (iv) each principal locality. Distinguish between urban and rural for (i), (ii) and (iii)

(*b*) Age: all ages; under 15 years; 15-19 years; 20-24 years; 25-29 years; 30-34 years; 35-39 years; 40-44 years; 45-49 years; 50-54 years; 55-59 years; 60-64 years; 65-69 years; 70-74 years; 75-79 years; 80-84 years; 90-94 years; 95-99 years; 100 years and over; not stated.

(*c*) Functional category: total not currently (or usually) active; homemaker; student; income recipient; other; not stated

(*d*) ex: both sexes; male; female

Metadata for this tabulation:

(*a*) Source of statistics:

> Traditional population census

> Register-based population census

> Registers/Surveys systems

> Rolling surveys

> Civil registration

(*b*) De jure or de facto population or a combination with detailed description

(*c*) Definition of urban and rural areas

Core topics:

> Place of usual residence or Place where present at time of census

> Sex

> Age

> Activity status (functional categories)

Note:

This tabulation provides data on the population not currently (or usually) active, classified by functional category. This data may be used for the analysis of potential sources of human resources that are not readily available at present but that may become so under different circumstances.

---

* The category "Under 15 years" should include all ages between the minimum age limit adopted by the country for census questions on economic activity and 14 years, if the minimum is below 15 years.

Group 8. Tabulations on disability characteristics

P8.1-R. Population with and without disabilities* by age and sex

Geographical division, sex and age (in years)	Total	With disabilities	Without disabilities	Not stated
Total country				
Both sexes				
All ages				
Under 1 year				
1-4				
5-9				
10-14				
15-19				
20-24				
25-29				
30-34				
35-39				
40-44				
45-49				
50-54				
55-59				
60-64				
65-69				
70-74				
75-79				
80-84				
85-89				
90-94				
95-99				
100 years and over				
Not stated				
Male (age groups as above)				
Female (age groups as above)				

Population included: total population

Classifications:
(*a*) Geographical divisions: (i) total country; (ii) each major civil division; (iii) each principal locality. Distinguish between urban and rural for (i), (ii) and (iii)
(*b*) Disability status: total; without disabilities; with disabilities; not stated
(*c*) Age: all ages; under 1 year; 1-4 years; 5-9 years; 10-14 years; 15-19 years; 20-24 years; 25-29 years; 30-34 years; 35-39 years; 40-44 years; 45-49 years; 50-54 years; 55-59 years; 60-64 years; 65-69 years; 70-74 years; 75-79 years; 80-84 years; 90-94 years; 95-99 years; 100 years and over; not stated.
(*d*) Sex: both sexes; male; female

Metadata for this tabulation:
(*a*) Source of statistics:
  > Traditional population census
  > Register-based population census
  > Registers/Surveys systems
  > Rolling surveys
  > Civil registration
(*b*) De jure or de facto population or a combination with detailed description
(*c*) Definition of urban and rural areas
(*d*) Exact question wording

Core topics:
  > Place of usual residence or Place where present at time of census
  > Sex
  > Age
  > Disability status

Note:
There is widespread interest in the prevalence of disability by age and sex in the population. This tabulation provides information for the calculation of prevalence rates distributed by geographical division, urban/rural residence and the living arrangements of persons with disabilities.

---

* Estimates of the population with and without disability are a function of the exact methods and question wording used in the data collection. Consult the metadata for information on the methods (include the specific questions) used.

P 8.2-R. Population 5 years of age and over, by disability status*, educational attainment, age and sex

Geographical division, sex, disability status and age (in years)	Educational attainment						
	No schooling	Primary education	Secondary education, first cycle	Secondary education, second cycle	Post-secondary education	Not classifiable by level and grade of education	Level not stated

Both sexes

Without disabilities

  All ages

  0-4

  5-9

  ...

  95-99

  100+

  Not stated

With disabilities
  (age groups as above)

Disability status not stated
  (age groups as above)

Male
(as for "Both sexes")

Female
(as for "Both sexes")

Population included: all persons at or above the usual age for entrance into school

Classifications:
(a) Geographical divisions: (i) total country; (ii) each major civil division; (iii) each principal locality. Distinguish between urban and rural for (i), (ii) and (iii)
(b) Disability status: without disabilities; with disabilities; disability status not stated
(c) Educational attainment: no schooling; primary education: by single grades and grade not stated; secondary education, first cycle: by single grades and grade not stated; secondary education, second cycle: by single grades and grade not stated; post-secondary education: by single grades/ years and grade not stated; not classifiable by level and grade of education; level of education not stated
(d) Age: all ages; 5-9 years; 10-14 years; 15-19 years; 20-24 years; 25-29 years; 30-34 years; 35-39 years; 40-44 years; 45-49 years; 50-54 years; 55-59 years; 60-64 years; 65-69 years; 70-74 years; 75-79 years; 80-84 years; 85-89 years; 90-94 years; 95-99 years; and 100 years over; not stated
(e) Sex : both sexes; male; female

Metadata for this tabulation:
(a) Source of statistics:
> Traditional population census
> Register-based population census
> Registers/Surveys systems
> Rolling surveys
> Civil registration
(b) De jure or de facto population or a combination with detailed description
(c) Definition of urban and rural areas
(d) Exact question wording

Core topics:
> Place of usual residence or Place where present at time of census
> Sex
> Age
> Disability status
> Educational attainment

Note:
The tabulation provides data for the comparison of the educational attainment of persons with and without disabilities. The percentage of people with disabilities who have no schooling can be compared with that of persons without disabilities. This gives information on the status of integration of persons with disabilities and on the opportunity that persons with disabilities have to participate in the economic, social and cultural development of the country.

---

* Estimates of the population with and without disability are a function of the exact methods and question wording used in the data collection. Consult the metadata for information on the methods (include the specific questions) used.

P 8.3-R.　Population …* years of age and over, by disability status**, current (or usual) activity status, age and sex

Geographical division, sex, disability status and age (in years)	Total …* years of age and over	Current (or usual) activity status									
		Economically active				Not economically active					Not stated
		Employed	Unemployed			Home-maker	Student	Income recipient	Other		
			Total	Worked before	Never worked before						

Both sexes

  Without disabilities

    All ages

    Under 15***

    15-19

    …

    95-99

    100 and over

    Not stated

  With disabilities
  (age groups as above)

  Disability status not stated
  (age groups as above)

Male
(as for "Both sexes")

Female
as for "Both sexes")

Population included:　population at or above the minimum age adapted for enumerating the economically active population

Classifications:

(a)　Geographical division: (i) total country; (ii) each major civil division; (iii) each minor civil division; (iv) each principal locality. Distinguish between urban and rural for (i), (ii) and (iii)

(b)　Disability status: without disabilities; with disabilities; disability status not stated

(c)　Activity status: economically active: (i) employed; (ii) unemployed (distinguishing persons who ever and never worked before); not economically active: (i) homemaker; (ii) student; (iii) income recipient; (iv) other; not stated

(d)　Age: all ages, 15 years and over; 15-19 years; 20-24 years; 25-29 years; 30-34 years; 35-39 years; 40-44 years; 45-49 years; 50-54 years; 55-59 years; 60-64 years; 65-69 years; 70-74 years; 75-79 years; 80-84 years; 85-89 years; 90-94 years; 95-99 years; and 100 years over; not stated. (The category "under 15 years" should include all ages between the minimum age-limit adopted by the country for census questions on economic activity and 14 years, if the minimum is under 15 years.)

(e)　Sex: both sexes; male; female

Metadata for this tabulation:

(a)　Source of statistics:
- Traditional population census
- Register-based population census
- Registers/Surveys systems
- Rolling surveys
- Civil registration

(b)　De jure or de facto population or a combination with detailed description

(c)　Definition of urban and rural areas

(d)　Exact question wording

Core topics:
- Place of usual residence or Place where present at time of census
- Sex
- Age
- Disability status
- Activity status

Note:
Access to paid work is crucial to achieving self-reliance and ensuring the well-being of the adult population, both of persons with disabilities as well as of those without disabilities. Tabulations by economic activity status provide a basic measure of the social and economic integration of the population with disabilities as compared with those without disabilities. Tabulations by urban/rural residence, age and sex are essential to identifying groups of the population that may be most disadvantaged.

---

　*　The minimum age adopted by the country for enumerating the economically active population.

　**　Estimates of the population with and without disability are a function of the exact methods and question wording used in the data collection. Consult the metadata for information on the methods (include the specific questions) used.

***　The category "Under 15 years" should include all ages between the minimum age limit adopted by the country for census questions on economic activity and 14 years, if the minimum is below 15 years.

Annex III
Recommended Tabulations for Housing Censuses

List of recommended tabulations for housing censuses[a],[b]

H1-R   Persons, by broad types of living quarters and number of roofless*

H2-R   Persons in collective living quarters by type

H3-R   Households in occupied housing units, by type of housing unit*

H4-R   Conventional dwellings by occupancy status

H5-R   Occupied housing units, by type of housing unit, cross-classified by type of ownership of the housing units

H6-R   Housing units, by number of rooms, cross-classified by type of housing unit and number of occupants per housing unit

H7-R   Occupied housing units, by type of housing unit, cross-classified by water supply system*

H8-R   Occupied housing units, by type of housing unit, cross-classified by main source of drinking water*

H9-R   Occupied housing units, by type of housing unit, cross-classified by type of toilet and type of sewage disposal*

H10-R   Occupied housing units, by type of housing unit, cross-classified by type of bathing facilities

H11-R   Occupied housing units, by type of housing unit, cross-classified by availability of kitchen and fuel used for cooking

H12-R   Occupied housing units, by type of housing unit, cross-classified by type of lighting and/or use of electricity

H13-R   Occupied housing units, by type of housing unit, cross-classified by main type of solid waste disposal

H14-R   Households in housing units, by type of housing unit occupied, cross-classified by number of households per housing unit

H15-R   Conventional dwellings by type of building, and construction material of outer walls

H16-R   Housing units by type and construction material of outer walls

H17-R   Households, by type of housing unit, cross-classified by sex and age of head or other reference member of household*

H18-R   Households in housing units, by type of housing unit, cross-classified by tenure of household and, for tenant households, ownership of housing unit occupied*

H19-R   Households in housing units, by type of housing unit, cross-classified by information and communication technology devices and access to Internet

[a] Recommended tabulations are identified by an "R" as part of the table number.
[b] An asterisk (*) represents a basic/essential tabulation.

H1.1-R.   Persons, by broad types of living quarters, and number roofless

H1.2-R.   Households, by broad types of living quarters, and number roofless

H1.3-R.   Living quarters, by broad types

Geographical division	Total living quarters	Type of living quarters				Roofless
		Housing units			Collective living quarters	
		Total	Conventional dwellings	Other housing units		
Total persons/households/living quarters						
Total						
Urban						
Rural						
Major civil division A*						
Urban						
Rural						
Minor civil division A1*						
Urban						
Rural						
Minor civil division A2*						
Major civil division B*						
Urban						
Rural						
Minor civil division B1*						
Urban						
Rural						
Minor civil division B2*						
(etc.)						
Major civil division Z*						
Urban						
Rural						
Minor civil division Z1*						
Urban						
Rural						
Minor civil division Z2*						
Urban						
Rural						
(etc.)						

For illustrative purposes, persons are shown as the units of tabulation in this table. Similar tables should be prepared using households, and living quarters as units of tabulation. Similar table, with family nuclei as unit of tabulation is listed as additional (in the set of additional tabulations)

Units of tabulation: persons; households; living quarters

Living quarters included: all living quarters

Persons and households included: all persons and all households

Classifications:
(a)   Geographical divisions: (i) total country; (ii) each major civil division; (iii) each minor civil division. Distinguish between urban and rural for (i), (ii) and (iii)
(b)   Type of living quarters
(c)   Roofless: separate class for the roofless

Metadata for this tabulation:
(a)   Source of statistics:
➤   Traditional housing census
➤   Register-based housing census
➤   Registers/Surveys systems
➤   Rolling surveys
(b)   De jure or de facto population or combination (provide detailed description)
(c)   Definition of urban and rural areas

Core topics:
➤   Place of usual residence or Place where present at time of census
➤   Living quarters—type of

Note:
This is a broad summary table designed to show in very general terms the type of housing occupied by persons and households and the number roofless. It provides background information as well as a control for preparation of more detailed tabulations for the categories shown. In fact, the magnitude of the number of households that occupy collective living quarters or are homeless and their geographical distribution provide an indication of the extent to which more detailed tabulations for these groups need to be prepared.

_____

*   Name of major or minor civil division.

H2.1-R. Persons in collective living quarters by type

H2.2-R. Collective living quarters by type

Geographical division	Total collective living quarters	Type of collective living quarters										
		Hotels	Hospitals	Correctional institutions	Military institutions	Religious institutions	Retirement homes	Student dormitories	Staff quarters	Camps and workers' quarters	Other
Total persons/collective living quarters												
Total												
Urban												
Rural												
Major civil division A*												
Urban												
Rural												
Minor civil division A1*												
Urban												
Rural												
Minor civil division A2*												
Urban												
Rural												
(etc.)												
Major civil division B*												
Urban												
Rural												
Minor civil division B1*												
Urban												
Rural												
Minor civil division B2*												
Urban												
Rural												
...												
Major civil division Z*												
Urban												
Rural												
Minor civil division Z1*												
Urban												
Rural												
Minor civil division Z2*												
Urban												
Rural												
(etc.)												

For illustrative purposes, persons and also collective living quarters are shown as the unit of tabulation in this table.

Units of tabulation: persons, collective living quarters

Living quarters included: collective living quarters

Persons included: persons living in collective living quarters

Classifications:
(a) Geographical divisions: (i) total country; (ii) each major civil division; (iii) each minor civil division. Distinguish between urban and rural for (i), (ii) and (iii)
(b) Type of collective living quarters

Metadata for this tabulation:
(a) Source of statistics:
   ➤ Traditional housing census
   ➤ Register-based housing census
   ➤ Registers/Surveys systems
   ➤ Rolling surveys
(b) De jure or de facto population or combination (provide detailed description)
(c) Definition of urban and rural areas

Core topics:
   ➤ Place of usual residence or Place where present at time of census
   ➤ Living quarters—type of

Note:
This is the only recommended table that displays all the categories of collective living quarters. It is recognized that the living conditions in different type of collective living quarters differ significantly, for example, in military camps and luxurious retirement homes. This table aims at showing the magnitude of institutional population in different types of institutions.

---

* Name of major or minor civil division.

H3.1-R.   Households in occupied housing units, by type of housing unit

H3.2-R.   Occupied housing units, by type of housing unit

H3.3-R.   Occupants of housing units, by type of housing unit

H3.4-R.   Family nuclei in occupied housing units, by type of housing unit

Geographical division*	Total housing units	Type of housing unit									Not stated
		Conventional dwelling			Other housing units						
								Informal housing unit			
		Total	Has all basic facilities	Does not have all basic facilities	Total	Semi-perm. dwellings	Mobile housing unit	Improvised	Permanent but not intended for habitation	Other	
Total households/occupied housing units/occupants/ family nuclei											
Total											
Urban											
Rural											
Major civil division A**											
Urban											
Rural											
Minor civil division A1**											
Urban											
Rural											
Minor civil division A2**											
Urban											
Rural											
(etc.)											
Major civil division B**											
Urban											
Rural											
Minor civil division B1**											
Urban											
Rural											
Minor civil division B2**											
Urban											
Rural											
...											
Major civil division Z**											
Urban											
Rural											
Minor civil division Z1**											
Urban											
Rural											
Minor civil division Z2**											
Urban											
Rural											
(etc.)											

For illustrative purposes, households, housing units, family nuclei and persons are shown as the units of tabulation.

Units of tabulation: households; housing units; family nuclei; occupants

Living quarters included: occupied housing units

Households, family nuclei and persons included: households, family nuclei and occupants

Classifications:
(*a*)   Geographical divisions: (i) total country; (ii) each major civil division; (iii) each minor civil division. Distinguish between urban and rural for (i), (ii) and (iii)

(*b*)   Type of housing unit

Metadata for this tabulation:
(*a*)   Source of statistics:
> Traditional housing census
> Register-based housing census
> Registers/Surveys systems
> Rolling surveys

(*b*)   De jure or de facto population or combination (provide detailed description)

(*c*)   Definition of urban and rural areas

Core topics:
> Place of usual residence or Place where present at time of census
> Living quarters—type of

Note:
This table distinguishes among various types of housing according to the level of housing standards. Also, its purpose is to describe the occupants in terms of aggregates, households and family nuclei. The tabulation is of primary importance for the formulation of housing programmes and is a prerequisite of calculation of indicators on housing conditions.

---

*   This table may be compiled for (i) total country; (ii) each major civil division; (iii) each minor civil division; (iv) each principal locality. Distinguish between urban and rural for (i), (ii) and (iii).

*   Name of major or minor civil division.

H4-R. Conventional dwellings by occupancy status

Geographical division* and type of conventional dwelling	Total conventional dwellings	Type of conventional dwellings										
		Occupied	Vacant									Not stated
			Seasonally vacant			Non-seasonally vacant						
			Holiday homes	Seasonal workers' quarters	Other	Secondary residences	For rent	For sale	For demolition	Other		

Total country

  Has all basic facilities

  Does not have all basic facilities

Urban
(as for "Total country")

Rural
(as for "Total country")

Units of tabulation: conventional dwellings

Living quarters included: conventional dwellings

Households and persons included: none

Classifications:
(a) Geographical divisions: (i) total country; (ii) each major civil division; (iii) each minor civil division. Distinguish between urban and rural for (i), (ii) and (iii)
(b) Type of conventional dwellings
(c) Occupancy status

Metadata for this tabulation:
(a) Source of statistics:
  ➤ Traditional housing census
  ➤ Register-based housing census
  ➤ Registers/Surveys systems
  ➤ Rolling surveys
(b) De jure or de facto population or combination (provide detailed description)
(c) Definition of urban and rural areas

Core topics:
  ➤ Place of usual residence or Place where present at time of census
  ➤ Living quarters—type of
  ➤ Occupancy status

Note:
This tabulation confines itself to data relating to conventional dwellings because all other types of housing units are required, by definition, to be occupied in order to fall within the scope of the census; a classification by occupancy would not therefore be applicable to them. In some housing censuses, vacancy information is recorded during the listing of sets of living quarters and summaries of these lists provide the aggregates furnished by this tabulation, although generally not in detail as far as reasons for vacancy are concerned. Such a procedure may provide an economic means of obtaining data, though every effort should be made to collect information in detail on vacant conventional dwellings.

---

* This table may be compiled for (i) total country; (ii) each major civil division; (iii) each minor civil division; (iv) each principal locality. Distinguish between urban and rural for (i), (ii) and (iii).

H5-R.　Occupied housing units, by type of housing unit, cross-classified by type of ownership of the housing units

Geographical division* and type of ownership	Total housing units	Conventional dwellings			Other housing units			Informal housing units			Not stated
		Total	Has all basic facilities	Does not have all basic facilities	Total	Semi-perm. dwellings	Mobile housing units	Impro-vised	Permanent but not intended for habitation	Other	

Total occupied housing units	*For illustrative purposes, housing units are shown as unit of tabulation in this table. A similar table could be prepared using households as units of tabulation, which is listed as additional (in the additional set of tabulations)*
Owner occupied	**Units of tabulation:**　housing units
Non-owner occupied	**Living quarters included:**　occupied housing units
Publicly owned	**Households and persons included:**　None
Privately owned	**Classifications:**
Communally owned	(*a*)　Geographical divisions: (i) total country; (ii) each major civil division; (iii) each minor civil division. Distinguish between urban and rural for (i), (ii) and (iii)
Cooperatively owned	(*b*)　Type of housing unit
Other	(*c*)　Type of ownership
	(*d*)　Use of housing unit

Metadata for this tabulation:
(*a*)　Source of statistics:
  › Traditional housing census
  › Register-based housing census
  › Registers/Surveys systems
  › Rolling surveys
(*b*)　De jure or de facto population or a combination with detailed description
(*c*)　Definition of urban and rural areas

Core topics:
  › Place of usual residence or Place where present at time of census
  › Living quarters—type of
  › Ownership—type of

Note:
This tabulation provides information on the type of ownership of the housing unit. It is intended to show the type of ownership according to the type of housing unit. Assessing the ownership of housing units is of paramount importance in establishing housing policies.

---

* This table may be compiled for (i) total country; (ii) each major civil division; (iii) each minor civil division; (iv) each principal locality. Distinguish between urban and rural for (i), (ii) and (iii).

H6-R. Housing units, by number of rooms*, cross-classified by type of housing unit and number of occupants per housing unit

Geographical division**, type of housing unit and number of occupants	Total housing units	Housing units with the following number of rooms*							
		Total	1	2	3	...	9	10+	Not stated

Total housing units

Housing units with the following number of occupants

  Total

    0

    1

    2

    3

    4

    5

    6

    7

    8

    9

    10+

Conventional dwellings with the following number of occupants
(classification of occupants as above)

Other housing units
(classification of occupants 1–10+)***

Not stated

Units of tabulation: housing units

Living quarters included: housing units

Classifications:
(a) Geographical divisions: (i) total country; (ii) each major civil division; (iii) each minor civil division. Distinguish between urban and rural for (i), (ii) and (iii)
(b) Type of housing unit
(c) Number of occupants per housing unit
(d) Number of rooms per housing unit

Metadata for this tabulation:
(a) Source of statistics:
    ➤ Traditional housing census
    ➤ Register-based housing census
    ➤ Registers/Surveys systems
    ➤ Rolling surveys
(b) De jure or de facto population or combination (provide detailed description)
(c) Definition of urban and rural areas

Core topics:
    ➤ Place of usual residence or Place where present at time of census
    ➤ Living quarters—type of
    ➤ Rooms—number of
    ➤ Occupants—number of

Note:
This tabulation provides for the selection of data concerning any desired level of density considered to be of significance, from extreme overcrowding to under-occupancy. In establishing the statistical indicators on housing conditions, the Statistical Commission and the Inter-Agency Working Party on Statistics for Social Programmes agreed that dwellings with densities of three or more persons per room should be considered overcrowded under any circumstances. For national use, this level may be raised or lowered according to circumstances; levels set for urban areas may be different from those for rural areas (the outdoor spaces in rural areas are sometimes considered to offset, to some extent, the high densities prevailing within the housing units).

---

* Excluding rooms used wholly for business or professional purposes.

** This table may be compiled for (i) total country; (ii) each major civil division; (iii) each minor civil division; (iv) each principal locality. Distinguish between urban and rural for (i), (ii) and (iii).

*** Since by definition it is required that housing units other than conventional dwellings be occupied in order to be included in the census, category 0 is not applicable.

H7-R. Occupied housing units, by type of housing unit, cross-classified by water supply system

Geographical division*, water supply system	Total housing units	Type of housing unit										
		Conventional dwellings			Other housing units							Not stated
									Informal housing units			
		Total	Has all basic facilities	Does not have all basic facilities	Total	Semi-permanent dwellings	Mobile housing units	Impro-vised	Permanent but not intended for habitation	Other		

Total occupied housing units

Piped water inside the unit
  From the community scheme
  From an individual source

Piped water outside the unit but within 200 metres
  From the community scheme
    For exclusive use
    Shared
  From an individual source
    For exclusive use
    Shared

Without piped water (including piped water beyond 200 metres)

For illustrative purposes, housing units are shown as unit of tabulation in this table. A similar table could be prepared using households and occupants as units of tabulation, which are listed as additional (in the additional set of tabulations)

Units of tabulation: housing units

Living quarters included: occupied housing units

Households and persons included: none

Classifications:
(a) Geographical divisions: (i) total country; (ii) each major civil division; (iii) each minor civil division. Distinguish between urban and rural for (i), (ii) and (iii)
(b) Type of housing unit
(c) Water supply system
(d) Source of water supply: on the basis of most frequent sources in country or area, but may include piped community-wide system; catchments tank; public well; private well; river, spring; and so forth

Metadata for this tabulation:
(a) Source of statistics:
  ➤ Traditional housing census
  ➤ Register-based housing census
  ➤ Registers/Surveys systems
  ➤ Rolling surveys
(b) De jure or de facto population or combination (provide detailed description)
(c) Definition of urban and rural areas

Core topics:
  ➤ Place of usual residence or Place where present at time of census
  ➤ Living quarters—type of
  ➤ Water supply system

Note:
From this tabulation, information may be derived on the number of persons and the number of households with ready access to water supply as well as the availability of piped water for each class of housing units. The classification of the source of the water supply in this tabulation is limited to the community scheme or an individual source. Many countries have found it useful to further elaborate this classification in order to provide more detailed information on the source of the water supply.

* This table may be compiled for (i) total country; (ii) each major civil division; (iii) each minor civil division; (iv) each principal locality. Distinguish between urban and rural for (i), (ii) and (iii).

H8-R. Occupied housing units, by type of housing unit, cross-classified by main source of drinking water

Geographical division* and main source of drinking water	Total housing units	Type of housing unit									
		Conventional dwellings			Other housing units						
								Informal housing units			
		Total	Has all basic facilities	Does not have all basic facilities	Total	Semi-permanent dwellings	Mobile housing units	Impro-vised	Permanent but not intended for habitation	Other	Not stated

Total occupied housing units

Piped water inside the unit
  From the community scheme
  From an individual source

Piped water outside the unit but within 200 metres
  From the community scheme
    For exclusive use
    Shared
  From an individual source
    For exclusive use
    Shared

Without piped water (including piped water beyond 200 metres)
  Borehole
  Protected well
  Protected spring
  Rainwater collection
  Vendor provided water
  Bottled water
  Tanker trucks
  Unprotected well/spring/ river/stream/lake pond, dam

For illustrative purposes, housing units are shown as unit of tabulation in this table. Similar tables could be prepared using households and occupants as units of tabulation, which are listed as additional (in the additional set of tabulations)

Units of tabulation: housing units

Living quarters included: occupied housing units

Households and persons included: None

Classifications:
(a) Geographical divisions: (i) total country; (ii) each major civil division; (iii) each minor civil division. Distinguish between urban and rural for (i), (ii) and (iii)
(b) Type of housing unit
(c) Water supply system
(d) Source of water supply: on the basis of most frequent sources in country or area, but may include piped community-wide system; catchments tank; public well; private well; river, spring; and so forth

Metadata for this tabulation:
(a) Source of statistics:
  ➤ Traditional housing census
  ➤ Register-based housing census
  ➤ Registers/Surveys systems
  ➤ Rolling surveys
(b) De jure or de facto population or combination (provide detailed description)
(c) Definition of urban and rural areas

Core topics:
  ➤ Place of usual residence or Place where present at time of census
  ➤ Living quarters—type of
  ➤ Drinking water—main source of

Note:
The importance of supply of drinking water was emphasized in a number United Nations documents and resolutions, most notably on Millennium Development Goals. This tabulation aims at assessing the source of drinking water used by households as it often differs from the source of water used for general purposes (see tabulation H7-R above).

---

* This table may be compiled for (i) total country; (ii) each major civil division; (iii) each minor civil division; (iv) each principal locality. Distinguish between urban and rural for (i), (ii) and (iii).

H9-R. Occupied housing units, by type of housing unit, cross-classified by type of toilet and type of sewage disposal

Geographical division*, type of toilet and sewage disposal	Total housing units	Type of housing unit									
		Conventional dwellings			Other housing units						
								Informal housing units			
		Total	Has all basic facilities	Does not have all basic facilities	Total	Semi-permanent dwellings	Mobile housing units	Impro-vised	Permanent but not intended for habitation	Other	Not stated
Total occupied housing units											
With toilet within the housing unit											
Flush/pour flush toilet											
Connected to a public sewerage plant											
Connected to a private sewerage plant											
Other											
Non-flush toilet											
Connected to a public sewerage plant											
Connected to a private sewerage plant											
Other											
With toilet outside the housing unit											
Flush/pour flush toilet											
Connected to a public sewerage plant											
Connected to a private sewerage plant											
Other											
Non-flush toilet											
Connected to a public sewerage plant											
Connected to a private sewerage plant											
Other											
No toilet available											
Not stated											

For illustrative purposes, housing units are shown as unit of tabulation in this table. Similar tables could be prepared using households and occupants as units of tabulation, which are listed as additional (in the additional set of tabulations)

Units of tabulation: housing units

Living quarters included: occupied housing units

Households and persons included: none

Classifications

(a) Geographical divisions: (i) total country; (ii) each major civil division; (iii) each minor civil division. Distinguish between urban and rural for (i), (ii) and (iii)

(b) Type of housing unit

(c) Type of toilet

(d) Sewage disposal system

Metadata for this tabulation:

(a) Source of statistics:
> Traditional housing census
> Register-based housing census
> Registers/Surveys systems
> Rolling surveys

(b) De jure or de facto population or a combination with detailed description

(c) Definition of urban and rural areas

Core topics:
> Place of usual residence or Place where present at time of census
> Living quarters—type of
> Toilet—type of
> Sewerage disposal

Note:

From this tabulation, data may be obtained on the number of housing units by type with the number of occupants, the type of toilet facilities available to them and the characteristics of the sewage system. The tabulation of toilet facilities shown provides the minimum data required for an evaluation of living quarters according to the facilities available. The information for dwellings is required for the computation of indicators of housing and its environment. If the number of sets of collective living quarters is large, it may be useful to prepare similar tabulations by type of collective living quarters. With respect to these units, however, separate tabulations that would also show the number of toilets in relation to the number of occupants may be more useful than information that merely indicates the availability of toilets and the type of toilet. Similar information may be tabulated for housing units occupied by more than a certain number of households. In many countries the classification has been elaborated to provide information on availability of particular types of toilets (other than flush) that are prevalent and characteristic of the country or area concerned and imply varying degrees of efficiency from a sanitary point of view.

---

* This table may be compiled for (i) total country; (ii) each major civil division; (iii) each minor civil division; (iv) each principal locality. Distinguish between urban and rural for (i), (ii) and (iii).

H10-R. Occupied housing units, by type of housing unit, cross-classified by type of bathing facilities

Geographical division* and type of bathing facilities	Total housing units	Type of housing unit									
		Conventional dwellings			Other housing units						Not stated
								Informal housing units			
		Total	Has all basic facilities	Does not have all basic facilities	Total	Semi-permanent dwellings	Mobile housing units	Impro-vised	Permanent but not intended for habitation	Other	

Total occupied housing units	*For illustrative purposes, housing units are shown as unit of tabulation in this table. Similar tables could be prepared using households and occupants as units of tabulation, which are listed as additional (in the additional set of tabulations)*
With fixed bath or shower within housing unit	**Units of tabulation:** housing units
Without fixed bath or shower within housing unit	**Living quarters included:** occupied housing units
	Households and persons included: none
Fixed bath or shower available outside housing unit	**Classifications:**
For exclusive use	(a) Geographical divisions: (i) total country; (ii) each major civil division; (iii) each minor civil division. Distinguish between urban and rural for (i), (ii) and (iii)
Shared	(b) Type of housing unit
	(c) Bathing facilities
No fixed bath or shower available	**Metadata for this tabulation:**
	(a) Source of statistics:

> Traditional housing census
> Register-based housing census
> Registers/Surveys systems
> Rolling surveys

(b) De jure or de facto population or a combination with detailed description

(c) Definition of urban and rural areas

Core topics:
> Place of usual residence or Place where present at time of census
> Living quarters—type of
> Bathing facilities

Note:
From this tabulation, data may be obtained on the number of housing units by and the type of bathing facilities available to occupants. This tabulation provides the minimum data required for an evaluation of living quarters according to the facilities available. The information for dwellings is required for the computation of indicators of housing and its environment. If the number of sets of collective living quarters is large, it may be useful to prepare similar tabulations by type of collective living quarters. With respect to these units, however, separate tabulations that would also show the number of fixed baths and showers in relation to the number of occupants may be more useful than information that merely indicates the availability of bathing facilities. Similar information may be tabulated for housing units occupied by more than a certain number of households.

---

* This table may be compiled for (i) total country; (ii) each major civil division; (iii) each minor civil division; (iv) each principal locality. Distinguish between urban and rural for (i), (ii) and (iii).

H11-R. Occupied housing units, by type of housing unit, cross-classified by availability of kitchen and fuel used for cooking

Geographical division*, availability of kitchen and fuel used for cooking	Total housing units	Type of housing unit										
		Conventional dwellings			Other housing units							Not stated
								Informal housing units				
		Total	Has all basic facilities	Does not have all basic facilities	Total	Semi-permanent dwellings	Mobile housing units	Impro-vised	Permanent but not intended for habitation	Other		

Total occupied housing units

With kitchen within the housing unit
- Gas
- Electricity
- Liquefied petroleum gas (LPG)
- Kerosene/paraffin (petroleum based)
- Oil (including vegetable oil)
- Coal
- Firewood
- Charcoal
- Animal dung
- Crop residue
- Other

With other space for cooking within the housing unit
(classification of fuel used for cooking as above)

Without kitchen or other space for cooking within the housing unit
(classification of fuel used for cooking as above)

For illustrative purposes, housing units are shown as unit of tabulation in this table. Similar tables could be prepared using households and occupants as units of tabulation, which are listed as additional (in the additional set of tabulations)

Units of tabulation: housing units

Living quarters included: occupied housing units

Households and persons included: none

Classifications:
(a) Geographical divisions: (i) total country; (ii) each major civil division; (iii) each minor civil division. Distinguish between urban and rural for (i), (ii) and (iii)
(b) Type of housing unit
(c) Cooking facilities
(d) Fuel used for cooking

Metadata for this tabulation:
(a) Source of statistics:
  ➤ Traditional housing census
  ➤ Register-based housing census
  ➤ Registers/Surveys systems
  ➤ Rolling surveys
(b) De jure or de facto population or combination (provide detailed description)
(c) Definition of urban and rural areas

Core topics:
  ➤ Place of usual residence or Place where present at time of census
  ➤ Living quarters—type of
  ➤ Kitchen—availability of
  ➤ Fuel used for cooking

Note:
The classifications used in this tabulation for equipment and fuel used for cooking should be formulated to conform to the types of equipment and types of fuel normally used in the country concerned. Data on fuel refer to the fuel most frequently used and it may be confined to the fuel used for preparing the principal meals. If information has been gathered on the number of kitchens or kitchenettes or the number of stoves in housing units occupied by more than a certain number of households and for collective living quarters, such as hotels, boarding houses and multi-household living quarters, it would be useful to tabulate this information according to the type of living quarters and the number of households.

* This table may be compiled for (i) total country; (ii) each major civil division; (iii) each minor civil division; (iv) each principal locality. Distinguish between urban and rural for (i), (ii) and (iii).

H12-R. Occupied housing units, by type of housing unit, cross-classified by type of lighting and/or use of electricity

Geographical division* and type of lighting and/or availability of electricity	Total housing units	Type of housing unit										
		Conventional dwellings			Other housing units							Not stated
								Informal housing units				
		Total	Has all basic facilities	Does not have all basic facilities	Total	Semi-permanent dwellings	Mobile housing units	Impro-vised	Perma nent but not intended for habitation	Other		

Total occupied housing units

Type of lighting

  Electricity

  Gas

  Oil lamp

  (Other types of lighting of significance to the country or area concerned)

Urban

  (type of lighting as above)

Rural

  (type of lighting as above)

For illustrative purposes, housing units are shown as unit of tabulation in this table. Similar tables could be prepared using households and occupants as units of tabulation, which are listed as additional (in the additional set of tabulations)

Units of tabulation: housing units

Living quarters included: occupied housing units

Households and persons included: none

Classifications:
(a) Geographical divisions: (i) total country; (ii) each major civil division; (iii) each minor civil division. Distinguish between urban and rural for (i), (ii) and (iii)
(b) Type of housing unit
(c) Type of lighting

Metadata for this tabulation:
(a) Source of statistics:
> Traditional housing census
> Register-based housing census
> Registers/Surveys systems
> Rolling surveys
(b) De jure or de facto population or combination (provide detailed description)
(c) Definition of urban and rural areas

Core topics:
> Place of usual residence or Place where present at time of census
> Living quarters—type of
> Lighting and/or electricity—type of

Note:
Countries and areas in all regions attach considerable importance to the source of energy used for lighting. This tabulation could provide planners with a useful indication of areas where community lighting needs to be extended. For housing units lit by electricity, additional information may be tabulated to show whether the electricity comes from a community supply, generating plant or some other source.

---

* This table may be compiled for (i) total country; (ii) each major civil division; (iii) each minor civil division; (iv) each principal locality. Distinguish between urban and rural for (i), (ii) and (iii).

H13-R. Occupied housing units, by type of housing unit, cross-classified by main type of solid waste disposal

Geographical division* and main type of solid waste disposal	Total housing units	Type of housing unit										Not stated
		Conventional dwellings			Other housing units							
									Informal housing units			
		Total	Has all basic facilities	Does not have all basic facilities	Total	Semi-permanent dwellings	Mobile housing units	Impro-vised	Permanent but not intended for habitation	Other		

Total occupied housing units

  Solid waste collected on regular basis by authorized collectors

  Solid waste collected on an irregular basis by authorized collectors

  Solid waste collected by self-appointed collectors

  Occupants dispose of solid waste in a local dump supervised by authorities

  Occupants dispose of solid waste in a local dump not supervised by authorities

  Occupants burn solid waste

  Occupants bury solid waste

  Occupants dispose solid waste into river/sea/creek/pond

  Occupants composting solid waste

  Other

Urban
(classification of solid waste disposal as above)

Rural
(classification of solid waste disposal as above)

For illustrative purposes, housing units are shown as unit of tabulation in this table. A similar table could be prepared using households and occupants as units of tabulation, which are listed as additional (in the additional set of tabulations)

Units of tabulation: housing units

Living quarters included: occupied housing units

Households and persons included: None

Classifications:
(a) Geographical divisions: (i) total country; (ii) each major civil division; (iii) each minor civil division. Distinguish between urban and rural for (i), (ii) and (iii)
(b) Type of housing unit
(c) Solid waste disposal

Metadata for this tabulation:
(a) Source of statistics:
   ➤ Traditional housing census
   ➤ Register-based housing census
   ➤ Registers/Surveys systems
   ➤ Rolling surveys
(b) De jure or de facto population or combination (provide detailed description)
(c) Definition of urban and rural areas

Core topics:
   ➤ Place of usual residence or Place where present at time of census
   ➤ Living quarters—type of
   ➤ Solid waste disposal—main type of

Note:
Disposal of solid waste and facilities for disposing of it have an extremely important impact on public health and on maintaining a safe environment. As for the classification of types of solid waste disposal, it consists of broad categories and may be further elaborated on the basis of prevalent systems in a specific country or area.

---

* This table may be compiled for (i) total country; (ii) each major civil division; (iii) each minor civil division; (iv) each principal locality. Distinguish between urban and rural for (i), (ii) and (iii).

## H14-R.	Households in housing units, by type of housing unit occupied, cross-classified by number of households per housing unit

Geographical division* and number of households per housing unit	Total housing units	Type of housing unit									
		Conventional dwellings			Other housing units						
								Informal housing units			
		Total	Has all basic facilities	Does not have all basic facilities	Total	Semi-permanent dwellings	Mobile housing units	Impro-vised	Permanent but not intended for habi-tation	Other	Not stated
Total households											
Households with the follow-ing number of households per housing unit :											
1											
2											
3+											
Not stated											

For illustrative purposes, households are shown as the unit of tabulation in this table. A similar table could be prepared using family nuclei as units of tabulation, which is listed as additional (in the additional set of tabulations).

Units of tabulation:	households

Households and family nuclei included:	households in housing units

Classifications:
(a)	Geographical divisions: (i) total country; (ii) each major civil division; (iii) each minor civil division. Distinguish between urban and rural for (i), (ii) and (iii)
(b)	Type of housing unit
(c)	Number of households per housing unit
(d)	Number of rooms per housing unit

Metadata for this tabulation:
(a)	Source of statistics:
  ➤	Traditional housing census
  ➤	Register-based housing census
  ➤	Registers/Surveys systems
  ➤	Rolling surveys
(b)	De jure or de facto population or combination (provide detailed description)
(c)	Definition of urban and rural areas

Core topics:
  ➤	Place of usual residence or Place where present at time of census
  ➤	Living quarters—type of
  ➤	Occupancy by one or more households

Note:
This tabulation provides information on the number of households that are sharing housing units with other house-holds and thus provides an important basis for estimating housing needs. The importance of a separate housing unit for each household that desires one is widely recognized. This tabulation shows the number of households that occupy the shared units.

---

*	This table may be compiled for (i) total country; (ii) each major civil division; (iii) each minor civil division; (iv) each principal locality. Distinguish between urban and rural for (i), (ii) and (iii).

H15-R. Conventional dwellings by type of building, and construction material of outer walls

Geographical division* and construction material of outer walls	Total buildings	Type of building							
		Containing a single housing unit		Containing more than one housing unit					Other
		Detached	Attached	Up to 2 floors	3-4 floors	4-10 floors	11+ floors		

Total conventional dwellings

Total country

  Material of outer walls

  Concrete

  Brick

  Wood

  Local vegetation material

  Other

Urban
(as for "Total country")

Rural
(as for "Total country")

Major civil division A**

Major civil division B**

...

Major civil division Z**

Units of tabulation: dwellings

Living quarters included: conventional dwellings

Classifications:
(a) Geographical divisions: (i) total country; (ii) each major civil division; (iii) each minor civil division. Distinguish between urban and rural for (i), (ii) and (iii)
(b) Type of building
(c) Period of construction
(d) Material of outer walls

Metadata for this tabulation:
(a) Source of statistics:
  ➤ Traditional housing census
  ➤ Register-based housing census
  ➤ Registers/Surveys systems
  ➤ Rolling surveys
(b) De jure or de facto population or combination (provide detailed description)
(c) Definition of urban and rural areas

Core topics:
  ➤ Place of usual residence or Place where present at time of census
  ➤ Building—type of
  ➤ Construction material of outer walls

Note:
This tabulation provides information on the number of dwellings by type of building where they are located and by material of construction of the walls of the building. The building is here an indirect but important unit of enumeration as it carries information on different types of buildings and the way to define them. The tabulation includes material of construction of external walls only, since this appears to be of the utmost significance as an indicator of durability. Information on the construction material of the roof and floor is also frequently collected in national housing censuses, particularly information on the former, but certain inconsistencies and complications have been noticed while tabulating construction material for more than one element of the dwelling.

* This table may be compiled for (i) total country; (ii) each major civil division; (iii) each minor civil division; (iv) each principal locality. Distinguish between urban and rural for (i), (ii) and (iii).
** Name of major or minor civil division.

H16-R. Housing units by type and construction material of outer walls

		Type of housing unit								
		Conventional dwellings			Other housing units					
								Informal housing units		
Geographical division* and construction material of outer walls	Total housing units	Total	Has all basic facilities	Does not have all basic facilities	Total	Semi-permanent dwellings	Mobile housing units	Impro-vised	Permanent but not intended for habitation	Other	Not stated
Total housing units											
Total country											
Material of outer walls											
Concrete											
Brick											
Wood											
Local vegetation material											
Other											
Urban (material as for "Total country")											
Rural (material as for "Total country")											
Major civil division A** (material as for "Total country")											
Major civil division B** (material as for "Total country")											
...											
Major civil division Z** (material as for "Total country")											

Units of tabulation: housing units

Living quarters included: housing units

Classifications:
(a) Geographical divisions: (i) total country; (ii) each major civil division; (iii) each minor civil division. Distinguish between urban and rural for (i), (ii) and (iii)
(b) Type of housing unit

Metadata for this tabulation:
(d) Source of statistics:
  ‣ Traditional housing census
  ‣ Register-based housing census
  ‣ Registers/Surveys systems
  ‣ Rolling surveys
(e) De jure or de facto population or combination (provide detailed description)
(f) Definition of urban and rural areas

Core topics:
  ‣ Place of usual residence or Place where present at time of census
  ‣ Type of housing units
  ‣ Construction material of outer walls

Note:
This tabulation provides information on the number material of construction of the outer walls cross-tabulated by the type of housing units. The main purpose of the tabulation is to provide an overview of the predominant construction material in regard to the type of housing unit. The tabulation includes material of construction of external walls only, since this appears to be of the utmost significance as an indicator of durability. Information on the construction material of the roof and floor is also frequently collected in national housing censuses, particularly information on the former, but certain inconsistencies and complications have been noticed while tabulating construction material for more than one element of the dwelling.

* This table may be compiled for (i) total country; (ii) each major civil division; (iii) each minor civil division; (iv) each principal locality. Distinguish between urban and rural for (i), (ii) and (iii).
** Name of major or minor civil division.

H17.1-R. **Households, by type of housing unit, cross-classified by sex and age of head or other reference member of household**

H17.2-R. **Occupants of housing units, cross-classified by sex and age of head of household**

Geographical division*, sex and age of head or other reference member of household	Total housing units	Type of housing unit									
		Conventional dwellings			Other housing units				Informal housing units		
		Total	Has all basic facilities	Does not have all basic facilities	Total	Semi-permanent dwellings	Mobile housing units	Impro-vised	Permanent but not intended for habitation	Other	Not stated
Total households/occupants											
Male head or other reference member of household											
All ages											
Under 15 years of age											
15-19											
20-24											
25-29											
30-34											
35-39											
40-44											
45-49											
50-54											
55-59											
60-64											
65-69											
70-74											
75-79											
80-84											
85-89											
90-94											
95-99											
100 years and over											
Not stated											
Female head or other reference member of household (age groups as above)											

Units of tabulation: households; occupants

Living quarters included: housing units

Households and persons included: all households and persons living in households

Classifications:

(*a*)   Geographical divisions: (i) total country; (ii) each major civil division; (iii) each minor civil division. Distinguish between urban and rural for (i), (ii) and (iii)

(*b*)   Age: under 15 years; 15-19 years; 20-24 years; 25-29 years; 30-34 years; 35-39 years; 40-44 years; 45-49 years; 50-54 years; 55-59 years; 60-64 years; 65-69 years; 70-74 years; 75-79 years; 80-84 years; 90-94 years; 95-99 years; 100 years and over; not stated

(*c*)   Type of living quarters

(*d*)   Sex of head or other reference member of household

Metadata for this tabulation:

(*a*)   Source of statistics:
- Traditional housing census
- Register-based housing census
- Registers/Surveys systems
- Rolling surveys

(*b*)   De jure or de facto population or combination (provide detailed description)

(*c*)   Definition of urban and rural areas

Core topics:
- Place of usual residence or Place where present at time of census
- Living quarters—type of
- Age
- Sex

Note:
It is assumed that the economic and demographic data required for housing tabulations will be obtained from the population census. In selecting characteristics to be used, the primary consideration should be their efficiency in providing insight into the housing requirements of the population as well as an indication of the possibilities that exist for meeting these requirements. This tabulation provides one component needed to compute headship rates specific for age and sex for the projection of number of households.

---

*   This table may be compiled for (i) total country; (ii) each major civil division; (iii) each minor civil division; (iv) each principal locality. Distinguish between urban and rural for (i), (ii) and (iii).

H18.1-R. Households in housing units, by type of housing unit, cross-classified by tenure of household and, for tenant households, ownership of housing unit occupied

H18.2-R. Occupants of housing units, by type of housing unit, cross-classified by tenure of household and, for tenant households, ownership of housing unit occupied

Geographical division*, tenure, and ownership of housing unit	Total housing units	Type of housing unit										
		Conventional dwellings			Other housing units							Not stated
									Informal housing units			
		Total	Has all basic facilities	Does not have all basic facilities	Total	Semi-permanent dwellings	Mobile housing units	Impro-vised	Permanent but not intended for habitation	Other	
Total households/occupants												
Tenure—member of household:												
Owns a housing unit												
Rents all or part of housing unit as:												
Main tenant in :												
Publicly owned												
Privately owned												
Communally owned												
Cooperatively owned												
Other												
Subtenant occupied												
Occupied free of rent												
Other tenure arrangements												
Not stated												

Units of tabulation: households; occupants

Living quarters included: housing units

Households and persons included: households and occupants of housing units

Classifications:
(*a*) Geographical divisions: (i) total country; (ii) each major civil division; (iii) each minor civil division. Distinguish between urban and rural for (i), (ii) and (iii)
(*b*) Type of housing unit
(*c*) Tenure
(*d*) Type of ownership

Metadata for this tabulation:
(*a*) Source of statistics:
  ➤ Traditional housing census
  ➤ Register-based housing census
  ➤ Registers/Surveys systems
  ➤ Rolling surveys
(*b*) De jure or de facto population or combination (provide detailed description)
(*c*) Definition of urban and rural areas

Core topics:
  ➤ Place of usual residence or Place where present at time of census
  ➤ Living quarters—type of
  ➤ Tenure
  ➤ Ownership—type of

Note
This tabulation yields data showing the type of tenure under which households occupy their living space. Data are tabulated in terms of households rather than housing units in order to show more clearly the tenure status of households sharing housing units. The number of owner-occupied housing units can be obtained from the tabulation H6-R using the corresponding figures for owner households in each category. Type of ownership of the housing unit occupied is shown in this table for renting households. Several variations of the classification of tenure have been found useful. Tenure data are sometimes classified so as to distinguish the tenure under which the living quarters are occupied from the tenure of land upon which they stand (*in* some countries such a classification may be of special significance). Owner-occupants are shown in some cases according to whether the housing unit is fully paid for or whether it is being paid for in instalments or is mortgaged.

---

* This table may be compiled for (i) total country; (ii) each major civil division; (iii) each minor civil division; (iv) each principal locality. Distinguish between urban and rural for (i), (ii) and (iii).

H19.1-R. Households in housing units, by type of housing unit, cross-classified by information and communication technology devices and access to Internet

H19.2-R. Occupants of housing units, by type of housing unit, cross-classified by information and communication technology devices and access to Internet

Geographical division* and information and communication technology devices	Total housing units	Type of housing unit										
		Conventional dwellings			Other housing units							
									Informal housing units			
		Total	Has all basic facilities	Does not have all basic facilities	Total	Semi-permanent dwellings	Mobile housing units	Impro-vised	Permanent but not intended for habitation	Other	Not stated
Total households/occupants												
Household having												
Radio												
Television set												
Fixed line telephone												
Mobile cellular telephone(s)												
Personal computer(s)												
Number of												
Household accessing Internet from												
Home												
Elsewhere												
Without access												

Units of tabulation: households; occupants

Living quarters included: housing units

Households and persons included: households; occupants

Classifications:
(a) Geographical divisions: (i) total country; (ii) each major civil division; (iii) each principal locality. Distinguish between urban and rural for (i), (ii) and (iii)
(b) Type of housing unit
(c) Ownership of information and communication technology devices
(d) Access to Internet

Metadata for this tabulation:
(a) Source of statistics:
  ➢ Traditional housing census
  ➢ Register-based housing census
  ➢ Registers/Surveys systems
  ➢ Rolling surveys
(b) De jure or de facto population or a combination with detailed description
(c) Definition of urban and rural areas

Core topics:
  ➢ Place of usual residence or Place where present at time of census
  ➢ Living quarters—type of
  ➢ Information and communication technology devices—availability of

Note
This tabulation presents the essential information on the ownership and availability of ICT devices to households in the country.

---

* This table may be compiled for (i) total country; (ii) each major civil division; (iii) each minor civil division; (iv) each principal locality. Distinguish between urban and rural for (i), (ii) and (iii).

Annex IV
Additional Tabulations for Population Censuses

List of additional tabulations for population censuses[a]

[a] Additional tabulations are identified by an "A" as part of the table number.

Group 1.   Tabulations on geographical and internal migration characteristics

P1.1-A   Native population, by major civil division of birth, age and sex

Group 2.   Tabulations on international migration and immigrant stock

P2.1-A   Foreign-born population, by marital status, age and sex

P2.2-A   Foreign-born population ... years of age and over, by current (or usual) activity status, age and sex

P2.3-A   Foreign-born population ... years of age and over, by educational attainment, age and sex

Group 3.   Tabulations on household and family characteristics

P3.1-A   Population in households, by household status, age and sex, and institutional population by age and sex

P3.2-A   Households and population in households, by size and type of household

P3.3-A   Multi-person households and population in such households, by type and size of household

P3.4-A   Households and population in households, by size of household and number of members under ... years of age

P3.5-A   Household population under 18 years of age, by age and sex and by whether living with both parents, mother alone, father alone, or neither parent

P3.6-A   Households and population in households, by sex, by size and type of household and number of persons 60 years of age and over

Group 4.   Tabulations on demographic and social characteristics

P4.1-A   Population, by religion, age and sex

P4.2-A   Population, by language (mother tongue, usual language or ability to speak one or more languages), age and sex

P4.3-A   Population, by ethnic group, age and sex

Group 5. Tabulations on fertility and mortality

P5.1-A Female population 10 years of age and over in their first marriage/union or married only once, by five-year duration of marriage/union group and number of children ever born alive by sex

P5.2-A Female population, by age at first birth, by current age and place of residence

P5.3-A Median age at first birth, by current age of women, place of residence and educational attainment

P5.4-A Mothers 10 years of age and over with at least one child under 15 years of age living in the same household, by age of mother and by sex and age of children

P5.5-A Female population … to 49 years of age, by age, number of live births by sex within the 12 months preceding the census and educational attainment

P5.6-A Population with mother alive (or dead), by age

Group 6. Tabulations on educational characteristics

P6.1-A Population that has successfully completed a course of study at the third level of education, by educational qualifications, age and sex

P6.2-A Population 15 years of age and over, by field of education, age and sex

Group 7. Tabulations on economic characteristics

P7.1-A Currently (or usually) active population, by activity status, main status in employment, place of work, main occupation and sex

P7.2-A Currently (or usually) active population, by activity status, institutional sector of employment, main industry and sex

P7.3-A Currently (or usually) active population, by activity status, main occupation, educational attainment, age and sex

P7.4-A Currently (or usually) active population, by activity status, main industry, educational attainment, age and sex

P7.5-A Usually active population, by activity status, sex, main status in employment and number of weeks worked in all occupations during the last year

P7.6-A Currently employed population by main status in employment, sex and number of hours worked in all occupations during the last week

P7.7-A Currently (or usually) active population, by activity status, main occupation, marital status, age and sex

P7.8-A Currently (or usually) active population, by activity status, main status in employment, marital status, age and sex

P7.9-A Currently (or usually) active population in the informal sector, by activity status, main status in employment, place of work, main occupation and sex

P7.10-A Usually active population, by monthly or annual income, main occupation and sex

P7.11-A Households and population in households, by annual income and size of household

P7.12-A   Population not currently active (in other words, not in the labour force), by primary reason for inactivity, age and sex

P7.13-A   Heads or other reference members of households … years of age and over, by economic activity status, age and sex

P7.14-A   Households and population in households, by size of household and number of currently (or usually) employed members

P7.15-A   Households, by size, number of currently (or usually) unemployed members and dependent children under 15 years of age in household

P7.16-A   Currently (or usually) active heads or other reference members of households … years of age and over, by activity status, main status in employment, main industry and sex

Group 8.   Tabulations on disability characteristics

P8.1-A   Total population by disability status, whether living in household or institution, age and sex

P8.2-A   Households with one or more persons with disabilities, by type and size of household

P8.3-A   Total population 15 of age years and over, by disability status, marital status, age and sex

P8.4-A   Population 5 to 29 years of age, by disability status, school attendance, age and sex

Group 1. Tabulations on geographical and internal migration characteristics

P1.1-A. Native population, by major civil division of birth, age and sex

Geographical division, sex and major civil division of birth	Age (in years)									
	All ages	Under 1	1-4	5-9	10-14	15-19	...	95-99	100 and over	Not stated

Both sexes

  Total country

    Major civil division A1*

    Major civil division B*

    Major civil division C*

    .

    .

    .

    Major civil division Z*

    Major civil division not stated

Male
(as for "Both sexes")

Female
(as for "Both sexes")

Population included: all persons born in the country

Classifications:

(*a*) Geographical division: (i) total country; (ii) each major civil division. Distinguish between urban and rural for (i) and (ii)

(*b*) Major civil division of birth: each major civil division of the country; not stated

(*c*) Age: all ages; under one year; 1-4 years; 5-9 years; 10-14 years; 15-19 years; 20-24 years; 25-29 years; 30-34 years; 35-39 years; 40-44 years; 45-49 years; 50-54 years; 55-59 years; 60-64 years; 65-69 years; 70-74 years; 75-79 years; 80-84 years; 85-89 years; 90-94 years; 95-99 years; and 100 years and over; not stated

(*d*) Sex: both sexes; male; female

Note:

Data on all persons born in the country are useful for internal migration studies with respect to providing indications of the magnitude of migration into, and out of, each major part of the country as well as of the ultimate origins of the migrants. In spite of important drawbacks, the data serve a useful purpose in countries where no other information on internal migration is available and their compilation is, accordingly, recommended for such countries. These drawbacks include failure to identify either duration of residence or prior place of residence and to provide much of the detailed information on internal migration that countries need to supply in particular information on migration to large cities, which is the most important kind of internal migration in many countries. Finally, it overlooks the fact that many foreign-born persons become internal migrants after their initial residence in the country.

---

*   Name of major civil division.

Group 2.   Tabulations on international migration and immigrant stock

P2.1-A.   Foreign-born population, by marital status, age and sex

Sex and marital status	All ages	Age (in years)							
		Under 15	15-19	20-24	25-29	...	95-99	100 and over	Not stated

Both sexes

  Total

    Single (never married)

    Married

    Widowed

    Divorced

    Separated

    Not stated

Male
  (as for "Both sexes")

Female
  (as for "Both sexes")

Population included: all foreign-born persons in the country for more than one year

Classifications:

(a)   Marital status: single (never married); married; widowed; divorced; separated; not stated

(b)   Age: all ages; under 15 years; 15-19 year; 20-24 years; 25-29 years; 30-34 years; 35-39 years; 40-44 years; 45-49 years; 50-54 years; 55-59 years; 60-64 years; 65-69 years; 70-74 years; 75-79 years; 80-84 years; 85-89 years; 90-94 years; 95-99 years; and 100 years and over; age not stated

(c)   Sex: both sexes; male; female

Note:

This tabulation is useful in studying the nuptiality patterns of the foreign-born population and the differentials by country of birth. Migration sometimes consists predominantly of single men and women. The pattern of migration, particularly whether it is family-type, may be inferred from such tabulation. This tabulation is the basis for assessing and projecting the effects of immigration on the distribution of the total population by age and sex. The data can be used to estimate the extent of family and household formation among the foreign-born population so as to assess the impact of immigration on housing requirements and the demand for various household goods and services. Cross-classification by country of birth may be made when the foreign-born population is large and diverse in the country of origin

P2.2-A   Foreign-born population …* years of age and over, by current (or usual) activity status, age and sex

| Sex and age (in years) | Foreign-born population … * years of age and over | Economically active | | | Not economically active | Not stated |
| | | Employed | Unemployed | | | |
			Total	Seeking work for the first time		
Both sexes						
All ages						
Under 15**						
15-19						
20-24						
25-29						
30-34						
35-39						
40-44						
45-49						
50-54						
55-59						
60-64						
65-69						
70-74						
75-79						
80-84						
85-89						
90-94						
95-99						
100 and over						
Age not stated						
Male (as for "Both sexes")						
Female (as for "Both sexes")						

Population included: all foreign-born persons in the country for more than one year who are at or above the minimum age adopted for enumerating the economically active population

Classifications:

(a)   Current (or usual) activity status: employed, unemployed (total and persons seeking work for the first time); not economically active; not stated

(b)   Age: all ages; under 15 years; 15-19 years; 20-24 years; 25-29 years; 30-34 years; 35-39 years; 40-44 years; 45-49 years; 50-54 years; 55-59 years; 60-64 years; 65-69 years; 70-74 years; 75-79 years; 80-84 years; 85-89 years; 90-94 years; 95-99 years; and 100 years and over; age not stated .

(c)   Sex: both sexes; male; female

Note:

These data provide information on the influence of the foreign-born population on the labour market of the receiving country. The labour force participation rates specific for each age and sex group are used particularly for making labour force projections in countries where immigration is occurring on a large scale. Comparison with the economic activity pattern of the native population provides information for identifying the relationship of immigration policy with changes in labour-market conditions that may pose special problems of adjustment for immigrants. Comparing the unemployment rates for the foreign-born and native populations may help in planning for the establishment of requisite vocational and other training programmes.

* The minimum age adopted by the country for enumerating the economically active population.

** The category "Under 15 years" should include all ages between the minimum age-limit adopted by the country for census questions on economic activity and 14 years, if the minimum is below 15 years.

P2.3-A.   Foreign-born population ...* years of age and over, by educational attainment, age and sex

Sex and educational attainment	Foreign-born population ...* years of age and over	Age (in years)								
		...*-9	10-14	15-19	20-24	25-34	...	95-99	100 and over	Not stated

Both sexes

  Total

  No schooling

  Primary level of education:

    Started but not completed

    Primary level of education completed

    Not stated

  Secondary level of education:

    First cycle started but not completed

    First cycle completed

    Second cycle started but not completed

    Second cycle completed

    Not stated

  Third level of education:

    First stage not completed

    First stage completed**

    Not stated

  Level not stated

Male
  (as for "Both sexes")

Female
  (as for "Both sexes")

Population included: all foreign-born persons in the country for more than one year and at or above the usual age of entrance into school

Classifications:

(*a*)   Educational attainment: no schooling; primary level of education: started but not completed; primary level completed; not stated; secondary level—first cycle of education started but not completed; second level—first cycle completed; secondary level—second cycle of education started but not completed; secondary level—second cycle completed; not stated; third level of education: first stage (UNESCO, International Standard Classification of Education (ISCED), category 5) started but not completed; first stage completed regardless of any education at the second stage of the third level (ISCED, category 6); not stated; level not stated

(*b*)   Age: ... -9 years; 10-14 years; 15-19 years; 20-24 years; 25-29 years; 30-34 years; 35-39 years; 40-44 years; 45-49 years; 50-54 years; 55-59 years; 60-64 years; 65-69 years; 70-74 years; 75-79 years; 80-84 years; 85-89 years; 90-94 years; 95-99 years; and 100 years and over; not stated

(*c*)   Sex: both sexes; male; female

Note:

These data provide the information needed to assess the educational level of the foreign-born population and the related impact on the economic and social development of the country. They provide profiles for comparison of the present educational attainment of recent immigrants with that of the total population of the country. Such comparisons are useful in determining immigration policy, taking into account the requirements for educated personnel with respect to undertaking various types of economic activity. The educational profile by age provided by the tabulation is useful in assessing differences in the educational attainment of younger and older immigrants, which may provide some indication of time trends in their educational attainment. These profiles are useful in formulating educational programmes and policies.

* The lower age-limit should be the usual age for entrance into school.
** Regardless of any education at the third level: second stage.

Group 3.   Tabulations on household and family characteristics

P3.1-A.   Population in households, by household status, age and sex, and institutional population by age and sex*

Geographical division, household status, institutional population	Total	Sex and age (in years)						Male (as for "Both sexes")	Female (as for "Both sexes")
		Both sexes							
		0-4	5-9	...	100 and over	Not stated			
Total population									
Person in a household with at least one family nucleus									
Husband									
Wife									
Lone mother									
Lone father									
Child living with both parents									
Child living with lone mother									
Child living with lone father									
Not a member of a family nucleus									
Living with relative(s)									
Living with non-relative(s)									
Person in a household with no family nucleus									
Living alone									
Living with others									
Living with sibling(s)									
Living with other relative(s)									
Living with non-relative(s)									
Institutional population									

Population included: total population

Classifications:

(a)   Geographical divisions: (i) total country; (ii) each major civil division; (iii) each minor civil division; (iv) each principal locality. Distinguish between urban and rural for (i), (ii) and (iii)

(b)   Household status: (i) persons in a household with at least one family nucleus: husband; wife; lone mother; lone father; child living with both parents; child living with lone mother; child living with lone father; not a member of a family nucleus, distinguishing living with relative(s), and living with non-relative(s); (ii) persons in a household with no family nucleus: living alone; living with others, distinguishing living with sibling(s); living with other relative(s); and living with non-relative(s)

(c)   Sex: both sexes; male; female

(d)   Age: 0-4 years; 5-9 years; ... five-year age groups up to 95-99 years; and 100 years and over; not stated

(e)   Institutional population: total number

Note:

This tabulation provides information on the extent to which persons live with relatives and non-relatives. The classification by age makes it possible to study specific population groups of interest such as dependent children, youth and the elderly, while disaggregation by sex allows gender aspects to come into focus.

---

*   This tabulation can also be compiled for family status, and also by marital status.

P3.2-A. Households and population in households, by size and type of household

Geographical division and size of household	Total		One person households	Type of household								
				Nuclear		Extended		Composite		Unknown	
	House-holds	Popula-tion		House-holds	Popula-tion	House-holds	Popula-tion	House-holds	Popula-tion	House-holds	Popula-tion
All households											
Households consisting of:											
1 person											
2 persons											
3 persons											
4 persons											
5 persons											
6 persons											
7 persons											
8 persons											
9 persons											
10 persons or more											
Not stated											

Population included: all members of households

Classifications:

(a) Geographical division: (i) total country; (ii) each major civil division; (iii) each minor civil division; (iv) each principal locality. Distinguish between urban and rural for (i),(ii) and (iii)

(b) Size of household: 1 person; 2 persons; 3 persons; 4 persons; 5 persons; 6 persons; 7 persons; 8 persons; 9 persons; 10 persons or more; not stated; and separately, the number of households of each size and the aggregate population by size of household

(c) Type of household: one-person household; nuclear household; extended household; composite household; unknown; and, separately, the number of households of each type and aggregate population by type of household

Note:

Details on household composition take into account not only the number of family nuclei, but also household members who are not part of a family nucleus. Furthermore, they set forth the relationship, if any, between the family nuclei in multinuclear households and between any nuclei and other members of the household. It is useful for in-depth examination of the demographic and social structure of households, which is essential for the formulation of measures designed to improve family living conditions.

P3.3-A. Multi-person households and population in such households, by type and size of household

Geographical division and type of household	Total		Households and population in households consisting of									
	Multi-person households	Population in multi-person households	2 persons		3 persons		...		10 persons or more		Not stated	
			House-holds	Popula-tion	House-holds	Popula-tion	...	...	House-holds	Popula-tion	House-holds	Popula-tion
All households												
Nuclear household												
Extended household												
One family nucleus and related persons												
Two or more related family nuclei without any other person												
Two or more related family nuclei and related persons												
Related persons without any family nuclei												
Composite household												
One family nucleus, related and non- related persons												
One family nucleus and non-related persons												
Two or more related family nuclei, related and non-related persons												
Two or more related family nuclei and non-related persons												
Two or more non- related family nuclei with or with-out any other persons												
Related persons without any nuclei and non-related persons												
Non-related persons												
Unknown												

Population included: all members of multi-person households

Classifications:

(*a*) Geographical division: (i) total country; (ii) each major civil division; (iii) each minor civil division; (iv) each principal locality. Distinguish between urban and rural for (i), (ii) and (iii)

(*b*) Type of household: nuclear household; extended household consisting of (i) one family nucleus and related persons, (ii) two or more related family nuclei without any other person, (iii) two or more related family nuclei and related persons, (iv) related persons without any family nuclei; composite household consisting of (i) one family nucleus, related and non-related persons, (ii) one family nucleus and non-related persons, (iii) two or more related family nuclei, related and non-related persons, (iv) two or more related family nuclei and non-related persons, (v) two or more non-related family nuclei with or without any other persons, (vi) related persons without any nuclei and non-related persons, (vii) non-related persons; unknown.

(*c*) Size of household: 2 persons; 3 persons; 4 persons; 5 persons; 6 persons; 7 persons; 8 persons; 9 persons; 10 persons or more; not stated; and, separately, the number of households of each size and the aggregate population by size of household

Note:

This tabulation provides details on household composition, taking into account not only the number of family nuclei, but also household members who are not part of a family nucleus. Furthermore, it sets forth the relationship, if any, between the family nuclei in multinuclear households and between any nuclei and other members of the household. It gives a more complete indication of household structure. It is particularly useful for countries with complex household structures. Hence, it is useful for in-depth examination of the demographic and social structure of households.

P3.4-A. Households and population in households, by size of household and number of members under ...* years of age

Geographical division and size of household	Total		Households with indicated number of children												
			0		1		...		4		5 or more		Not stated	
	House-holds	Popula-tion	House-holds	Popula-tion	House-holds	Popula-tion	...	...	House-holds	Popula-tion	House-holds	Popula-tion	House-holds	Popula-tion
All households														
Households consist-ing of:														
1 person														
2 persons														
3 persons														
4 persons														
5 persons														
6 persons														
7 persons														
8 persons														
9 persons														
10 persons or more														
Not stated														

Population included: all persons of multi-person households

Classifications:

(a)   Geographical division: (i) total country; (ii) each major civil division; (iii) each minor civil division; (iv) each principal locality. Distinguish between urban and rural for (i), (ii) and (iii)

(b)   Size of household: 1 person, 2 persons; 3 persons; 4 persons; 5 persons; 6 persons; 7 persons; 8 persons; 9 persons; 10 persons or more; not stated; and, separately, the number of households of each size and the aggregate population by size of household

(c)   Number of children: 0; 1; 2; 3; 4; 5 or more; not stated; and separately, the number of households by number of children and the aggregate population by number of children in the household.

Note:

This tabulation refers to all members of households; data are then disaggregated by geographical division. It could supplement tabulations on economic characteristics by showing the number of economically active persons and the number of household members below the age at which economic activity usually begins. With these data, the ratio of active household members to non-active members in the working ages and the ratio of active members to those below working age can be separately computed according to household size. Data on the number of children below working age, by size of household, are also useful in planning for the meeting of household needs and for household welfare measures.

* The minimum age adopted by the country for enumerating the economically active population.

P3.5-A. Household population under 18 years of age, by age and sex and by whether living with both parents, mother alone, father alone, or neither parent

Sex and age* (in years)	Total	Population aged under 18 years by whether				
		Living with both parents	Living with mother alone	Living with father alone	Living with neither parent	Not stated
Both sexes						
Total						
0-4 years						
5-9 years						
10-14 years						
15-17 years						
Males						
Total						
0-4 years						
5-9 years						
10-14 years						
15-17 years						
Females						
Total						
0-4 years						
5-9 years						
10-14 years						
15-17 years						

Population included: population under 18 years of age

Classifications:

(a)   Geographical division: (i) total country; (ii) each major civil division; (iii) each minor civil division; (iv) each principal locality. Distinguish between urban and rural for (i), (ii) and (iii)

(b)   Living arrangements: living with both parents; living with mother alone; living with father alone; living with neither parent; not stated

(c)   Age: total; 0-4 years; 5-9 years; 10-14 years; 15-17 years; not stated

(d)   Sex: both sexes; male; female

Note:

This tabulation provides information that can be used to study the extent to which children live with their mothers and fathers, one or neither parent. This information can also be used in studies of children's well-being and also of child-rearing responsibility and how it is shared between mothers and fathers. The classifications by age and also by sex are important for studying age and gender differences on this topic.

* Other age groupings may be used, and if possible data should be shown by single years of age.

P3.6-A. Households and population in households, by sex, by size and type of household and number of persons 60 years of age and over

Sex, type of household and number of persons 60 years of age and over	Total		Households by size													
			1		2		3		...		10 or more		Not stated	
	House-holds	Popula-tion	House-holds	Popula-tion	House-holds	Popula-tion	House-holds	Popula-tion	House-holds	Popula-tion	House-holds	Popula-tion	House-holds	Popula-tion
Both sexes														
Total														
One person														
0														
1														
Nuclear														
0														
1														
2														
3+														
Extended														
0														
1														
2														
3+														
Composite														
0														
1														
2														
3+														
Males (as for "Both sexes")														
Females (as for "Both sexes")														

Population included: population in households

Classifications:

(a) Geographical division: (i) total country; (ii) each major civil division; (iii) each minor civil division; (iv) each principal locality. Distinguish urban and rural for (i), (ii) and (iii)

(b) Size of household: 1 person; 2 persons; 3 persons; 4 persons; 5 persons; 6 persons; 7 persons; 8 persons; 9 persons; 10 persons or more; not stated

(c) Number of persons 60 years of age and over: 0; 1 person; 2 persons; 3 or more persons

(d) Sex: both sexes; male; female

Note:

Data on living arrangements for the elderly, one of the specific population groups, are important for assessing their well-being in terms of whom they live with. Tabulations provide material for the study of the distribution of the elderly by size and type of households, with particular reference to those living alone, which can be used to assess the availability of other persons in the household for taking care of the elderly.

Group 4. Tabulations on demographic and social characteristics

P4.1-A. Population, by religion, age and sex

Geographical division, sex and religion	All ages	Age (in years)						
		Under 5	5-9	10-14	...	95-99	100 and over	Not stated

Both sexes

   Total

      Each religion (and sect, if desired) of significance in the country

      All others

      No religion

      Not stated

Male
(as for "Both sexes")

Female
(as for "Both sexes")

Population included: total population

Classifications:
(a) Geographical division: (i) total country; (ii) each major civil division

(b) Religion: each religion (and sect, if desired) of significance in the country; all others; no religion; not stated

(c) Age: all ages; under 5 years; 5-9 years; ... five-year age groups up to 95-99 years; 100 years and over; not stated

(d) Sex: both sexes; male; female

Note:
The relative size and age-sex distribution of the different religious groups in the country provides information on countries where there are significant religious differences among the population. These data are useful for further investigation of the interrelationship between these characteristics and religious belief or affiliation.

P4.2-A. Population, by language (mother tongue, usual language or ability to speak one or more languages), age and sex

Geographical division, sex and language	All ages	Age (in years)						
		Under 5	5-9	10-14	...	95-99	100 and over	Not stated

Both sexes

  Total

    Each language or combination of languages for which separate information is required

    All others

    Not stated

Male
(as for "Both sexes")

Female
(as for "Both sexes")

Population included: total population

Classifications:

(a) Geographical division: (i) total country; (ii) each major civil division; (iii) each principal locality

(b) Language: each language or combination of languages for which separate information is required; all others; not stated

(c) Age: all ages; under 5 years; 5-9 years; … five-year age groups up to 95-99 years; and 100 years and over; not stated

(d) Sex: both sexes; male; female

Note:

Data on mother tongue are useful as an index to national and/or ethnic groups, whose existence is often reflected in the mother tongue of individuals long after those persons have assimilated other customs of the majority of the country's population. Data on usual language provide a measure of the linguistic homogeneity or differences in the population. When combined with data on place of birth, they are particularly useful in the study of rates of assimilation of the foreign-born population, which can indicate the possible need for measures to encourage such assimilation. Information on ability to speak one or more designated languages is needed in connection with handling problems of communicating with and educating linguistic minorities. Such data are especially important in countries where more than one official language is recognized and decisions must be taken about the language to be used in schools, in official communications and so on. Tabulation of persons unable to speak the official language of the country, according to their usual language, is particularly useful in connection with planning for teaching the official language of the country to linguistic minorities

P4.3-A. Population, by ethnic group, age and sex*

Geographical division, sex and ethnic group	All ages	Age (in years)					100 and over	Not stated
		Under 5	5-9	10-14	...	95-99		

Both sexes

  Total

    Each ethnic group for which information is required)

    All others

    Not stated

Male
(as for "Both sexes")

Female
(as for "Both sexes")

Population included: total population

Classifications:

(a) Geographical division: (i) total country; (ii) each major civil division

(b) Ethnic group: each group for which separate information is required, all others, not stated

(c) Age: all ages; under 5 years; 5-9 years; ... five-year age groups up to 95-99 years; and 100 years and over; not stated

(d) Sex: both sexes; male; female

Note:
For countries that are not ethnically homogeneous, this tabulation provides the basic information for a quantitative assessment of the relative size and age-sex distribution of the different ethnic groups. These data are the basis for further investigation of other characteristics of each group, which is needed in order to determine the variables connected with ethnic affiliation and to formulate policies designed to alleviate the social and economic handicaps affecting some of the groups.

* Depending on national circumstances, a similar table may be compiled to show indigenous populations.

Group 5.   Tabulations on fertility and mortality

P5.1-A.   Female population 10 years of age and over in their first marriage/union or married only once, by five-year duration of marriage/union group and number of children ever born alive by sex

Geographical division and duration of marriage/union (in years)	Total number of females	Female population with indicated number of children ever born alive								Total number of children ever born alive
		0	1	2	...	10	11	12 or more	Not stated	
Total country										
Children, both sexes										
Total										
0-4 years										
5-9										
10-14										
15-19										
20-24										
25-29										
30-34										
35 and over										
Not stated										
Children, males (age groups as above)										
Children, females (age groups as above)										

Population included: female population 10 years of age and over in their first marriage/union or married only once. (If the population included is restricted to ever-married females, this fact should be clearly stated.)

Classifications:

(a)   Geographical division: (i) total country; (ii) each major civil division; (iii) each intermediate division. Distinguish between urban and rural for (i), (ii) and (iii)

(b)   Duration of marriage/union: 0-4 years; 5-9 years; 10-14 years; 15-19 years; 20-24 years; 25-29 years; 30-34 years; 35 years and over; not stated.

(c)   Sex: both sexes; male and female children ever born alive

(d)   Number of children ever born alive: 0; 1 child; 2 children; 3 children; 4 children; 5 children; 6 children; 7 children; 8 children; 9 children; 10 children; 11 children; 12 or more children; not stated; and, separately, the aggregate number of children ever born alive by duration of marriage/union

Note:

The data are used to estimate fertility levels and patterns. This tabulation may be compiled in countries where experience has demonstrated that there has been substantial age-misreporting in past population censuses, which distorts fertility/mortality estimates based on children ever born and children living by age of women. This tabulation provides, for women in their first marriage, and for widowed, divorced and separated women who have had only one marriage, the data needed for computing all the measures of fertility described in connection with the recommended table P5.1-R. In countries where most births are legitimate, the tabulation is particularly useful for studies of trends in legitimate births, in association with information derived from current civil births, because of the information it provides on years of exposure to the risk of pregnancy.

P5.2-A. Female population, by age at first birth, by current age and place of residence

Geographical division, current age (in years), urban/rural	Females with no births	Female population by age (in years) at first birth								Median age at first birth
		Total	10-14	15-17	18-19	20-21	22-24	25 and over	Not stated	
Total country										
10 years and over, total										
10-14 years*										
15-19*										
20-24										
25-29										
30-34										
35-39										
40-44										
45-49										
50 years and over										
Not stated										
URBAN (age groups as above)										
RURAL (age groups as above)										

Population included: female population 10 years of age and over. (If the investigation is restricted to ever-married females, this fact should be clearly stated.)

Classifications:

(a)   Geographical division: (i) total country; (ii) each major civil division

(b)   Place of residence: (i) urban; (ii) rural

(c)   Age at first birth: total; 10-14 years; 15-17 years; 18-19 years; 20-21 years; 22-24 years; 25 years and over; not stated; and, separately, the total number of females with at least one child and the total number of females without children; and median age at first birth for each category

(d)   Current age: total 10 years and over; 10-14 years; 15-19 years; 20-24 years; 25-29 years; 30-34 years; 35-39 years; 40-44 years; 45-49 years; 50 years and over; not stated

Note:

The beginning of the childbearing period is an important determinant of fertility levels. Postponement of first births, reflecting a rise in age at marriage, can make an important contribution to overall fertility decline. From this table, the distribution of females by age at first birth by urban and rural background can be calculated. The urban/rural classification will lead to study of differentials with respect to the onset of childbearing.

*   May not be possible to calculate the median age at first birth because less than 50 per cent of females in this age group may not have had a birth at the initial age of the indicated age group.

P5.3-A. Median age at first birth, by current age of women, place of residence and educational attainment

Geographical division, place of residence, and educational attainment	Total	Median age at first birth by current age of females									
		10-14 years*	15-19**	20-24	25-29	30-34	35-39	...	95-99	100 and over	Not stated

Total country

Urban residence

Rural residence

Educational attainment

No schooling

Primary level of education:

Started but not completed

Primary level of education completed

Secondary level of education:***

First cycle started but not completed

First cycle completed

Second cycle started but not completed

Second cycle completed

Level not stated

Population included: female population 10 years of age and over with at least one child born alive. (If the population included is restricted to ever-married females, this fact should be clearly stated.)

Classifications:

(a) Geographical division: (i) total country; (ii) each major civil division

(b) Place of residence: (i) urban; (ii) rural

(c) Educational attainment: no schooling; primary level started but not completed; primary level completed; first cycle of secondary level started but not completed; first cycle of secondary level completed; second cycle of secondary level started but not completed; second cycle of secondary level completed (regardless of any education at the third level); level not stated

(d) Age: total; 10-14 years; 15-19 years; 20-24 years; 25-29 years; 30-34 years; 35-39 years; 40-44 years; 45-49 years; 50-54 year; 55-59 years; 60-64 years; 65-69 years; 70-74 years; 7575-79 years; 80-84 years; 85-89 years; 90-94 years; 95-99 years; and 100 years and over; not stated

Note:

The age at which childbearing starts is an important demographic indicator. If this indicator increases, then a decline in fertility is likely to occur. The median age at first birth, which is the age by which 50 per cent of women have had their first child for any group of women, is suggested for comparison purposes by background characteristics of women: urban; rural; educational attainment.

*May not be possible to calculate because less than 50 per cent of females in this age group may not have had a birth at the initial age of the indicated age group.

**Median age may not be calculated for this group because less than 50 per cent of women in the age group may have had a first child at 15 years of age.

*** Regardless of any education at the third level.

P5.4-A. Mothers 10 years of age and over with at least one child under 15 years of age living in the same household, by age of mother and by sex and age of children

Geographical division and age of mother (in years)	Total number of mothers	Children by age (in years) and sex							
		Total under15 years	Under 1 year	1	2	...	13	14	Not stated
Total country*									
Children, both sexes									
Total 10 years and over									
10									
11									
12									
13									
14									
10-14									
15									
16									
17									
18									
19									
15-19									
20									
21									
22									
23									
24									
20-24									
25									
26									
27									
28									
29									
25-29									
30-34									
35-39									
40-44									
45-49									
50-54									
55-59									
60-64									
65-69									
70 and over									
Not stated									
Children, males (age groups as above)									
Children, females (age groups as above)									

Population included: mothers 10 years of age and over with at least one child under 15 years of age living in the same household. (If the mothers included are restricted to ever-married mothers, this fact should be clearly stated.)

Classifications:

(a) Geographical division: (i) total country; (ii) each major civil division; (iii) each intermediate division. Distinguish between urban and rural for (i), (ii) and (iii)

(b) Age of mothers: 10 years; 11 years; 12 years ... single years to 29 (with subtotals for 10-14; 15-19, 20-24 and 25-29 years); 30-34 years; 35-39 years; 40-44 years; 45-49 years; 50-54 years; 55-59 years; 60-64 years; 65-69 years; 70 years and over; not stated

(c) Sex: both sexes; male and female children

(d) Age of children living with their natural mother: total under 15 years; under 1 year; 1 year; 2 years; 3 years; 4 years; 5 years; 6 years; 7 years; 8 years; 9 years; 10 years; 11 years; 12 years; 13 years; 14 years; not stated

Note:

This table refers to the female population 10 years of age and over (shown by single years from 10 to 29 years and by five-year age groups), with at least one child under 15 years of age living in the same household (shown by single years of age) distributed by geographical divisions and place of residence. This tabulation provides data to estimate fertility by the "own-children" method.

---

* This tabulation should be compiled for (i) total country, (ii) each major civil division. Distinguish between urban and rural for (i) and (ii).

P5.5-A. Female population …* to 49 years of age by age, number of live births by sex within the 12 months preceding the census and educational attainment

Geographical division, age (in years) and educational attainment	Total females …* to 49 years of age	Live births in the 12 months preceding the census		
		Total	Males	Females
Total country				
All levels of education				
Total, …* years and over				
Under 10 years**				
0-14				
15-19				
20-24				
25-29				
30-34				
35-39				
40-44				
45-49				
Not stated				
No schooling (age groups as above)				
Primary level of education:				
Started but not completed (age groups as above)				
Primary level of education completed (age groups as above)				
Secondary level of education:*				
First cycle started but not completed (age groups as above)				
First cycle completed (age groups as above)				
Second cycle started but not completed (age groups as above)				
Second cycle completed (age groups as above)				
Level not stated (age groups as above)				

Population included: female population between the minimum age limit adopted by the country for collecting information on current fertility and 49 years of age (If the population is restricted to ever-married females, this fact should be clearly stated.)

Classifications:

(a) Geographical division: (i) total country; (ii) each major civil division; (iii) each intermediate division. Distinguish between urban and rural for (i), (ii) and (iii)

(b) Live births by sex within the 12 months preceding the census: total number; total number of male births; total number of female births

(c) Age: total; under 10 years; 10-14 years; 15-19 years; 20-24 years; 25-29 years; 30-34 years; 35-39 years; 40-44 years; 45-49 years; not stated

(d) Educational attainment: no schooling; primary level started but not completed; primary level completed; first cycle of secondary level started but not completed; first cycle of secondary level completed; second cycle of secondary level started but not completed; second cycle of secondary level completed (regardless of any education at the third level); level not stated

Note:

This tabulation refers to female population between the minimum age limit adopted by the country for collecting information on current fertility and 49 years of age distributed among geographical divisions. It also provides data for investigating differentials in current age-specific fertility rates and current infant mortality rates by the educational attainment of mothers. It is particularly important as a supplement to vital rates or as an estimation for these rates where birth and death registration is defective or inadequate.

---

  * The minimum age adopted by the country for census questions on current fertility.

 ** All ages between the minimum age adopted by the country for census questions on current fertility if the minimum age is under 10 years.

*** Regardless of any education at the third level.

P5.6-A. Population with mother alive (or dead), by age

Geographical division, and age (in years)	Total population	Status of natural mother*		
		Living	Dead	Not stated
Total country				
Both sexes				
All ages				
Under 1 year				
1-4				
5-9				
10-14				
15-19				
20-24				
25-29				
30-34				
35-39				
40-44				
45-49				
50-54				
55-59				
60-64				
65-69				
70-74				
75-79				
80-84				
85-89				
90-94				
95-99				
100 and over				
Not stated				
Males (as for "Both sexes")				
Females (as for "Both sexes")				

Population included: total population

Classifications:
(a) Geographical division: (i) total country; (ii) each major civil division; (iii) each intermediate division. Distinguish between urban and rural for (i), (ii) and (iii)

(b) Mother alive (or dead): natural mother living; natural mother dead; not stated

(c) Sex: total; male; female

(d) Age: all ages; under 1 year; 1-4 years; 5-9 years; 10-14 years; 15-19 years; 20-24 years; 25-29 years; 30-34 years; 35-39 years; 40-44 years; 45-49 years; 50-54 years; 55-59 years; 60-64 years; 65-69 years; 70-74 years; 75-79 years; 80-84 years; 85-89 years; 90-94 years; 95-99 years; 100 years and over; not stated

Note:
This tabulation provides data for estimating the levels and patterns of adult female mortality, particularly in countries where death registration is defective or non-existent. The tabulation may be extended to estimate adult male mortality from data on survival of fathers.

* Tabulation should be based on responses of the eldest surviving child of its mother only and this fact should be clearly stated.

Group 6. Tabulations on educational characteristics

P6.1-A. Population that has successfully completed a course of study at the third level of education, by educational qualifications, age and sex

Geographical division, sex and educational qualifications	Total population that has successfully completed a course of study at the third level of education	Age (in years)							
		Under 20	20-24	25-29	30-34	...	95-99	100 and over	Not stated

Both sexes

All fields of education
(Classification of degrees, diplomas, certificates and so forth adopted by the country)
   General*
   Teacher training*
   Education science and teacher training*
   Fine and applied arts*
   Humanities*
   Religion and theology*
   Social and behavioural sciences*
   Commercial and business administration*
   Business administration and related programmes*
   Law and jurisprudence*
   Natural science*
   Mathematical and computer science*
   Medical diagnostic and treatment*
   Medical science*
   Trade, craft and industrial*
   Engineering*
   Architectural and town planning*
   Agricultural, forestry and fishing*
   Home economics (domestic science)*
   Transport and communications*
   Service trades*
   Mass communication and documentation*
   Other fields*
   Not stated*

Male (as for "Both sexes")

Female (as for "Both sexes")

Population included: all persons who have successfully completed a course of study at the third level of education

Classifications:

(a) Geographical division: (i) total country; (ii) each major civil division; (iii) each principal locality

(b) Educational qualifications: highest degree, diploma, certificate and so forth acquired and field of education

(c) Field of education

(d) Age: under 20 years; 20-24 years; 25-29 years; 30-34 years; 35-39 years; 40-44 years; 45-49 years; 50-54 years; 55-59 years; 60-64 years; 65-69 years; 70-74 years; 75-79 years; 80-84 years; 85-89 years; 90-94 years; 95-99 years; 100 years and over; not stated

(e) Sex: both sexes; male; female

Note:

These data supplement the data from recommended tabulation P6.1 by providing an important indicator of the nature of the skilled manpower available in the country. It allows estimates to be made of the stock and expected inflow of skilled manpower in different fields, for comparison with the skilled manpower needs of various sectors of the economy. The addition to the tabulation of a classification by occupation and by industry would furnish a useful supplement to tabulations on economic characteristics (group 7) by making information available on the extent to which specific skills are being used in the economic structure.

---

* As for "All fields of education".

P6.2-A. Population 15 years of age and over, by field of education, age and sex

Geographical division, sex and field of education	Total population 15 years and over	Age (in years)					
		15-19	20-24	25-29	....	100 and over	Not stated

Both sexes

  Total, all fields of education

    General programmes

    Education

    Humanities and arts

    Social sciences, business and law

    Science

    Engineering, manufacturing and
    construction

    Agriculture

    Health and welfare

    Services

    Not known or unspecified

Male
(Same as for "Both sexes")

Female
(Same as for "Both sexes")

Population included: all persons aged 15 years and over

Classifications :
(a) Geographical division: (i) total country; (ii) each major civil division; (iii) each principal locality. Distinguish between urban and rural for (i) and (ii)

(b) Field of education: The term "field of education" refers to the "broad groups of education" as presented in the most recent (1997) release of the International Standard Classification of Education (ISCED). For fields of education within the broad groups, refer to the latest release of UNESCO's ISCED

(c) Age: total 15 years and over; 15-19 years; 20-24 years; 25-29 years; 30-34 years; 35-39 years; 40-44 years; 45-49 years; 50-54 years; 55-59 years; 60-64 years; 65-69 years; 70-74 years; 75-79 years; 80-84 years; 85-89 years; 90-94 years; 95-99 years;100 years and over; not stated (but 15 years and over)

(d) Sex: both sexes; male; female

Note:
Data on field of study provide an important indication of the areas of specialization of the adult population and more particularly of qualified human resources available in the country. They provide input for estimate and projections of the stock and expected new entrants into the labour market with different specialization which, when matched with the skills needed in various sectors of the economy, can help to establish more effective education, training and employment policies for optimum development and utilization of human resources. Data on field of study when cross-classified with occupation and industries can furnish valuable information on the extent to which the qualified human resources with specific skills are being utilized in the national economy.

Group 7.   Tabulations on economic characteristics

P7.1-A.   Currently (or usually) active population, by activity status, main status in employment, place of work, main occupation and sex

Geographical division, activity status, sex, place of work and main occupation	Total	Main status in employment					
		Employer	Own-account worker	Employee	Contributing family worker	Member of producers' cooperative	Persons not classifiable by status
Total economically active population							
Both sexes							
All places of work							
Sub-major group 11							
Minor group 111							
Minor group 112							
(etc.)							
Sub-major group 21							
Minor group 211							
Minor group 212							
(etc.)							
...							
Sub-major group 91							
Minor group 911							
Minor group 912							
(etc.)							
Sub-major group 01							
Minor group 011							
Work at home							
(as for "All places of work")							
No fixed place of work							
(as for "All places of work")							
Fixed place, outside home							
(as for "All places of work")							
Unknown							
(as for "All places of work")							
Male (as for "Both sexes")							
Female (as for "Both sexes")							
EMPLOYED (as for "Total economically active population")							
UNEMPLOYED, TOTAL (as for "Total economically active population")							
UNEMPLOYED, WORKED BEFORE (as for "Total economically active population")							
UNEMPLOYED, NEVER WORKED BEFORE							
Both sexes							
Male							
Female							
(by definition, the occupational, place of work and main status in employment classifications above do not apply to this category; this category is required only as total for ensuring the consistency of the figure for total economically active population)							
NOT STATED (as for "Unemployed, never worked before")							

Population included: currently (or usually) active population at or above the minimum age adopted for enumerating the economically active population

Classifications:

(a)   Geographical division: (i) total country; (ii) each major civil division; (iii) each minor civil division; (iv) each principal locality. Distinguish between urban and rural for (i), (ii) and (iii)

(b)   Activity status: total economically active population; employed; unemployed (distinguishing persons who ever and never worked before); not stated

(c)   Status in employment: total; employer; own-account worker; employee; contributing family worker; member of producers' cooperative; persons not classifiable by status

(d)   Sex: both sexes; male; female

(e)   Occupation: according to, or convertible to, the latest revision of the International Standard Classification of Occupations (ISCO-88), at least to the minor groups (in other words, three-digit) level

(f)   Place of work: all places of work; work at home; no fixed place of work; fixed place of work outside home; unknown

Note:

This tabulation gives an indication of the nature of work being undertaken in places outside individuals' home, especially the employers and own-account workers' homes. Comparisons between urban and rural, or other administrative divisions, are also useful for determining which areas might need infrastructure development in the form either of business structures and related facilities or of networks of roads.

P7.2-A. Currently (or usually) active population, by activity status, institutional sector of employment, main industry and sex

Geographical division, activity status, sex and main industry	Institutional sector of employment					
	All sectors	Non-financial corporations	Financial corporations	General government	Non-profit institutions	Household sector
Total economically active population						
Both sexes						
Division 01						
Group 011						
Group 012						
(etc.)						
Division 02						
Group 021						
Group 022						
(etc.)						
...						
Division 99						
Group 990						
Male						
(as for "Both sexes")						
Female						
(as for "Both sexes")						
EMPLOYED						
(as for "Total economically active population")						
UNEMPLOYED, TOTAL						
(as for "Total economically active population")						
UNEMPLOYED, WORKED BEFORE						
(as for "Total economically active population")						
UNEMPLOYED, NEVER WORKED BEFORE						
Both sexes						
Male						
Female						
(by definition, the industrial and institutional sector of employment classifications above do not apply to this category; this category is required only as total for ensuring the consistency of the figure for total economically active population)						
NOT STATED						
(as for "Unemployed, never worked before")						

Population included: currently (or usually) active population at or above the minimum age adopted for enumerating the economically active population

Classifications:

(a) Geographical division: (i) total country; (ii) each major civil division; (iii) each minor civil division; (iv) each principal locality. Distinguish between urban and rural for (i), (ii) and (iii)

(b) Activity status: total economically active population; employed; unemployed (distinguishing persons who ever and never worked before); not stated

(c) Institutional sector of employment,: all sectors, non-financial corporations sector; financial corporations sector; general government sector; non-profit institutions serving households sector; household sector

(d) Sex: both sexes; male; female

(e) Industry: according to, or convertible to, the latest revision of the International Standard Industrial Classification of All Economic Activities (ISIC, Rev.3) to the level of groups (three-digit)

Note:

This tabulation may be used to monitor structural changes in the economy under different types of economic intervention programmes. The changes are recorded not only for the institutional sectors but also for industry and the interaction between the two, assessed separately for women and for men. The need for and the focus of any intervention programmes can therefore be targeted more specifically.

P7.3-A Currently (or usually) active population, by activity status, main occupation, educational attainment, age and sex

Geographical division, activity status, sex, educational attainment and age (in years)	Total	Main occupation							Armed forces
		Sub-major group 11			...	Sub-major group 91			
		Minor group				Minor group			
		111	112	etc.		911	912	etc.	

TOTAL ECONOMICALLY ACTIVE POPULATION	
Both sexes	
All levels of education	
All ages	
Under 15*	
15-19	
20-24	
...	
90-94	
95-99	
100 and over	
Not stated	

No schooling
(as for "All levels of education")

ISCED level 1: Primary education
(as for "All levels of education")

ISCED level 2: Lower secondary education
(as for "All levels of education")

ISCED level 3: Upper secondary education
(as for "All levels of education")

ISCED level 4: Post-secondary education
(as for "All levels of education")

ISCED level 5: First stage of tertiary education (as for "All levels of education")

ISCED level 6: Second stage of tertiary education (as for "All levels of education")

Level of education not stated
(as for "All levels of education")

Male (as for "Both sexes")

Female (as for "Both sexes")

EMPLOYED
(as for "Total economically active population")

UNEMPLOYED, TOTAL
(as for "Total economically active population")

UNEMPLOYED, WORKED BEFORE
(as for "Total economically active population")

UNEMPLOYED, NEVER WORKED BEFORE**
(*by definition, the occupational classification above does not apply to this category; this category is required only as total for ensuring the consistency of the figure for total economically active population*)

NOT STATED
(as for "Unemployed, never worked before")

Population included: currently (or usually) active population at or above the minimum age adopted for enumerating the economically active population

Classifications:

(a) Geographical division: (i) total country; (ii) each major civil division; (iii) each minor civil division; (iv) each principal locality. Distinguish between urban and rural for (i), (ii) and (iii)

(b) Age: all ages; under 15 years; 15-19 years; 20-24 years; 25-29 years; 30-34 years; 35-39 years; 40-44 years; 45-49 years; 50-54 years; 55-59 years; 60-64 years; 65-69 years; 70-74 years; 75-79 years; 80-84 years; 85-89 years; 90-94 years; 95-99 years;100 years and over; not stated.

(c) Activity status: total economically active population; employed; unemployed (distinguishing persons who ever and never worked before); not stated

(d) Educational attainment: all levels of education; no schooling; ISCED level 1: Primary education; ISCED level 2: Lower secondary education; ISCED level 3: Upper secondary education; ISCED level 4: Post-secondary education; ISCED level 5: First stage of tertiary education (not leading directly to an advanced research classification); ISCED level 6: Second stage of tertiary education (leading to an advanced research qualification); level of education not stated

(e) Sex: both sexes; male; female

(f) Occupation: according to, or convertible to, the latest revision of the International Standard Classification of Occupations (ISCO-88), at least to the minor groups (in other words, three-digit) level

Note:
This tabulation provides the data needed to analyse present requirements for educated personnel and the degree to which they are satisfied by the present human resources. It also furnishes information on the extent to which education is effectively utilized in the economic structure.

* The category "Under 15 years" should include all ages between the minimum age limit adopted by the country for census questions on economic activity and 14 years, if the minimum is below 15 years.

** The category "Unemployed, never worked before" should also be classified by sex: both sexes; male; female.

P7.4-A. Currently (or usually) active population, by activity status, main industry, educational attainment, age and sex

Geographical division, activity status, sex, educational attainment and age (in years)	Total	Main industry				
		Division 01		...	Division 99	
		Group			Group	
		011	012		990	

TOTAL ECONOMICALLY ACTIVE POPULATION

Both sexes

　All levels of education
　　All ages
　　Under 15*
　　15-19
　　20-24
　　...
　　90-94
　　95-99
　　100 and over
　　Not stated

　No schooling
　　(as for "All levels of education")

　ISCED level 1: Primary education
　　(as for "All levels of education")

　ISCED level 2: Lower secondary education
　　(as for "All levels of education")

　ISCED level 3: Upper secondary education
　　(as for "All levels of education")

　ISCED level 4: Post-secondary education
　　(as for "All levels of education")

　ISCED level 5: First stage of tertiary education (as
　　for "All levels of education")

　ISCED level 6: Second stage of tertiary education
　　(as for "All levels of education")

　Level of education not stated
　　(as for "All levels of education")

Male (as for "Both sexes")

Female (as for "Both sexes")

EMPLOYED
　(as for "Total economically active population")

UNEMPLOYED, TOTAL
　(as for "Total economically active population")

UNEMPLOYED, WORKED BEFORE
　(as for "Total economically active population")

UNEMPLOYED, NEVER WORKED BEFORE**
　(by definition, the industrial classification above
　does not apply to this category; this category is
　required only as total for ensuring the consistency of
　the figure for total economically active population)

NOT STATED
　(as for "Unemployed, never worked before")

Population included: currently (or usually) active population at or above the minimum age adopted for enumerating the economically active population

Classifications:

(a)   Geographical division: (i) total country; (ii) each major civil division; (iii) each minor civil division; (iv) each principal locality. Distinguish between urban and rural for (i), (ii) and (iii)

(b)   Age: all ages; under 15 years; 15-19 years; 20-24 years; 25-29 years; 30-34 years; 35-39 years; 40-44 years; 45-49 years; 50-54 years; 55-59 years; 60-64 years; 65-69 years; 70-74 years; 75-79 years; 80-84 years; 85-89 years; 90-94 years; 95-99 years;100 years and over; not stated.

(c)   Activity status: total economically active population; employed; unemployed (distinguishing persons who ever and never worked before); not stated

(d)   Educational attainment: all levels of education; no schooling; ISCED level 1: Primary education; ISCED level 2: Lower secondary education; ISCED level 3: Upper secondary education; ISCED level 4: Post-secondary education; ISCED level 5: First stage of tertiary education (not leading directly to an advanced research classification); ISCED level 6: Second stage of tertiary education (leading to an advanced research qualification); level of education not stated

(e)   Sex: both sexes; male; female

(f)   Industry: according to, or convertible to, the latest revision of the International Standard Industrial Classification of All Economic Activities (ISIC, Rev.3) to the level of groups (three-digit)

Note:

This tabulation provides the data needed to analyse present requirements of the main industrial sectors for educated personnel and the degree to which they are satisfied by the present human resources. It also furnishes information on the extent to which education is effectively utilized in the economic structure.

---

*   The category "Under 15 years" should include all ages between the minimum age limit adopted by the country for census questions on economic activity and 14 years, if the minimum is below 15 years.

** The category "Unemployed, never worked before" should also be classified by sex: both sexes; male; female.

P7.5-A. Usually active population, by activity status, sex, main status in employment and number of weeks worked in all occupations during the last year

Geographical division, activity status, sex and number of weeks worked	Total	Main status in employment					
		Employer	Own-account worker	Employee	Contributing family worker	Member of producers' cooperative	Persons not classifiable by status
TOTAL ECONOMICALLY ACTIVE POPULATION							
Both sexes							
Total weeks worked							
Less than 1 week							
1 to 4 weeks							
5 to 12 weeks							
13 to 24 weeks							
25 to 36 weeks							
37 weeks and over							
Not stated							
Male (as for "Both sexes")							
Female (as for "Both sexes")							
EMPLOYED (as for "Total economically active population")							
UNEMPLOYED, TOTAL (as for "Total economically active population")							
UNEMPLOYED, WORKED BEFORE (as for "Total economically active population")							
UNEMPLOYED, NEVER WORKED BEFORE** *(by definition, the main status in employment classification above does not apply to this category; this category is required only as total for ensuring the consistency of the figure for total economically active population)*							
NOT STATED (as for "Unemployed, never worked before")							

Population included: usually active population at or above the minimum age adopted for enumerating the economically active population

Classifications:

(a)   Geographical division: (i) total country; (ii) each major civil division; (iii) each minor civil division; (iv) each principal locality. Distinguish between urban and rural for (i), (ii) and (iii)

(b)   Activity status: total economically active population; employed; unemployed (distinguishing persons who ever and never worked before); not stated

(c)   Status in employment: total, employer; own-account worker; employee; contributing family worker; member of producers' cooperative; persons not classifiable by status

(d)   Sex: both sexes; male; female

(e)   Number of weeks worked: total; less than 1 week; 1 to 4 weeks; 5 to 12 weeks, 13 to 24 weeks; 25 to 36 weeks; and 37 weeks and over; not stated

Note:

This tabulation provides information for the analysis of potential underemployment, particularly among employees. It also makes available useful data for the planning of vocational training, insurance programmes and so forth. Information concerning the time worked in hours per week or in number of weeks per reference period by unpaid family workers is needed for comparative analysis of activity rates for females, particularly in view of the different practices followed by countries in defining and enumerating this group of workers in past censuses.

---

*   The category "Unemployed, never worked before" should also be classified by sex: both sexes; male; female.

P7.6-A. Currently employed population, by main status in employment, sex and number of hours worked in all occupations during the last week

Geographical division, sex and number of hours worked	Total	Main status in employment					
		Employer	Own-account worker	Employee	Contributing family worker	Member of producers' cooperative	Persons not classifiable by status
Both sexes							
Total hours worked							
Less than 8 hours							
9 to 16 hours							
17 to 24 hours							
25 to 32 hours							
33 to 40 hours							
41 to 48 hours							
49 hours and over							
Not stated							
Male (as for "Both sexes")							
Female (as for "Both sexes")							

Population included: currently employed population at or above the minimum age adopted for enumerating the economically active population

Classifications:

(*a*) Geographical division: (i) total country; (ii) each major civil division; (iii) each minor civil division; (iv) each principal locality. Distinguish between urban and rural for (i), (ii) and (iii)

(*b*) Status in employment: total, employer; own-account worker; employee; contributing family worker; member of producers' cooperative; persons not classifiable by status

(*c*) Sex: both sexes; male; female

(*d*) Hours worked: total; less than 8 hours; 9 to 16 hours; 17 to 24 hours; 25 to 32 hours; 33 to 40 hours; 41 to 48 hours; and 49 hours and over; not stated

Note:

This tabulation provides information for the analysis of potential underemployment, particularly among employees. It also makes available useful data for the planning of vocational training, insurance programmes and so forth. Information concerning the time worked in hours per week or in number of weeks per reference period by unpaid family workers is needed for comparative analysis of activity rates for females, particularly in view of the different practices followed by countries in defining and enumerating this group of workers in past censuses.

P7.7-A. Currently (or usually) active population, by activity status, main occupation, marital status, age and sex

Geographical division, activity status, sex, marital status and age (in years)	Total	Main occupation								Armed forces
		Sub-major group 11			...	Sub-major group 91				
		Minor group				Minor group				
		111	112	etc		911	912	etc		

TOTAL ECONOMICALLY ACTIVE POPULATION

Both sexes

All marital statuses

All ages

  Under 15 years*

  15-19

  ...

  95-99

  100 and over

  Not stated

Single (never married)
  (as for "All marital statuses")

Married
  (as for "All marital statuses")

Widowed
  (as for "All marital statuses")

Divorced
  (as for "All marital statuses")

Separated
  (as for "All marital statuses")

Marital status not stated
  (as for "All marital statuses")

Male (as for "Both sexes")

Female (as for "Both sexes")

EMPLOYED
  (as for Total economically active population)

UNEMPLOYED, TOTAL
  (as for "Total economically active population")

UNEMPLOYED, WORKED BEFORE
  (as for "Total economically active population")

UNEMPLOYED, NEVER WORKED BEFORE**
  (by definition, the occupational classification above does not apply to this category; this category is required only as total for ensuring the consistency of the figure for total economically active population)

NOT STATED
  (as for "Unemployed, never worked before")

Population included: currently (or usually) active population at or above the minimum age adopted for enumerating the economically active population

Classifications:

(a) Geographical division: (i) total country; (ii) each major civil division; (iii) each minor civil division; (iv) each principal locality. Distinguish between urban and rural for (i), (ii) and (iii)

(b) Activity status: total economically active: employed; unemployed (distinguishing persons who ever and never worked before); not stated

(c) Age: all ages; under 15 years; 15-19 years; 20-24 years; 25-29 years; 30-34 years; 35-39 years; 40-44 years; 45-49 years; 50-54 years; 55-59 years; 60-64 years; 65-69 years; 70-74 years; 75-79 years; 80-84 years; 85-89 years; 90-94 years; 95-99 years; 100 years and over; not stated.

(d) Marital status: all marital statuses; single (never married): married; widowed: divorced: separated; marital status not stated

(e) Occupation: according to, or convertible to, the latest revision of the International Standard Classification of Occupations (ISCO-88), at least to the minor group (in other words, three-digit) level

(f) Sex: both sexes; male; female

Note:

This tabulation provides material for the analysis of the relation of marital status to the broad occupation of economically active people and of the probable effect thereon of any anticipated changes in the distribution of the population by marital status. A similar tabulation by industry will also be useful in understanding the pattern of absorption, particularly of married women, into different industries. It should be noted that the present tabulation calls for occupation categories according to, or convertible to, only the major groups of ISCO. Data according to the more detailed minor groups give a more precise picture of the occupations where women are concentrated.

---

* The category "Under 15 years" should include all ages between the minimum age limit adopted by the country for census questions on economic activity and 14 years, if the minimum is below 15 years.

** The category "Unemployed, never worked before" should also be classified by sex: both sexes; male; female.

P7.8-A. Currently (or usually) active population, by activity status, main status in employment, marital status, age and sex

Geographical division, activity status, sex, marital status and age (in years)	Main status in employment						
	Total	Employer	Own-account worker	Employee	Contributing family worker	Member of producers' cooperative	Persons not classifiable by status
TOTAL ECONOMICALLY ACTIVE POPULATION							
Both sexes							
All marital statuses							
All ages							
Under 15 years*							
15-19							
...							
95-99							
100 and over							
Not stated							
Single (never married) (as for "All marital statuses")							
Married (as for "All marital statuses")							
Widowed (as for "All marital statuses")							
Divorced (as for "All marital statuses")							
Separated (as for "All marital statuses")							
Marital status not stated (as for "All marital statuses")							
Male (as for "Both sexes")							
Female (as for "Both sexes")							
EMPLOYED (as for "Total economically active population")							
UNEMPLOYED, TOTAL (as for "Total economically active population")							
UNEMPLOYED, WORKED BEFORE (as for "Total economically active population")							
UNEMPLOYED, NEVER WORKED BEFORE** (*by definition, the main status in employment classification above does not apply to this category; this category is required only as total for ensuring the consistency of the figure for total economically active population*)							
NOT STATED (as for "Unemployed, never worked before")							

Population included: currently (or usually) active population at or above the minimum age adopted for enumerating the economically active population

Classifications:

(a) Geographical division: (i) total country; (ii) each major civil division; (iii) each minor civil division; (iv) each principal locality. Distinguish between urban and rural for (i), (ii) and (iii)

(b) Activity status: total economically active population; employed; unemployed (distinguishing persons who ever and never worked before); not stated

(c) Age: all ages; under 15 years; 15-19 years; 20-24 years; 25-29 years; 30-34 years; 35-39 years; 40-44 years; 45-49 years; 50-54 years; 55-59 years; 60-64 years; 65-69 years; 70-74 years; 75-79 years; 80-84 years; 85-89 years; 90-94 years; 95-99 years;100 years and over; not stated.

(d) Marital status: all marital statuses; single (never married); married; widowed: divorced: separated; marital status not stated

(e) Status in employment: total; employer; own-account worker; employee; contributing family worker; member of producers' cooperative; persons not classifiable by status

(f) Sex: both sexes; male; female

Note:

This tabulation provides material for the analysis of the relation of marital status to the main status in employment of economically active people and of the probable effect thereon of any anticipated changes in the distribution of the population by marital status. Disaggregation of the table by sex will also be useful in understanding the pattern of women's employment status.

---

* The category "Under 15 years" should include all ages between the minimum age limit adopted by the country for census questions on economic activity and 14 years, if the minimum is under 15 years.

** The category "Unemployed, never worked before" should also be classified by sex: both sexes; male; female.

P7.9-A. Currently (or usually) active population in the informal sector, by activity status, main status in employment, place of work, main occupation and sex

Geographical division, activity status, sex, place of work, and main occupation	Total	Main status in employment					
		Employer	Own-account worker	Employee	Contributing family worker	Member of producers' cooperative	Persons not classifiable by status
TOTAL ECONOMICALLY ACTIVE POPULATION							
Informal sector, TOTAL							
Both sexes							
All places of work							
Sub-major group 11							
Minor group 111							
Minor group 112							
(etc.)							
...							
Sub-major group 91							
Minor group 911							
Minor group 912							
(etc.)							
Sub-major group 01							
Minor group 011							
Work at home (as for "All places of work")							
No fixed place of work (as for "All places of work")							
Fixed place, outside home (as for "All places of work")							
Place of work unknown (as for "All places of work")							
Male (as for "Both sexes")							
Female (as for "Both sexes")							
EMPLOYED (as for "Total economically active population")							
UNEMPLOYED, TOTAL (as for "Total economically active population")							
UNEMPLOYED, WORKED BEFORE (as for "Total economically active population")							
UNEMPLOYED, NEVER WORKED BEFORE* (*by definition, the occupational and main status in employment classifications above do not apply to this category; this category is required only as total for ensuring the consistency of the figure for total economically active population*)							
NOT STATED (as for "Unemployed, never worked before")							

Population included: currently (or usually) active population at or above the minimum age adopted for enumerating the economically active population, employed in the informal sector

Classifications:

(a) Geographical division: (i) total country; (ii) each major civil division; (iii) each minor civil division; (iv) each principal locality. Distinguish between urban and rural for (i), (ii) and (iii)

(b) Activity status: total economically active population; employed; unemployed (distinguishing persons who ever and never worked before); not stated

(c) Status in employment: total; employer; own-account worker; employee; contributing family worker; member of producers' cooperative; persons not classifiable by status

(d) Sex: both sexes; male; female

(e) Occupation: according to, or convertible to, the latest revision of the International Standard Classification of Occupations (ISCO-88), at least to the minor group (in other words, three-digit) level

(f) Place of work: all places of work; work at home; no fixed place of work; fixed place of work outside home; place of work unknown

Note:

Given the System of National Accounts definition of the production boundary, there is a substantial portion of the household sector that is attributable to non-market work. This tabulation provides information on the extent to which informal sector activities are conducted outside the home, to be used in formulating enterprise development and employment creation programmes. Urban and rural, or other administrative divisions, permit detailed analysis of this sector's activities.

---

* The category "Unemployed, never worked before" should also be classified by sex: both sexes; male; female.

P7.10-A. Usually active population, by monthly or annual income, main occupation and sex

Geographical division, sex and main occupation	Total usually active population	Monthly or annual income (Income classification adopted by the country)
Both sexes		
Sub-major group 11		
Minor group 111		
Minor group 112		
(etc.)		
Sub-major group 21		
Minor group 211		
Minor group 212		
(etc.)		
...		
Sub-major group 91		
Minor group 911		
Minor group 912		
(etc.)		
Sub-major group 01		
Minor group 011		
Male (as for "Both sexes")		
Female (as for "Both sexes")		

Population included: usually active population at or above the minimum age adopted for enumerating the economically active population

Classifications:
(a) Geographical division: (i) total country; (ii) each major civil division; (iii) each minor civil division; (iv) each principal locality. Distinguish between urban and rural for (i), (ii) and (iii)
(b) Income: income classification adopted by the country, preferably distinguishing approximately each fifth percentile or tenth percentile group
(c) Sex: both sexes; male; female
(d) Occupation: according to, or convertible to, the latest revision of the International Standard Classification of Occupations (ISCO-88), at least to the minor group (in other words, three-digit) level

Note:
This tabulation is needed for appraising variations in the income level of persons both within and among groups of occupations. The tabulation can be usefully expanded to include a cross-classification by broad age groups (for example, under 15 years, 15-64 years, and 65 years and over). It can usefully be expanded to include a classification by income of households and size of households. Such a tabulation is particularly useful for social policy studies and programmes focusing on households, particularly those of the poor.

P7.11-A. Households and population in households, by annual income and size of household

Geographical division*, and size of household	Annual income									
	Total		Less than ...		...		... and over		Not stated	
	House-holds	Popula-tion	House-holds	Popula-tion			House-holds	Popula-tion	House-holds	Popula-tion
All households										
Households consisting of										
1 person										
2 persons										
3 persons										
4 persons										
5 persons										
6 persons										
7 persons										
8 persons										
9 persons										
10 persons or more										
Not stated										

Population included: all members of households

Classifications:

(a)   Geographical division: (i) total country; (ii) each major civil division; (iii) each minor civil division; (iv) each principal locality. Distinguish between urban and rural for (i) and (ii)

(b)   Size of household: 1 person; 2 persons; 3 persons; 4 persons; 5 persons; 6 persons; 7 persons; 8 persons; 9 persons; 10 persons or more; not stated; and, separately, the number of households of each size and the aggregate population by size of household;

(c)   Income: income classification adopted by the country, preferably distinguishing approximately each fifth-percentile or tenth-percentile group

Note:

This tabulation provides information on annual income by the size of households. The information is useful, for instance, in obtaining indicators such as number of households by different percentile income groups. The tabulation will be useful in formulating a variety of social policies and measures. It may be expanded by classifying the annual income groups for urban/rural areas, which will be of further use in studies focusing on the development of disadvantaged areas.

*   This tabulation should be compiled for (i) total country, (ii) each major civil division. Distinguish between urban and rural for (i) and (ii).

P7.12-A. Population not currently active (in other words, not in the labour force), by primary reason for inactivity, age and sex

Geographical division, sex and age (in years)	Primary reason for inactivity					
	Total population not currently active	Attendance at educational institution	Engagement in household duties	Retirement or old age	Other reasons such as disability	Not stated
Both sexes						
All ages						
Under 15*						
15-19						
20-24						
25-29						
30-34						
35-39						
40-44						
45-49						
50-54						
55-59						
60-64						
65-69						
70-74						
75-79						
80-84						
85-89						
90-94						
95-99						
100 and over						
Not stated						
Male (as for "Both sexes")						
Female (as for "Both sexes")						

Population included: population not currently active at or above the minimum age adopted for enumerating the economically active population

Classifications:

(*a*) Geographical division: (i) total country; (ii) each major civil division; (iii) each minor civil division; (iv) each principal locality. Distinguish between urban and rural for (i) and (ii)

(*b*) Age: all ages; under 15 years; 15-19 years; 20-24 years; 25-29 years; 30-34 years; 35-39 years; 40-44 years; 45-49 years; 50-54 years; 55-59 years; 60-64 years; 65-69 years: 70-74 years: 75-79 years; 80-84 years; 85-89 years; 90-94 years; 95-99 years; and 100 and over; not stated.

(*c*) Primary reason for inactivity :total; attendance at educational institution; engagement in household duties; retirement or old age; other reasons such as disability; not stated

(*d*) Sex: both sexes; male; female

Note:
This tabulation provides data on the population not currently economically active classified by reason for inactivity. This data may be used for the analysis of potential sources of human resources that are not readily available at present but that may become so under different circumstances.

---

* The category "Under 15 years" should include all ages between the minimum age limit adopted by the country for census questions on economic activity and 14 years, if the minimum is under 15 years.

P7.13-A. Heads or other reference members of households* ... ** years of age and over, by economic activity status, age and sex

Geographical division, sex and age (in years) of head or other reference member of household	Total	Currently (or usually) active heads or other reference members of households	Currently (or usually) inactive heads or other reference members of households	Activity status not stated
Both sexes				
All households				
All ages				
Under 15***				
15-19				
20-24				
25-29				
30-34				
35-39				
40-44				
45-49				
50-54				
55-59				
60-64				
65-69				
70-74				
75-79				
80-84				
85-89				
90-94				
95-99				
100 and over				
Not stated				
Male (as for "Both sexes")				
Female (as for "Both sexes")				

Population included: all heads or other reference members of households at or above the minimum age adopted for enumerating the economically active population

Classifications:

(*a*) Geographical division: (i) total country; (ii) each major civil division; (iii) each minor civil division; (iv) each principal locality. Distinguish between urban and rural for (i), (ii) and (iii)

(*b*) Economic activity status: total; currently (or usually) active; currently (or usually) inactive; activity status not stated

(*c*) Age: all ages; under 15 years; 15-19 years; 20-24 years; 25-29 years; 30-34 years; 35-39 years; 40-44 years; 45-49 years; 50-54 years; 55-59 years; 60-64 years; 65-69 years; 70-74 years; 75-79 years; 80-84 years; 85-89 years; 90-94 years; 95-99 years; and 100 and over; not stated.

(*d*) Sex: both sexes; male; female

Note:

This tabulation provides information on the economic situation of households which provides for the calculation of the percentage of households and families headed by economically active men and women. Furthermore, the number of households and families headed by females is an important measure of the economic role of women in society. This information is also useful in planning for various facilities and services needed by women who work and maintain households. Similarly, data on households headed by the economically inactive such as retired persons are useful in formulating policies and programmes in social, housing and other sectors.

*Including one-person households (in other words, persons living alone).

**The minimum age adopted by the country for census questions on economic activity.

***The category «Under 15 years» should include all ages between the minimum age limit adopted by the country for census questions on economic activity and 14 years, if the minimum is below 15 years.

P7.14-A. Households and population in households, by size of household and number of currently (or usually) employed members

Geographical division, and size of household	Households with indicated number of currently (or usually) employed members											
	Total		0		1		...		5 or more		Not stated	
	House-holds	Popula-tion	House-holds	Popula-tion	House-holds	Popula-tion			House-holds	Popula-tion	House-holds	Popula-tion
All households												
Households consisting of												
1 person												
2 persons												
3 persons												
4 persons												
5 persons												
6 persons												
7 persons												
8 persons												
9 persons												
10 persons or more												
Not stated												

Population included: all members of households

Classifications:

(a) Geographical division: (i) total country; (ii) each major civil division; (iii) each minor civil division; (iv) each principal locality. Distinguish between urban and rural for (i) and (ii)

(b) Size of household: 1 person; 2 persons; 3 persons; 4 persons; 5 persons; 6 persons; 7 persons; 8 persons; 9 persons; 10 persons or more; not stated; and, separately, the number of households of each size and the aggregate population by size of household

(c) Number of currently (or usually) active members: 0; 1; 2; 3; 4; 5 or more; not stated

Note:

This tabulation provides information on the economic situation and size of households. The information is, for instance, useful in obtaining indicators such as the number of usually (or currently) employed and of dependent persons within households. Furthermore, the variations in dependency by the size of households can be examined. This tabulation will be useful in formulating a variety of social policies and measures. It may be expanded by classifying the employed by sex, which will be of further use in studies focusing on women and their twin roles in the household and the economy.

P7.15-A. Households, by size, number of currently (or usually) unemployed members and dependent children under 15 years of age in household

Geographical division, and size of households	Number of currently (or usually) unemployed members of household				Number of dependent children under 15 years of age in household				Total households	Total currently (or usually) unemployed	Total dependent children	Total population
	None	1	2	3 or more	None	1	2	3 or more				
All households												
Households consisting of												
1 person												
2 persons												
3 persons												
4 persons												
5 persons												
6 persons												
7 persons												
8 persons												
9 persons												
10 persons or more												
Not stated												

Population included: all members of households

Classifications:

(a)   Geographical division: (i) total country; (ii) each major civil division; (iii) each minor civil division; (iv) each principal locality. Distinguish between urban and rural for (i) and (ii)

(b)   Size of household: 1 person; 2 persons; 3 persons; 4 persons; 5 persons; 6 persons; 7 persons; 8 persons; 9 persons; 10 persons or more; not stated; and, separately, the number of households of each size and the aggregate population by size of household

(c)   Number of currently (or usually) unemployed members: 0, 1 member; 2 members; 3 or more members; and separately for total currently (or usually) unemployed by household size

(d)   Dependent (or not economically active) children under 15 years of age: the dependent children under 15 years of age should include all children not economically active in those ages; and separately aggregate dependent children by size of household

Note:

This tabulation provides basic information on the economic situation of households. Households in developing countries in particular include large numbers of dependent children and/or a considerable degree of unemployment and underemployment among their adult members. Therefore, such information as the number of unemployed members in households according to the size of households can serve as a basis for a variety of social programmes concerning the education and health of dependent children and for family allowance policies. This tabulation is also useful in focusing special attention on households containing several unemployed members and their needs, including unemployment assistance.

P7.16-A.   Currently (or usually) active heads or other reference members of households* … ** years of age and over, by activity status, main status in employment, main industry and sex

Geographical division, activity status, sex of active head or other reference member of household and main industry	Total	Main status in employment of active head or other reference member of household					
		Employer	Own-account worker	Employee	Contributing family worker	Member of producers' cooperative	Persons not classifiable by status
TOTAL ECONOMICALLY ACTIVE POPULATION							
Both sexes							
Households with active head or other reference member							
Division 01							
Group 011							
Group 012							
(etc.)							
Division 02							
Group 021							
Group 022							
(etc.)							
…							
Division 99							
Group 990							
(etc.)							
Male (as for "Both sexes")							
Female (as for "Both sexes")							
EMPLOYED (as for "Total economically active population")							
UNEMPLOYED, TOTAL (as for "Total economically active population")							
UNEMPLOYED, WORKED BEFORE (as for "Total economically active population")							
UNEMPLOYED, NEVER WORKED BEFORE							
Both sexes							
Male							
Female							
(by definition, the industrial and institutional sector of employment classifications above do not apply to this category; this category is required only as total for ensuring the consistency of the figure for total economically active population)							
NOT STATED (as for "Unemployed, never worked before")							

Population included: all currently (or usually) active heads or other reference members at or above the minimum age adopted for enumerating the economically active population

Classifications:
(a)   Geographical division: (i) total country (ii) each major civil division; (iii) each minor civil division; (iv) each principal locality. Distinguish between urban and rural for (i) and (ii)

(b)   Status in employment: total; employer; own-account worker; employee; contributing family worker; member of producers' cooperative; persons not classifiable by status

(c)   Activity status: total economically active population; employed; unemployed (distinguishing persons who ever and never worked before); not stated

(d)   Sex: both sexes; male; female

(e)   Industry: according to, or convertible to, the latest revision of the International Standard Industrial Classification of All Economic Activities (ISIC, Rev.3) to the level of groups (three-digit)

Note:
This tabulation furnishes information on the characteristics of heads or other reference members of households. It presents the type of industry, that is to say, agriculture, manufacturing, commerce, and so on, in which the head or reference member of the household is engaged and on which he or she is generally dependent for the support of his/her household. This tabulation also provides information on whether the head or reference member of the household is self-employed or an employee, reflecting the socio-economic status of households and means of livelihood.

* Including one-person households (in other words, persons living alone).
** The minimum age adopted by the country for census questions on economic activity.

Group 8.   Tabulations on disability characteristics

P8.1-A.   Total population by disability status*, whether living in household or institution, age and sex

Geographical division, urban or rural, households or institutions, age (in years) and sex	Total population		
	Without disabilities	With disabilities	Not stated
Total country			
All ages Both sexes			
Male			
Female			
0-4 (Sex as for "All ages")			
5-9 (Sex as for "All ages")			
...			
80-84 (Sex as for "All ages")			
85-89 (Sex as for "All ages")			
90-94 (Sex as for "All ages")			
95-99 (Sex as for "All ages")			
100 and over (Sex as for "All ages")			
Not stated (Sex as for "All ages")			
Population living in households (Sex and age as above)			
Population living in institutions (Sex and age as above)			
Not stated (Sex and age as above)			
Urban residence			
Population living in households (Sex and age as above)			
Population living in institutions (Sex and age as above)			
Not stated (Sex and age as above)			
Rural residence			
Population living in households (Sex and age as above)			
Population living in institutions (Sex and age as above)			
Not stated (Sex and age as above)			

Population included: total population

Classifications:

(a)   Geographical division: (i) total country; (ii) each major civil division; (iii) each minor civil division; (iv) each principal locality

(b)   Disability status: without disabilities; with disabilities; not stated

(c)   Age: all ages; 0-4 years; 5-9 years; 10-14 years; 15-19 years; 20-24 years; 25-29 years; 30-34 years; 35-39 years; 40-44 years; 45-49 years; 50-54 years; 55-59 years; 60-64 years; 65-69 years; 70-74 years; 75-79 years; 80-84 years; 85-89 years; 90-94 years; 95-99 years; and 100 and over; not stated

(d)   Sex: both sexes; male; female

Note:

There is widespread interest in the prevalence of disability in the population, by age and sex. This tabulation provides information for the calculation of prevalence rates distributed by geographical division, urban/rural residence and the living arrangements of persons with disabilities.

---

*   Estimates of the population with and without disability are a function of the exact methods and question wording used in the data collection. Consult the metadata for information on the methods (include the specific questions) used.

P8.2-A. Households with one or more persons with disabilities*, by type and size of household

Type of household, urban and rural areas	Total households		Size of household (persons)								
	Without disabilities	With disabilities	1	2	3	4	5	6	7	8 or more	Not stated

Total country

  Total households

    One-person household

    Nuclear family household

    Extended household

    Composite household

    Unknown

Urban areas
(Type of household as for "Total country")

Rural areas
(Type of household as for "Total country")

Population included: total population

Classifications:

(*a*)   Type of household: one-person household; nuclear household; extended household; composite household; unknown

(*b*)   Size of household: 1 person; 2 persons; 3 persons; 4 persons; 5 persons; 6 persons; 7 persons; 8 persons or more; not stated

Note:

This tabulation gives information on the number, type and size of households in which persons with disabilities live. The size of households and the distinction among the one-person household, the nuclear family household and the extended family household are useful for determining the economic and social provisions that may be needed for persons with disabilities living alone or with relatives. The tabulation also provides data for calculating prevalence of disability per household (*number of households with at least one person with disability per 1,000 households*).

---

*   Estimates of the population with and without disability are a function of the exact methods and question wording used in the data collection. Consult the metadata for information on the methods (include the specific questions) used.

P8.3-A. Total population 15 years of age and over, by disability status*, marital status, age and sex

Disability status, urban or rural, age (in years) and sex	Marital status (population 15 years of age and over)					
	Single (never married)	Married	Widowed	Divorced	Separated	Not stated
POPULATION WITHOUT DISABILITIES						
Total country						
All ages						
Both sexes						
Male						
Female						
15-19						
Both sexes						
Male						
Female						
.						
.						
.						
90-94						
Both sexes						
Male						
Female						
95-99						
Both sexes						
Male						
Female						
100+						
Both sexes						
Male						
Female						
Not stated						
Both sexes						
Male						
Female						
Urban areas (age and sex as above)						
Rural areas (age and sex as above)						
POPULATION WITH DISABILITIES (as for "Population without disabilities")						
NOT STATED (as for "Population without disabilities")						

Population included: total population

Classifications:

(a)   Marital status: single (never married); married; widowed; divorced; separated; not stated

(b)   Disability status: without disabilities; with disabilities; not stated

(c)   Age: all ages; 15-19 years; 20-24 years; 25-29 years; 30-34 years; 35-39 years; 40-44 years; 45-49 years; 50-54 years; 55-59 years; 60-64 years; 65-69 years; 70-74 years; 75-79 years; 80-84 years; 85-89 years; 90-94 years; 95-99 years; and 100 and over; not stated

(d)   Sex: both sexes; male; female

Note:

Information on the marital status of the persons with disabilities is important for understanding their social integration. This tabulation provides data on the marital status of persons with disabilities which are the basis for the calculation of age-sex specific marriage rates and divorce rates for comparison with persons without disabilities.

---

* Estimates of the population with and without disability are a function of the exact methods and question wording used in the data collection. Consult the metadata for information on the methods (include the specific questions) used.

P8.4-A. Population 5* to 29 years of age, by disability status, school attendance, age and sex**

Disability status, age (in years) and sex	Population* 5 to 29 years		
	Attending school	Not attending school	Not stated
Without disabilities			
All ages			
Both sexes			
Male			
Female			
5-9			
Both sexes			
Male			
Female			
.			
.			
25-29***			
Both sexes			
Male			
Female			
With disabilities			
(Age and sex as above)			
Not stated			
(Age and sex as above)			

Population included: all persons between the usual age for entering the first level of school and 29 years of age

Classifications:

(a)   Disability status: without disabilities; with disabilities; not stated

(b)   School attendance: attending school; not attending school; not stated

(c)   Age: all ages; 5-9 years; 10-14 years; 15-19 years; 20-24 years; and 25-29 years

(d)   Sex: both sexes; male; female

Note:

School attendance patterns for persons with disability are used to compare the current pattern of participation and non-participation in education for people with and without disability. The percentage of people with disability of the school-age population who attend school can also be compared among the different types of disability.

* Usual age for entering the first level of school.

** Estimates of the population with and without disability are a function of the exact methods and question wording used in the data collection. Consult the metadata for information on the methods (include the specific questions) used.

*** The higher age-limit may be adjusted: people with disability may attend school even in higher ages.

Annex V
Additional Tabulations for Housing Censuses

List of additional tabulations for housing censuses[a]

[a] Additional tabulations are identified by an "A" as part of the table number.

H1-A   Households in occupied housing units, by type of housing unit, cross-classified by type of household

H2-A   Households in collective living quarters, by type of living quarters

H3-A   Family nuclei, by broad types of living quarters and number of roofless family nuclei

H4-A   Family nuclei in housing units, by type of housing unit occupied, cross-classified by number of family nuclei per housing unit

H5-A   Households, by type of housing unit, cross-classified by activity status, occupation and sex of head or other reference member of household

H6-A   Homeless households, by age and sex of head or other reference member of household

H7-A   Vacant housing units, by type of vacancy

H8-A   Buildings, by year (or period) of construction of building, cross-classified by type of building and construction material of outer walls

H9-A   Housing units, by number of dwellings in the building

H10-A   Households in housing units, by type of housing unit occupied, cross-classified by number of households and number of rooms per housing unit

H11-A   Households in occupied housing units, by type of housing unit, cross-classified by type of ownership of the housing units

H12-A   Households in occupied housing units, by type of housing unit, cross-classified by type of bathing facilities

H13-A   Occupants of housing units, by type of housing unit, cross-classified by type of bathing facilities

H14-A   Households in occupied housing units, by type of housing unit, cross-classified by availability of kitchen and fuel used for cooking

H15-A   Occupants of housing units, by type of housing unit, cross-classified by availability of kitchen and fuel used for cooking

H16-A   Households in occupied housing units, by type of housing unit, cross-classified by water supply system

H17-A   Occupants of housing units, by type of housing unit, cross-classified by water supply system

H18-A   Households in occupied housing units, by type of housing unit, cross-classified by main source of drinking water

H19-A   Occupants of housing units, by type of housing unit, cross-classified by main source of drinking water

H20-A   Housing units, by type of housing unit occupied, cross-classified by type of toilet

H21-A   Occupants of housing units, by type of housing unit, cross-classified by type of toilet and type of sewage disposal

H22-A   Households in housing units, by type of housing unit, cross-classified by type of ownership of the housing unit, availability of piped water and availability of toilet facilities

H23-A   Households in occupied housing units, by type of housing unit, cross-classified by type of lighting and/or use of electricity

H24-A   Occupants of housing units, by type of housing unit, cross-classified by type of lighting and/or use of electricity

H25-A   Households in occupied housing units, by type of housing unit, cross-classified by type of solid waste disposal

H26-A   Occupants of housing units, by type of housing unit, cross-classified by type of solid waste disposal

H27-A   Renting households in housing units, by rent paid, cross-classified by type of ownership of the housing unit, whether space occupied is furnished or unfurnished and tenure of the household

H28-A   Renting households, classified by whether space occupied is furnished or unfurnished, and amount of rent paid monthly by the household, cross-classified by type of housing unit and number of households in housing unit

H29-A   Rented housing units, classified by whether space occupied is furnished or unfurnished, and amount of rent paid monthly for the housing unit, cross-classified by type of housing unit and number of rooms

H30-A   Rented housing units, classified by whether space occupied is furnished or unfurnished, and amount of rent paid monthly for the housing unit, cross-classified by type of housing unit, availability of piped water and availability of toilet facilities

H31-A   Occupied housing units, by type, cross-classified by available floor area and number of occupants

H1-A. Households in occupied housing units, by type of housing unit, cross-classified by type of household

Geographical division* and type of household	Total house-holds	Type of housing unit										
		Conventional dwellings			Other housing units							Not stated
								Informal housing units			
		Total	Has all basic facilities	Does not have all basic facilities	Total	Semi-permanent dwellings	Mobile housing units	Impro-vised	Permanent but not intended for habitation	Other	
Type of household												
One-person												
Nuclear												
Extended												
Composite												
Not stated												

Units of tabulation: households

Households included: households in occupied housing units

Classifications:
(a) Type of housing unit
(b) Type of household

Note:
This tabulation shows the type of household according to the type of housing units occupied. In itself, the tabulation provides useful insights into the housing patterns of the population. It could also be usefully combined with other tabulations to furnish a more detailed description of households in relation to certain aspects of housing, for example, characteristics of the head or other reference member of household (recommended tabulation H17.1-R and tabulation H5-A), number of rooms occupied or number of households occupying the housing unit (tabulation H10-A).

---

* This table may be compiled for (i) total country; (ii) each major civil division; (iii) each minor civil division; (iv) each principal locality. Distinguish between urban and rural for (i) and (ii).

H2-A.　Households in collective living quarters, by type of living quarters

| Geographical division | Total collective living quarters | Collective living quarters | | | | | | | | | |
		Hotels	Hospitals	Correc-tional institu-tions	Military institu-tions	Religious institu-tions	Retirement homes	Student dormito-ries	Staff quarters	Camps and workers' quarters	Other
Total households											

Units of tabulation:　households

Living quarters included:　collective living quarters

Households included:　households in collective living quarters

Classifications:
Type of collective living quarters

Note:
Whether or not this table is processed may depend upon the information provided in recommended tabulation H1.2-R, which shows the extent to which households occupy collective living quarters as well as geographical distribution of such households. Based on this information, it can be decided whether a tabulation by type of collective living quarters is necessary, for what geographical areas it should be prepared and the cross-classifications and level of detail required. Information concerning the institutional population is not included in this tabulation but information on the number of these persons is available from the population census tabulation programme. Their exclusion from this tabulation facilitates the identification of persons in households occupying collective living quarters

H3-A. Family nuclei, by broad types of living quarters and number of roofless family nuclei

Geographical division	Total persons	Type of living quarters				Roofless
		Total	Housing units		Collective living quarters	
			Conventional dwellings	Other housing units		
Total family nuclei						
Total country						
Urban						
Rural						
Major civil division A*						
Urban						
Rural						
Minor civil division A1*						
Urban						
Rural						
Minor civil division A2*						
Major civil division B*						
Urban						
Rural						
Minor civil division B1*						
Urban						
Rural						
Minor civil division B2*						
(etc.)						
Major civil division Z*						
Urban						
Rural						
Minor civil division Z1*						
Urban						
Rural						
Minor civil division Z2*						
Urban						
Rural						
(etc.)						

Units of tabulation: family nuclei

Living quarters included: all living quarters

Family nuclei included: all family nuclei

Classifications:

(a) Geographical divisions: (i) total country; (ii) each major civil division; (iii) each minor civil division. Distinguish between urban and rural for (i) and (ii))

(b) Type of living quarters

(c) Roofless: separate class for the roofless

Note

This is a broad summary table designed to show in very general terms the type of living quarters occupied by family nuclei and the number roofless. It provides background information as well as a control for preparation of more detailed tabulations for the categories shown. In fact, the magnitude of the number of family nuclei that occupy collective living quarters or are roofless and their geographical distribution provide an indication of the extent to which more detailed tabulations for these groups need to be prepared.

* Name of major or minor civil division.

H4-A. Family nuclei in housing units, by type of housing unit occupied, cross-classified by number of family nuclei per housing unit

Geographical division* and number of family nuclei per housing unit	Total house-holds	Type of housing unit									
		Conventional dwellings			Other housing units						Not stated
								Informal housing units			
		Total	Has all basic facilities	Does not have all basic facilities	Total	Semi-permanent dwellings	Mobile housing units	Impro-vised	Permanent but not intended for habitation	Other	
Total family nuclei											
Number of family nuclei per housing unit :											
1											
2											
3+											
Not stated											

Units of tabulation: family nuclei

Households and family nuclei included: family nuclei in housing units

Classifications:

(*a*) Geographical divisions: (i) total country; (ii) each major civil division; (iii) each minor civil division. Distinguish between urban and rural for (i), (ii) and (iii)

(*b*) Type of housing unit

(*c*) Number of family nuclei per housing unit

Note

This tabulation provides information on the number of family nuclei that are sharing housing units with other family nuclei and thus provides an important basis for estimating housing needs. The importance of a separate housing unit for each family nuclei that desires one is widely recognized. This tabulation shows the number of family nuclei that occupy the shared units.

*   This table may be compiled for (i) total country; (ii) each major civil division; (iii) each minor civil division; (iv) each principal locality. Distinguish between urban and rural for (i), (ii) and (iii).

H5-A. Households, by type of housing unit, cross-classified by activity status, occupation and sex of head or other reference member of household

Geographical division,* activity status, occupation and sex	Total house-holds	Type of housing unit										
		Conventional dwelling			Other housing units							Not stated
									Informal housing unit			
		Total	Has all basic facilities	Does not have all basic facilities	Total	Semi-permanent dwellings	Mobile housing unit	Impro-vised	Permanent but not intended for habitation	Other		

Total households

Economically active head or other reference member of household
   Employed
   Unemployed
  Male
   Employed
   Unemployed
  Female
   Employed
   Unemployed

Occupation—major group 01
  Male
  Female

Head or other reference member of household not economically active
  Male
  Female

Economic activity not stated

Units of tabulation: households

Living quarters included: all housing units

Households included: all households living in housing units

Classifications:

(a) Type of housing units

(b) Occupation of head of household: according to, or convertible to, the major groups of the International Labour Organization's International Standard Classification of Occupations, 1988

(c) Sex of head of household

(d) Economic activity of head or other reference member of household

Note

The relationships established in this tabulation provide data on the type of activity, occupation and sex of heads or other reference members of households occupying each type of housing unit, together with the number of households in each of the categories established. The tabulation attempts to isolate population groups in need of housing in terms of the occupation of economically active heads or other reference member of households and whether the head or other reference member is employed or not. In the absence of the data on income, which are not normally available in the population census, this tabulation may provide at least a general indication of socio-economic level. For the purpose of this presentation, only the total economically active heads or other reference member of household by sex are shown according to whether they are employed or unemployed. Where the number of unemployed is substantial, it may be useful to introduce the classification employed/unemployed for each occupational group.

---

* This table may be compiled for (i) total country; (ii) each major civil division; (iii) each minor civil division; (iv) each principal locality. Distinguish between urban and rural for (i), (ii) and (iii).

H6-A.   Homeless households, by age and sex of head or other reference member of household

Geographical division and unit of tabulation, head or other reference member of household, sex	Total house-holds	Age of head of household (in years)								
		Under 15 years	15-24 years	25-34 years	35-44 years	45-54 years	......	95-99 years	100 years and over	Age unknown

Total homeless households
 	
   Male head or other reference member of household
 	
   Female head or other reference member of household										

Units of tabulation: households

Households included: homeless households

Classifications:
(*a*)   Geographical division: depending on national needs
(*b*)   Sex of head or other reference member of household
(*c*)   Age of head or other reference member of household

Note:
This tabulation is prepared on the basis of the information furnished by the recommended tabulation H1.2-R on the number of homeless households and their geographical location. This information provides a basis for deciding what further tabulations of the homeless should be prepared, the most appropriate geographical areas for which the data should be tabulated and the household characteristics that should be included as well as the level of detail.

H7-A.   Vacant housing units, by type of vacancy

Geographical division* and dwellings	Total conventional dwellings	Type of vacancy						
		Seasonally vacant	Non-seasonally vacant					Not stated
			For rent	For sale	For demolition	Other		
Conventional dwellings								

Units of tabulation: Housing units

Living quarters included: vacant conventional dwellings

Classifications: Type of vacancy

Note:
This tabulation confines itself to data relating to conventional dwellings because all other types of housing are required, by definition, to be occupied in order to fall within the scope of the census; a classification by occupancy would not therefore be applicable to them. In some housing censuses, vacancy information is recorded during the listing of sets of living quarters and summaries of these lists provide the aggregates furnished by this tabulation, although generally not in detail as far as reasons for vacancy are concerned. Such a procedure may provide an economic means of obtaining data, though every effort should be made to collect information in detail on vacant conventional dwellings.

* This table may be compiled for (i) total country; (ii) each major civil division; (iii) each minor civil division; (iv) each principal locality. Distinguish between urban and rural for (i), (ii) and (iii).

H8-A. Buildings, by year (or period) of construction of building, cross-classified by type of building and construction material of outer walls

Geographical division,* type of building and construction material of walls	Total buildings	Year or period of building construction									
		Year prior to census**						Period***			Not stated
		0	1	2	...	8	9	I	...	IV	
Building coextensive with a single housing unit											
Material of walls:											
Material A											
Material B											
Material C											
Building coextensive with a single housing unit—detached											
Material of walls (as above)											
Building coextensive with a single housing unit—attached											
Material of walls (as above)											
Building with more than 1 unit											
Material of walls (as above)											
Building with more than 1 unit—up to 2 floors											
Material of walls (as above)											
Building with more than 1 unit—from 3-10 floors											
Material of walls (as above)											
Building with more than 1 unit—11 floors and over											
Material of walls (as above)											
Building for persons living in institutions											
Material of walls (as above)											
All other types of buildings											
Material of walls (as above)											
Not stated											
Conventional dwellings											
(Classifications of buildings and materials of walls as above)											
Other housing units											
(Classifications of buildings and materials of walls as above)											

Units of tabulation: buildings

Classifications:

(*a*) Construction material of outer walls: construction material of the walls (subclassified into types of construction material of significance for permanence and durability)

(*b*) Type of building

(*c*) Year or period of construction: single years for buildings constructed during the intercensal period immediately preceding (if it does not exceed 10 years) or during the preceding 10 years (where the intercensal period exceeds 10 years or where no previous census has been carried out); specified period for buildings constructed prior to this

Note:

This tabulation provides information on the number of dwellings by type of building in which the dwelling is located and by material of construction of the walls of the building cross-classified by the year or period of construction of the building. The inventory considered in terms of age and type of building provides a basis for estimating maintenance costs; it also provides insight into the housing patterns of the population, a factor that experience has shown should not be neglected in formulating housing programmes. The question whether to include only conventional and basic dwellings in the tabulation or other types of living quarters as well will depend upon the importance of the latter as far as the overall housing situation is concerned. In tropical countries where a substantial proportion of the population lives in housing units constructed of locally available material such as bamboo, palm, thatch and so forth, information on the rate of construction of temporary units may be considered sufficiently important for them to be included. Mobile and marginal units are not included, since the year or period of construction is of varying significance depending upon the type of unit.

The tabulation includes material of construction of external walls only, since this appears to be of the utmost significance as an indicator of durability. Information on the construction material of the roof and floor is also frequently collected in national housing censuses, particularly information on the former, but certain inconsistencies and complications have been noticed while tabulating construction material for more than one element of the dwelling.

---

* This table may be compiled for (i) total country; (ii) each major civil division; (iii) each minor civil division; (iv) each principal locality. Distinguish between urban and rural for (i), (ii) and (iii).

** Years preceding the census year, with 0 being the year of the census.

*** See paragraph 2.522

H9-A. Housing units, by number of dwellings in the building

Geographical division* and housing units	Total dwellings	Number of dwellings in the building						
		1	2	3-9	10-49	...	...	Not stated
Total housing units								
Conventional dwellings								
Other housing units								

Units of tabulation: Housing units

Living quarters included: all housing units

Classifications:
Number of dwellings per building: 1, 2, 3-9, 10-49 ... according to the needs of the country or area

Note:
A distribution of dwellings by the number of dwellings in the building in which dwellings are located provides a useful insight into the housing patterns of the population. The information required for this tabulation would normally be available from census control lists and would therefore not require any additional collection of data. This tabulation would normally be of significance only in urban areas and for localities of a certain size. Determination of the size of the locality as well as the distribution used in the tabulation would depend upon housing characteristics in the country concerned.

* This table may be compiled for (i) total country; (ii) each major civil division; (iii) each minor civil division; (iv) each principal locality. Distinguish between urban and rural for (i), (ii) and (iii).

H10-A. Households in housing units, by type of housing unit occupied, cross-classified by number of households and number of rooms per housing unit

Geographical division,* number of households and number of rooms	Total house-holds	Type of housing unit									
		Conventional dwellings			Other housing units						
								Informal housing units			
		Total	Has all basic facilities	Does not have all basic facilities	Total	Semi-permanent dwellings	Mobile housing units	Impro-vised	Permanent but not intended for habitation	Other	Not stated
Total households											
Households with the following number of households per housing unit :											
1											
In housing unit with the following number of rooms:											
1											
2											
3											
4											
5											
6											
7											
8											
9											
10+											
2											
(Classification of number of rooms as above)											
3+											
(Classification of number of rooms as above)											
Note stated											

Units of tabulation: households

Households included: households in housing units

Classifications:

(*a*)   Type of housing unit

(*b*)   Number of households per housing unit

(*c*)   Number of rooms per housing unit

Note:

This tabulation provides information on the number of households that are sharing housing units with other house-holds and thus provides an important basis for estimating housing needs. The importance of a separate housing unit for each household that desires one is widely recognized and is discussed under the uses for recommended tabulation H3.1-R. Tabulation H27-A, which shows the number of subtenant households, provides similar informa-tion, since subtenant households are households that share a housing unit with one or more households. However, this tabulation provides additional information, since it shows the number of households that occupy the shared units plus the number of rooms in the housing units.

---

* This table may be compiled for (i) total country; (ii) each major civil division; (iii) each minor civil division; (iv) each principal locality. Distinguish between urban and rural for (i), (ii) and (iii).

H11-A. Households in occupied housing units, by type of housing unit, cross-classified by type of ownership of the housing units

Geographical division* and type of ownership	Total	Type of housing unit										
		Conventional dwellings			Other housing units							Not stated
		Total	Has all basic facilities	Does not have all basic facilities	Total	Semi-permanent dwellings	Mobile housing units	Informal housing units				
								Impro-vised	Permanent but not intended for habitation	Other		
Total households												
Owner occupied												
Non-owner occupied												
Publicly owned												
Privately owned												
Communally owned												
Cooperatively owned												
Other												

Units of tabulation: households

Living quarters included: occupied housing units

Households included: households in occupied housing units

Classifications:

(a) Geographical divisions: (i) total country; (ii) each major civil division; (iii) each minor civil division. Distinguish between urban and rural for (i), (ii) and (iii)

(b) Type of housing unit

(c) Type of ownership

Note

This tabulation provides information on the type of ownership of the housing unit. It is intended to show the type of ownership according to the type of housing unit. Assessing the ownership of housing units is of paramount importance in establishing housing policies.

---

* This table may be compiled for (i) total country; (ii) each major civil division; (iii) each minor civil division; (iv) each principal locality. Distinguish between urban and rural for (i), (ii) and (iii).

H12-A.   Households in occupied housing units, by type of housing unit, cross-classified by type of bathing facilities

Geographical division* and type of bathing facilities	Total	Type of housing unit									
		Conventional dwellings			Other housing units						
		Total	Has all basic facilities	Does not have all basic facilities	Total	Semi-permanent dwellings	Mobile housing units	Informal housing units			Not stated
								Impro-vised	Permanent but not intended for habitation	Other	
Total housing units											
With fixed bath or shower within housing unit											
Without fixed bath or shower within housing unit											
Fixed bath or shower available outside housing unit											
For exclusive use											
Shared											
No fixed bath or shower available											

Units of tabulation: households

Living quarters included: Occupied housing units

Households included: households in occupied housing units

Classifications

(a)   Geographical divisions: (i) total country; (ii) each major civil division; (iii) each minor civil division. Distinguish between urban and rural for (i), (ii) and (iii)

(b)   Type of housing unit

(c)   Bathing facilities

Note

From this tabulation, data may be obtained on the number of housing units by type of bathing facilities available to occupants. This tabulation provides the minimum data required for an evaluation of living quarters according to the facilities available. The information for dwellings is required for the computation of indicators of housing and its environment. If the number of sets of collective living quarters is large, it may be useful to prepare similar tabulations by type of collective living quarters. With respect to these units, however, separate tabulations that would also show the number of fixed baths and showers in relation to the number of occupants may be more useful than information that merely indicates the availability of bathing facilities. Similar information may be tabulated for housing units occupied by more than a certain number of households.

* This table may be compiled for (i) total country; (ii) each major civil division; (iii) each minor civil division; (iv) each principal locality. Distinguish between urban and rural for (i), (ii) and (iii).

H13-A.   Occupants of housing units, by type of housing unit, cross-classified by type of bathing facilities

Geographical division* and type of bathing facilities	Total	Type of housing unit										
		Conventional dwellings			Other housing units							Not stated
		Total	Has all basic facilities	Does not have all basic facilities	Total	Semi-permanent dwellings	Mobile housing units	Informal housing units				
								Impro-vised	Permanent but not intended for habitation	Other		
Total number of occupants												
With fixed bath or shower within housing unit												
Without fixed bath or shower within housing unit												
Fixed bath or shower available outside housing unit												
For exclusive use												
Shared												
No fixed bath or shower available												

Units of tabulation: occupants

Living quarters included: housing units

Persons included: occupants of housing units

Classifications
(a)   Geographical divisions: (i) total country; (ii) each major civil division; (iii) each minor civil division. Distinguish between urban and rural for (i), (ii) and (iii)
(b)   Type of housing unit
(c)   Bathing facilities

Note
From this tabulation, data may be obtained on the number of housing units by type of bathing facilities available to occupants. This tabulation provides the minimum data required for an evaluation of living quarters according to the facilities available. The information for dwellings is required for the computation of indicators of housing and its environment. If the number of sets of collective living quarters is large, it may be useful to prepare similar tabulations by type of collective living quarters. With respect to these units, however, separate tabulations that would also show the number of fixed baths and showers in relation to the number of occupants may be more useful than information that merely indicates the availability of bathing facilities. Similar information may be tabulated for housing units occupied by more than a certain number of households

*   This table may be compiled for (i) total country; (ii) each major civil division; (iii) each minor civil division; (iv) each principal locality. Distinguish between urban and rural for (i), (ii) and (iii).

H14-A. Households in occupied housing units, by type of housing unit, cross-classified by availability of kitchen and fuel used for cooking

Geographical division*, availability of kitchen and fuel used for cooking	Total	Type of housing unit									Not stated
		Conventional dwellings			Other housing units						
								Informal housing units			
		Total	Has all basic facilities	Does not have all basic facilities	Total	Semi-permanent dwellings	Mobile housing units	Impro-vised	Permanent but not intended for habitation	Other	

Total households

With kitchen within the housing unit

  Gas

  Electricity

  Liquefied petroleum gas (LPG)

  Kerosene/paraffin (petroleum based)

  Oil (including vegetable oil)

  Coal

  Firewood

  Charcoal

  Animal dung

  Crop residue

  Other

With other space for cooking within the housing unit (classification of fuel used for cooking as above)

Without kitchen or other space for cooking within the housing unit (classification of fuel used for cooking as above)

Units of tabulation: households

Living quarters included: occupied housing units

Households included: households in occupied housing units

Classifications

(a) Geographical divisions: (i) total country; (ii) each major civil division; (iii) each minor civil division. Distinguish between urban and rural for (i), (ii) and (iii)

(b) Type of housing unit

(c) Cooking facilities

(d) Fuel used for cooking

Note

The classifications used in this tabulation for fuel used for cooking should be formulated to conform to the types of equipment and types of fuel normally used in the country concerned. Data on fuel refer to the fuel most frequently used and it may be confined to the fuel used for preparing the principal meals. If information has been gathered on the number of kitchens or kitchenettes or the number of stoves in housing units occupied by more than a certain number of households and for collective living quarters, such as hotels, boarding houses and multi-household living quarters, it would be useful to tabulate this information according to the type of living quarters and the number of households.

* This table may be compiled for (i) total country; (ii) each major civil division; (iii) each minor civil division; (iv) each principal locality. Distinguish between urban and rural for (i), (ii) and (iii).

H15-A. Occupants of housing units, by type of housing unit, cross-classified by availability of kitchen and fuel used for cooking

Geographical division*, availability of kitchen and fuel used for cooking	Total	Type of housing unit										Not stated
		Conventional dwellings			Other housing units							
		Total	Has all basic facilities	Does not have all basic facilities	Total	Semi-permanent dwellings	Mobile housing units	Informal housing units				
								Impro-vised	Permanent but not intended for habitation	Other		
Total number of occupants												
With kitchen within the housing unit												
Gas												
Electricity												
Liquefied petroleum gas (LPG)												
Kerosene/paraffin (petro-leum based)												
Oil (including vegetable oil)												
Coal												
Firewood												
Charcoal												
Animal dung												
Crop residue												
Other												
With other space for cooking within the housing unit (classification of fuel used for cooking as above)												
Without kitchen or other space for cooking within the housing unit (classification of fuel used for cooking as above)												

Units of tabulation: occupants

Living quarters included: housing units

Persons included: occupants of housing units

Classifications

(a) Geographical divisions: (i) total country; (ii) each major civil division; (iii) each minor civil division. Distinguish between urban and rural for (i), (ii) and (iii)

(b) Type of housing unit

(c) Cooking facilities

(d) Fuel used for cooking

Note

The classifications used in this tabulation for fuel used for cooking should be formulated to conform to the types of equipment and types of fuel normally used in the country concerned. Data on fuel refer to the fuel most frequently used and it may be confined to the fuel used for preparing the principal meals. If information has been gathered on the number of kitchens or kitchenettes or the number of stoves in housing units occupied by more than a certain number of households and for collective living quarters, such as hotels, boarding houses and multi-household living quarters, it would be useful to tabulate this information according to the type of living quarters and the number of households.

* This table may be compiled for (i) total country; (ii) each major civil division; (iii) each minor civil division; (iv) each principal locality. Distinguish between urban and rural for (i), (ii) and (iii).

H16-A. Households in occupied housing units, by type of housing unit, cross-classified by water supply system

Geographical division*, water supply system	Total	Type of housing unit									
		Conventional dwellings			Other housing units						
		Total	Has all basic facilities	Does not have all basic facilities	Total	Semi-permanent dwellings	Mobile housing units	Informal housing units			Not stated
								Impro-vised	Permanent but not intended for habitation	Other	
Total households											
Piped water inside the unit											
From the community scheme											
From an individual source											
Piped water outside the unit but within 200 metres											
From the community scheme											
For exclusive use											
Shared											
From an individual source											
For exclusive use											
Shared											
Without piped water (including piped water beyond 200 metres)											

Units of tabulation: households

Living quarters included: occupied housing units

Households included: households in occupied housing units

Classifications:

(a) Geographical divisions: (i) total country; (ii) each major civil division; (iii) each minor civil division. Distinguish between urban and rural for (i), (ii) and (iii)

(b) Type of housing unit

(c) Water supply system

(d) Source of water supply: on the basis of most frequent sources in country or area, but may include piped community-wide system; catchments tank; public well; private well; river, spring; and so forth

Note

From this tabulation, information may be derived on the number of households with ready access to water supply as well as the availability of piped water for each class of housing units. The classification of the source of the water supply in this tabulation is limited to the community scheme or an individual source. Many countries have found it useful to further elaborate this classification in order to provide more detailed information on the source of the water supply

* This table may be compiled for (i) total country; (ii) each major civil division; (iii) each minor civil division; (iv) each principal locality. Distinguish between urban and rural for (i), (ii) and (iii).

H17-A. Occupants of housing units, by type of housing unit, cross-classified by water supply system

Geographical division*, water supply system	Total	Type of housing unit									
		Conventional dwellings			Other housing units						
									Informal housing units		
		Total	Has all basic facilities	Does not have all basic facilities	Total	Semi-permanent dwellings	Mobile housing units	Impro-vised	Permanent but not intended for habitation	Other	Not stated
Total number of occupants											
Piped water inside the unit											
From the community scheme											
From an individual source											
Piped water outside the unit but within 200 metres											
From the community scheme											
For exclusive use											
Shared											
From an individual source											
For exclusive use											
Shared											
Without piped water (including piped water beyond 200 metres)											

Units of tabulation: occupants

Living quarters included: housing units

Persons included: occupants of housing units

Classifications:

(a) Geographical divisions: (i) total country; (ii) each major civil division; (iii) each minor civil division. Distinguish between urban and rural for (i), (ii) and (iii)

(b) Type of housing unit

(c) Water supply system

(d) Source of water supply: on the basis of most frequent sources in country or area, but may include piped community-wide system; catchments tank; public well; private well; river, spring; and so forth

Note:

From this tabulation, information may be derived on the number of persons with ready access to water supply as well as the availability of piped water for each class of housing units. The classification of the source of the water supply in this tabulation is limited to the community scheme or an individual source. Many countries have found it useful to further elaborate this classification in order to provide more detailed information on the source of the water supply

---

* This table may be compiled for (i) total country; (ii) each major civil division; (iii) each minor civil division; (iv) each principal locality. Distinguish between urban and rural for (i), (ii) and (iii).

H18-A. Households in occupied housing units, by type of housing unit, cross-classified by main source of drinking water

Geographical division* and main source of drinking water	Total	Type of housing unit									Not stated
		Conventional dwellings			Other housing units						
								Informal housing units			
		Total	Has all basic facilities	Does not have all basic facilities	Total	Semi-permanent dwellings	Mobile housing units	Impro-vised	Permanent but not intended for habitation	Other	
Total households											
Piped water inside the unit											
From the community scheme											
From an individual source											
Piped water outside the unit but within 200 metres											
From the community scheme											
For exclusive use											
Shared											
From an individual source											
For exclusive use											
Shared											
Without piped water (including piped water beyond 200 metres)											
Borehole											
Protected well											
Protected spring											
Rainwater collection											
Vendor provided water											
Bottled water											
Tanker trucks											
Unprotected well/spring/ river/stream/lake pond, dam											

Units of tabulation: households

Living quarters included: occupied housing units

Households included: households in occupied housing units

Classifications:
(a) Geographical divisions: (i) total country; (ii) each major civil division; (iii) each minor civil division. Distinguish between urban and rural for (i), (ii) and (iii)
(b) Type of housing unit
(c) Water supply system
(d) Source of water supply: on the basis of most frequent sources in country or area, but may include piped community-wide system; catchments tank; public well; private well; river, spring; and so forth

Note:
The importance of supply of drinking water was emphasized in a number United Nations documents and resolutions, most notably on Millennium Development Goals. This tabulation aims at assessing the source of drinking water used by households as it often differs from the source of water used for general purposes (see tabulation H5-R above).

---

* This table may be compiled for (i) total country; (ii) each major civil division; (iii) each minor civil division; (iv) each principal locality. Distinguish between urban and rural for (i), (ii) and (iii).

H19-A. Occupants of housing units, by type of housing unit, cross-classified by main source of drinking water

Geographical division* and main source of drinking water	Total	Type of housing unit										Not stated
		Conventional dwellings			Other housing units							
		Total	Has all basic facilities	Does not have all basic facilities	Total	Semi-permanent dwellings	Mobile housing units	Informal housing units				
								Impro-vised	Permanent but not intended for habitation	Other		

Total number of occupants

Piped water inside the unit

  From the community scheme

  From an individual source

Piped water outside the unit but within 200 metres

  From the community scheme

    For exclusive use

    Shared

  From an individual source

    For exclusive use

    Shared

Without piped water (including piped water beyond 200 metres)

  Borehole

  Protected well

  Protected spring

  Rainwater collection

  Vendor provided water

  Bottled water

  Tanker trucks

  Unprotected well/spring/ river/stream/lake pond, dam

Units of tabulation: occupants

Living quarters included: housing units

Persons included: occupants of housing units

Classifications:
(*a*) Geographical divisions: (i) total country; (ii) each major civil division; (iii) each minor civil division . Distinguish between urban and rural for (i), (ii) and (iii)
(*b*) Type of housing unit
(*c*) Water supply system
(*d*) Source of water supply: on the basis of most frequent sources in country or area, but may include piped community-wide system; catchments tank; public well; private well; river, spring; and so forth

Note:
The importance of supply of drinking water was emphasized in a number United Nations documents and resolutions, most notably on Millennium Development Goals. This tabulation aims at assessing the source of drinking water used by households as it often differs from the source of water used for general purposes (see tabulation H5-R above).

---

* This table may be compiled for (i) total country; (ii) each major civil division; (iii) each minor civil division; (iv) each principal locality. Distinguish between urban and rural for (i), (ii) and (iii).

H20-A. Housing units, by type of housing unit occupied, cross-classified by type of toilet

Geographical division* and type of toilet	Total house-holds	Type of housing unit										
		Conventional dwellings			Other housing units							Not stated
									Informal housing units			
		Total	Has all basic facilities	Does not have all basic facilities	Total	Semi-permanent dwellings	Mobile housing units	Impro-vised	Permanent but not intended for habitation	Other	
Total housing units												
With toilet within the housing unit												
Flush/pour toilet												
Non-flush toilet												
With toilet outside the housing unit												
Flush/pour toilet												
For exclusive use												
Shared												
Non-flush toilet												
For exclusive use												
Shared												
No toilet available												
Not stated												

Units of tabulation: housing units

Living quarters included: all housing units

Classifications:
(a) Type of housing unit
(b) Type of toilet

Note:
From this tabulation, data may be obtained on the number of housing units by type and the type of toilet facilities. The tabulation of toilet facilities shown provides the minimum data required for an evaluation of living quarters according to the facilities available. The information for dwellings is required for the computation of indicators of housing and its environment. If the number of sets of collective living quarters is large, it may be useful to prepare similar tabulations by type of collective living quarters. In fact, information concerning the availability of toilet facilities in institutions, hotels and so on is frequently collected in housing censuses. With respect to these units, however, separate tabulations that would also show the number of toilets in relation to the number of occupants may be more useful than information that merely indicates the availability of toilets and the type of toilet. Similar information may be tabulated for housing units occupied by more than a certain number of households. In many countries the classification has been elaborated to provide information on availability of particular types of toilets (other than flush) that are prevalent and characteristic of the country or area concerned and imply varying degrees of efficiency from a sanitary point of view.

---

* This table may be compiled for (i) total country; (ii) each major civil division; (iii) each minor civil division; (iv) each principal locality. Distinguish between urban and rural for (i), (ii) and (iii).

H21-A. Occupants of housing units, by type of housing unit, cross-classified by type of toilet and type of sewage disposal

Geographical division*, type of toilet and sewerage disposal	Total	Type of housing unit										Not stated
		Conventional dwellings			Other housing units							
									Informal housing units			
		Total	Has all basic facilities	Does not have all basic facilities	Total	Semi-permanent dwellings	Mobile housing units	Impro-vised	Permanent but not intended for habitation	Other		

Total number of occupants

With toilet within the housing unit

Flush/pour flash toilet

   Connected to a public sewerage plant

   Connected to a private sewerage plant

   Other

Non-flush toilet

   Connected to a public sewerage plant

   Connected to a private sewerage plant

   Other

With toilet outside the housing unit

Flush/pour flush toilet

   Connected to a public sewerage plant

   Connected to a private sewerage plant

   Other

Non-flush toilet

   Connected to a public sewerage plant

   Connected to a private sewerage plant

   Other

No toilet available

Not stated

Units of tabulation: occupants

Living quarters included: all housing units

Persons included: occupants of housing units

Classifications:

(*a*) Geographical divisions: (i) total country; (ii) each major civil division; (iii) each minor civil division. Distinguish between urban and rural for (i), (ii) and (iii)

(*b*) Type of housing unit

(*c*) Type of toilet

(*d*) Sewage disposal system

Note:

From this tabulation, data may be obtained on the number of housing units by type with the number of occupants, the type of toilet facilities available to them and the characteristics of the sewage system. The tabulation of toilet facilities shown provides the minimum data required for an evaluation of living quarters according to the facilities available. The information for dwellings is required for the computation of indicators of housing and its environment. If the number of sets of collective living quarters is large, it may be useful to prepare similar tabulations by type of collective living quarters. With respect to these units, however, separate tabulations that would also show the number of toilets in relation to the number of occupants may be more useful than information that merely indicates the availability of toilets and the type of toilet. Similar information may be tabulated for housing units occupied by more than a certain number of households. In many countries the classification has been elaborated to provide information on availability of particular types of toilets (other than flush) that are prevalent and characteristic of the country or area concerned and imply varying degrees of efficiency from a sanitary point of view

---

* This table may be compiled for (i) total country; (ii) each major civil division; (iii) each minor civil division; (iv) each principal locality. Distinguish between urban and rural for (i), (ii) and (iii).

H22-A. Households in housing units, by type of housing unit, cross-classified by type of ownership of the housing unit, availability of piped water and availability of toilet facilities

Geographical division,* type of ownership, availability of piped water, availability of toilet facilities	Total house-holds	Type of housing unit									Not stated
		Conventional dwellings			Other housing units						
								Informal housing units			
		Total	Has all basic facilities	Does not have all basic facilities	Total	Semi-permanent dwellings	Mobile housing units	Impro-vised	Permanent but not intended for habitation	Other	
Total households											
Household owning the housing unit it occupies											
Water supply:											
Piped water inside											
Toilet within housing unit											
Toilet outside housing unit											
Without toilet											
Piped water outside but within 100 metres (classification of toilet facilities as shown above)											
Without piped water (classification of toilet facilities as shown above)											
Household occupies a publicly owned housing unit (classifications of water supply and toilet facilities as shown above)											
Household occupies a privately owned housing unit (classifications of water supply and toilet facilities as shown above)											
Ownership not stated											

Units of tabulation: households

Living quarters included: housing units

Households and persons included: households occupying housing units

Classifications:
(*a*)   Type of housing unit
(*b*)   Type of ownership
(*c*)   Availability of piped water
(*d*)   Availability of toilet facilities

Note:
In this tabulation, households are tabulated according to the type of housing unit occupied, the principal facilities available in the housing unit and the type of owner. The information on toilet and water supply is cross-classified in order to show the number of households by owner of the housing unit according to whether the housing unit has piped water and/or toilet facilities or neither of these types of facilities. Ownership of housing units lacking basic facilities would be of particular interest and it would be useful to know whether these units are occupied by their owners or by tenants.

---

* This table may be compiled for (i) total country; (ii) each major civil division; (iii) each minor civil division; (iv) each principal locality. Distinguish between urban and rural for (i), (ii) and (iii).

H23-A. Households in occupied housing units, by type of housing unit, cross-classified by type of lighting and/or use of electricity

Geographical division* and type of lighting and/or use of electricity	Total	Type of housing unit										
		Conventional dwellings			Other housing units							Not stated
		Total	Has all basic facilities	Does not have all basic facilities	Total	Semi-permanent dwellings	Mobile housing units	Informal housing units				
								Impro-vised	Permanent but not intended for habitation	Other		

Total households

Type of lighting

  Electricity

  Gas

  Oil lamp

  Other types of lighting of significance to the country or area concerned

Urban
(classification of type of lighting as above)

Rural
(classification of type of lighting as above)

Units of tabulation: households

Living quarters included: occupied housing units

Classifications:
(a) Geographical divisions: (i) total country; (ii) each major civil division; (iii) each minor civil division. Distinguish between urban and rural for (i), (ii) and (iii)
(b) Type of housing unit
(c) Type of lighting and/or use of electricity

Note:
Countries and areas in all regions of the world attach considerable importance to the source of energy used for lighting. This tabulation could provide planners with a useful indication of areas where community lighting needs to be extended. For housing units lit by electricity, additional information may be tabulated to show whether the electricity comes from a community supply, generating plant or some other source.

---

* This table may be compiled for (i) total country; (ii) each major civil division; (iii) each minor civil division; (iv) each principal locality. Distinguish between urban and rural for (i), (ii) and (iii).

H24-A. Occupants of housing units, by type of housing unit, cross-classified by type of lighting and/or use of electricity

Geographical division* and type of lighting and/or use of electricity	Total	Type of housing unit										
		Conventional dwellings			Other housing units							Not stated
		Total	Has all basic facilities	Does not have all basic facilities	Total	Semi-permanent dwellings	Mobile housing units	Informal housing units				
								Impro-vised	Permanent but not intended for habitation	Other		

Total number of occupants

Type of lighting
  Electricity
  Gas
  Oil lamp
  Other types of lighting of significance to the country or area concerned

Urban
  (classification of type of lighting as above)

Rural
  (classification of type of lighting as above)

Units of tabulation: occupants

Living quarters included: housing units

Classifications
(a)   Geographical divisions: (i) total country; (ii) each major civil division; (iii) each minor civil division. Distinguish between urban and rural for (i), (ii) and (iii)
(b)   Type of housing unit
(c)   Type of lighting and/or use of electricity

Note
Countries and areas in all regions of the world attach considerable importance to the source of energy used for lighting. This tabulation could provide planners with a useful indication of areas where community lighting needs to be extended. For housing units lit by electricity, additional information may be tabulated to show whether the electricity comes from a community supply, generating plant or some other source.

---

*   This table may be compiled for (i) total country; (ii) each major civil division; (iii) each minor civil division; (iv) each principal locality. Distinguish between urban and rural for (i), (ii) and (iii).

H25-A. Households in occupied housing units, by type of housing unit, cross-classified by type of solid waste disposal

Geographical division* and main type of solid waste disposal	Total	Type of housing unit									
		Conventional dwellings			Other housing units						Not stated
		Total	Has all basic facilities	Does not have all basic facilities	Total	Semi-permanent dwellings	Mobile housing units	Informal housing units			
								Impro-vised	Permanent but not intended for habitation	Other	
Total households											
Solid waste collected on regular basis by author-ized collectors											
Solid waste collected on an irregular basis by author-ized collectors											
Solid waste collected by self-appointed collectors											
Occupants dispose of solid waste in a local dump supervised by authorities											
Occupants dispose of solid waste in a local dump not supervised by authorities											
Occupants burn solid waste											
Occupants bury solid waste											
Occupants dispose solid waste into river/sea/creek/pond											
Occupants composting solid waste											
Other											
Urban (classification of solid waste disposal as above)											
Rural (classification of solid waste disposal as above)											

Units of tabulation: households

Living quarters included: occupied housing units

Classifications
(a) Geographical divisions: (i) total country; (ii) each major civil division; (iii) each minor civil division. Distinguish between urban and rural for (i), (ii) and (iii)
(b) Type of housing unit
(c) Type of solid waste disposal

Note:
Disposal of solid waste and facilities for disposing of it have an extremely important impact on public health and on maintaining a safe environment. As for the classification of types of solid waste disposal, it consists of broad categories and may be further elaborated on the basis of prevalent systems in a specific country or area.

---

* This table may be compiled for (i) total country; (ii) each major civil division; (iii) each minor civil division; (iv) each principal locality. Distinguish between urban and rural for (i), (ii) and (iii).

H26-A. Occupants of housing units, by type of housing unit, cross-classified by type of solid waste disposal

Geographical division* and main type of solid waste disposal	Total	Type of housing unit									Not stated
		Conventional dwelling			Other housing units						
								Informal housing unit			
		Total	Has all basic facilities	Does not have all basic facilities	Total	Semi-permanent dwellings	Mobile housing unit	Impro-vised	Permanent but not intended for habitation	Other	

Total number of occupants

Solid waste collected on regular basis by authorized collectors

Solid waste collected on an irregular basis by authorized collectors

Solid waste collected by self-appointed collectors

Occupants dispose of solid waste in a local dump supervised by authorities

Occupants dispose of solid waste in a local dump not supervised by authorities

Occupants burn solid waste

Occupants bury solid waste

Occupants dispose solid waste into river/sea/creek/pond

Occupants composting solid waste

Other

Urban (classification of solid waste disposal as above)

Rural (classification of solid waste disposal as above)

Units of tabulation: occupants

Living quarters included: housing units

Persons included: occupants of housing units

Classifications
(a) Geographical divisions: (i) total country; (ii) each major civil division; (iii) each minor civil division. Distinguish between urban and rural for (i), (ii) and (iii)
(b) Type of housing unit
(c) Type of solid waste disposal

Note:
Disposal of solid waste and facilities for disposing of it have an extremely important impact on public health and on maintaining a safe environment. As for the classification of types of solid waste disposal, it consists of broad categories and may be further elaborated on the basis of prevalent systems in a specific country or area.

* This table may be compiled for (i) total country; (ii) each major civil division; (iii) each minor civil division; (iv) each principal locality. Distinguish between urban and rural for (i), (ii) and (iii).

H27-A. Renting households in housing units, by rent paid, cross-classified by type of ownership of the housing unit, whether space occupied is furnished or unfurnished and tenure of the household

Geographical division,* type of ownership and tenure	Total renting households	Monthly rent paid by household					
		Scale of rents					
		Category 1	Category 2	Category 3	Category 4	Not stated
Publicly owned housing units							
Privately owned housing units							
Tenant							
Furnished							
Unfurnished							
Subtenant							
Furnished							
Unfurnished							
Tenure not stated							

Units of tabulation: households

Living quarters included: housing units

Households: renting households

Classifications:

(*a*) Rent paid: a scale of rents established in accordance with the range of rent normally paid and the currency in the country concerned and an indication of whether the premises are rented furnished or unfurnished

(*b*) Type of ownership

(*c*) Tenure

Note:
In this tabulation, households are tabulated according to the rent paid by the household and the type of ownership of the dwelling occupied. Households renting privately owned housing units are further classified according to whether the household is a main tenant or a subtenant and whether the premises are rented furnished or unfurnished. These latter classifications would not normally apply to publicly owned housing units. Data on type of ownership and rent paid provide an opportunity to review the part played by the public and private sectors in providing housing for the population and the cost of such housing.

---

* This table may be compiled for (i) total country; (ii) each major civil division; (iii) each minor civil division; (iv) each principal locality. Distinguish between urban and rural for (i), (ii) and (iii).

H28-A. Renting households, classified by whether space occupied is furnished or unfurnished, and amount of rent paid monthly by the household, cross-classified by type of housing unit and number of households in housing unit

Geographical division,* type of housing unit and number of households	Total renting households	Monthly rent paid by household							
		Unit or part of the unit occupied by household rented furnished				Unit or part of the unit occupied by household rented unfurnished			
		Scale of rents				Scale of rents			
		1	2	3	4	1	2	3	4
Total housing units									
Housing units with the following number of households per unit									
1									
2									
3+									
Conventional dwellings (Classification of households as above)									
Other housing units (Classification of households as above)									
Semi-permanent dwellings (Classification of households as above)									
Mobile housing units (Classification of households as above)									
Informal housing units (Classification of households as above)									
Type of housing unit not stated (Classification of households as above)									

Units of tabulation: households

Living quarters included: housing units

Households: renting households

Classifications:
(a) Furnished or unfurnished housing unit
(b) Type of housing unit
(c) Rent paid: a scale of rents established in accordance with the range of rent normally paid and the currency in the country concerned
(d) Households per housing unit

Note:
In this tabulation, rent paid refers to the amount paid monthly by the household for the space it occupies. The amount of rent paid is related to the number of households occupying the housing unit and the type of housing unit. However, it may also be related to the occupation or industry of the heads of households, particularly where these characteristics provide a significant indication of the income levels of large sectors of the population. The tabulation may be further expanded to show whether the rent includes the cost of utilities such as gas, electricity and heat, where this information has been collected.

* This table may be compiled for (i) total country; (ii) each major civil division; (iii) each minor civil division; (iv) each principal locality. Distinguish between urban and rural for (i), (ii) and (iii).

H29-A. Rented* housing units, classified by whether space occupied is furnished or unfurnished, and amount of rent paid monthly for the housing unit, cross-classified by type of housing unit and number of rooms

Geographical division,** type of housing unit and number of rooms	Total rented housing units	Monthly rent paid by household							
		Unit or part of the unit occupied by household rented furnished				Unit or part of the unit occupied by household rented unfurnished			
		Scale of rents				Scale of rents			
		1	2	3	4	1	2	3	4
Total housing units									
Housing units with the following number of rooms									
1									
2									
3									
4									
5									
6									
7									
8									
9									
10+									
Conventional dwellings (Classification of rooms as above)									
Other housing units (Classification of rooms as above)									
Semi-permanent dwellings (Classification of rooms as above)									
Mobile housing units (Classification of rooms as above)									
Informal housing units (Classification of rooms as above)									
Type of housing unit not stated (Classification of rooms as above)									

Units of tabulation: housing units

Living quarters included: rented housing units

Classifications:
(a)   Furnished or unfurnished housing unit
(b)   Type of housing unit
(c)   Rent paid: a scale of rents established in accordance with the range of rent normally paid and the currency in the country concerned
(d)   Rooms per housing unit

Note:
In this tabulation, rent paid is related to the number of rooms in the housing unit, since space is an important factor in determining the cost of housing. It may be useful, however, to expand the tabulation so that it includes not only the number of rooms in the housing unit, but also an indication of the availability of certain basic facilities such as piped water, toilet and bathing facilities (*H30-A*). If information has been collected showing whether or not the rent is controlled, this could usefully be included in the tabulation.

---

* "Rented" in this case means wholly rented and does not refer to housing units occupied by an owner who rents part of the unit to another household.

** This table may be compiled for (i) total country; (ii) each major civil division; (iii) each minor civil division; (iv) each principal locality. Distinguish between urban and rural for (i), (ii) and (iii).

H30-A. Rented* housing units, classified by whether space occupied is furnished or unfurnished, and amount of rent paid monthly for the housing unit, cross-classified by type of housing unit, availability of piped water and availability of toilet facilities

Geographical division,** type of housing unit, availability of piped water and availability of toilet facilitiess	Total housing units	Monthly rent paid by household							
		Unit or part of the unit occupied by household rented furnished				Unit or part of the unit occupied by household rented unfurnished			
		Scale of rents				Scale of rents			
		1	2	3	4	1	2	3	4
Total housing units									
Housing units with the following facilities:									
Piped water inside									
Toilet inside									
Toilet outside									
No toilet									
Piped water outside (classification of toilet facilities as above)									
No piped water (classification of toilet facilities as above)									
Conventional dwellings (classification of water and toilet facilities as above)									
Other housing units (classification of water and toilet facilities as above)									
Semi-permanent dwellings (classification of water and toilet facilities as above)									
Mobile housing units (classification of water and toilet facilities as above)									
Informal housing units (classification of water and toilet facilities as above)									
Type of housing unit not stated (classification of water and toilet facilities as above)									

Units of tabulation: housing units

Living quarters included: rented housing units

Classifications:
(a)   Furnished or unfurnished housing unit
(b)   Type of housing unit
(c)   Rent paid
(d)   Availability of piped water
(e)   Availability of toilet facilities

Note:
Comments concerning the amount of rent paid outlined in connection with tabulation see tabulation H29-A are also applicable to the present tabulation. The purpose of this tabulation is to relate the cost of housing to the adequacy of basic services -- in this case, the availability of piped water and toilet facilities.

* "Rented" in this case means wholly rented and does not refer to housing units occupied by an owner who rents part of the unit to another household.

** This table may be compiled for (i) total country; (ii) each major civil division; (iii) each minor civil division; (iv) each principal locality. Distinguish between urban and rural for (i), (ii) and (iii).

H31-A. Occupied housing units, by type, cross-classified by available floor area and number of occupants

Geographical division,* and type of housing unit	Total housing units	Floor area (in square metres (m2))						Total floor area	Total occupants	Floor area (m2) per occupant
		Less than 20	20-29	30-39	...	100-119	120 and over			
Total housing units										
Conventional dwellings										
Other housing units										
Semi-permanent dwellings										
Mobile housing units										
Informal housing units										
Type of housing unit not stated										

Units of tabulation: housing units

Living quarters included: occupied housing units

Persons included: occupants of housing units

Classifications:
(a) Type of housing unit
(b) Available floor area

Note:
This tabulation provides information on the total useful area of housing units, the distribution of housing units according to the floor area, the total number of occupants and the average floor area per occupant. That information is required to assess overcrowding and this tabulation is designed to complement the information provided by recommended tabulation H6-R. It is recommended that data be tabulated in geographical detail because of the importance of the topic and the use to which the information yielded may be put. This is particularly important since less crowded and overcrowded housing units may be found in relative proximity to each other. For collective living quarters, it would be more useful to collect information on the useful living floor space per occupant of the collective living quarters. Data should be derived by dividing the total useful floor space by the number of occupants using it.

* This table may be compiled for (i) total country; (ii) each major civil division; (iii) each minor civil division; (iv) each principal locality. Distinguish between urban and rural for (i), (ii) and (iii).

References

Blacker, J. G. C. (1977). The estimates of adult mortality in Africa from data on orphanhood. *Population Studies*, vol. XXXI, No. 1 (March).

Brass, William and K. Hill (1973). Estimating adult mortality from orphanhood. *International Population Conference*, vol. 3. Liège, Belgium: International Union for the Scientific Study of Population.

Dorrington, Rob, Tom A. Moultrie, and Ian M. Timæus (2004). Estimation of mortality using the South African Census 2001 data. *CARe Monograph No. 11*. Centre for Actuarial Research, University of Cape Town.

Food and Agriculture Organization of the United Nations (2005). World Programme for the Census of Agriculture 2010. *A system of Integrated Agricultural Censuses and Surveys, Volume 1*. FAO Statistical Development Series No. 11. Rome: FAO.

Hill, Kenneth H. and T. James Trussel (1977). Further developments in indirect mortality estimation. *Population Studies*, vol. XXXI, No. 2 (July).

Horiuchi, Shiro (1991). Assessing the effects of mortality reduction of population ageing. *Population Bulletin of the United Nations*, Nos. 31/32, pp. 38-51. Sales No. E.91.XIII.18.

Hussmanns, R., F. Mehran and V. Verma (1990). *Surveys of the Economically Active Population, Employment, Unemployment and Underemployment: An ILO Manual on Concepts and Methods*. Geneva: International Labour Office.

International Labour Office (1990). *International Standard Classification of Occupations (ISCO-88)*. Geneva: International Labour Office.

_____ (2000). *Current International Recommendations on Labour Statistics*. Geneva: International Labour Office.

_____ (2003). Resolution on household income and expenditure statistics. Report of the 17th International Conference of Labour Statisticians, Geneva, 24 November to 3 December 2003.

Krotki, K., ed. (1978). *Developments in Dual System Estimation of Population Size and Growth*. Alberta, Canada: University of Alberta Press, 1978.

National Academy of Sciences, Committee on Population and Demography (1981). *Collecting Data for the Estimation of Fertility and Mortality, Report No.6*. Washington D. C.: National Academy Press.

Stanton, Cynthia, et al (2001). Every death counts: Measurement of maternal mortality via a census. *Bulletin of the World Health Organization*. 79(7): 657-664.

Timaeus, Ian and Wendy Graham (1989). Measuring Adult Mortality in Developing Countries. A Review and Assessment of Methods. *World Bank Working Paper, No. 155*. Washington, D.C.: World Bank.

Timaeus, Ian M. (1991). Measurement of adult mortality in less developed countries: A comparative review. *Population Index*, vol. 57, No. 4 (winter), pp. 552-568.

United Nations (1952). Manuals on methods of estimating population. *Manual I: Methods of Estimating Total Population for Current Dates*. Sales No. E.52.XIII.5.

_____ (1956). Manuals on Methods of Estimating Population. *Manual II: Methods of Appraisal of Quality of Basic Data for Population Estimates*. Sales No. E.56. XIII.2.

_____ (1956). Manuals on Methods of Estimating Population. *Manual III: Methods for Population Projections by Sex and Age*. Sales No. E.56.XIII.3.

_____ (1956). Report of the Statistical Commission at its ninth session. *Official Records of the Economic and Social Council, Twenty-second Session, Supplement No. 7. E/2876*.

_____ (1962). *Statistical Indicators of Housing Conditions*, Studies in Methods, No. 37, Sales No. 62.XVII.7.

_____ (1965). *General Principles for National Programmes of Population Projections as Aids to Development Planning*. Sales No. E.65.XIII.2.

_____ (1969). *Methods of Analysing Census Data on Economic Activities of the Population*. Sales No. E.69.XIII.2.

_____ (1970). Manuals on Methods of Estimating Population. *Manual VI: Methods of Measuring Internal Migration*. Sales No. E.70.XIII.3.

_____ (1973). Manuals on Methods of Estimating Population: *Manual VII: Methods of Projecting Households and Families* Sales No. E.73.XIII.2.

_____ (1977*). The Organization of National Statistical Services: A Review of Major Issues*, Studies in Methods, No. 21, Sales No. E.77.XVII.5.

_____ (1979). *Improving Social Statistics in Developing Countries: Conceptual Framework and Methods*, Studies in Methods, No. 25, Sales No. E.79.XVII.12.

_____ (1979). *The Development of Integrated Data Bases for Social, Economic and Demographic Statistics*, Studies in Methods, No. 27, Sales No. E.79.XVII.14.

_____ (1983). *Manual X: Indirect Techniques for Demographic Estimation*. Population Studies, No. 81. Sales No. E.83.XIII.2.

_____ (1983).*The World Programme of Action concerning Disabled Persons*. New York: United Nations.

_____ (1984). *Compiling Social Indicators on the Situation of Women*. Studies in Methods, No. 32. Sales No. E.84.XVII.2.

_____ (1984). *Handbook of Household Surveys (Revised Edition)*, Studies in Methods, No. 31, Sales No. E.83.XVII.13.

_____ (1984). *Improving Concepts and Methods for Statistics and Indicators on the Situation of Women*. Studies in Methods, No. 33. Sales No. E.84.XVII.3.

_____ (1985). *Socio-economic Differentials in Child Mortality in Developing Countries*. Sales No. E.85.XIII.7.

_____ (1985). *Statistical Indicators on Youth*. Statistics on Special Population Groups, No. 1. Sales No. E.85.XVII.12.

_____ (1988). *First Marriage: Patterns and Determinants.* (ST/ESA/SER.R/76).

_____ United Nations (1989). *Handbook for National Statistical Data Bases on Women and Development.* Social Statistics and Indicators, No. 6. Sales No. E.89. XVII.9.

_____ (1989). *Handbook on Social Indicators*, Studies in Methods, No. 49, Sales No. E. 89.XVII.6.

_____ (1989). *Projection Methods for Integrating Population Variables into Development Planning*, vol. I: *Methods for Comprehensive Planning, Module One: Conceptual issues and methods for preparing demographic properties.* ST/ESA/SER. R/90.

_____ (1990). *Step-by-step Guse to the Estimation of Child Mortality.* Population Studies, No. 107. Sales No. E.89.XIII.9.

_____ (1991). *The World's Women: Trends and Statistics, 1970-1990.* Social Statistics and Indicators, No. 8. Sales No. E.90.XVII.3.

_____ (1992). *Handbook of Population and Housing Censuses, Part II.* Studies in Methods, No. Sales No. E.91.XVII.9.

_____ (1993). *Internal Migration of Women in Developing Countries.* Sales No. E.94.XIII.3.

_____ (1993). *Methods of Measuring Women's Economic Activity: Technical Report.* Studies in Methods, No. 59. Sales No. E.93.XVII.6.

_____ (1994). *The Standard Rules on the Equalization of Opportunities for Persons with Disabilities.* Adopted by the United Nations General Assembly at its 48th session on 20 December 1993 (Resolution 48/96).

_____ (1995). *Report of the International Conference on Population and Development, Cairo, 5-13 September 1994.* Sales No. E.95.XIII.18.

_____ (1995). *The World's Women 1995: Trends and Statistics.* Social Statistics and Indicators, No. 12. Sales No. E.95.XVII.2.

_____ (1996). *Costing Aspects of Population and Housing Censuses in Selected Countries in the UN/ECE Region.* Statistical Standards and Studies, No. 46. United Nations publication, Sales No. E.96.II.E.15.

_____ (1996). *Handbook of Population and Housing Censuses, Part IV: Economic Activity Status.* Studies in Methods, No. 54. United Nations publications, Sales No. E.96.XVII.13.

_____ (1996). *Indicators of Sustainable Development Framework and Methodologies.* Sales No. E.96.II.A.16.

_____ (1996). *Manual for the Development of Statistical Information for Disability Programmes and Policies.* Statistics on Special Population Groups, No. 8. Sales No. E. 96.XVII.4.

_____ (1996). *Report of the Fourth World Conference on Women, Beijing, 4-15 September 1995.* Sales No. E.96.IV.13.

_____ (1996). *Report of the World Summit for Social Development, Copenhagen, 6-12 March 1995.* Sales No. E.96.IV.8.

_____ (1996). *The Beijing Declaration and the Platform for Action.* Fourth World Conference on Women, Beijing, China, 4-15 September 1995.

_____ (1998). *Principles and Recommendations for Population and Housing Censuses, Revision 1*, Statistical Papers, No. 67/Rev. 1, Sales No. E.98.XVII.8.

_____ (1998). *Recommendations on Statistics of International Migration, Revision 1*. Statistical Papers, No. 58/Rev. 1, Sales No. E.98.XVII.14.

_____ (1999). *Country or Area Codes for Statistical Use*. Statistical Papers, No. 49, Rev.4. Sales number: 98.XVII.9.

_____ (2000). Handbook on Geographic Information System and Digital Mapping Studies in Methods, No. 79, Sales No. E.00.XVII.12.

_____ (2000). *The World's Women 2000: Trends and Statistics*. Social Statistics and Indicators, No. 16. Sales No. E.00.XVII.14.

_____ (2001). *Guidelines and Principles for the Development of Disability Statistics*. Statistics on Special Population Groups, No. 10. Sales No. E.01.XVII.15.

_____ (2001). *Handbook on Census Management for Population and Housing Censuses*, Studies in Methods, No. 83, Sales No. E.00.XVII.15 Rev. 1.

_____ (2001). *Handbook on Population and Housing Census Editing*. Studies in Methods, No. 82. Sales No. E.00.XVII.9.

_____ (2001). *Principles and Recommendations for a Vital Statistics System, Revision 2*. Sales No. E.01.XVII.10).

_____ (2001). Report on the thirty-second session. *Economic and Social Council, Official Records, 2001, Supplement No. 4*. E/2001/24 and E/CN.3/2001/25

_____ (2003). *Handbook of Statistical Organization, Third Edition: The Operation and Organization of a Statistical Agency*, Studies in Methods, No. 88, Sales No. E.03.XVII. 7.

_____ (2004). *System of National Accounts, 1993-CD ROM*, Sales No. 96.XVII.3.

_____ (2005). *The Inequity Predicament: Report on the World Social Situation 2005*. Sales No. E. 05.IV.5.

_____ (2006). *The World's Women 2005: Progress in Statistics*. Sales No. E.05.XVII.7

United Nations and International Labour Office (2002). *Collection of economic characteristics in population censuses*. Technical Report. ST/ESA/STAT/119.

United Nations Development Programme (1996). *Human Development Report, 1996*. New York, Oxford University Press.

_____ (2004). *Human Development Report 2004*. New York.

United Nations Economic and Social Commission for Asia and the Pacific (1984). *National Migration Surveys, Manuals I-IX: Comparative Study on Migration, Urbanization and Development in ESCAP Region*. Bangkok.

United Nations Economic Commission for Africa (1977). *Study on special techniques for enumerating nomads in African censuses and surveys*. Conference of African Statisticians at its tenth session. E/CN.14/CAS.10/16.

United Nations Economic Commission for Europe (2006). *Conference of European Statisticians Recommendations for the 2010 Censuses of Population and Housing*. ECE/CES/STAT.NONE/2006/4.

United Nations Educational, Scientific and Cultural Organization (2005). *Education for All: Global Monitoring Report, 2006.* Paris: United Nations Educational, Scientific and Cultural Organization.

United Nations General Assembly (2001). *Road map towards the implementation of the United Nations Millennium Declaration.* Report of the Secretary General, 6 September 2001 (A/56/326).

United States Department of Commerce, Bureau of the Census (1985). *Evaluating Censuses of Population and Housing.* Statistical Training document ISP-TR-5. Washington, D.C.

World Health Organisation (2001). *International Classification of Functioning, Disability and Health*, Geneva: WHO.

World Health Organization and UNICEF (2005). *Water for life: making it happen.*

INDEX

Note: Reference numbers are to part and paragraph numbers. An "n." following a reference number refers to a footnote. "P" references refer to the Population tabulations in Annexes 2 and 4; "H" references refer to Housing tabulations in Annexes 3 and 5. "P" and "H" references are in order of Recommended (R) tabulations followed by Additional (A) tabulations, for example, "H15-R, H8-A"

DATE DUE

DEMCO, INC. 38-2931